P9-DUK-076

Economic Growth in History

SURVEY AND ANALYSIS

Economic Growth in History

SURVEY AND ANALYSIS

J. D. Gould

METHUEN & CO LTD
LONDON

First published 1972
by Methuen & Co Ltd
11 New Fetter Lane London EC4
Printed in Great Britain
by Richard Clay (The Chaucer Press) Ltd,
Bungay, Suffolk.
© 1972 J. D. Gould

SBN 416 66030 4 (hardback)
SBN 416 66040 1 (paperback)

Distributed in the USA by
HARPER & ROW PUBLISHERS INC
BARNES & NOBLE IMPORT DIVISION

To Sheila and Chris

Contents

List of Figures

List of Tables

Preface

It is an author's custom, and his pleasure, to record his thanks to those who have helped him to write his book. If I desist from writing here a long list of names, it is not because my indebtedness is smaller or less warmly acknowledged, but because it is so widely diffused. Whatever merit this book may have it owes to the work of many hundreds of scholars, both economists and historians, living and dead, whose names are scattered throughout the text and the notes. If I do not name them all here it is because they are too numerous, not because I do not feel the weight of my indebtedness.

Here I should like to name only one individual, my colleague Gary R. Hawke, who has read each chapter in typescript and saved me from many errors. Those which remain are mine. I also wish to thank the Council of the Victoria University of Wellington for granting me a period of sabbatical leave in 1970–1 which freed me for a time from routine duties to concentrate on researching and writing the book, and the Chairman and Faculty of the Department of Economics at Duke University, North Carolina, U.S.A., for making it possible for me to spend this leave on a campus where the Faculty, the atmosphere, and library and other facilities all helped me to reap maximum advantage from it. A different and even greater obligation I try, inadequately, to acknowledge in the dedication of this book.

J. D. GOULD

Introduction

One of the sources of the renewed intimacy between economics and economic history which has developed over the last couple of decades is the revival of interest in growth and development on the part of economists. So long as economists concerned themselves only with problems of static equilibrium there was no need to court the friendship of economic historians. But it is manifestly impossible, if one's interest centres on problems of growth, to ignore the lessons of the past. Unfortunately the writings of economic historians of pre-World War II generations were in many ways ill-attuned to provide ready answers to the sorts of questions economists posed about the historical experience of economic growth. A resulting feature of the economic historiography of the last few decades is that a good deal of it, especially of the more quantitatively-oriented studies, has been written by economists. Economic historians, for their part, have been inevitably influenced by the distinctive orientation of effort and analytical penetration which characterize these historical forays of the economist, and their own recent work has in many instances developed a 'growth-centred' stance and an analytical style which it rarely adopted a generation ago.

These changes of interest have been reflected, quite properly, in the structure of university courses. It is now common for courses in economics to provide for some modest exposure to economic history, and for students specializing in economic history to be required to study at least one year of economic theory. This is as it should be. Yet the compulsion to know something of each other's ways has not, perhaps, brought to either economist or economic historian quite the advantages which might have been hoped. One would hesitate to call it a shot-gun marriage; yet the renewed intimacy is one in which neither partner as yet feels quite at home with the other.

This book is primarily intended for the economics student who is not quite sure what he has learned from economic history; for the student of economic history who thinks he knows what he has learned from economics, but does not quite see how it applies to history; and for their teachers. It is an attempt to present some of the facts of modern (and a little pre-modern) economic history in a growth-oriented analytical framework. The plan of the book is simple. Chapter 1 is, for the most part, descriptive, and summarizes what we know in quantitative terms about the historical experience of growth and structural change which today's more highly-developed countries have undergone. The four central chapters of the book adopt a more analytical approach and investigate, in turn, the contribution to economic growth made by a number of particular sectors or economic activities. The final chapter, Chapter 6, reviews some general theories of growth and development.

It should be conceded at the outset that no firm general conclusion is reached as to why some countries have experienced more rapid and sustained growth than others – though it is certainly hoped that some *partial* explanations of the general record, and some explanations of particular accelerations and decelerations, will emerge in the course of Chapters 2 to 6. For example, there is no simple and agreed answer to the question: why have Sweden and Japan experienced a rate of growth of *per capita* income of more than 2 per cent per annum over the past hundred years, whereas Australia has not been able to manage even 1 per cent? We do not even know, with any certainty, why most countries have experienced more rapid growth in the past twenty years than they did before World War II, even though the reasons for international differences in growth rates in the past quarter-century have been very widely and expertly discussed. There is still no general agreement whether the recent acceleration in the rates of growth of, say, West European countries has its origin in the higher and more sustained level of demand on which, for example, Mr Maddison lays stress; or in the higher rates of capital formation which many countries have experienced; or in the distinctive labour market conditions which Professor Kindleberger places at the centre of his scheme of explanation; or in the 'catching-up' mechanism which Mr Denison advances as one of the reasons why European growth has outstripped that of the U.S.A. in recent decades.

If explanations of fast and slow growth on a very general level are as yet not widely agreed, there has nevertheless been a great deal of investigation of the relationship between particular factors and economic growth in individual countries and over shorter periods. It is research of this type, in fact, which has provided much of the material for the four middle chapters of the book. The first of these deals with agriculture – as is appropriate, since almost all poor countries are predominantly agricultural and the role of agriculture in the early stages of economic growth is therefore particularly critical. The next chapter, Chapter 3, discusses the role of capital in a very broad framework. Much of the argument turns on the frequently-discussed question of the relationship between rates of investment and rates of growth of output, but there are also separate sections on savings and institutional changes in the mobilization of capital, and on foreign borrowing.

Chapter 4 deals with the foreign sector and economic growth, a topic which is dealt with at considerable length because so many developing countries of the present day believe that more favourable trading conditions provide the key to improving their growth achievement. Finally, Chapter 5 deals principally, and again at considerable length, with what an increasing number of economists and historians view as the most important single source of economic growth: namely, invention and technological change. While not dissenting from this opinion, Chapter 5 emphasizes, however,

how difficult it is to separate out the contribution of technological change from other, often-overlooked factors influencing the rate of growth of output. This discussion of 'residual'
factors in economic growth owes much to recent debates
among (particularly) American economists and especially to
the work of E. F. Denison.

Chapter 6 is of a rather different character from the others
in that it subjects to critical review a number of broad interpretations of economic growth and development put forward
by other scholars. However, the discussion of these theories is
related as closely as possible to both the empirical information
and the more specific and limited theories which have been
discussed in earlier chapters of the book. Further, the
opportunity is taken to refer briefly to one or two less
obvious influences on economic performance which do
not conveniently fit into the framework of the other
chapters.

Perhaps one should finish a brief summary of what the
book is about by an even briefer reference to what it is *not*
about. The search for the sources of economic growth can be
conducted, so to say, on a number of different 'levels'.* This,
in fact, is one of the chief reasons why they have proved so
elusive. For example, one often encounters the view that the
'true' sources of economic backwardness lie in social and
psychological features of traditional societies rather than in
characteristics which fall within the province of the economist. There is a 'level' of explanation in which a given rate
of growth can be 'explained' quite rigorously in terms of
economic variables; but underlying these variables are other
characteristics of the society in question which we may well
think of, if we choose, as in some sense more fundamental.
For example, the savings ratio is an observable economic
characteristic which can be measured and incorporated in
simple models analysing the achieved rate of economic
growth. But no one will deny that the propensity to save
itself arises from and reflects certain deeper attributes of the
members of the society in question, attributes which may, for

* On this, see further, pp. 435-8.

example, be intimately related to the prevailing pattern of religious belief.

This book deals only with the restricted range of economic variables lying close, so to speak, to the surface of these various layers of explanation. In deliberately restricting its scope in this way, I do not in the least intend to deny that non-economic characteristics may in some sense be more fundamental causes of the level of economic achievement. It is partly that I am not competent to enter this more diffuse and difficult area. It is also that an examination of even the more obvious 'economic' sources of growth is in itself an ample theme for one book, even a large one – so much so, indeed, that we had better turn at once to that purpose.

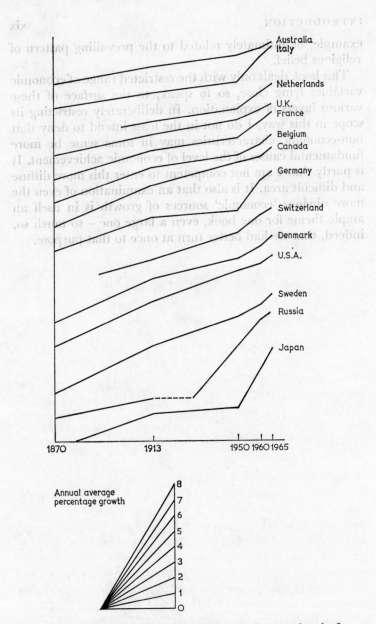

FIGURE 1.1 The growth of real product per head of population, 1870–1965

1 Growth and Development in History

This book is about economic growth. Some of the facts – or more accurately, some of our beliefs – about modern economic growth are presented visually in fig. 1.1, which plots rates of growth for fourteen advanced countries over a period of about 100 years. It is tempting to jump straight into our subject by commenting at once on some of the main features of this diagram and of Table 1.1 (pp. 22-3), in which the data on which it is based, and some others which are relevant, are more precisely presented. Unfortunately, the derivation, the meaning and the limitations of these data call for discussion, both urgent and extended, and it would be as irresponsible as it is tempting to launch into descriptions and explanations based on these data before subjecting them to the required exegesis. So we had better begin again.

Economic growth and economic development

This book is about economic growth. By 'growth' is intended, primarily, a *sustained increase in real* per capita *incomes. Sustained*, because short-lived and reversible improvements due to (e.g.) a run of good harvests or a temporary improvement in the terms of trade do not greatly interest us. *Real*, because we wish to focus on a society's power to produce increasing quantities of goods and services, and this is not correctly portrayed by a measure of the money value of such goods and services unadjusted for changes in their average prices. *Per capita*, because on the whole it is an increasing enjoyment of goods and services by the individual member of a society which (in the view taken here) is the chief justification for being concerned about economic growth and considering it a 'good thing'. But we shall relax our insistence on the '*per capita*' part of the definition from time to time to cast sidelong glances at the growth of *total* real income – not only because there are points of view from which this is an object of interest in its own right (e.g. if we are interested in a country's capacity to wage war or to finance a national museum or library or symphony orchestra of outstanding calibre), but because there are circumstances in which the rate of growth of *per capita* product might be regarded as in part a 'passive' outcome of an economically-determined rate of increase of aggregate real product and an exogenously-determined rate of population increase.

While 'sustained increase in real *per capita* incomes', or something like it, is the most widely accepted definition of economic growth, there are those who would prefer to envisage this, alternatively or in a complementary sense, in terms of structural changes such as a persistent decline in the proportion of the labour force employed, or national product generated, by the agricultural sector, and corresponding increases in manufacturing. This view of growth is one which appeals particularly to some economists in low-income countries oriented to agriculture or mining, especially if they are also small or if there has been a history of economic dependence on foreign capital. There is a temptation to view true economic *development* in such societies as involving not merely rising *per capita* incomes but also diversification of economic structure away from primary activity, towards the industrial and services sectors, perhaps by way of import substitution and a reduced dependence on trade. Such 'development' may be desired for economic reasons – as providing a greater safeguard against fluctuating terms of trade or to reduce dependence on a non-reproducible resource such as oil; or for reasons of national prestige or military security; or simply for its own sake – as offering greater variety of employment and scope for differing talents and styles of living. Thus William Demas summarized the first of his four brilliant lectures on *The Economics of Development in Small Countries* by proposing, firstly, that 'The criterion of development or underdevelopment of a country is the extent to which it has achieved structural transformation'. Secondly, but *only* secondly, 'Structural transformation is usually associated with an increase in real output and real income per head'; and we are reminded, thirdly, that 'A country can have a high *per capita* income without having undergone structural transformation, if it is an enclave economy or a small economy relying on exports of valuable natural-resource products'.[1]

It is understandable that Mr Demas should espouse such views, for at the time of writing he was Head of the Economic Planning Division of the Government of Trinidad and Tobago, a country whose relative prosperity was heavily dependent on oil wells then expected to run dry in ten to fifteen years. History confirms the need to make a distinction between growth of income and structural change; for there are undoubtedly instances of countries which have enjoyed a high level of, and sustained increases in, *per capita* incomes, while continuing to be characterized by somewhat 'undeveloped' and unchanging structures – Australia and New Zealand between, say, 1870 and 1938 are cases in point. Even more dramatically, possession of a valuable resource like oil can ensure a high level of *per capita* income even to a country of highly unbalanced, and largely backward, structure: not the U.S.A. but Kuwait has enjoyed the highest average *per capita* income in the world in recent years.

It would undoubtedly be convenient to have separate words to denote these two differing concepts, say *growth* (for sustained increase in real *per capita* incomes) and *development* (for sustained structural change). Such a linguistic usage would not of course imply any denial that the two processes are usually intimately linked, but it would accord well with the historical fact that substantial 'growth' can occur without substantial 'development', and (less certainly) vice versa, and that even in so far as the two *are* but opposite sides of the same

coin, our interest at a particular time may legitimately focus
on one side only, and be served by having terminology
capable of reflecting this preference.

Unfortunately, the English language has been debased and
impoverished in this, as in so many similar ways. Later economists have not followed the example of Schumpeter, who
drew a sharp distinction – similar to, though not identical
with, that suggested here – between 'development' and
'Growth',[2] which in *Business Cycles* is always referred to,
curiously, with a capital 'G'. (Growth in this sense, incidentally, was of quite minor concern in Schumpeter's scheme.)
Today, one must agree with Meier and Baldwin that the
terms are used as synonyms.[3] Thus, the first chapter of an
excellent introductory text with the title *Economic Development,
Past and Present* begins with the sentence: 'The meaning and
implications of rapid economic growth have become increasingly clear . . .'[4] It is clear from the context that the author
uses the two words indifferently, for the sake of stylistic
variety. Again, the best-selling of all modern texts on the
subject, Walt W. Rostow's well-known *The Stages of Economic
Growth*, ought certainly to be titled *The Stages of Economic
Development* if the linguistic usage envisaged here were current.

Nor is it only the English language whose power to dis-
criminate between concepts has been eroded in this way. The
French use their words *croissance* and *développement* as indis-
criminately as the English use 'growth' and 'development';
Perroux' famous *pôles de croissance* would be *pôles de développement* in the more discriminating usage. The Germans are less
worried by repetition: *Wachstum* (growth) normally does
service for both concepts, and few have followed Schumpeter
in using *Entwicklung* (development) in an economic context.
The same is true of Italy, but there it is the word for development (*sviluppo*) which serves both purposes. Only the Latin
Americans display any wish to preserve shades of meaning,
doubtless because of all major groupings of economists it is
they who place most emphasis on the structural change
aspect of growth/development, regarding this as the key not
only to *long-run* growth but to the preservation of economic

and indeed cultural and political national identity and self-respect. (In many respects West Indian economists share the outlook of Latin Americans, for obvious reasons of history and geography.) Accordingly, though even here usage is not uniformly precise, *crecimiento* is usually used for 'growth' and *desarrollo* for 'development' as defined in the preceding paragraphs.

But it is too much to hope that a textbook should succeed in inducing a change in language. Such works more often contribute to the further debasement than to the refinement of terminology, and having made one's point there is no sense in labouring it. We do need to be clear, however, that though this is *predominantly* a book about *growth* it will not ignore *development*, where that seems the more relevant concept; and the degree of attention to the first would be less and to the second more, were it not that as yet there are fewer satisfactory historical data on development than on growth.

Growth and welfare

The desire not to rely too exclusively on changes in real *per capita* incomes as one's measure of historical change can only be strengthened when we consider both that strong exception has been taken to the use of *per capita* income as an index of welfare, and that grave difficulties impede its historical measurement. This is not the place for an exhaustive discussion of the first of these problems, but three criticisms of the use of real *per capita* income as a welfare measure must receive more than cursory notice. It has been claimed that measures of real income pay regard only to material enjoyments, neglecting (for example) spiritual values and other non-material benefits. It is suggested that even in so far as material satisfactions are concerned, the volume of goods and services consumed by two societies cannot be regarded as a measure of the respective degrees of satisfaction derived unless it can be assumed that 'wants' are identical, which need not be and usually is not the case. And it is pointed out that the measure of changing real income derived from orthodox national accounting totals may be deficient in failing to allow for offsetting 'social costs' (such as pollution) which are not charged against production in the accounts of constituent units, and by counting as part of output certain items such as travelling to work, which from a welfare point of view ought to be reckoned as costs and subtracted from the value of final product rather than added to it.

The first of these issues is one which involves value judgments as well as questions of fact lying outside the province of either the economic historian or the economist. The point to be made, however, is that economic development may be systematically related to cultural and religious change, as it certainly is to social change. A complete balance sheet of a period of economic growth would in that event call for the inclusion of measures not only of changes in real income but also of development in the spiritual and other areas which may have been either the consequence of, or necessary conditions for, the economic improvement in question. Thus J. L. Hammond, when his original assertion that the industrial revolution had led to a decline in the standard of living in Britain was challenged and (as it seemed) disproved by statistics, fell back on the argument that industrialization had wrought social dislocation and spiritual and aesthetic impoverishment which offset any material improvement there may have been.[5] Our purpose here is not to adjudicate in this or any similar debate, but simply to point out that if there is, indeed, a systematic relationship between the material and non-material aspects of life, Hammond's insistence on counting spiritual losses (or conceivably gains) as well as material improvement is logically compelling.

Even within the material area, however, the question of the possible inconstancy of wants raises doubts about the propriety of translating real values of aggregate consumption into terms of 'satisfactions'. Here, more than with the first point, it seems probable that the issue is particularly acute in historical as opposed to cross-country comparisons. In respect of the latter it has sometimes been claimed that cross-country estimates of income elasticities of demand for various classes of consumer goods prove that international differences in tastes and needs are not as great as commonly supposed.[6] This may be so – inference from such estimates poses conceptual problems, especially those concerning levels and distribution of disposable income and the width of the commodity categories to which the elasticities relate – but in any event it is more difficult to believe in the constancy of wants over time. Indeed, unless exceedingly broad classifications of types of expenditure are employed, the mere appearance of new commodities over time must ensure inconstancy. It is possible (though it does not seem likely) that in these days of developed communications and the 'demonstration factor' the Brazilian peasant may feel exactly the same intensity of desire for a direct-dial telephone as a middle-class American suburbanite, and that if he got one it would be appropriate to add as much to the measure of his welfare as we would subtract from that of the suburbanite whose instrument was removed for non-payment of the rental. But it is surely absurd to consider the whole world deficient in satisfaction by a similar amount per head throughout the centuries in which no such instrument as the telephone was conceived, and in which no one was capable of experiencing a 'want' for it.

Historical (and anthropological) evidence abounds of the mutability of wants over time. The deliberate stimulation of new 'wants' in order to induce effort, a tactic repeatedly employed in situations of interaction between two cultures, is predicated upon this mutability. Ragnar Nurkse voiced a widespread belief when he surmised that too ready a capacity to learn new wants, and too complete and rapid an exposure to new forms of expenditure, might maintain the propensity to consume at so high a level, even with rising incomes, as to frustrate efforts to increase the savings rate in low income countries to a level capable of sustaining self-financed growth.[7] At the same time, societies seem to have differed – for sociological reasons which are little understood – in their capacity to resist or absorb new wants: American society has always been characterized by the rapidity and relative thoroughness with which the desire to acquire new consumption goods has spread, whereas some economic historians

have explained Japan's characteristically high savings rates
as arising from the relative willingness of her consumers to
perpetuate a pattern of traditional consumption.

As we move back in time, it is surely evident that we
approximate the Japanese, rather than the American, experience of cultural diffusion. Before the late nineteenth century
the whole apparatus of mass communications and the advertising specialists who exploit it did not exist; and before the
coming of the railway and of cheap sea travel personal
mobility was also far more restricted than at the present day.
In such circumstances Nurkse's 'demonstration factor' was
severely circumscribed by the mere lack of the technology
required to permit its operation, not to mention the possibility
of greater resistance to it from internalized habits of tradition.
As against this, however, it is possible that the typically wider
spread of disposable incomes in less developed countries and
the less marked tendency to geographical separation of class-
demarcated living areas, and also the greater importance of
domestic service in the pattern of employment, afforded
greater opportunity for the face-to-face dissemination of
knowledge of the expenditure patterns of richer classes. On
balance, however, it seems certain not merely that there were
fewer commodities in earlier centuries which could be the
object of 'wants', but that the geographical and social diffusion of new wants was much more beset by impediments than
in our own times.

Let us couple with this conclusion the assumption that
'satisfaction' (in its material aspect) is a function not just of
the absolute level of consumption of goods and services but
of the *proportion* of those wants actually experienced which
can be satisfied. (This is an assumption which seems to be
warranted by everyday experience and which is in fact
implicit in many existing economic hypotheses, such as
Duesenberry's 'relative income' explanation of the propensity to save.) It then follows that the average level of 'satisfaction' has not increased over time as much as the growth
of real *per capita* income would suggest, for while the *absolute*
quantity of wants satisfied parallels the growth of real income,

the multiplication of wants ensures that the *proportion* of wants satisfied does not increase by the same factor, and indeed may not increase at all. This reasoning may seem tenuous to support so important a conclusion, and certainly some historical research on the hypothesis would be welcome (though what would be an appropriate and, data-wise, feasible criterion for judging the level of 'satisfaction' is indeed a puzzle). But that the average inhabitant of a rich industrial state of today enjoys ten to twenty times more 'satisfaction' than his forbear of two centuries ago, as the rise of *per capita* real income would suggest, appears quite at variance with all sorts of 'qualitative' historical evidence (as well as being, doubtless, a near-meaningless statement).

The third objection to translating the historical course of real income into welfare terms is based on the notion of 'social cost' and on alleged conceptual deficiences of national accounting viewed from a welfare aspect. This whole area is one which is undergoing critical rethinking by specialists at the present time – not to mention the public discussion aroused by such issues as conservation and pollution. In view of this, and of the present lack of (for example) cost/benefit studies with a substantial historical dimension, it would seem imprudent to speculate how much allowance it would be proper to make for these factors in historical comparisons. But it seems very difficult to resist the belief that from this point of view the historical course of real incomes overstates the rise in welfare which has been achieved. To take the case of social costs: the most widely-publicized examples, such as pollution, loss of natural environment, traffic congestion and accidents, have clearly resulted from industrialization and modern technology, and have no obviously important analogues in pre-industrial societies. Moreover, the more work that is done on 'traditional' peasant societies, the clearer does it become that these societies have often achieved an almost miraculous accommodation with nature, balancing present use and preservation for the future with a degree of success which the modern economic machine has rarely approached.

The three criticisms reviewed in the foregoing paragraphs cast considerable doubt on the legitimacy of using estimates of *per capita* income as measures of change in welfare in historical comparisons. When we further bear in mind the difficulty of obtaining data from which to construct such estimates – and this, evidently, is a difficulty which in general increases the further back in time we move – the question of whether the subject we propose for this book is one which is worth exploring cannot be suppressed. There are indeed signs at the present time of a growing scepticism, a scepticism manifested both in the dissatisfaction of specialists with some of the conceptual bases of national accounting, and in the increasing insistence on the part of the public generally and of local communities specifically on weighing social costs much more carefully when considering the establishment of new industrial enterprises.* It is possible that a substantial 'backlash' against the uncritical acceptance of economic growth as an important objective of economic policy is in process of developing; and this book, indeed, may prove to be a masterpiece of ill-timing in that its writing has been delayed until the very point of time at which its subject, which has stood on a pedestal of high public and professional esteem for a generation or so, is now toppling into disfavour or even ridicule.

But it remains to be seen how far this backlash will go. Even in the wealthiest countries there are powerful forces making for a continued emphasis on growth. Not only are there huge areas of squalor and poverty in such countries which growth has so far failed to eradicate – a consideration, of course, which cuts both ways – but profits are so much

---

* What might be thought one of the most dramatic manifestations of this new public mood, the local outcry against the proposed siting of the third London international airport in the English Midlands, is in fact not a good example, for here the difficulty was rather that the community which would have borne almost all of the social costs of the site would have enjoyed a small fraction of its benefits. More pertinent examples are, however, becoming an almost weekly feature of the Press in the U.S.A. and Britain.

easier to come by in an expanding than in a stagnating economy that the whole weight of business influence will continue to be brought to bear on government to follow expansionary policies. Further, the burden of defence expenditure and of such non-military international rivalries as the space programme enable growth to be plausibly wrapped up in the flag, and indeed in a world where several powerful nations are experiencing rapid growth, any one of them is in the situation of Alice and the Red Queen – having to run very hard just to stay in the same place. In any event, deriding economic growth is a luxury which as yet only a handful of countries are rich enough to indulge. The poor countries, which collectively comprise by far the larger part of the world's population, are likely to pay little heed to philosophical musings from their rich neighbours that perhaps economic growth is not after all an object worth pursuing. It seems certain therefore that such misgivings notwithstanding, the present concern to accelerate growth will continue to be felt in many parts of the world, and so long as it is many economists will bend their efforts to seeking to understand better its sources and processes. That economic history, in turn, should have some part to play in this inquiry can scarcely be doubted.

The measurement of economic growth

The question still remains open, however, whether there may not be some measure, more defensible from a welfare standpoint and less prone to data difficulties, which we could substitute for *per capita* income as derived from national accounting studies? There have in fact been several attempts to find an alternative. In the earlier post-war years M. K. Bennett, noting the conceptual deficiencies of national accounts and their unavailability or poor quality in many cases, proposed a method of comparing countries in respect of their standard of living by calculating an average of their rankings in respect of each of a number of 'non-monetary' indicators, such as number of passenger cars, postal traffic and school enrolment ratios.[8] The chief objection to Bennett's procedure (which produced, however, a ranking close to that suggested by national income comparisons) is that there is no theoretical justification either for the particular collection of items included or, still less, for their combination into an unweighted average. More recently Wilfred Beckerman has sought to improve on Bennett's procedure by using regression analysis to test which non-monetary indicators, of the almost infinite variety available for cross-country comparison, correlate most closely with total consumption, and then using the indicators selected and their regression coefficients to 'predict' consumption levels for countries where appropriate money data do not exist.[9] This procedure has the attraction of being theoretically more defensible and also of requiring many fewer data than Bennett's, and the results seem to suggest that even with as few as two or three 'indicators' extremely accurate prediction of consumption levels can be achieved.

In view of the paucity and unreliability of estimates of national income for earlier historical periods, some investigation of the possibility of using an approach similar to that of Beckerman for the purpose of historical, rather than cross-country, comparisons is certainly warranted. (Incidentally, Beckerman's method is *not* as novel as he claims, for in 1960 F. Seton published an estimate of Soviet industrial growth obtained by regressing three quantity indicators – fuel consumption, steel produced and electric power generated – on indices of total industrial output in twelve Western countries, and then using the equation yielding the best fit to 'predict' the historical trend of Soviet industrial production.[10])

Unfortunately, it is possible to see substantial difficulties in historical exercises of this type. This is at once apparent in that the three non-monetary indicators in Beckerman's best-fitting equation are steel consumption, the stock of telephones and the number of road vehicles. Clearly this particular collection of commodities would not take us far back in time. The indicators in question were selected, however, by regressing various possible candidates on contemporary (post-World War II) estimates of total consumption for a group of Western countries. To find indicators apt for *historical* prediction we would need to select them and estimate their coefficients from equations using time series drawn from the history of those countries for which appropriate expenditure and consumption data exist. In the case of the Beckerman study, the 'control group' comprised in the main the nine countries for which Milton Gilbert and associates[11] made estimates of real consumption levels in the post-war years. The distinctive feature of the Gilbert studies was an attempt to overcome the distortion introduced by comparing consumption levels by conversion of national income data at official exchange rates – which, as is well known, fail to reflect real differences to price levels. Unfortunately, no comparable studies exist for earlier historical periods, nor in all probability are the price deflators used to construct price time-series of national income really appropriate, in many instances, to their purpose. The significance of this is that in the absence of a control group for which *real* consumption or income levels, over time and as between countries at any one point of time, are known, any distortions which afflict the presently available estimates would be transmitted into the predicting equation derived from them, so that the procedure would do nothing to eradicate the deficiencies of existing series. At best, it would merely permit similarly deficient predictions of trends in income and consumption levels to be made for countries for which such estimates, via conventional national income accounts, do not presently exist.

There is another difficulty which is absent, or less pressing, in contemporary cross-country comparisons, namely that arising from the mutability of wants over time, a feature we have already discussed. There is no need to repeat what has already been said on this subject. The implication is that to the extent that the pattern of tastes and preferences changes over time, the chance of finding any (small) collection of items of expenditure highly correlated with total expenditure throughout the period in question is correspondingly reduced. Even were a satisfactory control group available, therefore, the Beckerman approach would be conceptually

B

less promising in time-series than in cross-country comparisons. This, indeed, is acknowledged by Beckerman himself, who writes:

> . . . there are powerful reasons for believing that the relationships over time, when techniques, tastes, etc., are all changing are not the same as those existing over space, even with widely different income levels.[12]

Even if all these difficulties were overcome, however, the attraction of a measure of real income derived from non-monetary indicators is diminished by the difficulty of using it in that sort of analysis of the sources and contours of growth which we wish to perform. As a means of readily calculating estimates of the growth of consumption or real income, avoiding some of the data deficiencies and conceptual uncertainties of the conventional national income approach, the use of non-monetary indicators might be warmly welcomed by the economic historian, could the difficulties mentioned in the preceding paragraphs be surmounted. But the attraction of national accounting is that its systematic, interlocking and internally-consistent character facilitates the integration of sectoral or single-factor studies with that of the growth of the whole economy. By contrast it is hard to see how any ready integration of (e.g.) capital inputs could be effected with what is in effect a 'proxy' for real income, or how this proxy could be disaggregated, as we so often wish, to yield estimates of the components of the aggregate for which it *is* a proxy. It seems, then, that not only are we stuck with economic growth whether we think it a thing worth striving for or not; we are also stuck – at least for analytical purposes – with the national accounting measure of it. That being so, a closer look at some of the difficulties specific to historical estimates of real national income is called for.

National income accounting: progress, promise and pitfalls

Evidently the first and major difficulty is the insufficiency of data on which to construct reliable estimates for more than a relatively few recent decades. Although attempts to estimate the national income or 'dividend' – early terminology was, evidently, inexact – date from at least as early as the exercises of Petty and King in England in the later seventeenth century,[13] inquiry along these lines, though increasingly frequent, remained the province of isolated individuals until after World War I. Possibly the only *official* estimates of national income prior to that war, curiously enough, were those of the Victorian and New South Wales Government Statisticians, Hayter and Coghlan, in the last decade of the nineteenth and first years of the twentieth centuries.[14] These early experiments, however, gave valuable experience of the problems of using data originally gathered for other purposes in the construction of income estimates, and also insight into the possibility and respective merits of the three major alternatives, the product, income and expenditure approaches. Unfortunately economic theory had meanwhile added relatively little to the conceptual bases of national accounting.

In the years between the wars a number of countries inaugurated official national income estimates, not necessarily on an annual basis. The spread of the practice was assisted by the depression of the 1930s and the sharp increase in government intervention in economic life which it prompted. In pre-World War II years, too, the publication of Keynes' *General Theory* and the debate which it inaugurated directed the attention of economic theorists sharply towards macro-economic magnitudes and their interrelationships. Finally, the demands of the war economy called for greater knowledge and more conscious planning of the allocation of national economic resources; the Kingsley-Wood budget of 1941 was the first in the United Kingdom to be intended as a major instrument of economic management along Keynesian lines, and this concept involved framing it against an estimate of the national income which was prepared at the British Treasury under Keynes' direction. After World War II, more and more governments began to make annual estimates of the national income, and such series are now available for the large majority of nations – though subject, without doubt, to widely-varying degrees of reliability.

Several countries which made no official estimates prior to World War II have seized a later opportunity to construct an estimate for a pre-war year, usually 1938–9, for purposes of comparison.

The situation is therefore that we have official estimates for a large number of countries for a varying span of post-World War II years. The number of such estimates for pre-war years is, however, much smaller, and for most countries we are dependent for the inter-war years, and for all countries before 1914, on reconstructions attempted in recent years. In some cases these reconstructions have themselves been performed officially, but in more they are the work of private individuals or research teams. In perhaps the majority of cases these reconstructions have employed the output approach, production statistics being better for most countries than the tax or wage and salary data required by the income approach. In the case of the United Kingdom, however, the relative poverty of production data and the unusually early introduction of income tax, due to the need to find an alternative source of revenue when free trade was espoused in the 1840s, have led to a preference for the income approach. Few countries can boast a combination of income, output and expenditure estimates such as Professor Hoffmann has made available for Germany. In a few instances scholars have also made use of, or have republished with commentary and perhaps some reworking, one or more of the better of the estimates made by the earlier pioneers of national accounting.

There exist, then, more or less continuous estimates of pre-1914 income or product, of varying complexity and reliability, for some fourteen or fifteen countries. Most of these begin no earlier than the middle of the nineteenth century, some even later. Only in a few instances are series available for years before the mid-nineteenth century, and mostly they take the form of reworking of contemporary estimates. Even in the case of the U.S.A., the scholarly and careful attempts to carry knowledge of the major economic magnitudes back to the early nineteenth century have not generated complete agreement on the course of these aggregates,[15] while the oft-quoted estimates of King and his eighteenth-century successors in England are really only intelligent guesses. But uncertainty is not confined to these earlier figures, for continuing research suggests from time to time the need for possibly substantial revision of series for later periods too. Notably, the original estimates by Ohkawa and his associates for Japanese income in the Meiji years have been queried from several quarters, and are now fairly generally agreed to have been substantially too low.[16] More recent work has not, however, produced a consensus as to what the true rate of growth was, and we are compelled for the time being to regard all pre-1914 estimates for Japan as provisional.

In the case of Japan, whose early growth was estimated essentially via the product approach, it is disagreement as to the volume of output of some major sectors, and also the alleged implausibility of some assumptions about the tertiary sector, which led to the call for revision of the original estimates. In the case of the United Kingdom, however, Dr Phyllis Deane has proposed a major revision of earlier views on the nineteenth-century growth of real income chiefly for a different reason, namely that an inappropriate (in her view) price deflator was used to convert from current to constant prices.[17] The twin problems of price deflators and weighting procedures do indeed constitute an even more formidable hurdle to one estimating the historical trend of real incomes than to those concerned to effect cross-country comparisons at a particular point of time. In the case Dr Deane is concerned with, and doubtless in many others where the possible need for revision has not yet been so clearly perceived, the immediate problem is the paucity or unreliability of *appropriate* price indices for deflating the various components of income or transforming volume into value series through time. But this data problem may well be less serious than the *conceptual* difficulty posed by the combination of changing relative prices and changing composition of output.

The difficulty here is analogous with that encountered in

comparing output or consumption measures in two countries. It has become well known in recent years that comparisons of *per capita* incomes translated at official exchange rates tend to give a false picture of relative real incomes because the rates in question do not accurately reflect the differences in purchasing power of the national currencies.[18] But equally, comparisons of the aggregate value of, say, consumption do not result in the same picture if measured in the prices of Country *A* as when measured in the prices of Country *B*. Generally, measurement in Country *A*'s prices results in a comparison less flattering, relatively, to Country *A* than if measurement is undertaken in Country *B*'s prices. This is because not only the *general* level of prices may differ in the two countries, but also *relative* prices of different classes of commodities. Consumers tend to adjust rationally to these relative differences, buying in each country more of the goods and services which are relatively cheap and less of those which are relatively dear. Estimating Country *A*'s overall consumption level *vis-à-vis* Country *B*'s in the prices of Country *A* therefore results in an unflattering comparison, since it attaches a relatively *small* weight to those goods and services of which *A* consumes relatively more and a relatively *large* weight to those of which it consumes relatively less.

A similar problem arises in comparing consumption (or output) levels for the same country at two points of time, if the structure of output and relative prices is changing. Aggregating output in prices of an early year, say year 1, allots weights to the various components according to relative prices in that year. This will result in a downward bias compared with output in some later year, say year 2, measured in year 1 prices, *if* the trends of output and of prices for various categories of goods and services between years 1 and 2 are inversely related – if, that is to say, the output of those goods which were *relatively* dear in year 1 grows faster than average and the output of those goods which were *relatively* cheap in year 1 grows more slowly than average (*relatively*, that is, to year 2 in each case). This is likely, since a relatively falling price for a commodity usually indicates that it is experiencing an above-average rate of growth of productivity, which is usually associated with an above-average rate of growth of output; and also since consumers (including the export market) will tend to buy more of goods which are becoming relatively cheaper and less of those which are becoming relatively dearer. Hence comparing the output for any two years in prices of the earlier year tends to depress the measure of output for that year relative to the later year, while comparison in the prices of the later year has the opposite effect. It follows in turn from this that if a compound rate of growth is calculated from the output level of the earlier year to that of the later, measurement in prices of the *earlier* year will suggest a higher rate of growth than if prices of the later year are used.

How important this effect may be when the rate of change in the output mix and in relative prices is rapid has been shown by alternative calculations by Western scholars of the rate of growth of Soviet output during the early five-year plans. Over the interval 1928–37, Soviet G.N.P. is estimated to have risen by 174·6 per cent, a compound rate of growth of 11·9 per cent per annum, if measured in 1928 prices; but by only 71·6 per cent, a growth rate of 6·2 per cent per annum, if measured in 1937 prices. (It is noteworthy that very little difference, in contrast, is made to measures of post-1937 Soviet growth by the use of 1937 or 1950 price weights; the big disparity is that which arises from the use of alternative weights for the period of dramatic change in economic structure and relative prices under the early five-year plans.) Despite the shortness of this interval, the disparity is big enough to result in substantially different appraisals of Soviet growth achievement over the whole interval 1928–61, the compound rate of increase of G.N.P. being 6·7 per cent in 1928 prices to 1937, and 1937 prices thereafter, but only 5·2 per cent in 1937 prices throughout. When we turn, of course, to estimate the trend of Soviet *productivity*, an even greater proportionate difference is implied by the choice between the two alternative measures of output.[19]

Unfortunately, it is not only in respect of the analysis of Soviet growth itself that the calculations just discussed suggest the need for caution. For while few if any countries have experienced in a mere decade as profound and rapid a change in economic structure as that achieved by the Soviet Union from 1928 to 1937, present-day industrial countries have of course undergone similar degrees of transformation over longer periods. Regrettably there is no theoretical justification for expecting that the mere lengthening of the time interval over which a given degree of structural change has taken place should reduce the sensitivity of the estimates of output over it to the system of weights adopted. In this respect the disquieting fact is that there have been no explicit tests in capitalist countries comparable in care and scholarship with those of the leading Western students of Soviet growth, of the difference which the choice of alternative weights would make to estimates of economic growth in such a country. The one experiment of some magnitude which has been performed, Alexander Gerschenkron's measure of U.S. machinery and vehicles output between 1899 and 1939, produced far from reassuring results.[20] It is true that 'machinery' is a sector of unusually heterogeneous composition and one subject, over the interval in question, to rapid technological change. These features would lead one to expect an abnormally high sensitivity of the measure of output change to the weighting procedure chosen. But even allowing for this, one can take little comfort from the result of Gerschenkron's calculations, which showed the output of the sector concerned multiplying more than fifteen-fold in 1899 prices, but barely doubling in the prices of 1939! While one can readily see political and other reasons for the unusual degree of attention lavished by Western scholars on Soviet economic growth, the interests of scholarship cry out for the extension of similar types of inquiry to some of the leading Western countries.

There are several further considerations of some importance in measuring long-term growth, especially those turning upon quality changes and the introduction of new commodities over time, which would warrant considerable discussion. But already the modest evidence we have to offer on long-term growth, previously offered visually in fig. 1.1 and now to be presented in tabular form, has been overwhelmed by a deluge of comment, qualification and cautionary admonition. We therefore desist from further discussion along such lines and for what it is worth present Table 1.1, which assembles some data on the growth of total product, of product per head of the population and of product per man-hour (all in constant prices) for a number of contrasting countries over the years 1870–1965. Before making some interpretative comments, a few remarks on the sources of this table are called for, though detailed reference to the works drawn on is relegated to the notes to the table on p. 23.

The growth of income in modern times

There have been many presentations of the evidence on the long-run course of historical growth, among the best known being the series of studies by Simon Kuznets;[21] an article by Angus Maddison, whose data have been subsequently extended and revised in two books;[22] and a paper in the *National Institute Economic Review* by Paige, Blackaby and Freund.[23] Due allowance made for differences of coverage and timing, these various studies present an essentially similar picture of the contours of long-term economic growth – an agreement which is not surprising considering that they are all based in the last resort on estimates of growth of product in individual countries contained in the same series of monographs, several of them inspired and helped by the United States Social Science Research Council. Choice between these sources can therefore be exercised on relatively trivial grounds of convenience rather than in the light of more fundamental considerations.

Our table is drawn predominantly, for the years before 1960, from Mr Maddison's works. The reasons for preferring this source were these: (1) Maddison's chronological presentation of his data does not vary from country to country, as does that of Kuznets, and is more appropriately subdivided

TABLE 1.1 *The growth of product, 1870–1965 (annual average percentage growth)*

	1870–1913			1913–1950			1950–1960			1960–1965		
	Total	Per head of population	Per man-hour	Total	Per head of population	Per man-hour	Total	Per head of population	Per man-hour	Total	Per head of population	Per person employed
	1	2	3	4	5	6	7	8	9	10	11	12
Australia	3.5	0.8	—	2.0	0.6	—	3.9	1.5	—	4.5	2.3	—
Canada	3.8	2.0	2.1	2.8	1.3	2.1	3.9	1.2	2.5	5.5	3.6	2.6
France	1.6	1.4	1.8	0.7	0.7	1.6	4.4	3.5	3.9	5.1	3.8	4.6
Germany	2.9ᵃ	1.7ᵃ	2.1ᵃ	1.2	0.4	0.9	7.6	6.5	6.0	4.8	3.5	4.1
Italy	1.4	0.7	1.2	1.3	0.6	1.9	5.9	5.3	4.1	5.1	4.3	4.5
Japan	2.7ᵇ	1.7ᵇ	2.0ᵇ	1.7	0.3	—	9.5	8.2	—	9.6	8.5	8.3
Sweden	3.0	2.3	2.7	2.	1.6	2.0	3.3	2.6	3.5	5.1	4.4	4.1
U.K.	2.0	1.0	1.2	1.3	0.8	1.3	2.6	2.2	2.0	3.3	2.3	2.5
U.S.A.	4.3ᵃ	2.2ᵃ	2.4ᵃ	2.9	1.7	2.4	3.2	1.8	1.6	4.5	3.0	2.9
Russia/U.S.S.R.	2.5	0.9	—	6.4ᶜ	5.5ᶜ	3.5ᶜ	7.5	5.6	6.6	4.9f	3.3f	—
Belgium	2.7	1.7	2.0	1.0	0.7	1.4	2.9	2.3	2.5	4.5	3.8	3.5
Denmark	3.2	2.1	2.6	2.1	1.1	1.5	3.3	2.6	2.9	4.9	4.1	3.8
Netherlands	2.2ᵈ	0.8ᵈ	1.1ᵈ	2.1	0.7	1.1	4.9	3.6	3.7	4.8	3.4	3.2
Switzerland	2.4ᵉ	1.3ᵉ	1.6ᵉ	2.0	1.5	1.9	5.1	3.7	4.2	5.3	3.1	2.9

— = not available

Notes:

$a = 1871\text{–}1913$

$b = 1879\text{–}1913$: line 6, column 3 = growth rate of product per person employed.

$c = 1928\text{–}1950$ $d = 1900\text{–}1913$ $e = 1890\text{–}1913$ $f = 1960\text{–}1964$

Column 12 measures output per person employed, *not* output per man-hour (as in columns 3, 6 and 9).

Sources:

Lines 1–3, 5–14, column 1: calculated from Maddison (1969), Table B–1, pp. 154–5.

Line 1, column 2: population relatives from Maddison (1969), Table C–1, p. 157.

Line 1, columns 4, 5, 7, 8, 10, 11: calculated from *ibid.*, Table B–1, pp. 154–5; population data from *Official Yearbook of the Commonwealth of Australia*.

Lines 2, 3, 5, 7, 9, 11–14, columns 2–9: line 4, columns 3–9: line 8, columns 7–9: Maddison (1964), Tables I–1, p. 28; I–3, 30; I–7, p. 37.

Lines 2–9, 11–14, columns 10, 12: *Economic Growth 1960–1970: A Mid-decade Review of Prospects* (Paris, O.E.C.D., 1966), Table V, p. 28.

Lines 2–14, column 11: population data from U.N. *Demographic Yearbook*.

Line 4, columns 1, 2: calculated from Hoffmann (1965), Table 103, pp. 454–5; Table 1, pp. 172–4.

Lines 6, 10, column 2: Maddison (1969), Table 8a, p. 31.

Line 6, column 3: persons employed from K. Ohkawa and associates, *The Growth Rate of the Japanese Economy since 1878* (Tokyo, Kikokuniya Bookstore, 1957), Table 3, p. 19.

Line 6, columns 4, 5, 7, 8: calculated from Maddison (1969), Table B–1, pp. 154–5; population data from *ibid.*, Table C–1, p. 157, and U.N. *Demographic Yearbook*.

Line 8, column 2: population data from B. R. Mitchell and Phyllis Deane, *Abstract of British Historical Statistics* (Cambridge, Cambridge U.P., 1962), 9–10.

Line 8, columns 3–6: calculated from Maddison (1969), Table B–1, pp. 154–5; man-hours calculated from Maddison (1964), Tables F–1, G–1, G–2, pp. 224, 228; population relatives from Maddison (1964), Table B–1, pp. 205–6.

Line 10, columns 4–9: calculated from Moorsteen and Powell (1966), Tables T–47, T–48, pp. 361–3, and Table T–51, p. 365. Population data from Abram Bergson, *The Real National Income of Soviet Russia Since 1928* (Cambridge, Mass., Harvard U.P., 1961), Table K–1, p. 442 (1938 and 1950), and U.N. *Demographic Yearbook* (1960).

Line 10, column 10: calculated from Abraham S. Becker, *Soviet National Income 1958–1964* (University of California Press, 1969), Table K–1, pp. 526–7 (G.N.P. at 1958 Adjusted Factor Cost).

for our purposes than that of the *National Institute Economic Review* paper; (2) Maddison attempts an estimate of rates of growth per man-hour, as well as total and per head of the population, which is worth reproducing even though the evidence is sketchy and the values suggested must be regarded with extreme reserve; (3) his data are the most up to date in the sense both of being calculated to very recent terminal years and of incorporating the latest single-country revisions to hand; (4) Mr Maddison's position on the staff of O.E.C.D. probably ensures that his figures are conceptually comparable (save for being basically on a G.D.P. rather than a G.N.P. basis) with later estimates for 1960–5 made by that organization, and these estimates can therefore readily be included in the table.

A few comments on individual countries must be made. The figures for German total product and product per head 1871–1913 have been calculated direct from Professor Hoffmann's book, in order to avoid the necessity of making an adjustment to Hoffmann's 1870 figures for the omission of Alsace-Lorraine, an adjustment which has to be based on its share of *population* (rather than of product), which is Mr Maddison's procedure. The growth estimates for the United Kingdom incorporate recent revisions mentioned elsewhere in the text, the necessity for which is argued by Phyllis Deane.[24] Regrettably, reliable estimates for Great Britain alone (i.e. excluding Ireland) are not yet available, despite Professor Butlin's convincing demonstration that the confounding of Great Britain and Ireland may result in an average which is misleading if it is explanations of *British* growth which are the focus of interest.[25]

The most serious and controversial revision in Mr Maddison's latest book (and incorporated in Table 1.1) is that applied to the estimates of Japanese growth, particularly for the years before 1913. It now seems virtually certain that the pioneering study by Professor Ohkawa and others substantially overstated the rate of Japanese growth, especially for the Meiji period. The estimates of agricultural productivity, in particular, have been strongly criticized by Nakamura, and though Nakamura himself is now under challenge, an important part at least of his case – that alleging an under-estimate of arable acreage in the early Meiji period – appears to carry complete conviction. Indeed, a later revision by Ohkawa and Rosovsky tacitly accepts the need for a sharp downward revision of the original estimate of agricultural growth and proposes a substantially lower overall rate of growth for 1879–1913, though one still above the figure borrowed here from Maddison. Secondly, Shionoya has more recently produced a new index of manufacturing output for the period 1874–1940 which shows a dramatically lower growth rate than the old Nagoya index used by Ohkawa for the period up to 1929. Finally, Maddison himself argues, convincingly it seems, that the rates of growth both of productivity and of employment in the services sector are substantially exaggerated even in the revised Ohkawa–Rosovsky estimates.[26] All in all, while the continuation of active research and debate on Japanese economic growth enjoins caution, particularly on the part of the non-specialist, it does seem probable that even the *revised* Ohkawa–Rosovsky estimates, and certainly the original Ohkawa and associates ones, inflate the Japanese achievement, especially before 1913. That achievement is still remarkable; but it is less miraculous than previously thought, *both* because the rate of growth was lower *and* because the starting-point *c.* 1878 was higher and thus less unpropitious. In Table 1.1 we have used the estimate offered by Maddison in *Economic Growth in Japan and the USSR* in the belief that it is substantially closer to the truth than the original Ohkawa figure, and probably than the revised Ohkawa–Rosovsky figure.

Finally, we have preferred to calculate the rate of Soviet growth in the period 1928–50 direct from the major study by Moorsteen and Powell, using the estimates of product in 1928 prices for the interval 1928–37 and in 1937 prices thereafter. Here our procedure differs from that both of Maddison and of Kuznets, who use the estimates in 1937 prices throughout. The choice is far from a trivial decision since, as already explained, estimates of the Soviet rate of growth under the early five-year plans differ substantially according to whether 1928 or 1937 price weights are used. The belief underlying our decision is that since Soviet economic history in the years in question had *de facto* the character of a dramatic and ruthless pursuit of industrialization, and since it was the *intention* of Soviet policy makers to pursue such a goal, it is appropriate to judge performance of the Soviet economy in that period in the light of the speed of its transformation towards the 1937 'output mix' – and this, broadly, is what is measured by output in 1928 prices. Output in 1937 prices, by contrast, measures the economy's changing capacity to produce the 1928 product mix – that, that is to say, of an underdeveloped agricultural society – which seems a less appropriate measure of Soviet achievement.

In making this choice, however, it should be stressed that it too is open to substantial criticism, and is in no sense to be absolutely preferred to the alternative.[27] Further, the reader should recall that as yet alternative estimates using different weights are not available for non-communist countries, in some of which long-run growth rates covering a period of pronounced structural change would probably reveal a similar sensitivity as in the case of the Soviet Union to alternative weighting systems. The effect of our choice, at all events, is to suggest a higher rate of Soviet growth during the whole interval 1928–50 than either Maddison or Kuznets envisage, though the choice of different periods by these writers would conceal the discrepancy from the casual reader. (It may be added that Russia is the only country in Table 1.1 for which estimates are not continuous, there being no provision in it for the interval 1913–28. Some scholars believe that the level of real *per capita* income may have been *about* the same in 1928 as in 1913.)

A few comments on the table can at last be made. It can be seen that rates of growth, both of total and of *per capita* income, have shown a considerable dispersion both over time and between countries. In the forty-odd years before World War I, rates of growth of aggregate product ranged between annual averages of 1·6 (France) and of 4·3 (U.S.A.) per cent; for product per head of population the range was between 0·7 (Italy) and 2·3 (Sweden) per cent. There was a slight tendency for rates of growth of total product to 'cluster' around the middle of the range, seven of the fourteen countries recording rates between 2·4 and 3·2 per cent, but no such tendency in the case of *per capita* growth rates, save that three countries happened to have the same rate (1·7 per cent). There is fully as much dispersion among the countries in the following period, 1913–50, in respect of both total and *per capita* growth. It is noteworthy that aggregate growth in this period was lower – substantially so in most cases – than before 1913 for all countries except Russia, where the growth rates shown refer, in fact, to the years 1928–50. *Per capita* growth rates were also lower than before 1913 in all cases except Russia and Switzerland, but for some countries less markedly lower – a contrast resulting, of course, from a widespread decline in birth rates in Western countries during the inter-war period.

It seems clear, however – despite the somewhat adventurous nature of Mr Maddison's calculations here – that the rate of growth of post-1913 output per man-hour was not as much below the corresponding pre-1913 figure as that of either total or *per capita* product. In all cases except that of the Soviet Union after 1928, output per man-hour rose more rapidly than *per capita* output throughout the pre-1950 period, a fact which reflects the general shortening of the working week. Actually, this shortening proceeded more rapidly in most cases than might be casually inferred from these figures, since the widespread fall of the birth rate between the wars implied in most countries a fall in the proportion of the population aged 0–14 and a rise in the share of those in the working years of life (15–64). This change in age structure would of course have led *ceteris paribus* to an increase in man-hours per head of (total) population; that these in fact declined thus implies a more rapid trend towards greater leisure than might at first have been thought.[28] The implication of the relatively more buoyant trend of output per man-hour than of total or *per capita* output between 1913 and 1950 is that the tendency towards a retardation of productivity improvement was less pronounced than might be thought from the figures of aggregate output: to some extent the decline in the rate of growth of the latter resulted from a slower growth of labour inputs reflecting a rising valuation of leisure. This, in turn, seems easy to explain in terms of rising real incomes, the growing power of trade unions, and perhaps the rise of entertainment industries, though this last was clearly as much result as cause.

The case of the Soviet Union from 1928 to 1950 stands out in sharp contrast; as we shall see, the rapid growth rate during that interval was achieved principally by a rapid increase of inputs, including an especially rapid increase of man-hours brought about by the elimination of unemployment, the reduction of rural *under*employment, and a sharp rise in the paid employment of women. By contrast, the improvement in productivity was somewhat less impressive (though according to the particular estimates we have chosen, output per man-hour nevertheless rose faster in the Soviet Union than in any other country before 1950). Reflecting these facts, Soviet output per man-hour, in contrast with that of other countries, rose very substantially less not only than total output, but also than output per head of the population.

The rates of growth shown for the interval 1913–50 were, of course, much more affected by war than those for any of the other three periods shown, and perhaps also by depression, though of course some would regard the latter as a 'normal' element of the growth process. There has been a good deal of discussion as to what allowance, if any, would be proper for such events in calculating long-term 'normal' growth rates. To the economic historian it seems that any proposal for making a single adjustment for all countries, or in the case of war for, say, all belligerents, is ruled out by the differing effects the events in question had on different countries. Any such adjustment would result in quite arbitrary 'normal' rates. Of the countries listed, for example, only the Soviet Union and Japan suffered little if any damage from the world economic crisis of 1929–33, but the extent to which other countries experienced a loss of real income varied a good deal from case to case, and one major country (U.K.) suffered relatively little loss only, it seems, because it had been relatively less prosperous than other industrial countries in the years immediately preceding the depression. In the light of such divergent experiences, to make any uniform across-the-board adjustment for the effect of the depression seems quite unwarranted.

This conclusion holds even more strongly for the effect of the world wars on growth, where the experience of individual countries diverged yet more sharply. To mention only extreme cases, World War II led to a marked increase in U.S. output, whereas in Japan it brought about a catastrophic setback which put national product in the immediate post-war years back to the level of the mid-1920s. (It was this alone which accounts for the relatively modest Japanese growth recorded in Table 1.1 for 1913–50; excluding the years 1937–47 the Japanese growth record is an outstanding one throughout.) These differences of experience *during* the wars were to some extent counteracted by contrary offsetting experiences afterwards; there is evidence that *some* part of the very high growth rates recorded for, e.g., Japan and Germany since about 1950 represents a 'rebound' from the unusually adverse effect of the war on their economies, whereas the war lifted the U.S. economy to a 'ceiling' level of performance from which further rapid growth in the post-war years was much more difficult. To allow for the war by, say, omitting the years 1939–45 from consideration and calculating long-term growth from the record of peace years only is therefore inadmissible, in so far as the impact of major war on long-term growth is *not* confined to its direct effect on output during the war years alone. To make matters even more complicated, the two world wars did not affect each individual nation in the same degree or even in the same direction. The U.S. economy, on the whole, benefited from both world wars, but more from the second than from the first. Russia suffered in both, but probably more from the first than from the second (it is difficult here to disentangle effects of the war from those of the Revolution and the Civil War). Japan's economy suffered catastrophically from the effects of bombing in World War II, but was on the whole strengthened, like that of the U.S.A. and for much the same reasons, in its predecessor.

In the light of such diverging experiences the first instinct of the economic historian is to abandon the search for any easy formula for allowing for the effects of major crises and, indeed, the very concept of a 'normal' rate of growth, and to rest satisfied with charting and explaining the growth record of each individual country and *possibly* (though the usefulness of this operation is much open to question) speculating what the economic history of the country concerned *might have been* like if the war or other crisis had not occurred. There would be merit, however, in adopting a slightly less agnostic position than this by experimenting with groupings designed to capture, in some degree, the differing impact of depression or of war. For example, there is at once some gain in systematic understanding if we subdivide countries during war years into even three groups:

1. belligerents who were subjected to prolonged and heavy aerial bombardment and/or invasion;
2. belligerents exempt from such attack;
3. non-belligerents.

It is easy now to discern and explain *some* similarities of experience within each group as evidenced in the economic history from *c.* 1939 to 1945 of, respectively, Japan and Russia; the U.S.A. and Australia; Sweden and Argentina. More, we can account immediately for the differing fortunes of Japan in World War I (when she was in group 2) and in World War II (when she was in group 1). Analysis along these lines would counter the popular dictum that no one wins twentieth-century wars by contending that in the two world wars there were *military* victors and vanquished and *economic* victors and vanquished, but that in neither case were either the two lists of victors or the two lists of vanquished identical.

When we turn to the two post-World War II subdivisions of Table 1.1, the salient feature is of course the sharp acceleration of growth both of *total* and of *per capita* product. This emerges with clarity in the graphical presentation in fig. 1.1. With the sole exception of the U.S.A. the rate of growth of total product during the 1950s exceeded that in both earlier subdivisions; even for the U.S.A. growth was faster than in 1913–50. In several cases the contrast in respect of *per capita* growth rate is even more marked, though Canada now joins the U.S.A. in recording slower *per capita* growth than in one or both earlier periods. Between 1960 and 1965 both North American countries join the rest in experiencing faster total and *per capita* growth than before 1950, and while some continental European countries experienced slightly slower growth in the first half of the 1960s than in the 1950s, the relatively slowly-growing countries like Australia, the United Kingdom, Belgium and the U.S.A. improved their performance somewhat, thus contributing to a narrowing of the range of growth rates and the achievement of an even more impressive 'average' for these advanced countries.

It has already been suggested that this post-war experience of 'explosive growth' or 'super-growth', as it has been variously christened,[29] has in some cases and in part the character of a 'rebound' from wartime dislocation and destruction. The notion here, in general terms, is that badly-hit belligerent countries inherited from pre-war years certain necessary conditions for higher output which were ineffectual because of the absence of other necessary conditions. If the latter could be made good relatively cheaply and quickly, rapid growth might for a time ensue without the appearance of too much effort. For example, the physical destruction of capital in countries such as Japan and Germany, though extensive, was not total, but some of the capital which survived was rendered non-productive by the

destruction of complementary capital: railway track without
the wagons to run on it, or wagons without engines to pull
them. In such a case the whole system might be made productive once again by relatively modest investments in complementary assets. More generally, a country such as Germany
inherited from the past a tremendous stock of *human* capital
embodied in the skills of technologists, business leaders and
skilled workers, which provided the basis for rapid growth
once the requisite material inputs were forthcoming. It is
along such lines that many would explain the brilliant
effectiveness of the moderate injections of U.S. capital under
the Marshall Plan, as opposed to the much more equivocal
record of success achieved by subsequent (and larger)
programmes of aid to countries lacking the inherited skills of
Western Europe.

But rapid growth has now gone on sufficiently long for it
to be impossible to ascribe its continuance to any 'rebound'
effect from a war which finished more than a quarter of a
century ago. The sources of rapid growth in the post-war
years, especially in Western Europe, in Russia, and in Japan,
have already become the subject of a considerable literature
which cannot be summarized here. But we can anticipate
later discussion by referring to three characteristics of the
post-war economic world which are certainly to be linked
with this rapid growth as cause or, in part, as effect: the
accelerated pace of technological advance;[30] the achievement by many countries of investment ratios substantially in
excess of previously recorded levels;[31] and – in contrast with
several preceding decades of opposing experience – an
expansion of world trade at a rate considerably outstripping
the growth of world output.[32]

. The estimates of the rate of growth over the whole period
from the later nineteenth century to 1965 implied by Table
1.1 must be viewed with considerable reserve in view of the
conceptual and data uncertainties discussed earlier. Grouping the rates for the fourteen countries into ranges, so as to
remind ourselves of the considerable margin of uncertainty
in the results, and ordering countries in descending rate of

growth of *per capita* product calculated from starting year to 1965, we have the following picture:

TABLE 1.2   *Growth rates, later nineteenth century to 1965*

Annual average growth of real *per capita* income	Countries
≥2·0 per cent	Russia
	Japan
	Sweden
	United States
1·5 < 2·0 per cent	Denmark
	Switzerland
	Germany
	Canada
	Belgium
1·0 < 1·5 per cent	Netherlands
	France
	Italy
	United Kingdom
<1·0 per cent	Australia

In general, this ordering is easy to reconcile with what we know as to present-day differences of real *per capita* income and with the more qualitative and partial indications as to such differences in the mid-nineteenth century. Thus, for example, the pre-eminence of the United States at the present day in respect of *per capita* income reflects a very high standing in regard to the same measure a century ago, combined with a high rate of *per capita* growth; Canada doubtless started at a slightly lower level and has also grown somewhat more slowly. The United Kingdom was probably slightly ahead of both these countries in the starting year but has clearly fallen behind owing to its much lower long-run growth rate. Sweden, on the other hand, was behind all three countries mentioned in the mid-nineteenth century but has overhauled the United Kingdom and approached closer to the other two thanks to its rapid and well-sustained growth. The three major countries of Western Europe – the United

Kingdom, France and Germany – started from nineteenth-century positions of respectively decreasing affluence; but growth rates of respectively increasing rapidity brought them to roughly similar levels of *per capita* product during the 1960s. Italy, whose average long-run growth rate most closely resembles that of France, started from a position of distinctly greater backwardness and poverty than any of these three *c.* 1870, and was accordingly still behind in the 1960s, though catching up fast on Britain. The moderate levels of *per capita* product in present-day Russia and Japan, in conjunction with their outstanding growth achievements, suggest – as all other evidence would confirm – starting points of exceptional backwardness in the later nineteenth century (or in Russia's case, indeed, in 1928). Possibly the most interesting and unfamiliar case is that of Australia, whose very high present level of relative real income and very low growth rate combine to suggest that this country may have headed the international table of real *per capita* income in the mid-nineteenth century* – a position which, if New Zealand's domestic product had been reliably estimated for years prior to 1918, as it has not, she would probably be found to have shared with Australia.

Economic growth before the mid-nineteenth century

What of the years before 1870? On this, of course, Table 1.1 affords no direct evidence, and the indications which do

---

* *Direct* comparisons between modern estimates of mid-nineteenth-century income levels in different countries are impeded by the lack of estimates of exchange rates calculated to equalize purchasing power of national currencies. The inadequacy of official exchange rates for such comparisons in recent years has been shown by the studies of Milton Gilbert and associates. It is a matter for conjecture whether purchasing-power-parity rates would have been further removed from official rates in the mid-nineteenth century than a hundred years later, or not. A possibly lower level of integration of international markets and higher relative transport costs would suggest a wider spread; generally lower tariffs and other impediments to trade (in the 1850s and 1860s), a smaller distorting influence from government intervention (e.g. agricultural subsidies) and the lesser role of the service sector would tell in the opposite

exist for a few countries have not been reproduced because of their generally low level of reliability. It has been pointed out, however, that evidence such as that in the table casts an indirect but still powerful light on this problem by suggesting that it is impossible that the long-run growth rates over the last century should have been sustained for long periods prior to the mid-nineteenth century. This is very clearly true of Japan and Russia, for a *per capita* growth rate even of 2 per cent per annum, which both countries have exceeded according to Table 1.1, implies a more than seven-fold rise of average real income in a century, and a more than fifty-fold increase in 200 years. Given the very low starting level of these countries *c*. 1870 it is clearly impossible that they should have experienced sustained growth at anything like the average 1870–1965 rate for more than a few decades before this, for this would imply an implausibly low earlier level – one at which life could not have been sustained, and one much less capable of serving as a springboard for rapid growth.

In the case of West European countries this argument via backward extrapolation is slightly less convincing, in so far as both their mid-nineteenth-century levels of real *per capita* income substantially bettered those of Japan or Russia, and their average long-run growth rates since *c*. 1870 have been lower. Even here, however, there is quite a severe limit to the amount of sustained pre-1870 growth which we can

direction. Conceivably the latter influences preponderated in the case of nations which were close neighbours and the former in the case of those which were not.

A comparison of the latest estimate by Phyllis Deane of the United Kingdom national product in 1870 with that of Butlin for Australia suggests a *per capita* level of about £33·9 for the United Kingdom against about £48·25 (or 43·2 per cent higher) for Australia, at current prices and a par exchange rate. (I have adjusted the Butlin estimate to a factor cost basis.) The older Feinstein estimates would give Australia a very substantially greater lead. The view of Australian wealth in the mid-nineteenth century adopted here is shared by Noel G. Butlin in *Australian Economic Development in the Twentieth Century*, ed. C. Forster (London, Allen & Unwin, 1970), 298.

contemplate. Compound interest at 1·5 per cent cumulates to a more than four-fold increase in a century and a nineteen-fold increase in two centuries; even 1 per cent growth yields a 2½-fold rise in less than 100 years or a seven-fold increase in less than 200. It is hard to believe that any of the eight European countries listed within the long-run growth ranges 1·0 < 2·0 per cent per annum could have started in the later seventeenth century at a level which a backward extrapolation of the average c. 1870–1965 growth rate would imply. (For Australia, Canada and even the U.S.A. the question of a seventeenth-century starting-point, of course, hardly arises.)

This backward-looking technique may seem an insecure line of argument on which to base one's judgment as to the course of economic growth in earlier periods for which direct quantitative evidence is lacking or inadequate. But the logic is impeccable: only the estimates of nineteenth-century starting-point and of long-run growth rate are suspect. In any event there is really no conflict; for what we *do* know of conditions of life in Europe in earlier centuries, albeit in a more qualitative and impressionistic way, entirely confirms these inferences from backward extrapolation. There is no warrant, in historical studies of diet, of housing, of general conditions of life and work, for supposing that modern European growth had continued for centuries at something like the average 1870–1965 rate, or even the average 1870–1913 rate, where that was smaller. The peasantry of England and the urban craftsmen of southern Germany and northern Italy in the medieval period were ignorant of modern affluence, and may have lived lives which were in many ways nasty, brutish and short, but the picture we have of them does not suggest average conditions of abject, hopeless poverty such as *per capita* real incomes even one-seventh, let alone one-fiftieth, of mid-nineteenth-century levels would imply.

But let us be clear what such an exercise in backward extrapolation suggests. It implies *only* that a long-sustained growth at post-1870 rates cannot, in most cases, have taken place immediately prior to 1870. It does not rule out the possibility of pre-1870 *fluctuations* in the rate of growth in the course of which some countries may have enjoyed a long-continued improvement in *per capita* income from which there was later retrogression. This, rather than centuries-long stagnation or near stagnation, is what history seems to suggest in some instances. Impressionistic or partial though the evidence is, there is reason to believe that some north Italian city-states, particularly Venice, suffered economic decline when the geographical discoveries of the late Middle Ages changed the currents of international trade, removing them from the mainstream of commercial life and leaving them in a backwater. In the case of Spain the Golden Century was followed by a long period in which the scrappy evidence available suggests an economic retrogression accompanying, and doubtless partly causing, her loss of military supremacy; this decline has been attributed to various causes, among them the expulsion of the Moors, the decline of imports of the precious metals from the New World, and bad government.[33]

In neither of these cases does the evidence permit us to speak with assured confidence of a sustained or substantial decline of real *per capita* incomes. In other cases, however, studies have been made which offer evidence of a more rigorous character in favour of that experience. The outstanding case in point is the study of real wage rates in England by Professor Phelps Brown and Miss Hopkins, which extends over the uniquely long period of seven centuries.[34] The graph in which they express the changing real value of wage rates (of building craftsmen in southern England) is reproduced in fig. 1.2. It can be seen that prior to the onset of 'modern' economic growth during the industrial revolution these real wage rates traced a fluctuating course, enjoying a secular rise to a remarkably high level in the later fifteenth century – a level which was not recaptured until the last years of the nineteenth century – followed by an almost catastrophic decline under the Tudors and early Stuarts to a level, *c.* 1640, barely 40 per cent of the

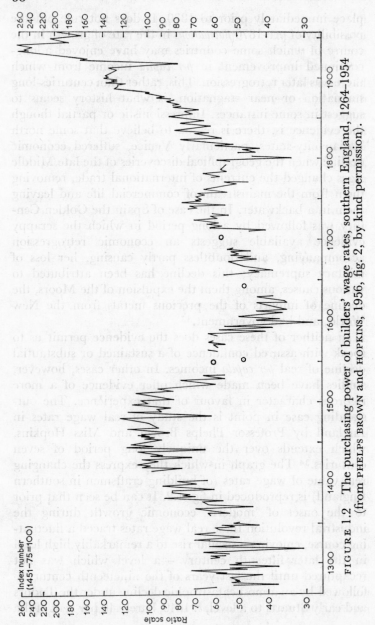

FIGURE 1.2 The purchasing power of builders' wage rates, southern England, 1264–1954 (from PHELPS BROWN and HOPKINS, 1956, fig. 2, by kind permission).

fifteenth-century peak. Thereafter there was a slow recovery to about the mid-eighteenth century, followed by a further decline in the early decades of industrialization.

Some of the limitations of this research – a similar inquiry has been made, yielding similar results, for France[35] – will be discussed in the following chapter. To anticipate the points made there, wage *rates* are a different matter from *earnings*, and even the earnings of a particular class of craftsmen are not necessarily representative of those of all wage earners, and still less – in a society predominantly agricultural for most of the time-span covered – of incomes generally. All qualifications made, however, it remains true that these studies reconcile more easily with the hypothesis that the period of modern economic growth was preceded by marked secular fluctuations of real income, impressive improvements being cancelled by later and equally impressive declines, *rather* than with the alternative to which the technique of backward extrapolation would compel us, namely that envisaging centuries-long stagnation or growth at a rate infinitesimally above zero. These studies, moreover, suggest a reason for these fluctuations: the changing man/land ratio as pre-industrial population rose and fell.

It is natural to ascribe a large importance to the *per capita* supply of land in a dominantly agricultural society where levels of technology are low and little capital is employed. Agricultural techniques may improve or non-agricultural pursuits develop, but too slowly to offset the depressive effect of a falling supply of land per head when population rises, even slowly, in a country with no large reserves of unoccupied land. A *decline* in population, on the other hand, such as was experienced by many parts of Western Europe in the late Middle Ages, will reinforce whatever improvement emanates from rising agricultural productivity or from the development of the non-agricultural sector. It may well be that an exogenously-determined rise of population, at a rate in excess of that of the improvement of agricultural technology, has been a more common and widespread cause of pre-modern economic downswings than the rather special circumstances which led to the subsequent decline of Venice or of Spain from their medieval and sixteenth-century pre-eminence.

This line of explanation helps to answer a question which the hypothesis of pre-modern secular fluctuations provokes: is the growth which Western countries have enjoyed in the nineteenth and twentieth centuries a genuinely novel phenomenon? Or is it rather merely a further secular up-swing comparable to those of England in the later fourteenth and fifteenth centuries or between *c.* 1650 and *c.* 1750? After all, even those Western countries with the longest-sustained records of modern growth have not as yet experienced documented growth for a period as long as that which the Phelps Brown and Hopkins graph would suggest for England between *c.* 1300 and the late fifteenth century.

There are in fact reasons for answering this question optimistically. The least important is that, as we have already surmised and as the Phelps Brown and Hopkins data confirm, modern economic growth has been not only sustained, but *more rapid* overall than in pre-industrial cen-turies. (In interpreting fig. 1.2 it has to be remembered that the United Kingdom has been among the slowest-growing countries, in terms of *per capita* real income, in the past century.) This of course has resulted in present-day levels of affluence in such countries far in excess of any previous historical experience. Secondly, modern growth has not had the adventitious character of earlier upswings caused, in part at least, by an improving man/land ratio. Rather, modern growth has in fact occurred *simultaneously* with a hitherto unparalleled rise in population and a correspondingly un-precedented decline in land/man ratios. It has been achieved largely by developments in non-agricultural sectors which have caused the land/man ratio to lose much of its former importance. Thirdly, while the positive origins of recent improvements in output per head defy easy analysis and vary from case to case, probably everyone would agree that broadly speaking the accumulation of capital and the ad-vance of science and technology are among the most important. As to the former, real income levels are now high enough to permit savings and investment ratios to be sustained at levels substantially above any previous historical experience; while as to the latter, technological advance has accelerated and modern science is harnessed to economic ends to an extent which many people actually find disquieting. For all of these reasons it seems fair to say that in today's higher-income countries modern economic growth has not only quantitatively exceeded, but is qualitatively different from, any advances won in the pre-industrial era, and that it holds a promise of irreversibility which even long-sustained improvements in earlier centuries lacked.

Forty years ago one would have been inclined to doubt this judgment because modern economic systems, in eliminating or reducing age-long threats of an exogenous character to man's attempt to better his conditions of life, seemed to have invented new threats of a more built-in character which could bring the process of sustained improvement to a halt. However, economic science, like other sciences, has made great progress in recent decades, and many would now feel considerable confidence that a recurrence of a major world economic depression like that of 1929–34 can be avoided. It remains to be seen, it is true, whether the demon of inflation can be exorcized as readily as the devil of depression; and the problem of international liquidity, though perhaps its solution poses difficulties of a political rather than an economic order, also reminds us that the growth of economic understanding has not yet necessarily sufficed to overcome all the interruptions to sustained growth which the modern economic system may itself generate. Nevertheless, the more *likely* threats to the continuance and wider spread of rapid economic growth may seem to emanate from different directions than these, namely from the possibility of destruction on a global scale in the course of a third, nuclear, world war; and from the constraints posed by the Earth's diminishing stock of non-reproducible resources and limited area of productive land.

The first of these threats is indeed a possibility to be

reckoned with, but not one which it falls to the lot of the economic historian to speculate on. On the second, however, history has a point to make, and it is that the striking economic achievements of the industrial countries in the past century or so have been to a significant degree dependent on a successful avoidance of the Malthusian trap, an avoidance which may prove difficult to perpetuate. In several instances the early stages of industrialization were accompanied by, and probably in part caused, an unprecedented growth in population which proved supportable only because new low-cost sources of food supply and raw materials opened up in other parts of the world. In the nature of things this method of escaping the trap cannot be repeated; there are no longer rich, unused areas of the globe apt for easy settlement and exploitation as there were in the mid-nineteenth century, and at a time when 'the population explosion' is a phrase on everyone's lips one does not need to be persuaded that the Malthusian threat has been postponed rather than permanently averted.

Nevertheless, realism equally enjoins that we should recognize the presently *regional* nature of the problems of population and food supply. Europe's increasing dependence in the late nineteenth century on food imported from other continents was largely a matter of relative cost, reflecting differences in the price of land rather than an absolute inability to feed itself. In the mid-twentieth century sharp rises in agricultural productivity have tended to make Western Europe as a whole more, rather than less, self-sufficient, the rise of population notwithstanding, and it seems improbable that for the next few decades at least food supply will impose any severe constraint on European growth, still less on North American, even admitting the possibility of some deterioration in the schedule of supplies imported from other continents. Only Japan and possibly Russia, among the presently industrialized countries, appear to face at all imminent threats from that quarter. A more likely cause of difficulty will be from the side of raw materials, especially of minerals such as oil.

The demographic factor and economic growth

These speculations, however, are not for the historian. But a few comments *are* called for as to the historical evidence on the impact of population trends on economic growth and income levels *other than* that exerted through the obvious change in man/land ratios which they imply. This is a matter which has been well analysed theoretically,[36] and it is easy to find in the comparative economic history of the past century or two illustrations of most of the relationships which theory has envisaged. To mention only a few: in the nineteenth century such areas as the U.S. West, Australia and New Zealand – often referred to collectively as the 'regions of recent settlement' – were characterized by high rates of natural increase and large-scale immigration, and their history admirably confirms that the largest capital investments are those called for to meet the 'social overheads' of population growth, extended settlement and urbanization. The same countries also confirm the expectation that domestic *per capita* savings can be high where the age structure of population is skewed towards the younger working ages – most saving being done by those of working age and most dis-saving by the retired. America for most of the nineteenth century, Australia in the 1880s, confirm that a high rate of population increase induces an optimistic business climate and a high propensity to invest, while the opposite demographic experience has often been put forward as one reason for the very different outlook on the part of investors and entrepreneurs which is held to have contributed to the world economic crisis of 1929–34.

Imbalances between the sexes are less frequent than changes in age structure, but they were not insignificant in countries of heavy immigration or emigration when, as was usually the case in the nineteenth century, males predominated heavily in the migrant stream. (The New Zealand ratio was only just over one female to every two males following the inrush of men to the goldfields in the early 1860s.) Perhaps a more important imbalance between the sexes is that which has characterized the demography of the

Soviet Union for most of its existence. Here it is *men* who have been in short supply. The succession of war and civil war, the slaughter and deportation of kulaks during the era of forced collectivization, Stalin's purges, and war again kept the male/female ratio permanently below par, and down to less than 8 : 10 in early post-World War II years. The well-known importance of women in the Soviet labour force has been variously explained – by communist apologists as a victory for socialism which offers to all citizens, regardless of sex or other differences, the opportunity to engage in meaningful toil; and by critics of the Soviets as evidence of Russia's need for ruthless mobilization of all possible factor inputs to secure economic growth in an economy of low productivity. While there may be some truth in both contentions, the more obvious explanation is that a large minority of Soviet womenfolk have had to seek employment in industry or in service activity merely because there have not been enough men to go round.

Closer to the man/land balance theme is the pressure placed, not only on food supply but on employment, by population growth in densely-settled peasant regions: hence the huge out-migrations from Ireland in the second half of the nineteenth century and from southern Italy and European Russia during *c.* 1890–1914, across the Atlantic in the first two instances and to Siberia in the third. The problem in Tsarist Russia was made graver by the country's dependence on food exports; the growing population ate the potential exports, as they have been doing in Argentina since 1945.

It would be easy to extend this list of historical illustrations of the ways in which population change impinges on the level and growth of *per capita* incomes. But, in fact, the channels through which this demographic influence is brought to bear are not much in dispute, and theory does not perhaps entertain great hopes of discovering unfamiliar relationships from history. What *is* uncertain, and what theory *would* willingly learn from history if it could, is whether there is any systematic *net* gain or loss, on balance, from a given demographic experience.

The economic historian would wish to answer this question – in so far as he feels that present evidence warrants any answer at all – first by drawing a distinction between pre-industrial and industrial societies. In respect of the former, we have seen that there is evidence, in the cases of England and of France, of a negative correlation in the trend between population size and level of average income. But not too much should be read into this suggestion. Not only is the finding subject (as we have seen) to qualification, but at best the evidence relates to only two countries, or even (it might be said) to two *regions*. There is no certainty that a similar relationship held, or holds, in pre-industrial societies where, given the level of agricultural technology, population was or is below the level at which all land has to be farmed in order to secure an adequate food supply. There are those who believe, as we shall see in the next chapter, that in such a situation the *beneficial* influences of rising population density outweigh the adverse effects from the side of food supply. Moreover, the restriction, 'given the level of agricultural technology', is an illegitimate one, in so far as even without substantial change of technology in the sense of 'applied science', traditional agriculture gives scope for considerable increases in output per acre by simpler organizational changes which thus permit some elasticity of supply in the face of population increase. (This, again, will be discussed at greater length in the next chapter.) As against this, however, it is easy to think of societies in which, despite the lack of firm statistical information, all the historical evidence suggests that the net effect of rising population on income was dominated by the downward pressure applied *via* the falling land/man ratio: pre-Famine Ireland and late nineteenth-century Russia spring to mind.

In industrial societies, on the other hand, this particular linkage progressively loses importance, and the net economic effect of a given trend of population represents the outcome of a wider range of possibly conflicting influences. Consequently, the likelihood increases that the net effect of a given demographic experience will vary from country to country

C

and perhaps from time to time since the relative importance and even direction of the various effects cannot be presumed constant in all situations. For example, the effect of changes in age structure on the average savings ratio may have (more or less) favourable or (more or less) unfavourable economic implications according to whether the economy in question is operating in conditions of full employment and inflation, or of demand deficiency and depression.

An impression of the overall effect of population growth at varying rates of increase – since there are no examples of *falling* population amongst the countries and in the time-span covered by Table 1.1 – has been sought by ranking the fourteen countries in this table in two lists, based respectively on rate of growth of output per head of population and on rate of population growth. This has been done for each of the four chronological subdivisions of Table 1.1 separately, and the Spearman coefficient of rank correlation between the two lists has been calculated in each case. The results are as follows:

Period	Coefficient of rank correlation	Level of statistical significance
1870–1913	−0·02	Not significant
1913–1950	−0·07	Not significant
1950–1960	−0·14	Not significant
1960–1965	−0·59	5%

It can be seen that while the coefficient suggests a negative correlation throughout between rate of population growth and rate of growth of real *per capita* income, only in the last and shortest period is the coefficient statistically significant, and then only at the 5 per cent level. Even in this last period the correlation between the two variables cannot be regarded as inspiring any confidence *analytically*, since measurement of the rate of growth by reference to the levels of income in the end years only is liable to lead to appreciable distortion over so short a period. Thus, the only safe conclusion to be

drawn from the data is that there is no proof here of any
systematic *net* impact of a given rate of population growth on
the rate of growth of *per capita* income.

This conclusion is in line with some earlier comments, but
not with others. Kuznets, for example, seems to harbour
slightly ambivalent opinions on this matter. In the empirical
survey undertaken in the first of his series of papers, 'Quantitative Aspects of the Economic Growth of Nations', he concluded that there was a 'lack of clear-cut association between
rates of growth of population and of *per capita* product.'[37]
Specifically, the rank correlations between the two measures
which he computed were all lacking in statistical significance
save for seven 'larger' countries during the twentieth century,
for which a positive association significant at the 5 per cent
level was suggested. Writing in more analytical vein in
Modern Economic Growth, on the other hand, he presents a list
of possible interactions which leaves the reader with a distinct
expectation of a positive association.[38] Finally, a still later
paper explicitly dealing with 'Population and Economic
Growth' appears not to be able to make up its mind on the
subject: in seeming defiance of his earlier empirical work he
assumes a positive though 'quite loose' association for the
years before 1930, but presents evidence based on U.N. data
which suggests, for the years since World War II and for
various assortments of countries, either a clear *negative*
association ('all' countries, and 'all developed' countries) or
no significant association ('developed' countries excluding
Canada, the U.S.A., Australia, New Zealand and 'non-
developed' countries).[39]

Another leading American economist, Joseph J. Spengler,
adopted in his 1965 Presidential address to the American
Economic Association a much firmer, neo-Malthusian
stance.[40] (Professor Spengler's treatment is interesting for its
suggestion that excessive population growth, especially
massive urbanization, poses threats to a country's political
and social health as well as to its economic growth.) However, Spengler had little new comment to offer on the
influence of population on economic growth in history; his

emphasis was on tracing the changing opinions of economists from Malthus onwards on the subject, and when his attention turned to the world of events rather than of thought, the future interested him more than the past. By contrast, the members of the staff of the British National Institute of Economic and Social Research, whose paper was referred to earlier, largely eschewed theory and speculation and based their comments directly on scrutiny of the aggregative historical evidence of the past 100 years.[41] Since the basic data largely overlap with those of our own study, it is not surprising that the conclusion is broadly similar: the authors found that 'neither over the whole period nor in either sub-period before or after 1913 is there any significant correlation between rate of growth of output per head and that of population of working age'. (Though the authors do not themselves perform, or at any rate do not report, any formal statistical test to support this conclusion, calculation of the Spearman rank correlation coefficient between the rankings in the relevant columns of their Table 2, and of its level of statistical significance, completely vindicates this assertion.) There seems, therefore, to be a fairly general consensus that over the past century or so, and for those countries for which we have reasonable national product and population data, growth of population and of product per head have not by and large been significantly related. However, there is some indication that for the most recent sub-period, since World War II, there may have been a negative association.

Structural change in history

We have now squeezed about as much interpretative juice out of our collection of statistics on modern product growth as they will yield, and it is time to turn to the alternative aggregative measure, that of 'development' in terms of changing sectoral shares. Here, however, comments will be very much briefer, and that for two reasons. First, much less work has been done as yet on sectoral shares than on the growth of incomes; and secondly, some comments on the shares of particular sectors in the pattern of employment and/

or generation of product will be offered in later chapters – on the agricultural share in Chapter 2, and on the manufacturing share in Chapters 5 and 6. In this chapter comment will be restricted to a few general remarks and to some observations on the 'services' or 'tertiary' sector, which is not the subject of more extended discussion in any later chapter of this book.

The practice of subdividing the economy into broad industrial classifications on the basis of the type of end product (that is, an *industrial* rather than an *occupational* grouping) is well known, and widely used as a handy if crude indicator of economic structure. The division can be made either in respect of the components of national product, or of employment. At the crudest level of aggregation stands the classification which will be discussed here, that which breaks down the economy into agricultural, industrial and service activities, or *primary*, *secondary* and *tertiary* sectors.

Curiously enough, this latter classification seems to have been introduced into economic terminology from the everyday language of public discussion in Australia and New Zealand, where the respective merits of 'primary' and 'secondary' industries were the subject of debate in the years between the great wars. The terms were pioneered among economists by A. G. B. Fisher and Colin Clark, two British economists who have spent substantial proportions of their careers in Australasia.[42] In Fisher's exposition, which was not entirely free from ambiguity, however, the terms seem to have related to the degree of urgency of the human wants which they satisfied – primary industries catering for the most essential needs, secondary industries for less essential ones and so on. Fisher then argued that as a country's real *per capita* incomes rose it should devote its resources increasingly to secondary and then to tertiary activity; and, in the conditions of underemployment prevailing at the time, his analysis of the place of the tertiary sector seemed both to provide an explanation for underemployment and to suggest a means of combating depression.

While Fisher's instinct did not lead him entirely astray in

relating industrial structure to differing income elasticities of demand for various products, modern practice has rather followed Clark in defining the sectors more rigorously – though still not very rigorously – in terms of the intrinsic nature of the end product, rather than of some market characteristic. Thus the primary sector, broadly, is that which produces food and raw materials; the secondary sector that which processes primary materials into other material products; and the tertiary sector, that which produces non-material commodities like medical care or hotel service.

As yet there has been rather less systematic work on structural change in history than on the growth of incomes. Estimates of the contribution of the various sectors to the national product are of course generated by studies of the growth of the national income by the product approach, but these estimates have on the whole attracted less attention in recent discussions than has the overall growth rate and the relation to it of capital and other inputs. As for the changing historical shape of the structure of *employment*, this is still relatively unexplored, partly because both the data deficiencies and the conceptual uncertainties turn out to be surprisingly daunting. For a good many countries estimates of employment by sector still have to be taken from the pioneering work of Colin Clark.

Sectoral origins of national product and sectoral distribution of employment for nine countries from the mid-nineteenth to the mid-twentieth centuries are plotted in fig. 1.3. The data have predominantly been drawn from Kuznets' *Modern Economic Growth: Rate, Structure, and Spread*. Kuznets, in turn, drew largely, for his data on product shares, upon the monographic studies of individual countries with which Table 1.1 has already made us familiar; his data on labour force shares, however, are in most cases calculated from Colin Clark's figures.

The chief features of these diagrams are well known. In all cases except one the share of the agricultural sector, both in product and in the labour force, declines over time.

Figure 1.3 (1)

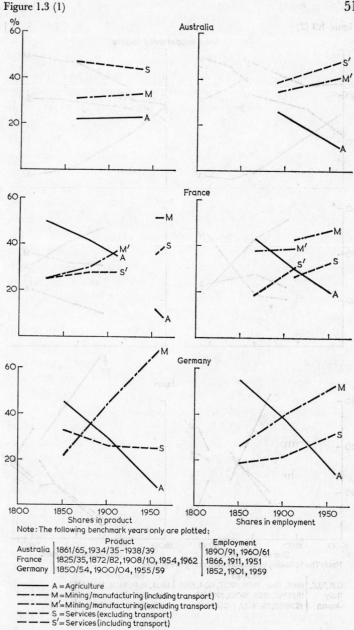

Note: The following benchmark years only are plotted:

	Product	Employment
Australia	1861/65, 1934/35-1938/39	1890/91, 1960/61
France	1825/35, 1872/82, 1908/10, 1954, 1962	1866, 1911, 1951
Germany	1850/54, 1900/04, 1955/59	1852, 1901, 1959

————— A = Agriculture
—·—·— M = Mining/manufacturing (including transport)
—··—··— M′ = Mining/manufacturing (excluding transport)
— — — S = Services (excluding transport)
— — — S′ = Services (including transport)

FIGURE 1.3 Sectoral shares in product and employment, nine-teenth and twentieth centuries

52

Figure 1.3 (2)

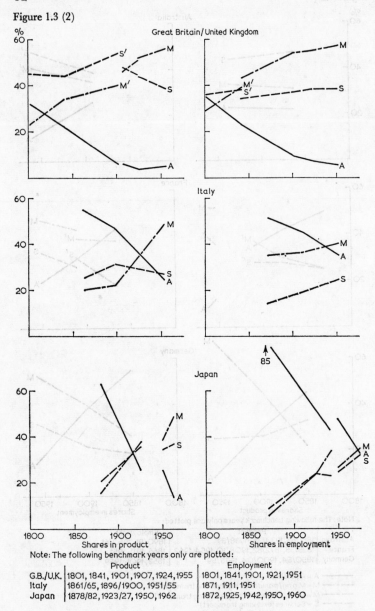

Note: The following benchmark years only are plotted:

	Product	Employment
G.B./U.K.	1801, 1841, 1901, 1907, 1924, 1955	1801, 1841, 1901, 1921, 1951
Italy	1861/65, 1896/1900, 1951/55	1871, 1911, 1951
Japan	1878/82, 1923/27, 1950, 1962	1872, 1925, 1942, 1950, 1960

Figure 1.3   Sectoral shares in product and employment, nineteenth and twentieth centuries

Figure 1.3 (3)

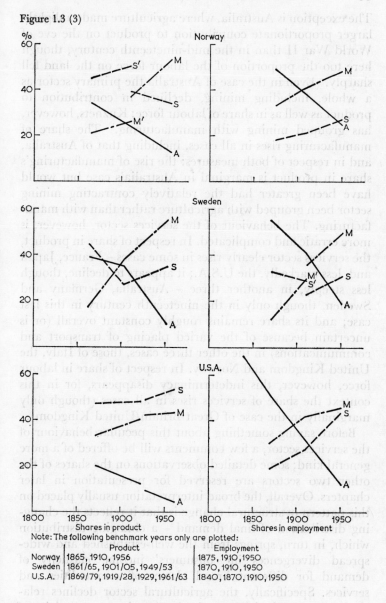

Note: The following benchmark years only are plotted:

	Product	Employment
Norway	1865, 1910, 1956	1875, 1910, 1950
Sweden	1861/65, 1901/05, 1949/53	1870, 1910, 1950
U.S.A.	1869/79, 1919/28, 1929, 1961/63	1840, 1870, 1910, 1950

The exception is Australia, where agriculture made a slightly larger proportionate contribution to product on the eve of World War II than in the mid-nineteenth century, though here too the proportion of the labour force on the land fell sharply. (Even in the case of Australia the primary sector as a whole, including mining, declined in contribution to product as well as in share of labour force: Kuznets, however, has grouped mining with manufacturing.) The share of manufacturing rises in all cases, including that of Australia, and in respect of both measures: the rise of manufacturing's share in product is marginal in Australia's case but would have been greater had the relatively contracting mining sector been grouped with agriculture rather than with manu-facturing. The behaviour of the services sector, however, is more erratic and complicated. In respect of share in product, the services sector clearly rises in some cases – France, Japan and, less markedly, the U.S.A.; it appears to decline, though less steeply, in another three – Australia, Germany and Sweden, though only in the nineteenth century in this last case; and its share remains roughly constant overall (or is uncertain because of the varied placing of transport and communications) in the other three cases, those of Italy, the United Kingdom and Norway. In respect of share in labour force, however, this indeterminacy disappears, for in this context the share of services rises in all cases (though only marginally in the case of Great Britain/United Kingdom).

Before saying something about this peculiar behaviour of the services sector, a few comments will be offered of a more general kind; some detailed observations on the shares of the other two sectors are reserved for presentation in later chapters. Overall, the broad interpretation usually placed on this pattern of structural change is that it reflects the chang-ing distribution of final demand – a changing distribution which, in turn, springs from the well-established and wide-spread divergences in consumers' income elasticity of demand for different broad classes of commodities and services. Specifically, the agricultural sector declines rela-tively as *per capita* incomes rise because income elasticity of demand for food is typically less than one, while manufacturing grows because elasticity of demand for its products is typically greater than one. There is certainly an important element of validity in this explanation, though as we shall see in later chapters it is not adequate on its own, particularly if no account is taken of the importance of resource endowment, density of population and the pattern of international trade to an open economy. To the extent, however, that this explanation is valid it would lead us to expect the pace of structural change to be positively related to the rate of growth of *per capita* incomes. This expectation would be strengthened, in the case of a country progressing from moderately low to high income levels, by reinforcing changes in the coefficients of income elasticity of demand for different classes of commodities; the marginal propensity to spend on food falls beyond a certain level of income, a fact sometimes obscured in budget or inter-country studies by the tendency towards more expensive packaging and processing of food at higher income levels. Such activities, of course, form part of the output of the manufacturing, not of the agricultural, sector.

There is perhaps a suggestion of this expected positive association between rates of growth of *per capita* income and of structural change in the diagrams: Japan and Sweden, the fastest-growing economies, both experienced rapid structural change, whereas Australia, the country with the lowest rate of *per capita* growth, experienced very little. (Australia, in fact, is the outstanding proof, among the countries for which quantitative data are offered in this chapter, of the need to draw a distinction between *growth* and *development*. Slow though its growth was, real *per capita* incomes rose by something like two-thirds between the early 1860s and the later 1930s, but this achievement was accomplished within a framework of remarkably stable economic structure.) In the Australian case, the strong resource bias towards farming encouraged a dominating pattern of international specialization which reinforced the tendency arising from the income side for structural change to be very slow. In the case of

Britain the influence of resources, population and trade has evidently worked in the opposite direction, that is it has tended to promote a *more* substantial structural change than Britain's relatively slow rate of income growth would have caused.

Structural change and sectoral productivity

In interpreting the diagram the reader must bear in mind that in the interests of visual clarity the data have *not* been plotted on a ratio scale. The *slopes* of the curves do not therefore alone suffice to permit inter-country comparisons of the rate of structural change; the position of each portion of each curve on the vertical axis has also to be taken into account. This applies also when comparing, for any one country, structure in terms of share of product and in terms of share of employment. Subject to this caution, the latter comparison permits rough estimates of respective *levels* and *rates of change* of labour productivity of the three sectors in each country. The estimates will be only very rough, for the two sets of data, share in product and share in labour force, are of different vintage and from the pens of various authors, and without doubt incorporate some differences of coverage and classification. Nor are the benchmark years the same, in most cases, as between the two measures of structure. Still, within wide margins of error it is true that for any given country and sector a higher vertical position of the share of product line than of the share of labour force line implies for that sector a level of labour productivity above the country-wide average, and vice versa. Similarly, a greater proportionate increase (or lesser fall) in product share than in employment share over a given period implies an above-average rise of labour productivity, and again conversely.

The number of comparisons of these sorts which could be made is of course very large. Suffice here to underline a few recurring patterns. First, the line depicting the agricultural share in employment generally lies above the corresponding line depicting its share in product, indicating that labour productivity in agriculture is usually lower than the country-wide average. This is of course a familiar conclusion. The outstanding exception is again Australia, where a level of agricultural productivity predominantly above the national average is implied. This is consistent with Bellerby's finding that Australia is (or was) one of the very few countries in the world in which the average farm income has exceeded that in the remainder of the economy.[43] (Bellerby's similar and even more emphatic finding for New Zealand confirms one's suspicion that the comments made about Australian economic structure and growth in this chapter would also be found to apply to New Zealand, were similar aggregate historical data available for that country, as they are not.) Comparison of the two Australian diagrams also reveals that in this country, alone out of the nine represented, labour productivity in agriculture improved at a rate substantially in excess of that of the nation-wide average. It is sometimes suggested that countries such as Australia before World War II were 'stunted' in their economic development because commitment to the exploitation of comparative advantage in a particular sector inhibited structural diversification. While this may be true, and while if true it may have had disadvantageous *indirect* consequences for Australia's long-term growth prospects, in the more direct sense the high level and high rate of growth of labour productivity of Australian agriculture made, in the years before World War II, an outstanding contribution to Australia's enviable level of *per capita* incomes and to such growth of them as she did enjoy.

While Australia is outstanding in this respect, however, the rate of growth of labour productivity in agriculture over time, as opposed to its relative level, has been by no means as unsatisfactory as one might be tempted to infer from some widely-held views about agriculture's role in economic growth. Rather, the rate of improvement of labour productivity in agriculture seems to have kept pace with or bettered that of the economy as a whole almost as often as not. The conclusion would certainly be even more favourable to agriculture if the very rapid improvement of labour productivity in that sector since about 1950, characteristic of

many advanced countries, were added to the data.[44] Nor is
the relative performance of manufacturing quite as outstanding, according to these data, as one might expect from
the prestige which this sector enjoys in many development
plans: it can be seen from the respective levels of the product
and employment curves that labour productivity in the manufacturing sector has by no means always been above the
country-wide average. However, the *time* trend of relative
labour productivity in this sector has been generally favourable, rising sharply in some countries and deteriorating
appreciably in none. Moreover, one must bear in mind that
the 'manufacturing' sector as defined by Kuznets is in fact
much wider than manufacturing industry proper, and that
the improvement in its productivity has been impeded by
the inclusion of activities characterized by notoriously slow
productivity growth, such as construction.

Since agricultural labour productivity has grown at about
the same rate as the nation-wide average while that of
'manufacturing' has commonly exceeded it, it follows that
the growth of productivity of the services sector must have
been below average. This indeed is what the diagrams
suggest: the fact that services' share in product rose but
slowly or actually fell, whereas their share in employment
generally rose sharply, leads to the same conclusion. It is
right to emphasize, however, that the *direct* measurement of
productivity in service industries is in its infancy even for
recent years, let alone for the remoter past. For this fact the
nature of service industries is largely to blame, for in respect
of some it is conceptually unclear what 'output' consists of,
and some comprise a characteristically large component of
self-employed from whom data collection is difficult. Work
recently inaugurated on novel measures of output and
productivity in service industries at the present day promises
new light on these matters in the not-too-distant future,[45]
and doubtless in the years to come these new approaches will
increasingly be brought to bear on historical data. For the
present, we must regard the indications of our data with
respect to the historical course of productivity in the services

sector as quite the least well-established aspect of the analysis.

Yet the belief that services industries *are* characterized by slow rates of productivity improvement is widespread; and it cannot be said that there is any correspondingly wide agreement why this should have been so. The puzzle is the greater since, as we shall see in a moment, the composition of the sector has been changing in a way which, one would have thought, would have improved matters: more 'modern' service sectors such as banking have grown in relative importance while such low-productivity activities as domestic service, hand-laundering and huckstering and petty trading have declined. On the other hand it is true that there *are* service activities (such as much office routine) which have been relatively untouched, until very recent decades at least, by productivity-enhancing technical change; and there are others, such as the practice of medicine or teaching, in which 'output' per worker perhaps changes little save in terms of qualitative improvements which are not captured by the measure of output applied. And where 'output' is measured, more or less directly, by the incomes of those producing it, as has regrettably often been the case in regard to the professions and administration, the widespread tendency for the salaries of professional workers and public servants to fall through time relative to average incomes would naturally tend to produce the kind of relative 'productivity' movement in question.[46]

The 'services' sector

A feature of the services sector more amenable to explanation is the tendency, already noted, for its share in product and sometimes in employment too to be less strongly correlated with income than the shares of either of the other sectors. It is sometimes suggested that this feature arises because the relative sizes of the agricultural and industrial sectors are both strongly correlated, the former negatively and the latter positively, with *per capita* real income, the share of services thus resulting passively from the interaction of these two offsetting influences and not being, itself, strongly correlated one way or the other with income. It is of course true that since the 'shares' of the three sectors must needs add up to 100 per cent they are simultaneously determined, and it is thus possible that the 'share' of any one of the sectors should be increased or diminished by some contractionary or expansive factor working on either or both of the others. There is in fact some appeal in this simple explanation of the fickleness of the services share, in so far as that sector consists *in part* of 'residuary' employment which people engage in when there is nothing else for them to do and give up when there is. But this is a characteristic which could be postulated even more generally of agriculture, especially in poor societies of high rural population density. (The increase in farm employment in some advanced countries during the world economic crisis of 1929–33 testifies that agriculture's role as a sector of residuary employment can be revived even at high income levels.) And in any event we can proffer a more satisfying explanation of the behaviour of the share of the services sector than that which regards it as merely a passive arithmetical reflection of the shares of the other sectors: the movements are directly and economically rather than residually and arithmetically determined.

The essential point is that the 'services' sector is not homogeneous; the activities which it includes are of very diverse nature, with very different technological and economic characteristics, and differently related to the level of *per capita* incomes. *Broadly* we may distinguish what might be called 'traditional' and 'modern' sub-divisions of the services sector. The former includes such activities as petty trading and hawking, hand-laundering, domestic service and the like. Economically speaking the characteristic of this type of activity is that it is a labour-intensive method of performing distributive tasks and personal services which is justified by prevailing conditions of capital scarcity and a low opportunity cost of unskilled labour. The 'modern' sub-division of services, by contrast, consists of activities geared to the distributive and financial needs of a developed economy and to the demand of its citizens for educational, medical and similar services. It is highly plausible to conjecture that these two types of employment are both significantly correlated with *per capita* incomes, but the former negatively and the latter positively. 'Traditional' service activities decline as incomes rise, partly because the growth of communications and of modern intermediaries of high productivity 'competes down' the traditional way of performing them – the street trader ousted by the supermarket – and partly because as employment in the modern sector rises, over-employment in residuary agricultural and service occupations is reduced, the opportunity cost of labour in such activities rises, and they thus become less attractive.

Unfortunately, confirmation of the hypothesized relation of these two sectors is hard to come by since many 'traditional' service occupations are not recorded by available statistics. This is notably the case in so far as such activities are performed by members of peasant families whose holdings are insufficiently large to occupy the whole household on the land the whole time. Both in present-day under-developed societies and historically, substantial labour inputs to secondary and tertiary activity have come from those who would regard themselves, and whom official statistics and censuses regard, as 'peasants'. This division of labour represents a lack of clear-cut specialization of economic function very characteristic of pre-industrial societies which can even result, as in late Tsarist Russia, in 'peasants' spending more than half their annual working time on non-agricultural pursuits. It is really inappropriate to apply to the labour force of such economies a rigid classificatory scheme based on the assumption that each person has only one occupation capable of being clearly allocated to one of three types of activity; and it is because of this that some economists and historians regard the primary–secondary–tertiary or agricultural–manufacturing–services scheme as misleading or positively obfuscating in its application to less highly developed societies.

Despite the lack of satisfactory statistical evidence for

many 'traditional' service activities, proof of the contraction of such employment as incomes rise is not confined to the testimony, impressionistic even if extremely well-informed, of such observers as Bauer and Yamey, whose brilliant article, 'Economic Progress and Occupational Distribution', based on the authors' direct observation of traditional employment in tropical, especially West African, economies, pioneered a more realistic view of the relationship of structural change to the growth of incomes.[47] Lacking in quantitative precision though it may be, the historical evidence speaks clearly of increasing specialization of function and of the decline of such divisions of labour time as those upon which internal distribution in the medieval period or the domestic industry of early modern England were based. Further, there is one numerically important occupation which shares the essential characteristics of the 'traditional' services sector, about which systematic statistical information *has* been compiled for a few countries: namely, domestic service. In its essentials this is a 'traditional' service occupation in that it consists of unskilled, labour-intensive work finding its economic justification in a very low opportunity-cost for the labour involved. It is somewhat less typical in that the category is not characterized by self-employment, as so many traditional service occupations are, and that the supply of labour is often governed not merely by macro-economic considerations, but also by elements of sex, caste or racial discrimination. Despite these idiosyncracies, domestic service has behaved as traditional service occupations are here envisaged as behaving in the course of economic growth, and it seems reasonable to argue that it can in some degree act as a proxy for the behaviour of this traditional subsector as a whole, and in doing so confirm the explanation propounded here of the otherwise puzzling behaviour of the tertiary (or services) sector as conventionally conceived.

Fig. 1.4 shows, for a number of benchmark years, the shares in national product and employment in Germany and in Britain of the service sector as a whole, and also of domestic services and of services *other than* domestic service separately.

While the two countries differ somewhat, the divergent experiences of the 'domestic service' and 'other services' sectors stand out sharply in both instances. In Germany the share in product of the services sector as a whole has declined, but this experience is shown to have been entirely caused by the dramatic shrinkage of the output generated by domestic service. In respect of employment, services as a whole rose markedly, but the growth of services employment *excluding* domestic service was in fact even more dramatic, being masked somewhat by the decline of the latter. In Britain the share in product of the services sector as a whole was remarkably stable during most of the nineteenth century, once government expenditure had retreated from the high level attained during the French wars; only in the twentieth century has there been a pronounced rise. Again, however, a clearly divergent experience as between domestic and other services is apparent from about the 1840s.[48] In the pattern of British employment the services sector as a whole seems to have been responsible for a remarkably stable share, but again this results from the offsetting experiences of the 'domestic service' and 'other services' groups. (The 1801 share of the latter was inflated, and of the former doubtless depressed, by high employment in the armed services during the French wars.)

While comparisons between the 'share in product' and 'share in employment' diagrams should not be pressed too hard, the suggestion is that in both countries the ratio of earnings in domestic service to those in the remainder of the economy declined through time. In Germany domestic service earnings appear (surprisingly) to have been a little above the country-wide average in the mid-nineteenth century; by the late 1950s they were less than one-third of it. In Britain the comparable ratio was about one half in the early nineteenth century, falling to little more than one-quarter in the 1950s. In both countries domestic service clearly became a less attractive occupation from the point of view of those who performed it, and one which could increasingly be dispensed with as the functions of the domestic

Figure 1.4 (1)

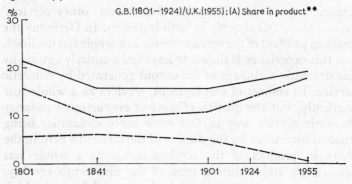

G.B.(1801–1924)/U.K.(1955); (A) Share in product**

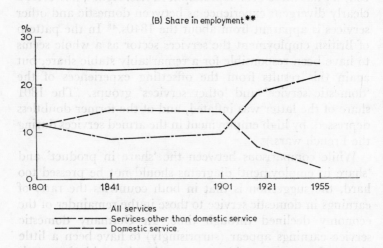

(B) Share in employment**

———— All services
— · — · — Services other than domestic service
– – – – Domestic service

servant were usurped by technological change (domestic appliances) or the development of specialist and more capital-intensive services outside the home.

It remains only to remind the reader that these estimates of domestic service are available only because of the numerical importance of that particular employment until very recent years; there are no comparably systematic estimates relating

Figure 1.4 (2)

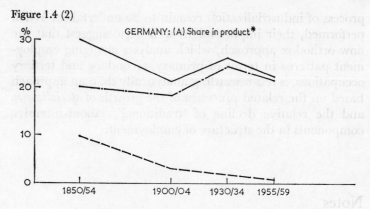

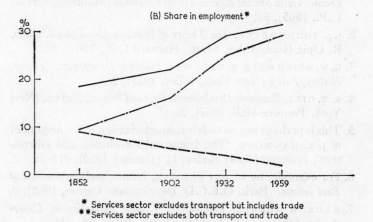

* Services sector excludes transport but includes trade
** Services sector excludes both transport and trade

FIGURE 1.4   Share of the services sector in product and employment, Germany and Great Britain/United King-
dom, nineteenth and twentieth centuries

to other 'traditional' service occupations, partly because
these are so often subsidiary employments undertaken by
those who appear in census or similar returns under some
other classification. Systematic quantitative (or even qualitative) studies of the course of such employments during the

process of industrialization remain to be undertaken. When performed, their impact might well be to suggest that the now orthodox approach, which analyses changing employment patterns in terms of primary, secondary and tertiary occupations, is less rewarding analytically than an approach based on the related processes of the growth of *specialization* and the relative decline of 'traditional', labour-intensive components in the structure of employment.

Notes

1. WILLIAM G. DEMAS, *The Economics of Development in Small Countries with Special Reference to the Caribbean* (Montreal, McGill U.P., 1965), 37.

2. J.A. SCHUMPETER, *The Theory of Economic Development*, trans. R. Opie (Cambridge, Mass., Harvard U.P., 1961), 63.

3. G. M. MEIER and R. E. BALDWIN, *Economic Development: Theory, History, Policy* (New York, Wiley, 1957), 2.

4. R. T. GILL, *Economic Development, Past and Present*, 2nd ed. (New York, Prentice-Hall, 1967), 3.

5. This is perhaps not an unfair characterization of the argument of J. L. HAMMOND, 'The Industrial Revolution and Discontent', *Economic History Review*, II (January 1930), 215–28.

6. For example, by W. BECKERMAN, *International Comparisons of Real Incomes* (Paris, O.E.C.D. Development Centre, 1966), 9.

7. RAGNAR NURKSE, *Problems of Capital Formation in Underdeveloped Countries* (Oxford, Blackwell, 1953), Ch. III.

8. M. K. BENNETT, 'International Disparities in Consumption Levels', *American Economic Review*, XLI (September 1951), 632–49.

9. BECKERMAN, *op. cit.*; see also W. BECKERMAN and R. BACON, 'International Comparisons of Income Levels: A suggested New Measure', *Economic Journal*, LXXVI (September 1966), 519–36.

10. F. SETON, 'Soviet Progress in Western Perspective', *Soviet Studies*, XII (October 1960), 126–44.

11. MILTON GILBERT and associates, *Comparative National Products and Price Levels* (Paris, O.E.E.C., 1958).

12. BECKERMAN, *International Comparisons . . .*, 27.

13. PHYLLIS DEANE, 'The Implications of Early National Income Estimates for the Measurement of Long-Term Economic Growth in the United Kingdom', *Economic Development and Cultural Change*, IV (November 1955), 3–38.

14. BUTLIN (1962), 36–7.

15. See PAUL A. DAVID, 'The Growth of Real Product in the United States before 1840: New Evidence, Controlled Conjectures', *Journal of Economic History*, XXVII (June 1967), 151–2.

16. See pp. 24–5.

17. DEANE, 1968.

18. See especially, MILTON GILBERT and associates, *op. cit.*

19. The values mentioned are calculated from MOORSTEEN and POWELL (1966), Tables T–47, 48, 49, 360–3; see also the discussion in Ch. 10, sections 1 and 2.

20. A. GERSCHENKRON, *A Dollar Index of Soviet Machinery Output, 1927–28 to 1937* (Santa Monica, Calif., Rand Corporation, Report R–197, 1951), Ch. 4. An illustration of the difference made to the calculation of the rise of industrial output in the U.S.A., 1909–37, made by use of base-year or end-year weights, is given in SALTER (1960), 170.

21. A convenient and recent summary of Kuznets' findings is to be had in KUZNETS, 1966. For details of the sources drawn on to compile the table of product growth rates, the reader is referred back to S. KUZNETS, *Postwar Economic Growth* (Cambridge, Mass., Harvard U.P. (Belknap Press), 1964), Table 4, 63–6.

22. A. MADDISON, 'Economic Growth in Western Europe 1870–1957', *Banca Nazionale del Lavoro Quarterly Review*, XII (March 1959), 58–102; MADDISON, 1964 and 1969.

23. D. C. PAIGE, F. T. BLACKABY and S. FREUND, 'Economic Growth: the Last Hundred Years', *National Institute Economic Review*, 16 (July 1961), 24–49.

24. DEANE, 1968.

25. N. G. BUTLIN, 'A New Plea for the Separation of Ireland', *Journal of Economic History*, XXVIII (June 1968), 274–91.

26. The works referred to in the text are: K. OHKAWA and associates, *The Growth Rate of the Japanese Economy since 1878* (Tokyo, Kikokuniya Bookstore, 1957); NAKAMURA, 1966; Y. HAYAMI and S. YAMADA, 'Technological Progress in Agriculture', in *Economic Growth: The Japanese Experience since the Meiji Era* (eds) L. KLEIN and K. OHKAWA (Homewood, Ill., Richard D. Irwin, 1968), 135–61; K. OHKAWA and H. ROSOVSKY, 'Economic Fluctuations in Prewar Japan: A Preliminary Analysis of Cycles and Long Swings', *Hitotsubashi Journal of Economics*, III (October 1962), 10–33; Y. SHIONOYA, 'Patterns of Industrial Development', in KLEIN and OHKAWA (eds), *op. cit.*, 69–109; MADDISON (1969), 30–2, 150–1.

27. cf. the discussion in MOORSTEEN and POWELL (1966), 179–82.

28. MADDISON (1964), 29–36.

29. The first term belongs to Mr Maddison, the second to Professor Kindleberger.

30. See p. 126 below.

31. See pp. 135–151 below.

32. See pp. 285–7 below.

33. On Spain's economic decline, see EARL J. HAMILTON, 'The Decline of Spain', *Economic History Review*, VIII (May 1938), 168–79.

34. E. H. PHELPS BROWN and SHEILA V. HOPKINS, 'Seven Centuries of the Prices of Consumables, Compared with Builders' Wage-Rates', *Economica*, N.S. XXIII (November 1956), 296–314.

35. DENIS RICHET, 'Croissance et blocages en France du XVe au XVIIIe siècle', *Annales*, 23 (July/August 1968), 766–8.

36. See, for example, SIMON KUZNETS, 'Population and Economic Growth', *Proceedings of the American Philosophical Society*, Vol. III, No. 3 (June 1967), 170–93; JOSEPH J. SPENGLER, 'The Economist and the Population Question', *American Economic Review*, LVI (March 1966), 1–24.

37. S. KUZNETS, 'Quantitative Aspects of the Economic Growth of Nations. I: Levels and Variability of Rates of Growth', *Economic Development and Cultural Change*, V (October 1956), 28–31.

38. KUZNETS (1966), 56–63.

39. In *Proceedings of the American Philosophical Society*, 1967. (See note 36 above.)

40. See note 36 above.

41. See note 23 above.

42. See especially ALLAN G. B. FISHER, *The Clash of Progress and Security* (London, Macmillan, 1935), 25–43, and 'Production, Primary, Secondary and Tertiary', *Economic Record*, XV (June 1939), 24–38; COLIN CLARK, *The Conditions of Economic Progress*, 1st ed. (London, Macmillan, 1940), 6–7 and Ch. X. For a discussion of the views of Fisher, Clark and some other writers, and of Australian service industries in the twentieth century, see J. A. DOWIE, 'The Service Ensemble', in *Australian Economic Development in the Twentieth Century*, ed. C. FORSTER (London, Allen & Unwin, 1970).

43. J. R. BELLERBY and associates, *Agriculture and Industry: Relative Income* (London, Macmillan, 1956), 18–19.

44. See further below, p. 407.

45. VICTOR R. FUCHS (ed.) *Production and Productivity in the Service Industries* (N.B.E.R., *Studies in Income and Wealth*, Vol. 34, 1969).

46. TIBOR SCITOVSKY, 'An International Comparison of the Trend of Professional Earnings', *American Economic Review*, LVI (March 1966), 25–42.

47. P. T. BAUER and B. S. YAMEY, 'Economic Progress and Occupational Distribution', *Economic Journal*, LXI (December 1951), 741–55.

48. In comparing fig. 1.4 with fig. 1.3, the different placing of *Transport* should be borne in mind.

2 Agriculture in Economic Growth

The role of agriculture

The role of agriculture in economic development has been the subject of disagreement from the point of view both of analysis and of policy. Those concerned with measures to promote economic development in today's low-income countries have often tended to belittle the contribution which the agricultural sector can make. Whether this attitude is justified or not, it is not difficult to see reasons for its appeal. The world which such policy-makers see is one in which most rich nations are highly industrialized and nearly all poor ones overwhelmingly agricultural. The temptation to draw an obvious, if possibly invalid, conclusion is strengthened by the knowledge that in countries with substantial non-agricultural sections income per head in the latter has usually been appreciably higher than in the agricultural sector.[1] Moreover, it is believed – on quite inadequate grounds, historically speaking, as we have already hinted and shall demonstrate further – that the rate of growth of productivity has been appreciably higher in industry than in agriculture; and so far as tropical countries are concerned – and most poor countries lie between Cancer and Capricorn – the stock of technology available for 'free borrowing' from advanced countries is greater in manufacturing than in agriculture if only because the advanced countries are located in the temperate zone, and have oriented their agricultural research to crops and types of livestock which are generally unsuited to tropical climates and tastes. There are other reasons too: but enough has been said to show that there is a respectable case for the 'development equals (or at least implies) industrialization' standpoint.

The opposite view, however, also numbers many adherents, especially in advanced countries. It is argued that precisely because the agricultural sector generates such a large fraction of national income productivity gains in this sector must, as a matter of simple arithmetic, be the chief determinant of the rate of overall growth in poor countries. And it is easy to show that where the large majority of the work force is engaged in agriculture, the rapid rate of population increase characteristic of today's low income countries implies that even given an extremely high rate of growth in the manufacturing sector, agriculture's proportionate role will reduce only slowly, and the *absolute* numbers working on the land will continue to increase for many decades.[2] The dominant agricultural sector, moreover, is potentially the greatest market for industrial products, especially in view of the generally poor outlook for the export of such products by developing countries; and if industrial growth is not to be thwarted by an insufficiency of demand, a rise in productivity capable of generating an appropriate increase in agriculture's purchasing power must be achieved. Finally, poor countries are typically short of capital, of entrepreneurial talent and of skilled workers. These shortages limit the scope for industrial growth and compel greater emphasis on sources of growth which make smaller demands on these scarce resources.

Both of these points of view have enlisted the support of highly knowledgeable and intelligent scholars; both can muster plausible-sounding arguments and an array of seemingly persuasive facts in support. That this should be so arises partly because the economic and social interrelationships between agriculture and the rest of the economy are complex; they permit of causal influences flowing in both directions, and there is room for debate as to what, in any given situation, are the most strategic links. But it also reflects a diversity which is not commonly – or easily – taken account of in economic models limited to portraying possible patterns of interaction between a restricted number of variables. Agriculture is of its nature profoundly subject to environmental influences which can safely be ignored in considering manufacturing industry. A steel mill is a steel mill, with a roughly similar technology, similar input/output linkages, similar factor requirements, and giving rise to a somewhat similar array of managerial problems, whether it be in capitalist America or communist Russia, in sparsely-populated Australia or densely-populated India, in temperate Luxembourg or tropical Venezuela. But the structure, output and technology of farming are bound to differ not merely from country to country, but often even from micro-region to micro-region, in response to facts of physical geography over which man has only very restricted control, as well as to facts of human geography (such as the density of population) which, if not ordained by nature like precipitation or temperature, must yet be accepted as ineluctable data for many years to come. It is obvious to anyone, on reflection, that agriculture is likely to play a different role in the economic growth of New Zealand and of Kuwait, of Iceland and of Ceylon. But the economic historian – and the geographer – are professionally more accustomed to taking such differences into account than the model-building economist.

The contraction of the agricultural sector

Despite these disagreements, it is almost invariably contended that as economic development gets under way, the shares of agriculture in national income and in employment must decline. Stanley Lebergott struck a very unaccustomed note when he told a conference of economic historians that 'U.S. experience reveals no higher law at work forcing a decline of the labour force in agriculture during economic growth'; and he was quickly challenged by Brinley Thomas, the commentator on his paper, who said: 'This assertion is unwarranted. It can be shown to be wrong both theoretically and empirically.'[3]

At first sight the historical record does indeed seem fully to support the orthodox view. Countries like Great Britain, for which estimates of labour force distribution are available over a long period of time, seem to have experienced a progressive decline in agriculture's share in employment from a level commonly between 65 and 80 per cent in pre-industrial days to 20 per cent or less when industrialization is very advanced. It is extremely hard to find, even for a fairly short time-interval, a documented case of a *rising* agricultural share in employment in a developing country – Mexico between 1895 and 1930 is a rare and important exception[4] – and even a virtually constant share is rare. Logically, of course, this correlation, marked though it is, does not prove that economic development *causes* a decline in agriculture's share in employment. It might be that the causal influence works the other way round. Or, more plausibly, it might be argued that all the countries which have experienced substantial economic development in the past 200 years have also experienced substantial population increase, and that it is this population growth and a (usually) more or less unchanging area of cultivable land which have combined to cause the decline in agriculture's proportionate share, by placing a ceiling on the absolute numbers who can find work on the land at a time when the total labour force is growing.

This suggestion is lent some plausibility by cases like that of New Zealand where, after growing substantially since the first settlement of the country, the area of occupied farm land and with it the number of agricultural holdings reached a plateau about half a century ago. The number of holdings has remained virtually unchanged at 85,000 to 90,000 ever since. It is this constancy in the number of farms – predominantly family concerns employing little outside labour – which in combination with rapid aggregate labour force growth has 'caused', arithmetically speaking at least, the proportionate decline in agricultural employment in twentieth-century New Zealand. It would also be interesting to have information on the relevant magnitudes for the relatively few cases of substantial population *decline* in modern or near-modern times, such as England in the century following the Black Death or Ireland in the half-century following the famine of 1846. It is not impossible that in these instances substantial increases in *per capita* real incomes were combined with stagnant or even (in the first case) rising agricultural shares in employment.[5]

However, the hypothesis which links agriculture's relative shrinkage solely with population increase seems to be ruled out by two other facts: first, countries which have experienced substantial population increase but *not* substantial economic development have not manifested the same pattern of labour force change; and secondly, absolute numbers in agriculture have rarely remained unchanged for long in advanced industrial countries. The more common pattern has been absolute growth in agricultural employment to an all-time peak (which has often come quite late: *c*. 1851 in Britain and *c*. 1917 in the U.S.A.) followed by absolute decline. Absolute numbers working on the land in Britain today are less than half what they were in the mid-nineteenth century. It is therefore clear that the placing by the limited area of land of an absolute 'ceiling' on employment cannot be the only reason for agriculture's declining share in a growing labour force.

Proponents of the orthodox account of agricultural shrinkage buttress their argument not only by statistics, but also by proffering Engel's Law as an explanation for the inverse correlation between agriculture and degree of development: rich countries spend a smaller proportion of their income on food, and hence have a smaller proportion of their labour force in agriculture. This logic is not compelling. In the first place, the fact that the proportion of *income* spent on food is falling does not necessarily mean, for a country which has no spare land, that the proportion of the labour force in agriculture will decline. For one thing, land produces commodities other than food. Further, if the economy is closed (and so must be self-sufficient in food) and if the supply of land is fixed, labour and/or capital will have to rise proportionately *more* than output (and therefore than population) unless aggregate productivity can be increased. But more generally, the logic fails because it neglects foreign trade. Employment on the land can naturally be expected to be higher in New Zealand, which in the late 1960s exported between 64 per cent (beef and veal) and 96 per cent (wool) of the output of its major pastoral products,[6] than in Britain, which imports getting on for half its food supply.

The share of the labour force in agriculture cannot therefore be expected to be a very accurate reflection either of degree of development or of *per capita* income, and familiar historical data indicate that it is not. In the twentieth century agriculture's share in the labour force has consistently been more than twice as high in the U.S.A. as in Britain; but this does not mean that the latter is twice as rich, or twice as 'developed', as the former. Nor would one argue that because Khruschev's Russia used two-fifths or more of its labour force on the land it was more backward than England during the Napoleonic wars, which made do with about one-third.

Peasant artisans and peasant traders

Greater analytical significance might be expected, however, if instead of measuring simply the number of people *primarily* engaged in this or that sector – which is what these percentages actually refer to – we measure the fraction of total labour-time devoted to different pursuits. The point behind this suggestion is that in most historical periods and in most countries the total working-time of any one individual, and still more of any one family, has generally been divided among two or more pursuits. The most common combination has been agriculture and some small-scale industrial pursuit such as weaving. In the 'domestic system' of industry which prevailed in many parts of Europe before the industrial revolution (and in some industries survived until a quite late date) a very substantial fraction of the output of manufacturers was produced in this fashion by part-time agriculturists. In some instances there was a more thoroughgoing and clear-cut division of the working year between agriculture and larger-scale industry, perhaps on a seasonal basis as in late Tsarist Russia.

There are many interlocking reasons on the side both of labour supply and of demand for the prevalence of such combinations of agricultural and non-agricultural work. Where population pressure is great and the supply of farm-land inadequate, many holdings may not offer full-time employment. Even where the average farm is larger, the marked seasonal fluctuations which characterize farm work mean that many workers may be underemployed for part of the year; this was especially the case before the peak operations of the arable farming year – ploughing, sowing and harvesting – were mechanized. There are always inclement days and long hours of winter darkness in which a poor peasant can usefully occupy his time on work other than farming. And sometimes climate dictates longer absences from the fields, as in Tsarist Russia where the soil in many regions was frozen too hard to be worked by hand implements for several months each year. On the demand side, man does not live by bread alone; and the poverty of a peasantry which, given prevailing technology and the farm area at its disposal, cannot produce a surplus to sell for cash, or which has no means of exporting it, dictates that requirements such as shelter and clothing must be met in other ways. Some-times the practice of peasant crafts through the centuries builds up a body of inherited skill which makes possible the domestic production of articles of sufficient quality to serve as a source of cash income, as in the *kustar* industry of Tsarist Russia or the traditional crafts of South Asia. And where economies of scale are unimportant, underemployed peasants and their families offer to industrial capitalists a source of labour which is not only low-cost in itself but which also reduces the need for heavy expenditures on fixed capital such as factory buildings.

The extent of the divergence between agricultural employment as recorded by the number of workers *primarily* engaged in agriculture and the number of man-hours per annum actually devoted to agricultural tasks has not, unfortunately, been studied systematically. It can well be understood that the data for such a study are forbiddingly scarce. But acquaintance with the economic history of, say, late Tsarist Russia or Tudor England generates a strong qualitative impression that the divergence would be very substantial. Kahan suggests, in his study of labour inputs in Soviet agriculture, that only about 120 days a year were worked on the land for every agricultural worker during the New Economic Policy (N.E.P.) of the 1920s.[7] Some scholars have observed an even smaller percentage utilization of potential labour-time in tropical agriculture, especially of the shifting variety,[8] and this situation has often prevailed also in conditions of sedentary agriculture if, as in pre-colonial Ghana, land is relatively abundant and distributed in an egalitarian manner.[9] But the phenomenon is not confined to very backward societies or to early periods of history. As late as the 1950s agricultural–industrial workers in Poland commuted long distances to towns by rail to supplement their work on the land by part-time factory employment.[10]

Even in default of systematic studies, it is perfectly obvious *in what direction* an appropriate correction for this divergence would tend: the trend has been for the difference between apparent and actual labour inputs in agriculture to narrow through time as the allotment of time by agricultural workers to non-agricultural pursuits, or to 'leisure', has been reduced. Kahan found that man-days p.a. per worker in Soviet agriculture increased *c.* 50 per cent between the 1920s and 1950s,[11] though even in the latter decade the Russian figure was exceptionally low in international terms. There have been several reasons for this trend. As the capital intensity of industry increased, it became increasingly uneconomic to employers to tolerate part-time or seasonal employment. A study of the Moscow textile industry in the late 1880s showed clearly how seasonal employment continued to prevail in handloom weaving sheds, but was being inexorably driven out in favour of a full-time proletariat in steam-powered factories.[12] Peasant industry gradually succumbed to the competition of cheaper or better-quality

D

factory products, whether made within the country as in Russia, or imported as in British India.[13] In the temperate zone, particularly, the mechanization of the peak-period operations – ploughing, sowing and harvesting – has permitted a narrowing of the difference between labour needs at these periods and in the 'off-season', while in tropical agriculture the need for increasing intensity of cultivation as population densities have increased, and particularly the growth of double-cropping, have reduced the time which peasants have free to devote to non-agricultural pursuits. And whenever real wages and employment opportunities in non-agricultural occupations have increased relatively, the opportunity cost of peasant leisure has increased and, to the extent that workers have been drawn off from agriculture, the marginal productivity of the remaining agricultural workers has risen.

A recalculation of sectoral shares in employment and output making appropriate allowance for the widespread practice of dividing time between two or more occupations would quite possibly make a substantial difference in many cases to the behaviour of such shares in economic development through time, or in comparative international studies. It might (or might not) improve the accuracy of agricultural share as an indicator of degree of development. Appropriate allowance for non-agricultural production by 'agricultural' workers might significantly affect estimates of rates of growth of output and international comparisons of output. It is now generally agreed, even by Soviet commentators, that official Soviet estimates overstated the rate of industrial growth in the early five-year plans *partly* because they neglected or underestimated the output of peasant industry which the Soviet style of industrialization rapidly demolished. Some early estimates of India's national product suffered from a similar defect,[14] and a major recent study accuses the received estimates of the growth of output in Meiji Japan of the same bias.[15] It is likely that this bias is very general in estimates of the growth of output of economies undergoing industrial transformation and in comparisons between dominantly agricultural and highly industrialized economies. Attention would have to be paid, however, to the extent to which the non-agricultural time of 'agricultural' workers was devoted to other productive activity or on the other hand – as was perhaps more common in primitive societies practising shifting agriculture – to leisure.

Systems of land tenure and inheritance

It has sometimes been suggested that the extent to which division of labour-time between agriculture and industry occurs is a function not only of such factors as climate or the density of agricultural population (and thus the size of the average holding) but also of the pattern of land tenure and of inheritance. It has been suggested that where the inheritance system favours or prescribes partition between descendants landholdings become fragmented and, if population is increasing, reduced in aggregate area, but that there is nevertheless a tendency for peasants to remain on the land because of the security it offers and also, perhaps, for reasons of an economically less rational nature. In such circumstances rural underemployment may develop, favouring the growth of peasant crafts or 'domestic' industry. Under primogeniture, however, landless heirs have an incentive to leave the village in search of employment, and the growth of urban industry and a true industrial proletariat is favoured.

Only wide-ranging comparative research will confirm or deny the validity of this hypothesis, and such research would encounter the difficulty that so many other factors influence the type of industrial development which occurs that it is difficult to disentangle the influence of any one factor. Dr Thirsk has made some suggestive – and corroborative – remarks regarding the differing types of industrial structure which characterized the various regions of early modern England, in which the system of inheritance varied from one region to another.[16] There can be no question of the effects of partible inheritance on the structure of landholding, especially where population is increasing. France, until very recent decades, clearly showed the effects of the *Code*

Napoléon in its small-scale, highly-fragmented peasant farming and – surely not entirely coincidental? – its relatively low level of urbanization.

A striking example of the disadvantages of the multiplication of land titles under partible inheritance is the case of the New Zealand Maori. His land has suffered from the combination of the culturally alien system of individual land titles, imposed by the European settlers of New Zealand in the nineteenth century to suit their own purposes, with the Maori's own strong psychological preferences for retaining a claim to some piece of land, however small, and for equal division of property at death. In the nineteenth century the potential dangers of this combination were concealed by the slow decline of Maori numbers; but the massive demographic resurgence of the race in the twentieth century has led to a classic situation of fragmentation of land and multiplicity of titles. Nor is the damage confined to the technological disadvantages of the fragmentation and dispersal of claims: these features in turn inhibit credit agencies from lending on the security of Maori land, which thus suffers a lack of capital. Only the best efforts of New Zealand's predominantly white rulers to undo the harm which the anthropological blindness of their nineteenth-century forebears caused averted the complete breakdown of Maori farming in the inter-war decades. At the same time, the continued claim to *some* piece of land, however small, and the possibility of supplementing its meagre returns by seasonal work such as shearing or by sporadic employment in forestry and the like, are facts which help to explain the lower level of urbanization and lack of integration with the rest of the economy which have characterized Maoridom until very recent years.[17]

Agricultural productivity before the industrial age

What 'contribution' does agriculture make to economic growth? Can one justify the belief, often encountered and critical to the 'growth *equals* or *implies* industrialization' school of thought, that increasing productivity is harder to secure in agriculture than in other occupations?

We may preface discussion of the scattered and un-satisfactory evidence on these issues, which are of obvious importance to us, by stressing the obvious: that agriculture is more important to the welfare of less developed than of highly-developed societies. The level of productivity, rate of growth and liability to short-term fluctuations of a sector responsible for, say, half of total output and two-thirds or more of employment will clearly be more crucial than those of a sector with shares of 10 per cent or less in both. The annual fluctuations to which agriculture is subjected by the vagaries of climate are in the literal sense of the word vital to poor communities. As Professor Ashton wrote of eighteenth-century England – by no means one of history's poorest countries – 'What was happening at Westminster or in the City was of small account compared with what was happening in the heavens.'[18] What made harvest fluctuations such a serious concern to many pre-industrial societies was not merely the amplitude of these fluctuations but also the fact that the basic food grains of tropical and temperate zones are essentially *bulky* products which could not economically be transported for substantial distances by land.[19] Hence, the area over which yields were 'averaged' was relatively restricted, and dearth, even killing famines, could be essentially *local* affairs. Moreover, for the temperate zone grains at least, yield ratios (the ratio of harvest yield to seed sown) have increased substantially through the centuries,[20] so that in earlier times a higher proportion of the harvest had to be held back for next season's sowing, thus increasing the amplitude of the fluctuations of that part of the output available for consumption this season.

It is tempting to transfer this argument from short-run fluctuations to secular trends of real income, and to adopt the pseudo-Malthusian position that the ratio of cultivable land to population has been the chief determinant of the level of real income of pre-industrial societies. Exceptions could naturally be envisaged in favour of such special cases as medieval Venice, but the generalization would still enjoy sufficiently wide applicability to be worth making. It is theoretically appealing, in particular, in relation to societies where the level of agricultural technology is low, for here capital by definition makes relatively little contribution and it is reasonable to suppose that labour productivity will be chiefly determined by the *per capita* quantity of the major co-operant factor, land. History, too, lends some support to the thesis. In a widely-quoted study, Professor Phelps Brown and Miss Hopkins presented an estimate of the changing purchasing-power of the wage rates of building labourers in Southern England over a period of seven centuries.[21] Their graph, reproduced on p. 38 above, shows a great secular improvement from the mid-fourteenth century to the late fifteenth; a sharp decline to a level barely two-fifths of the fifteenth-century peak under the early Stuart kings; a slow recovery to a less impressive peak in the mid-eighteenth century, followed by more than half a century of decline; and finally a strong upswing to an all-time peak in the mid-twentieth century, the fifteenth-century peak being passed, however, only towards the end of the nineteenth century.

Economic historians will readily agree that the improvement of the last century or more has been brought about by industrialization, capital accumulation and technological advance over a broad spectrum of economic activity. But it is tempting to relate the great secular fluctuations of the first five and a half centuries *primarily* to changes in the ratio of population to land. *Some* allowance can be made for a slowly-rising trend of output per acre – mid-eighteenth-century England achieved a higher level of real income than that of the early fourteenth despite a population between 50 and 100 per cent higher – but otherwise there would seem to be a marked inverse correlation between purchasing power and population density. The favourable situation of the fifteenth century would be explained by the demographic retreat caused by the exceptional ravages of plague in the mid- and later fourteenth century; the unhappy experience of the sixteenth century would reflect the rapid recovery of population, and the slow improvement thereafter a combination of decelerating population growth and (probably)

an upward tilt in the secular trend of output per acre.
Resumed, and more rapid, population growth would
partially account for the further decline after about 1750,
which was arrested and reversed only in the nineteenth
century by the great structural and technological changes of
the industrial revolution.

Needless to say, many technical criticisms have been made
of Phelps Brown and Hopkins' bold enterprise. One major
correction which might be necessary in translating their
estimates of real wages into estimates of real *per capita*
incomes would allow for the increasing regularity and
intensity of employment following the Reformation and the
reduction in the number of 'holy-days'; indeed, the significance of this economic aspect of the Reformation has probably
been grossly underestimated.[22] Such a correction might
mitigate the deterioration in the sixteenth century, the
magnitude of which many historians of the period find
difficult to accept, and lift all subsequent values by a substantial margin. The fall of the later eighteenth century
would not be readily conceded, to put it mildly, by many
economic historians of the period, and in any event should
be ascribed in part to factors other than population density.[23]

It must also be pointed out that for most of Phelps Brown
and Hopkins' period the great majority of the working
population were *not* non-agricultural wage labourers. Indeed, given the overwhelming weight of agricultural products
in the basket of consumables used it might well be said that
what their index really measures is the internal terms of
trade of industry – which, in a predominantly agricultural
society, makes it illegitimate to treat the findings as in any
way representative of average real income per head for the
whole community. Still, the big secular swings in prosperity
which the Phelps Brown–Hopkins studies suggest are difficult
to argue away entirely. Similar results have been arrived at
by a French study.[24] It is easy to think of other historical
examples of the dire consequences of a combination of
increasing population density and technical stagnation in a
predominantly agricultural society: Ireland in the first half

of the nineteenth century and Russia in the second spring to mind. And in our own day, of course, many have been converted to neo-Malthusianism on a global scale by the population explosion.

Yet a contrary view continues to find adherents. In a challenging recent monograph[25] Ester Boserup has argued that population growth can promote improvements in land use which increase output per acre, and if they reduce output per man-hour do so in circumstances in which they imply inroads only on leisure rather than on other productive activity. The greater intensity of cultivation thus encouraged may have side effects which are distinctly beneficial to economic development, such as the encouragement of better work habits and the inculcation of an 'economizing' frame of mind more prone to weighing the costs and benefits of alternative courses of action. By the same token, the advantages of specialization and exchange may be discovered and advertised. Above all, population densities in conditions of primitive agriculture are often not great enough to support industrialization. This contention, obscured though it often is by the obvious difficulties posed to low-income countries by rapid population growth, is still valid even in 1971 over very large areas of South America and Africa, and even in parts of Asia. Under this interpretation, agricultural technology becomes in part at least a function of population density, with recourse successively to hoe and to plough, and capital works such as irrigation or drainage undertaken only when cruder and more shiftless methods no longer suffice.

The neo-Malthusian will quickly complain that this view ignores the clear evidence of near-starvation in so many densely-populated areas of the tropical world today. Clearly enough, too, improvements in agricultural productivity in the last century or so have *not* all been 'endogenous' in the sense here envisaged: the mechanization of the peak operations of temperate-zone farming in the nineteenth and twentieth centuries, which did so much to raise labour productivity in agriculture, came as a response to labour shortages inflicted on agriculture by developments in the rest of the economy, while agriculture, like other sectors of the economy, has benefited enormously in recent decades from the 'spin-off' of advances in scientific knowledge. All the same, the record of history shows clearly enough that agriculture in its pre-scientific and pre-mechanical centuries has been able, though not always immediately, to respond to demographic growth by modifying the system of land use and other organizational changes. Thus as population densities increased, sedentary cultivation gradually superseded the stages of primitive hunting and of nomadic pastoralism which still, however, survive in a few places. The sedentary farmer, in turn, successively adapted his techniques as pressure on the land increased. At first, he needed no more than the 'shifting cultivation', still practised in many areas of low population density, which Pierre Gourou so vividly described in his famous book *The Tropical World*[26] – a work, however, which despite its date of publication essentially deals with the tropics of the 1920s and 1930s. In conditions of greater density, 'slash and burn' no longer sufficed, for the fallow period became dangerously shortened, and more controlled rotations using animal droppings for soil enrichment were necessary.

The 'open field' system of farming, so widespread in Europe in the medieval and early modern periods, provided for a primitive rotation with fallow periods every second, third or fourth year in a system of mixed farming. When even a fourth-year fallow could no longer be tolerated, a more sophisticated rotation involving temporary leys, and later root crops and legumes, permitted the complete elimination of fallow and, as a bonus, the better maintenance of soil fertility. At the same time more careful cultivation, the elimination of the time-wasting defects of open-field husbandry, and stock improvement were facilitated by the consolidation and enclosure of 'open-field' farms which permitted the incentive of personal gain to be better harnessed to those ends. It was chiefly in these pre-scientific and pre-mechanical ways that England increased its food supply to keep pace with population growth until it finally became a more than marginal and occasional food importer during the industrial revolution. That England and other Western European countries achieved considerable increases in per acre output by such methods is shown not only by their success in feeding growing populations from a relatively unchanging land area but by historical studies which have revealed secularly rising crop yields.[27]

In tropical countries with their different crops and techniques increases in output have been achieved in somewhat different ways. In lightly-populated and very backward areas the natural response, once the limits of clearing virgin land have been reached, has been to increase the ratio of years of cultivation to fallow years. Elsewhere, if rainfall allows, advantage has been taken of the high air and soil temperatures to take two or even more crops annually off the same piece of land. In the densely-populated, highly-productive, flat – often deltaic – areas where paddy rice is grown, a dry crop may be planted after the paddy. Nor are such possibilities entirely confined to tropical countries. An important contribution to the growth of agricultural output in early Meiji Japan came from the extension and northward movement of the practice of double-cropping.[28]

Such possibilities of expanding agricultural output heighten one's reluctance to accept the findings of Professor Phelps Brown and Miss Hopkins as a measure of trends in real income per head, for such an interpretation seems to do inadequate justice to this ability of pre-scientific agricultural output to respond to the challenge of growing population densities. But the refutation is far from complete. Agricultural output *may* be able to respond – but as the limits (and there must surely be limits) of pre-scientific productivity are approached the response may be less than complete; and in any event it may come too slowly if population densities increase even moderately quickly. Enclosure and consolidation of open-field holdings, which played a vital part in the increase of output of pre-scientific English farming, were retarded by many legal, technical and physical problems, and the failure of the movement to progress rapidly enough surely helps to explain the problem of agricultural supply in late Tudor England. Only in the later seventeenth century did more rapid technological advance – turnips, clovers, irrigation, drainage – combine with slower population growth to enable agricultural output to 'catch up'.[29] The dramatic fall in industrial real wages which Phelps Brown and Hopkins postulate for Shakespeare's England was therefore only *partly* a matter of the internal terms of trade. Nor have the increments to output been achieved without cost. In tropical countries, in particular, the over-exposure of poor soils to direct sun and heavy rainfall and the cultivation or over-grazing of too-steep slopes have destroyed larger areas of the surface of our ravaged planet than the more-publicized derelictions of modern industry.[30]

Agricultural productivity in recent times

These summary remarks about the output of 'pre-scientific' agriculture fail, it need hardly be said, to convey a proper sense of the infinite variations woven in differing environments upon these basic themes. The sources of growth in modern agriculture are perhaps even more difficult to generalize about. Increasing scientific knowledge and mechanical inventions have of course improved productivity in agriculture as they have in other areas; but the extent to which they have been able to be applied has varied much more than in manufacturing industry or transportation because of the greater importance of climatic and other environmental differences. These have posed an impediment to technological borrowing in agriculture such that individual countries or even individual regions have often been unable to use, without substantial modification, knowledge or tools fashioned for other environments.

The most evident of such obstacles is that posed by the climatic differences between tropical and temperate countries. The substantial lead of the latter in science and technology has offered to the former much less opportunity for 'free borrowing' in agriculture than in other activities because agricultural research has naturally been oriented to crops which do not thrive in tropical latitudes, or which must be cultivated in substantially different ways if they do. Only in respect of plantation crops have Europe and America had much, until recent decades, to offer to tropical agriculture; and even now that this situation is beginning to be altered, it is humiliating to recall the many failures of Western 'experts' in attempting to transfer good laboratory findings to unfamiliar habitats. It has been suggested, too, that the disposition of the great landmasses, and in particular the separation from each other by thousands of miles of ocean of the earth's three great areas of tropical farming – in South Asia, in Africa, and in Latin America – has made it difficult for these areas to learn even from each other.

But it is not only in tropical latitudes that the diffusion of agricultural knowledge encounters difficulties. Much of the knowledge of mixed temperate-zone farming which the English settlers of Australia and New Zealand brought with them proved as much of a hindrance as a help in the new environment; the techniques of extensive pastoral farming and even of arable farming had to be fashioned almost from scratch to suit soils and climates which were more different than they seemed at first acquaintance.[31] The environmental differences affected tools and machines as well as stock and crops. The plains of South Australia must have looked at first sight very like the Great Plains of North America, and tempted the use of the same ploughing and harvesting machinery. But the ploughshares caught in the tree stumps left after the mallee scrub had been burnt off, and it was left to local initiative to invent a device to feel along the ground in advance and operate an upward-tripping mechanism when such an obstruction was detected: the 'stump-jump plough'.[32] Such adaptations come easily enough to inventive, educated communities; but among an illiterate and tradition-bound peasantry the need for them poses a severer obstacle to progress.

It is doubtless for such reasons that the opinion has become so widespread that advances in productivity are doomed to be less spectacular in agriculture than in industry. Yet there is little evidence in rigorous quantitative analyses so far conducted which would support this belief. It is, of course, perfectly true that agricultural output has progressively declined as a percentage of G.N.P. in most developing economies; under the orthodox definitions of 'development' they would not be developing if it did not. But this does not necessarily mean that agricultural *productivity* is falling or even growing relatively slowly; it may be merely that a smaller proportion of resources is devoted to agriculture as its products become relatively less important in the pattern of final demand.

This raises the question, however: which is the most revealing measure of productivity to apply in the case of agriculture? In many discussions of economic growth, scholars incline to use output per head (of total population, of the labour force) as the chief measure of statistical comparison and assessment. Since 'growth' is conceived in terms of changes in *per capita* real incomes, this is a natural tendency, and it is also convenient since employment and total population are relatively easily measurable. But it is not very satisfactory, even for appraising the performance of a whole economy, since it ignores such complications as time preference and the valuation of leisure. Economy A may achieve a higher level of output per head than economy B by adopting more capital-intensive techniques. But this capital has to be created, serviced and replaced, and the ability to satisfy consumers' wants may be no higher in A than in B. A level of aggregate output per head, which seems satisfactory in terms of international comparisons or in comparison with some earlier period, may have been won by subjecting the consumers in the preceding period to intolerable hardships designed to permit a very high level of capital formation, as under the early five-year plans in Russia. Or it may be sustained only by a prodigal use of irreplaceable resources and a neglect of current investment which may imperil the welfare of future generations, or by enforcing, by appeals to patriotism or threats of punishment, a level of labour force participation or intensity of work higher than that which producers would freely choose.* In appraising *sectoral* economic performance, output per head is even less satisfactory: a high level of output per head may be achieved in a given sector by raising, say, its capital/labour ratio beyond the point where the marginal productivity of capital in that sector is equal to its marginal productivity in other uses. Thus the favoured sector may score high marks for output per head only by drawing to itself co-operant factors which could have made a greater contribution to the level of the output of the whole economy if deployed elsewhere.

In the case of agriculture the strategy has often been to maximize output per acre rather than output per head. In the case of poor and densely-populated countries the reasons for this are obvious, given the uniquely 'vital' importance of agriculture's chief products. Even if the marginal product of labour in agriculture is extremely low, it may be impossible to employ labour more productively in other uses because of the shortage of some co-operant factor, or the lack of an adequate infrastructure, or of skills. And even if this difficulty does not exist, it is necessary that any non-agricultural commodities produced with the aid of labour transferred out of agriculture should be capable of being marketed if the import of food from other countries or regions is to be financed. For a variety of reasons this may be impossible. In either of these cases maximizing output per acre up to the point of zero marginal productivity of agricultural labour is quite rational.

We feel disinclined to say, however, that even a sustained increase in output per man or output per acre achieved in such circumstances represents a 'contribution' of agriculture to economic growth. For evidence of this we prefer to turn to a measure of aggregate factor productivity. This is also important to the economic historian, of course, in interpreting historical patterns of international trade, but here the relative prices of factors are also relevant. European farming

* In some countries, dramatic increases in productivity were achieved during World War II by some of the methods mentioned in the text.

in the late nineteenth century wilted under the competition of American grain and beef and of wool, meat and dairy produce from the southern hemisphere; but output per acre in these new lands was certainly substantially lower than in Europe, and had factor prices been equal all over the world, even aggregate factor productivity might well have been seen to be lower there. What enabled the new regions to compete was the (rational) adoption of factor combinations which took maximum advantage of the relative cheapness of land.

In an economy developing through time, we take the difference between the growth of output and the growth of aggregate factor inputs to be a measure of the improvement wrought by technical and organizational improvements.[33] This seems to be the most appropriate measure to adopt in assessing the contribution of any particular sector, for it abstracts from any increases in output per head or per unit of capital achieved in that sector by diverting to it a disproportionate share of co-operant resources. It is therefore at first sight surprising that so little work has been done in attempting to measure changes in aggregate factor productivity, especially in respect of particular sectors. This surprise evaporates, however, when one considers the daunting statistical complexities, data deficiencies and conceptual obscurities which impede the analysis of aggregate factor productivity.

The problems are clearly brought home to the reader of Moorsteen and Powell, *The Soviet Capital Stock 1928–1962*, a monumental work which offers not only a major addition to our knowledge of Soviet economic growth but also a wealth of valuable insights into the methodological perplexities of its subject.[34] Dealing with the productivity of the whole economy, different methods of computing the growth of output and of aggregate inputs yield total productivity growth estimates for the Soviet economy, 1928–61, ranging from $+0.1$ per cent to $+3.2$ per cent per annum. This extremely wide range permits no international comparisons more conclusive than that 'Soviet rates . . . are likely to bracket single rates calculated for advanced economies'.[35] Although Moorsteen and Powell doubtless did not intend any covert criticism in choosing this form of words, the reader could well take from it a useful reminder that the 'single rates' calculated for some such countries have been arrived at by methods which ride relatively roughshod over the difficulties which Moorsteen and Powell bring explicitly to the reader's attention: estimates for other countries would frankly not *be* single rates, but rather a more or less wide range of plausible rates, had the same degree of skill, industry and intellectual rigour been lavished on their estimation as Moorsteen and Powell have bestowed in the Russian case.

What is even more noteworthy is that even this magisterial study declines to offer any explicit estimate of the growth of aggregate productivity in the agricultural sector alone. The authors permit themselves nothing more than the guarded and unobtrusive comment that 'the productivity changes in agriculture implied by our estimates, while not statistically reliable, do nevertheless show considerable conformity in their broad fluctuations to those of the non-agricultural sectors. The total series is not, so far as we can judge, an average of greatly disparate changes in agriculture and in all other sectors.'[36] This conclusion was doubtless generated by comparing the estimates of productivity of aggregate inputs for the whole economy and for the non-agricultural sectors as presented in Tables T-64 and T-65 (378–9). Here total productivity in 1937 prices is shown to have risen from 85·1 in 1928 to 151·6 in 1961 with interest at 8 per cent, or from 89·7 to 125·6 with interest at 20 per cent (1937=100 in all cases). Non-agricultural productivity rose from 79·6 to 147·7 or from 84·5 to 122·2 over the same period. It can be seen that these increases, respectively of 78·1 or of 40 per cent for the whole economy and of 85·6 or of 44·6 per cent for the non-agricultural sectors, imply (given the relatively large share of agriculture in the total in 1928) not too widely disparate rates of aggregate productivity growth in agriculture and in the rest of the economy, though the achievement of the latter was somewhat more impressive.

Moorsteen and Powell do not state systematically and explicitly the reasons for their reluctance to offer a direct estimate of the growth of agricultural productivity, though their exposition suggests to the reader that it is in part connected with the scepticism with which they view their implied estimate of agricultural fixed capital. But it seems fairly evident that in many cases the estimate of inputs in the agricultural sector would be unusually sensitive to the choice made between alternative methods of weighting and aggregating inputs. Such a choice is less crucial in a sector in which the factors employed grow in roughly equiproportional fashion, so that the capital/labour ratio, for example, changes only relatively slowly. But in an advanced industrial country the case with agriculture is usually that the input of land remains roughly constant, while that of capital grows sharply and that of labour declines. These divergent movements lead one to expect a calculation of total inputs and therefore of aggregate factor productivity in agriculture to be influenced in an exceptional degree by the method adopted for weighting and aggregating inputs. Hence estimates of total productivity in agriculture need to be considered with an even greater degree of caution than similar estimates for other sectors or for the whole economy. The fact remains that this outstanding study gives no warrant for supposing that total productivity in Soviet agriculture has grown *markedly* less rapidly than that of other sectors of the economy, despite the widespread belief that the deficiencies of Soviet planning and control mechanisms have been especially harmful to this sector of the economy. If Soviet agriculture has indeed been a lagging sector holding back the growth of the economy this is less, the message seems to be, because its productivity has remained stubbornly low than because the Soviet decision-makers have simply refused to accord it sufficiently high priority in the allocation of inputs.

Another well-known study of productivity is that by Kendrick on the U.S. economy. Kendrick's findings suggest a slightly inferior relative performance for agriculture, a (roughly) three-fold improvement from 1869 through 1957, against a four-fold gain for the whole economy. But Kendrick is aware of the element of arbitrariness in adopting particular weighting conventions and warns the reader against undue reliance on his single-value estimates. Moreover, most of the lead of the non-agricultural sectors over agriculture was achieved in the first two decades of the present century, when agricultural productivity declined slightly. Over the remaining seven decades there was little to choose overall, and it is striking that since 1929, and especially since 1937, the increase in aggregate productivity has been greater in agriculture than in the economy as a whole.[37] There seem in fact to be as yet no firm empirical grounds for believing that agriculture is *inherently* incapable of generating increases in productivity comparable to those in the non-agricultural sectors, however plausible this belief may seem in the light of the distinctive organizational rigidities of farming, the greater impediments to technological diffusion, the intractability of Nature, and other such considerations. Yet it has to be added that this may well be because sufficient, and sufficiently reliable, econometric analyses have not as yet been undertaken.

The sources of productivity improvement

In the meantime it seems possible to offer with reasonable confidence a few generalizations about the sources of productivity improvement in temperate-zone farming in the 'scientific' period. The first phase was a 'mechanical' one, in which agricultural tools and machinery began to share in the benefits of the advances in engineering skill associated with the industrial revolution, and experiments were made in harnessing the new sources of power to its needs. Generally these innovations were labour-saving in character, and economically they found their justification in the fact that in the mid-nineteenth century agriculture for the first time began to experience difficulties in recruiting an adequate labour supply at an acceptable wage rate. In the early stages of the industrial revolution the labour force in manufacture and mining was so small relative to agriculture that factory and mine generally posed little threat to farm in the search for an adequate labour force. Further, with the increase in the rate of population growth, and given the small numbers employed in the secondary and tertiary sectors, the number of those engaged on the land was bound to increase absolutely for many decades, despite the quickening pace of industrialization.[38] The permanent agricultural work force in England did not begin to decline until about the time of the 1851 Census. But by then the rise of real wages in industry, and particularly the growth of manufacturing employment relative to that on the land, had begun to exert a marked upward pressure on agricultural wage rates and to reduce the elasticity of the supply of farm labour, especially of the extra seasonal labour needed at harvest and other peak periods of the farming year. Innovation therefore naturally concentrated at first on minor adaptations to the kit of agricultural implements designed to increase labour productivity at harvesting.[39] Attempts were naturally made, too, to adapt the new source of power to agricultural purposes, but by and large they failed, chiefly because the power/weight ratio of the steam engine was inadequate for the peculiar needs of agriculture. Only where the engine could remain stationary on a hard standing, notably in threshing, did steam power make a really successful contribution.

In the regions of recent settlement, however, these relatively modest adaptations were inadequate, since labour was much dearer than in the older countries, and as farming moved westwards in America, away from the great centres of population, the elasticity of supply of seasonal labour was extremely low. At the same time cheap virgin land and the freedom to fashion farm layout untrammelled by any inherited pattern of hedges and ditches permitted a size both of farm and of field on which more fundamental labour-saving machinery could be pioneered with the hope of profit. Since America had also by far the largest population of any region of recent settlement in the mid-nineteenth century, and therefore by far the largest stock of potential inventors and innovators, it is not surprising that the major labour-saving inventions, especially harvesting machinery, were made in the U.S.A. American reapers, binders and combine-harvesters were, however, quickly adopted – though often, as we have seen, alterations were needed to suit local conditions – in other regions of recent settlement with similar factor endowments.

The effect of these advances was to improve labour productivity in temperate grain farming. A remarkable paper by Parker and Klein analysing the sources of productivity improvement in American grain production in the later nineteenth century[40] shows clearly how much was owing to these technological advances. Over half the total gain in labour productivity in wheat, oats and corn alike was due directly to mechanization alone. Further, since mechanization was not equally effective – or applicable – in all regions, the growing importance in total output of those regions where it was *most* effective was an additional source of productivity improvement. Directly or in interaction with other changes mechanization was thus by far the most important source of labour productivity gain in American grain farming in the later nineteenth century, and one may guess that this conclusion will prove to hold also for other major areas of temperate grain farming.

Livestock farming has been even less studied than arable farming from the standpoint of productivity, but it seems clear that there were fewer dramatic improvements of the type which so increased labour productivity in grain farming, at least until the later nineteenth century. This is understandable, for the care of livestock is of its nature less prone to mechanization. Bateman, indeed, reports a 50 per cent increase in annual milk yields per cow in U.S. dairying between 1850 and 1910, but suggests that this was brought about primarily by labour-intensive changes such as an increase in the annual lactation period and by an averaging-up of techniques towards the level of the best (1850) performance, and that labour productivity (in terms of milk yield) actually declined.[41] It seems clear that we have here the sort of change – improving land but declining labour productivity – by which increases in grain output had been achieved in earlier centuries. The U.S.A., however, is perhaps not a shining example of high achievement in dairying; more impressive gains were registered in the Scandinavian countries, especially Denmark, and in some parts of the southern hemisphere, especially New Zealand. In Denmark, for example, milk yield per cow and butterfat content per gallon both doubled over the years 1870–1914;[42] in New Zealand, dairying was transformed from a backward part of the pastoral economy into the major farm sector, earning nearly half of the Dominion's export receipts, by the early 1930s. It seems quite certain that these developments reflect large productivity increases, though the appropriate analysis has not yet been undertaken. It also appears that the usual type of productivity analysis might fail adequately to measure the 'improvements' achieved in so far as the development of export-oriented dairy industries depended to an extent unusual in trade in farm products on achieving a high and consistent level of quality, a feature which had been markedly absent in the earlier period of farm dairy production in these countries.

The sources of productivity gain were also more complex than in grain farming. Innovations on the processing and marketing side were essential elements, these including improved cream separators and factory machinery and (in the case of the southern hemisphere producers) refrigeration on ocean-going ships. On the farm, the only important and distinctive machinery was the milking machine, which again was labour-saving in bias and had the effect of increasing the size of herd which could be coped with on these predominantly family-labour farms. For the rest, increasing productivity was essentially a matter of raising the level of butterfat production per acre, which subdivides into the possibilities (a) of increasing the butterfat content of the milk; (b) of raising milk yields per cow; (c) of increasing stock-carrying capacity per acre. (Bateman's work on U.S. dairying, incidentally, is of limited application as it in effect confines itself to only the second of these improvements.) A necessary prerequisite to the first was the invention of a reliable and easily-administered test of butterfat content, which was accomplished in the last two decades of the nineteenth century. Beyond this, improvements in one or more of the directions indicated were achieved by diverse means, such as improvement of the sward by seed selection or applications of fertiliser; herd improvement; improved grazing routines (such as movable electric fences to permit controlled rotational grass use); and the discovery of optimum stocking rates.

It is noteworthy that productivity improvement in dairying (unlike that in nineteenth-century grain farming) here begins to impinge on the second major phase in the improvement of productivity of temperate-zone farming, namely that of the replacement of animal power by mechanical (including electrical) energy, and of the application of advances in chemistry and genetics to agricultural purposes. Before leaving pastoral farming, however, it may be stressed that a common feature of the improvements in dairying to which we have referred, and in meat production, is that they were very much a response to, and had as a necessary condition, substantial changes on the demand side. In Denmark the particular initiating factor was the impossibility of perpetuating the old reliance on grain exports in the face of the competition of Russian and American supplies. In the southern hemisphere the essential starting-point for export-oriented frozen meat and dairy industries was the advent of refrigerated cargo vessels capable of carrying highly-perishable products across the Equator. In the highly-urbanized countries of North America and Western Europe, town milk supply was transformed, or almost in some cases created, by railways and refrigerated railroad cars.[43] And lying behind all of this was the secular growth of population and of incomes in these countries, increasing their market size and transforming the structure of consumer demand away from the staple bread grains towards more expensive foods such as meat, milk and dairy products. Technological change in these forms of agriculture, even though it involved much experiment and innovation at the farm level, was essentially supplied by science and prompted by market opportunity – a far cry from the 'endogenous' agricultural advance in response to increasing population densities on which Boserup lays stress.

It has been said that the second phase of improvement in the productivity of temperate-zone farming consisted in the application of inanimate and electrical energy, and of chemical and genetic science, to agricultural purposes. Despite the fact that agricultural research had its institutional origins in the nineteenth century, *substantial* gains from these directions seem to have been forthcoming only in the twentieth century, and in most countries indeed from the beginning of the second quarter of this century onwards. It is this period, for example, which has witnessed the supersession of the horse by the tractor and the introduction of electricity on the farm (for example in power milking machines); the application of greatly increased resources to the furthering and diffusion of scientific knowledge relating to agriculture, forestry and fisheries; an enormous increase in the rate of application of fertilisers and of insecticides and fungicides; and the application to farming of the principles of scientific management.

These changes, which are still very much continuing and indeed in some branches of farming still accelerating, have had obvious and major consequences for the level of farm production in the advanced countries. While the embarrassing surpluses of some products – grain in the U.S.A.; dairy produce in Europe – which in some countries piled up in post-World War II years arose in part because of government policies channelling towards agriculture an inappropriate share of total inputs, they more fundamentally reflect the rapid growth of productivity achieved by such changes as those just summarized. The fault of policy has chiefly lain in impeding the modifications to the total size of and combination of factor inputs in the agricultural sector which would have been appropriate. Evidence of the increases in productivity which have been achieved in the last three or four decades can be found, for example, in Kendrick's study: his table showing total productivity in U.S. agriculture suggests two periods of particularly marked improvement since 1869, the first exhausting itself by the early 1890s, the second, and greater, beginning about 1929, accelerating after 1937 and still continuing at the end of his study (1957). The less well-known work of Loomis and Barton, which suggests a broadly similar path for total productivity growth since 1870, differs chiefly in attributing less improvement to the earlier period and more to the years 1930–60.[44]

Agricultural productivity and the growth of the economy

How are changes in agricultural productivity related to the growth of the whole economy? Simon Kuznets has suggested that agriculture's contribution to growth can be subdivided into a 'product', a 'market' and a 'factor' contribution.[45] In the first case we regard an increase in agricultural productivity as leading to a rise in agricultural output and thus enlarging the national product directly; in the second, attention is focused on the agricultural sector as a source of demand for the products of other sectors, whether by way of inputs or of the spending of farmers as consumers; while in the third, a rise in agricultural productivity permits agricultural output to be maintained while factors are released to the benefit of other sectors. While this is a useful analytical classification, it must of course be remembered that although a given increase in agricultural productivity can be *divided* between various possible benefits, it cannot be counted twice.[46] The same increase cannot *both* permit a proportionate increase in agricultural output *and* be used to release factors of production to other sectors. In practice it is also difficult, because of the paucity of appropriate studies, to separate out increases in productivity and increases brought about by enlarging factor inputs. With these provisos, however, it can be said that Kuznets' scheme does help us to see the differing ways in which rising agricultural productivity has been 'taken out' in different historical situations.

Where the market opportunity has been favourable, as in most of New Zealand's history, rising productivity was allowed to generate increased output for export and rising farm incomes formed a major part of the demand for the product of other sectors. In the case of Meiji Japan, output also increased with rising productivity, but generated increased exports only to a lesser degree, most of the increased output being absorbed by a rising population. At the same time, a large fraction of agriculture's rising receipts was taxed away to provide capital for infrastructural development and industrial credits.[47] In Tsarist Russia agriculture played a somewhat similar role, but the chief emphasis was on maximizing agricultural exports at the expense, if necessary, of domestic consumption. In Soviet Russia, on the other hand, the chief achievement of collectivization was to raise *labour* productivity by rapid mechanization so as to permit both labour and a larger fraction of food output – there being both fewer men and fewer horses left in the rural areas – to be siphoned off to permit the growth of urban industry. And in many industrial countries the unprecedented growth of industry since World War II has been made possible by using the growth of agricultural productivity in part to permit a massive withdrawal of labour from the land.

A major factor determining how increasing agricultural productivity has been 'shared' between various possible benefits has been the shape of the demand schedule for agricultural products. A country with a strong comparative advantage in a particular type of farming, like New Zealand in pastoral farming, would not be prosperous if it were permanently blockaded and unable to trade, for one cannot become rich *merely* by producing, however cheaply, meat and dairy produce, or even wool, which cannot be exported. The late nineteenth and early twentieth century formed a period when there were exceptional opportunities for countries like New Zealand to achieve growth by specializing in export-oriented primary products; demand conditions in the industrial countries, the marked fall of ocean freights, and a

series of technological advances headed by refrigeration
enabled them to exploit the comparative advantage offered
by their relatively abundant land. As late as the eve of
World War II New Zealand's economy was dominated by
pastoral farming; there was no other major centre of
autonomous economic activity. In saying this, it is not
intended to assert that the pastoral sector directly accounted
for the greater part of employment, any more than one
wishes to claim that their respective industries were directly
responsible for the bulk of employment in referring to
nineteenth-century Pittsburgh as a steel town or to nineteenth-century Manchester as a cotton town. In all rich and
complex societies most people work in such places as shops,
banks, or central and local government offices, or in the
building or transport industries, or they teach the children
of those who do, or provide other services for them. But these
activities are linked by 'derived' demand to, or they supply,
consume or carry the inputs and outputs of, the 'autonomous'
economic activity which gives each region or city its economic
raison d'etre, be it cotton in Manchester, steel in Pittsburgh or
pastoral farming in New Zealand.

Where this autonomous economic activity is the production of some primary product for export, it has sometimes
been the custom to refer to the latter as the 'staple'. Some
economic historians have argued that the economic structure
and development of such societies are best understood by
analysing them in terms of these relationships of their 'staple'
products; the mode of analysis referred to is sometimes called
'staple theory'. The first important application of this
approach was by Harold Innis, who in two major books and
a series of articles analysed the chief periods and patterns of
Canadian economic development in terms of the 'staples'
which were produced and exported.[48] More recently,
writers such as North[49] in America and McCarty[50] in
Australia have found 'staple theory' useful in analysing the
economy of their respective countries, and the 'theory' has
been more systematically presented by North, Baldwin and
Watkins.[51] Actually, 'theory' is perhaps a slightly pre-

tentious term to bestow on the limited array of theoretical tools and concepts involved; these are in no sense a novel or even a closely-knit segment of the whole corpus of economic theory, but merely an *ad hoc* selection which is particularly valuable for analysing the ways in which a dominant sector influences the structure of the economy as a whole. Nor is there in principle any reason why this dominant sector should be agricultural (or mineral); it is merely that most of the rather simple societies of the past which 'staple theory' has proved useful in illuminating have been dominantly primary producers.

With these reservations, the staple approach has been useful in explaining at least some facets of the economies of export-oriented primary producers. It concentrates chiefly on two sorts of relationship: the type of income distribution and of demand generated by the structure of the dominant sector, and the input/output linkages to which its technology gives rise. These relationships, due regard paid to the pattern of the spatial distribution of production and to freight charges, are held to throw light on (for example) the structure of international or inter-regional trade, the degree of urbanization, and the pattern of commodity demand and thus the style and size of the impetus given to the development of industry and services.

It is a feature, and a recommendation, of staple theory that it helps to explain economic differences between the various regions of a large country such as America. Such regional differences were a more prominent feature of such economies in earlier times than they are today, and the need for a theoretical framework capable of explaining them is correspondingly strongly felt. North, in particular, has persuasively argued that their distinctive agricultural sectors are largely responsible for the differing income levels, growth rates, and degrees of urbanization and industrialization of the American South and West. The latter was characterized by a greater variety of agricultural and mining activities, lacking the overwhelming comparative advantage in any one crop which kept so much of the South tied to cotton even in bad years. The West, again, had a structure of family farms which generated a relatively egalitarian distribution of income more favourable to the development of local service and manufacturing industry than the extreme inequality of the large-scale Southern plantation, with its small class of rich owners sharply contrasting with the majority, most of them slaves, who exercised little if any market demand. The tendency for the former class to import their requirements from outside the region was accentuated by the cheap back-haul on the ships which carried the cotton out, whereas the West's industry received greater natural protection from freight costs. Further, the staple products of the latter exercised much greater demand on internal transport facilities and on industries producing agricultural machinery, and gave rise to processing industries with locational advantages in intra-regional sites.

The staple approach, in fact, is one which readily commends itself to the historical geographer, for it throws unusual emphasis on the significance not only of spatial relationships but also of natural endowment. It is for this latter characteristic, however, that it has been criticized by some. Thus Butlin has argued that staple theory is based on a *fixed* pattern of comparative advantage arising essentially from a given natural endowment and the assumption (*inter alia*) of fixed factor proportions.[52] But growth, in Butlin's contention, is essentially a matter of *changing* factor proportions and of *changing* comparative advantage. He charges McCarty, specifically, with an inability to explain Australia's nineteenth-century growth in terms of staple theory, though conceding that this can 'cast interesting light on some aspects of social and economic structure'. Butlin's contention seems to be that staple theory is on its own an *inadequate* framework for explaining development in the specific sense of structural change, rather than that it is invalid or even unhelpful in explaining growth of total product or product per head.

In Kuznets' terms, 'staple theory' concentrates on the 'market' aspect of agriculture's contribution to development, with some reference too to the 'factor' contribution in so far as forward linkages are concerned. A somewhat more aggregate view of agriculture's 'market' contribution is implied in the doctrine of 'balanced growth'. The 'balanced v. unbalanced growth' controversy of the 1950s and early 1960s is, in the opinion of many, decently interred;[53] the concepts involved are held to have been overtaken by the greater sophistication of more recent thinking. Yet the views of the 'balanced growth' theorists have been quietly absorbed by the school which advocates the parallel growth of agriculture and industry as the best grand strategy for today's low-income countries. This school rests its case, in part, on two arguments. First, given the poor prospects for exporting manufactures which face most low-income countries, the demand for the output of the manufacturing sector must be sought at home, and must in large part be forthcoming from the agricultural sector, in view of the very large share of this in total income. But equally, if agriculture is to be encouraged to improve its productivity, an expanding urban and industrial market must be ready to buy its products, both food and raw materials, and offer in exchange an array of consumer goods to serve as an incentive to expand money earnings in agriculture.

The economic historian very readily appreciates the force of this argument for the symbiotic growth of agriculture and industry, for history seems to show obvious instances of the advantages of such growth and of the disadvantages of its absence. An outstanding instance of the latter is that of Russia. For a variety of economic, social and geographical reasons, rural Russia in Tsarist days was remarkably self-sufficient, the *mir* (Russian village community) producing not only the great bulk of its food requirements but also, through peasant industry, the bulk too of consumer manufactures and agricultural implements. Consequently domestic demand for the products of capitalist industry was very small relative to population, particularly since the rich imported many of their purchases. In the late Tsarist period the State adopted a policy of stimulating industrial growth, and with marked success, especially in the 1890s when the rate of growth of factory production, at some 8·0 per cent per annum, was higher than in either Germany or the U.S.A. This forced industrialization was achieved, however, at the expense of the peasantry, constituting perhaps four-fifths of the population, who were compelled to produce grain for export and to pay heavy taxes to finance capital formation. Industrial growth was therefore largely confined to industries producing for export, for State purchase, or for capital formation, while the mass of the people depended as much as ever on peasant industry.

These developments led to an outstanding example of a 'dual economy', and it would be an apt exercise for practitioners of counterfactual history to speculate whether, had war and revolution not intervened, the promising start of Tsarist industrialization might have proved abortive because of the deficiency of internal demand to absorb industrial production and the failure of agricultural productivity to guarantee a continuing rise of food and raw material supplies for urban industry. In their economic aspect – though political motives were uppermost – Stolypin's reforms following the 1905 revolution were in part calculated to amend this situation, by encouraging individualization of titles, the formation of compact, enclosed farms, and the rise of a class of richer peasants oriented to market production. It is interesting, too, that as early as 1902 a critic of Witte, who as Minister of Finance had been chiefly responsible for the forced industrialization policies of the preceding decade, had argued that the poverty of the peasant market was the chief restraint on Russian industrialization and that for successful development, industry and agriculture must grow in step. What is clear is that after the Revolution and the Civil War the failure of agriculture and factory industry to achieve a steady growth permitting reciprocal and mutually satisfactory exchange emerged as the major threat to Soviet economic growth. The peasantry, sullen from the experience of forced levies during the Civil War and disenchanted by the failure of industry to offer sufficient quantities of consumer goods at acceptable prices, retreated into self-sufficiency, while industry and the towns were starved of food and raw materials notwithstanding the drastic reduction of grain exports below pre-1914 levels. A way out of the dilemma was ultimately found only in the terrible expedient of forced collectivization. But it is interesting that the protagonists in the 'industrial debate' which raged in the mid-1920s not only correctly identified the essence of the problem, but also anticipated most of the more important arguments which have been rediscovered in the 'balanced *v.* unbalanced growth' and 'big push' debates of recent decades.[54]

In contrast to the Russian experience the countries which achieved smoother industrialization, whether early or late starters – Great Britain, the U.S.A., Japan – all apparently enjoyed substantial increases in agricultural output during the period of early industrialization. Their methods of achieving it varied widely according to their geography and the chronology of their 'take-off'; British agricultural output, at least until the mid-nineteenth century, seems to have risen chiefly by organizational changes (enclosures and tenant farming) and by increasing intensity of cultivation as absolute numbers in agriculture rose; the U.S.A. drew on its immense land reserves, causing a fall in average man/acre ratios but inventing new capital and land-intensive techniques appropriate to Western farming; Japan's agricultural output increased thanks to a combination of extension of the total cultivated area, a northwards extension of double cropping, and modest yield increases.[55] The use made of these increases also varied from case to case; in Japan they were largely 'siphoned off' by taxation and by exploiting low-cost underemployed farm labour as a 'factor' contribution to small-scale industry, whereas in the U.S.A. the farm sector, at least in the West and North, was clearly a big source of demand for industrial products and transportation services and stimulated industrial growth by its relatively strong forward linkages. In the case of Britain, too, the modern interpretation is once again placing considerable emphasis on the agricultural sector's 'market' contribution to total demand.[56]

In many countries, here including Russia, agriculture has also played an important role in foreign trade during the industrialization process. Even in the British case, grain exports represented a not inconsiderable fraction of total exports for several decades, while in the later eighteenth and early nineteenth century the need for food imports was greatly restrained by increasing domestic production. Later industrializers whose 'take-off' occurred at a time of more capital-intensive industrial techniques and after the invention of railways experienced greater needs, and had greater opportunities, for imports of capital goods than Britain did, and hence faced a more critical need to expand import capability until a domestic iron/steel and heavy engineering industry had been created. They met this need, in some cases, partly by borrowing abroad; but to the extent that this solution was unavailable or unwanted, a corresponding burden was thrown on the expansion of exports. Since it is difficult for a newly-industrializing country to develop exports of manufactures against established competitors in world markets, and since by definition such countries are starting from a predominantly agricultural base, this meant in most cases expanding primary exports. As late as the last decade of the nineteenth century, by which time it was already the world's leading industrial power, nearly three-quarters of the U.S.A.'s exports were classified as foodstuffs or primary produce, while in the case of Japan raw silk alone accounted for 30 per cent of aggregate exports over the whole period 1870–1930. In Russia, too, agricultural exports still constituted 60 per cent of the total in 1913, with industrial raw materials and semi-manufactures (including lumber and petroleum) accounting for a further 34½ per cent. An additional reason for the Soviet resort to a crash programme of development of metallurgy and heavy engineering in 1929 was the apparent impossibility of restoring the pre-1914 pattern of financing capital goods imports by primary exports, in view of the difficulties both of producing and marketing an agricultural surplus. It should be added, how-ever, that some nineteenth-century industrializers, notably Germany, had greater success in developing manufactured exports at an early stage and may have owed less to agri-cultural progress.

Finally, we stress once again the most obvious aspect of agriculture's 'product' contribution to economic growth: that where it is much the largest sector, agriculture will have much the largest weight in determining the rate of growth of total output. The rate of growth of output of any sector must, of course, be multiplied by the fraction representing that sector's share in total output in calculating its effect on the latter. Hence, even a very rapid growth rate of a given sector, say manufacturing industry, will have little impact on total product if that sector is only a very small fraction of the total economy; whereas if a slowly-growing agricul-ture is responsible for more than half of total output, as in many pre-industrial societies, it will pull down the aggregate growth rate even if other, smaller, sectors are growing very quickly. It was precisely this combination which damped down the achievement of Russia before the Revolution, despite the impressive advances of Tsarist industry.[57]

It has been stressed by Folke Dovring, and following him by Bruce Johnston, that the arithmetical implications are even more impressive in considering the pattern of employ-ment in less developed countries.[58] If population is increas-ing, and if we make the (reasonable) assumption that agri-culture is a 'residual' occupation, that is that most people are born in farming families and stay on the land *unless* the growth of non-agricultural activity affords them employment elsewhere, total agricultural employment will increase. For now the increased numbers in the agricultural labour force induced by the natural increase of population will all be 'credited' to agriculture except in so far as the growth of employment in other sectors exceeds the rate of natural increase in those sectors. If employment in non-agricultural sectors is growing proportionally faster than the total labour

E

force, the agricultural share in employment must, of course, decline in proportionate terms; but if the total labour force is growing, *absolute* numbers on the land may continue to increase for some years. The relationship may be expressed as

$$L'_a = \left\{ L'_t - L'_n \right\} \frac{1}{L_a/L_t} + L'_n ,$$

where L'_a, L'_t, L'_n are the rates of change of agricultural, total and non-agricultural employment, and L_a/L_t is the initial share of agriculture in total employment. It can be seen that the rate of increase of employment in agriculture will be greater the faster the rise of total employment, and the larger agriculture's initial share in the labour force. It is for this reason that in modern industrial societies, where rising population so generally accompanied the process of industrialization, absolute employment on the land still continued to increase, often for many decades, and until a quite advanced stage of structural transformation was achieved. This fact in turn explains why in the agricultural sector of such societies increases in output could be won in essentially labour-intensive ways, labour-saving agricultural innovations being unnecessary until this advanced stage was reached. Only in countries like the U.S.A., where land reserves were large enough to permit acreage to increase more rapidly than agricultural employment, did labour shortage become acute at an earlier stage of industrialization, and only there was there an overwhelming incentive for labour-saving agricultural innovations. This, in turn, has important implications for the level of (non-agricultural) wage rates, but these will be considered elsewhere in this book.[59] It may also be pointed out that in present-day societies with very high rates of population increase and a large fraction of the labour force in agriculture, even the most wildly optimistic estimates of the possible rate of industrialization may still imply continued increase in total numbers on the land for many decades to come. But this, fortunately, is not a topic which it falls to the historian to discuss.

Notes

1. See above, pp. 56–7, and J. R. BELLERBY, *Agriculture and Industry: Relative Income* (London, Macmillan, 1956), Ch. XVI and *passim*.

2. See above, pp. 109–10.

3. S. LEBERGOTT, 'Labour Force and Employment, 1800–1960', in N.B.E.R. (1966), 131, and the 'General Comment' by BRINLEY THOMAS, *ibid.*, 206.

4. DONALD B. KEESING, 'Structural Change Early in Development: Mexico's Changing Industrial and Occupational Structure from 1895 to 1950', *Journal of Economic History*, XXIX (December 1969), 723.

5. M. POSTAN, 'Some Economic Evidence of Declining Population in the Later Middle Ages', *Economic History Review*, Sec. Ser. II (1950), 221–46; NOEL G. BUTLIN, 'A New Plea for the Separation of Ireland', *Journal of Economic History*, XXVIII (June 1968), 285 ff.

6. *New Zealand and an Enlarged EEC* (N.Z. Monetary and Economic Council *Report No. 19*, June 1970), Appx. II, Table 1, 74.

7. ARCADIUS KAHAN, 'Changes in Labor Inputs in Soviet Agriculture', *Journal of Political Economy*, 67 (October 1959), 457.

8. GOUROU (1961), 28.

9. STEPHEN H. HYMER, 'Economic Forms in Pre-Colonial Ghana', *Journal of Economic History*, XXX (March 1970), 37.

10. DOREEN WARRINER, *The Economics of Peasant Farming*, 2nd ed. (New York, Barnes & Noble, 1964), xxi–xxii.

11. KAHAN, *loc. cit.*

12. JAMES MAVOR, *An Economic History of Russia*, 2nd ed. (London, Dent, 1925), Vol. II, 391.

13. cf. STEPHEN A. RESNICK, 'The Decline of Rural Industry Under Export Expansion: A Comparison among Burma, Philippines, and Thailand, 1870–1938', *Journal of Economic History*, XXX (March 1970), 51–73.

14. DANIEL THORNER, 'Long-term Trends in Output in India', in S. KUZNETS *et al.* (eds), *Economic Growth: Brazil, India, Japan* (Durham, N.C., Duke University Press, 1955), 111–12, 117–18.

15. NAKAMURA (1966), 128–9.

16. J. THIRSK, 'Industries in the Countryside', in *Essays in the*

Economic and Social History of Tudor and Stuart England, ed.
F. J. FISHER (Cambridge, Cambridge U.P., 1961).

17. For nineteenth-century sales of Maori land, see M. P. K.
    SORRENSON, 'Land Purchase Methods and Their Effect on
    Maori Population, 1865–1907', *Journal of the Polynesian Society*,
    65 (September 1956), 183–99; for recent experience, J. K.
    HUNN, *Report on Department of Maori Affairs* (Wellington,
    Government Printer, 1961), 52–76.

18. T. S. ASHTON, *Economic Fluctuations in England 1700–1800*
    (Oxford, Clarendon Press, 1959), 2.

19. The statement in the text is not, however, intended to apply
    to eighteenth-century England, where the wheat market, at
    least, appears to have been relatively well integrated: C. W. J.
    GRANGER and C. M. ELLIOTT, 'A Fresh Look at Wheat
    Prices and Markets in the Eighteenth Century', *Economic
    History Review*, Sec. Ser. XX (August 1967), 257–65.

20. B. H. SLICHER VAN BATH, *Yield Ratios, 810–1820*, Afdeling
    Agrarische Geschiedenis *Bijdragen*, Vol. 10 (1963).

21. PHELPS BROWN and HOPKINS, 1956.

22. See CHRISTOPHER HILL, *Puritanism and Revolution* (London,
    Secker & Warburg, 1965), 43.

23. For a temperate discussion of a sometimes intemperate debate,
    see A. J. TAYLOR, 'Progress and Poverty in Britain, 1750–
    1850: A Reappraisal', *History*, XLV (1960), 16–31.

24. DENIS RICHET, 'Croissance et blocages en France du XVe au
    XVIIIe siècle', *Annales*, 23 (July/August 1968), 766–8.

25. ESTER BOSERUP, *The Conditions of Agricultural Growth*
    (London, Allen & Unwin, 1965).

26. GOUROU, 1961.

27. VAN BATH, *op. cit.*

28. NAKAMURA (1966), 49.

29. The view that England's agricultural revolution should be
    dated in the seventeenth rather than the eighteenth century
    is championed by ERIC KERRIDGE, *The Agricultural Revolution*
    (London, Allen & Unwin, 1967).

30. GOUROU (1961), *passim*.

31. e.g. D. W. MEINIG, *On the Margins of the Good Earth: The South
    Australian Wheat Frontier 1869–1884* (Skokie, Ill., Rand Mc-
    Nally & Co. for the Association of American Geographers,
    1962), 113–15.

32. *ibid*, 104.

33. See further below, Ch. 5.

34. MOORSTEEN and POWELL, 1966.

35. *ibid.*, 293.

36. *ibid.*, 267.

37. KENDRICK (1961), Tables 34 (136–7), A–XX (331), B–I (362–4), and p. 10.

38. cf. above, pp. 109–10.

39. E. J. T. COLLINS, 'Harvest Technology and Labour Supply in Britain, 1790–1870', *Economic History Review*, Sec. Ser. XXII (December 1969), 453–73.

40. W. N. PARKER and J. L. V. KLEIN, 'Productivity Growth in Grain Production in the United States, 1840–60 and 1900–10', in N.B.E.R. (1966), 523–80.

41. FRED BATEMAN, 'Improvement in American Dairy Farming, 1850–1910: A Quantitative Analysis', *Journal of Economic History*, XXVIII (June 1968), 255–73; 'Labor Inputs and Productivity in American Dairy Agriculture, 1850–1910', *ibid.*, XXIX (June 1969), 206–29.

42. A. J. YOUNGSON, *Possibilities of Economic Progress* (Cambridge, Cambridge U.P., 1959), 208.

43. For the U.S.A., BATEMAN, 'Improvement . . .', *loc. cit.*, 259; for the United Kingdom, E. H. WHETHAM, 'The London Milk Trade, 1860–1900', *Economic History Review*, Sec. Ser. XVII (December 1964), 369–80.

44. KENDRICK (1961), 362–4; R. A. LOOMIS and G. T. BARTON, *Productivity of Agriculture, United States, 1870–1958*, quoted in WAYNE D. RASMUSSEN, 'The Impact of Technological Change on American Agriculture, 1862–1962', *Journal of Economic History*, XXII (December 1962), 585.

45. SIMON KUZNETS, 'Economic Growth and the Contribution of Agriculture: Notes on Measurements', in EICHER and WITT, 1964.

46. cf. CHARLES P. KINDLEBERGER, *Economic Growth in France and Britain, 1851–1950* (Cambridge, Mass., Harvard U.P., 1964), 209.

47. The classic exposition of the Japanese experience – many times repeated with only slight variations, and now under challenge by Nakamura – is in B. F. JOHNSTON, 'Agricultural

Productivity and Economic Development in Japan', *Journal of Political Economy*, LIX (December 1951), 498–513.

48. For references to Innis' work and to some critiques, see the article by Watkins listed in note 51 below.

49. D. C. NORTH, 'Agriculture in Regional Economic Growth', in EICHER and WITT (1964), 69–78. See also NORTH, *The Economic Growth of the United States 1790–1860* (Englewood Cliffs, N.J., Prentice-Hall, 1961).

50. J. W. MCCARTY, 'The Staple Approach in Australian Economic History', *Business Archives and History*, IV (February 1964), 1–22.

51. D. C. NORTH, 'Location Theory and Regional Economic Growth', *Journal of Political Economy*, LXIII (June 1955), 243–58; R. E. BALDWIN, 'Patterns of Development in Newly Settled Regions', *Manchester School of Economic and Social Studies*, XXIV (May 1956), 161–79; M. H. WATKINS, 'A Staple Theory of Economic Growth', *Canadian Journal of Economics and Political Science*, XXIX (May 1963), 141–58.

52. NOEL G. BUTLIN, 'Growth in a Trading World: The Australian Economy, Heavily Disguised', *Business Archives and History*, IV (August 1964), 138–58.

53. cf. PAUL STREETEN, 'Unbalanced Growth: A Reply', *Oxford Economic Papers*, N.S. 15 (March 1963), 66–73.

54. cf. ALEXANDER ERLICH, *The Soviet Industrialization Debate* (Cambridge, Mass., Harvard U.P., 1960).

55. NAKAMURA (1966), *passim*.

56. D. E. C. EVERSLEY, 'The Home Market and Economic Growth in England, 1750–1780', in E. L. JONES and G. E. MINGAY (eds), *Land, Labour and Population in the Industrial Revolution* (London, Arnold, 1967).

57. R. W. GOLDSMITH, 'The Economic Growth of Tsarist Russia, 1860–1913', *Economic Development and Cultural Change*, 9 (April 1961), 441–75.

58. FOLKE DOVRING, 'The Share of Agriculture in a Growing Population', in EICHER and WITT (1964), 78–98; B. F. JOHNSTON, 'Agriculture and Economic Development in Japan: Its Relevance to the Developing Nations', *Food Research Institute Studies*, 6 (1966), 251–312.

59. See below, pp. 361–2.

3　The Role of Capital

(A) INVESTMENT AND ECONOMIC GROWTH

The unimportance of capital?

In December 1955 Moses Abramovitz presented a paper to the sixty-eighth annual meeting of the American Economic Association in which he calculated that by far the greater share of the increase of output in the U.S.A. from 1869–78 to 1944–53 had come from a rise in aggregate productivity rather than from the increase of inputs.[1] Abramovitz characterized this result as 'surprising' and commented that it should be 'sobering, if not discouraging, to students of economic growth'.

His surprise reflected a background of thought in which it had been customary to assume that the increase in the stock of capital per worker had been the chief reason for the rise of labour productivity. Since analysis had centred on the classical three-factor approach, and since the importance of land was clearly small in the typical activities of highly industrialized economies and could hardly have grown relatively, it seemed natural to look at the increment of capital to explain the great secular rise in output per worker which was known to have occurred. Schumpeter, in his insistence on the role of the entrepreneur as a fourth factor of production and in his remarkable historical grasp of technological and organizational change, was clearly reaching out for something more, but his finest book had the misfortune to appear only three years after Keynes' *General Theory* and failed to make the impact it deserved to make on growth analysis.[2] This new branch of economics first made its appearance in the years immediately preceding World War II, and it took the form rather of an attempt to extend Keynesian analysis from the static to the dynamic field.

This approach, pioneered by Keynes' friend and biographer Roy (later Sir Roy) Harrod, began with the formulation of simple equations in which the rate of growth of output was determined by the propensity to save and the output-generating power of capital. If the value of the stock of capital in a given time period is divided by the value of output in the same period, we derive a 'capital coefficient' or 'capital/output ratio'. If the net *increase* in the value of the stock of capital is divided by the increase in income we have a marginal or *incremental* capital/output ratio ($=ICOR$). It is then tautological to say that the rate of growth of income in any previous period is the product of the rate of investment, expressed as a ratio of income, and the reciprocal of the *ICOR*. If, however, there is some reason for believing that the *ICOR* is stable, at least for a certain period, then we can use this tautology to *predict* potential rates of growth for various levels of savings. In a climate of thought in which capital was viewed as the chief agent of growth, it seemed natural to assume that the ratio of capital to output was governed essentially by technological considerations, and that for a given state of technology, at least, the *ICOR* could be regarded as a fundamental parameter.

In the early post-war period events and problems in several areas conspired to focus attention on capital formation. The brilliant recovery of war-devastated Europe after about 1948 was widely ascribed to injections of American capital under the 'Marshall Aid' programme, and thus as testifying to the growth-promoting power of investment. In the 1950s attention shifted to the problems of the 'third world', where it was natural to ascribe the low level of income to the shortage of capital goods which leapt to the eye of any observant traveller. The problems of the low-income countries assumed greater urgency, in the eyes of Western nations, in the measure that European recovery progressed and that cold-war tensions shifted from a more and more stable Europe to a more and more unstable Asia and Africa. Here the progress of 'decolonization' brought both political turmoil and world-wide publicity. The belief was fostered that in helping the emergent nations to achieve a satisfactory rate of economic growth lay the best hope of securing their allegiance to the democratic camp. As a further step in the analysis, it was suggested that the shortage of capital in these countries stemmed from their low level of income, which did not permit a sufficient margin of savings above irreducible consumption needs, so that they were caught in a vicious circle of poverty from which escape was to be looked for only in the direction of foreign capital.

The most influential exposition of this line of thought was perhaps Ragnar Nurkse's Rio de Janeiro lectures of 1951, later published (in 1953) as *Problems of Capital Formation in Underdeveloped Countries*.[3] Many of those who took up Nurkse's arguments on the political level failed to note the qualifications with which Nurkse, a fine historian, hedged his assertions as to the role of capital in economic growth, even though he stated them explicitly in the first paragraph of his book, which ended with the sentence: 'Capital is a necessary but not a sufficient condition of progress.' Nurkse's views found apparent confirmation from several directions. Arthur Lewis, who had done distinguished work in economic history as well as in development economics, wrote in his 1955 essay *The Theory of Economic Growth* that increasing the rate of net investment from 5 per cent or less to 12 per cent or more 'is what we mean by an Industrial Revolution', and again that 'The central problem in the theory of economic growth is to understand the process by which a community is converted from being a 5 per cent to a 12 per cent saver'.[4] (One suspects, incidentally, that these sentences, torn out of context, have been more frequently quoted – and criticized – than Lewis might have wished.) Among the economic historians proper, W. W. Rostow made an increase in the rate of investment from 5 to 10 per cent an essential ingredient of his 'take-off' stage,[5] while some years earlier Professor T. S.

Ashton, who probably knew more about the English industrial revolution than anyone in the world, had stressed the importance for industrial investment of the low rate of interest characteristic of the eighteenth century, and had written: 'If we seek – it would be wrong to do so – for a single reason why the pace of economic development quickened about the middle of the eighteenth century, it is to this we must look.'[6]

It can well be understood that against this background the assertion that capital had been responsible for only a small fraction of American growth should have come as something of a shock. But Abramovitz's findings quickly received confirmation in other studies. In 1957 Solow claimed that over the period 1909–49 gross output per man doubled in the private, non-agricultural sector of the U.S. economy, and that seven-eighths of the improvement had been due to an upward shift in the production function, and only one-eighth to increased capital per man.[7] Solow's paper elicited some methodological discussion, but John W. Kendrick, using a somewhat different technique and a different coverage, came to not dissimilar conclusions: total factor productivity had been responsible for somewhat less than half of the U.S. growth, 1889–1953, but for more than half over the interval 1919–53.[8] (At the time of writing these words, preliminary findings of an extension of the Kendrick study have been made public: they suggest that of a total growth of American N.N.P. of 4·1 per cent per annum over the years 1948–66, more than half – 2·3 per cent – was achieved by the annual growth of total factor productivity.[9])

Studies for other countries have, in the main, reached similar findings. Aukrust, for example, found increased labour inputs responsible for 0·46 of Norway's twentieth-century growth of 3·4 per cent per annum; capital contributed 1·12 and productivity 1·81 per cent.[10] Hoffmann placed the annual growth of aggregate factor productivity at 1·5 per cent for Germany before World War I, and at 4·0 per cent since 1950, compared with N.D.P. growth at 2·6 and 6·6 per cent respectively.[11] Matthews showed the 'residual' responsible for the greater part of British growth of output per man year in three of his four sub-periods over the interval of 1886–1962, the exception being 1899–1913 when growth was minimal and the contribution of the 'residual' actually negative.[12] Finally, Denison's study, *Why Growth Rates Differ*,[13] suggested estimates of the contribution of increased capital inputs to the growth of nine countries over the interval 1950–62 as shown in Table 3.1:

TABLE 3.1 *Contribution of Capital to Growth, 1950–62*

	U.S.A.	N.W. Europe*	Italy
	%	%	%
Growth of Total Income	3·32	4·78	5·96
Contribution of capital to above	0·83	0·86	0·70
Growth of Income per Worker	2·15	3·80	5·36
Contribution of capital to above	0·60	0·65	0·57

* Belgium, Denmark, France, Germany, Netherlands, Norway, United Kingdom.
Source: Denison (1967), Tables 21–1, p. 298; 21–3, p. 300; 21–19, p. 316.

Some conceptual and measurement problems

It may seem churlish to question what is by way of becoming a firmly-established generalization of seemingly universal application, but it is necessary to point out that perhaps the most outstanding study of capital and its economic significance yet undertaken for any country, Moorsteen and Powell's *The Soviet Capital Stock*, points to the need for caution in the interpretation of these findings. Different methods of calculating the growth rates of Soviet output and input yield estimates of aggregate factor productivity growth ranging from 0·1 to 3·2 per cent per annum. These extreme values are generated, respectively, by combining the upper limit estimate for the growth of aggregate inputs with the lower limit estimate for the growth of output, and the lower limit estimate for the growth of aggregate inputs with the upper limit estimate for the growth of output. It is doubtful that either of these extreme combinations can be analytically justified, and probable therefore that the 'true' rate of Soviet productivity growth – if that means anything – lies somewhere in between. It is quite possible, indeed, that the 'true' rate of Soviet productivity growth lies within the same range, say 1·4–1·8 per cent, in which many long-term estimates for Western economies fall. Since Soviet growth since 1928 has been, overall, faster than that of Western countries in the long run, this would still leave a relatively larger, indeed preponderant, role for the growth of factor inputs, thus separating off Soviet experience from that of most if not all Western countries.

But the chief importance of the Moorsteen and Powell study is to indicate how sensitive the results of these econometric exercises may be to the particular conventions adopted in, for example, weighting the various segments of final output, weighting the different inputs, allowing for improvements to the quality of labour, converting to a constant price basis and the like. It is a sad reflection that for no Western country do we have anything like the range of reasoned alternatives which these scholars have provided for the U.S.S.R. One of the few attempts made to calculate alternatives for a segment of a Western economy, Gerschenkron's estimate of U.S. machinery production over the years 1899–1939 in prices of 1899, 1909, 1923 and 1939, was far from reassuring, for it generated alternative estimates of the increase of output ranging from a doubling to a fifteen-fold increase![14] Machinery, admittedly, is a sector with a particularly heterogeneous output-mix – precisely the feature which one would expect to create abnormal sensitivity to weighting procedures – and one might be justified in hoping that (as indeed is true in the Soviet case) alternative estimates of the growth of total output would not be subject to quite as big a discrepancy as this.[15] However, it would be as well to bear in mind Moorsteen and Powell's comments that 'All the problems in international comparisons of output or input growth rates are compounded in the comparison of productivity rates', and that 'Estimates in alternative prices are not available for the United States which extend into the early periods in which weight sensitivity is likely to be large.'[16]

Since we have already injected a note of caution into the discussion, it may be well at this point to recall that there is a host of conceptual and data problems which beset the measurement of capital, and particularly of changes in the capital stock or capital inputs over time. This is a vast and much traversed area which it is beyond the scope of this study or the competence of its author to enter fully; but it is necessary to point to a few of the difficulties which are more particularly relevant to our purposes. Some are conceptual. Should the capital stock be valued at what it cost to supply, or in terms of its output-generating capacity? The former has the advantage of making it possible to link investment with savings and also of making it possible in some sense to separate the increase in present output achieved by sacrificing past consumption to investment from that brought by improvements in the efficiency of the physical assets purchased. The point is worth stressing because, as Deane and Cole remind us, many contemporary estimates of the stock of capital in earlier times – and the modern estimates which are partly or wholly based on them – have been made by capitalizing current incomes.[17] What justification there is for using estimates so grounded to calculate capital/output ratios or for combining them with estimates for later dates calculated on a conceptually different basis to form an impression of trends is difficult to see.

One is tempted to say that what one really wants in constructing time series of capital is an index showing the changing cost from year to year of supplying an (unchanging) unit of capital. Then all gains achieved by technical progress will be thrown into the 'residual' (the fraction of growth *not* achieved by increasing factor inputs) where they can be measured up against the cost, say, of research and development and of public education. But what – over a long period of time when new types of machines have been introduced, old ones have ceased to be used, and those used throughout have undergone drastic changes of design and efficiency – can this unchanging unit of capital be considered as consisting of? In practice it usually comes down to crude formulae such as the cost of a more or less random assortment of steel machines weighing 1,000 tons; and we are then in danger of subtracting a pure statistical artefact from a magnitude of real analytical significance and merely hoping that the remainder is itself meaningful.

Other difficulties are of a more statistical order or arise from data deficiencies. Capital is a less tangible and (for the individual firm) less homogeneous concept than volume of production or labour force, and even at the present time it is difficult to frame questions concerning capital which can be included in an industrial census and are capable of being answered with any reliability by the average industrial concern. The treatment of depreciation and retirement raises particularly difficult issues, for everything we know – which as far as these matters are concerned is surprisingly little – suggests that the rate at which capital deteriorates (in terms of its ability to produce a stream of output) and also the age at which it is retired, either because it is physically beyond repair or because it has become technologically obsolete, vary enormously from one type of asset to another. The convenient but crude method of applying the depreciation provisions of tax laws, which like all such measures are framed in part in deference to political considerations and which may be consciously unrealistic to foster development ends, almost certainly leads to major errors. Barna's work suggests that the life of industrial plant is considerably longer than normally assumed; this factor possibly explains one-half of the difference of 50 per cent by which his estimate of British manufacturing capital in 1955, based on a direct sample, exceeds that of Redfern, based on the 'perpetual inventory' method.[18]

It can well be assumed that if discrepancies of this magnitude exist in the valuation of the capital stock of one sector of the economy of an advanced country at a recent date, estimates for less developed countries at remoter periods are extremely fragile. In particular, the facts that in most countries company income was not taxed before the later nineteenth or twentieth centuries, and that (partly because of the circumstance just mentioned) accountancy had no developed or satisfactory procedures for handling capital expenditures or valuing capital assets, mean that there is little guidance to be looked for in company or governmental records. However, this problem may be less crippling than appears at first sight in that rates of depreciation and retirement were probably lower in earlier periods than today. This is partly because there has been in all developed countries a gradual change in the composition of assets, residential and other structures with long service lives becoming relatively less important and industrial equipment and similarly short-lived assets becoming relatively more important. Further, the service life of equipment has probably tended to become shorter because the more rapid progress of technology characteristic of recent times has added technological obsolescence to physical decay as a reason for retirement. There are very few industrial assets today for which one would predict a service life as long as that of the Newcomen engines which, in some parts of England, continued to supply power up to a century and a half after they had been installed. It is for such reasons that the ratio of net to gross capital formation has tended to decline in the past century or so: Deane and Cole suggest about 0·8 for the 1860s compared with the (British) Central Statistical Office's estimate of less than 0·5 for the 1950s,[19] *despite* the fact that the increase in the rate of British capital formation since World War II would have led one to expect an above-trend net/gross ratio in recent years. Hence estimating uncertainties arising out of the treatment of depreciation and retirement were probably less important in earlier than in more recent times.

The difficulty of allowing for non-monetized investment (for example, agricultural improvements such as hedges and ditches wrought by peasant labour) has on the contrary almost certainly diminished through time, and thus imposes a greater and greater impediment as one seeks to push estimates of capital formation or the capital stock back into earlier periods. This is admittedly an impressionistic judgment, necessarily so in the absence of quantitative evidence. In making it one has in mind the greater relative importance in earlier centuries of the agricultural sector, in which non-monetized investment is probably particularly conspicuous, and also the fact that as one goes back through time more and more economic activities, including the creation of capital assets, were not monetized; for example, the compulsory labour of serfs and tenure of land in return for predial services on the land of manorial lords, or collective responsibility for the upkeep of roads and other public capital in medieval times. Since it has been estimated that as late as 1950–1 non-monetized investment may have accounted for as much as a quarter of net domestic capital formation in India,[20] the need for major allowances in respect of earlier centuries may be indicated.

Finally, one needs to emphasize the need for care in choosing appropriate, and comparable, measures of capital. For despite the discouragements just reviewed modern interest in problems of capital and economic growth has generated so bewildering a variety of estimates as (in Professor Domar's whimsical comment) 'to make the exercise of their consumers' choice a fascinating, if not an easy, occupation.'[21] We have already noticed, for example, the tendency for the ratio of net to gross capital formation to decrease through time: it makes an appreciable difference to the appearance of the long-term trend of U.S. capital formation and capital stock proportions whether these are measured gross or net. We shall see, too, that these trends are in some cases decisively influenced by measurement in *current* or in *constant* prices, and analogously, differences in the ratio of investment good prices to the overall price level make international comparisons of capital formation or capital stock proportions highly sensitive, in some instances, to the price weighting adopted. Kuznets, for example, reported the Italian G.C.F./G.N.P. ratio for 1950 as 19·2 per cent in Italian price weights, but only 13·8 per cent in U.S. weights.[22] Capital goods are *relatively* cheaper in the U.S.A. than in most other countries and measurement of capital formation in U.S. prices usually results in lower estimates than in national prices. The distinction between *domestic* and *national* capital formation proportions is also important, particularly in considering the period before World War I and particularly in respect of major international borrowers such as Australia and Canada. Finally, inter-country and inter-temporal comparisons are bedevilled by differences in coverage of the estimates: for example, inventories are often neglected but in some cases (e.g. U.S.S.R.) are large enough to make a substantial difference in comparisons with other countries.

The difficulties just reviewed certainly seem to authorize caution, if not outright scepticism, in entertaining analytical argument as to the role of capital in growth predicated on the quantitative measures discussed. It is indeed in considering capital formation that one is seized most frequently by a mood of cynicism generated by the suspicion that the whole apparatus of econometric research at the 'macro' level, particularly in its historical dimension, is something of a complicated parlour game for intellectuals in which points are scored according to the degree of skill shown in marshalling evidence to support a pre-determined result. Re-reading one or other of the works of massive and patient scholarship to which this book owes so much usually dispels this mood of cynicism, however; and it seems better to plod on hopefully with what evidence one has, framing one's conclusions cautiously and undogmatically and reminding oneself at frequent intervals that only *slightly* different measures may point in *substantially* different directions.

Capital/output ratios, cross-country and over time

In conformity with this modest mood one may start by indicating that there appears to be no clear and universal trend, at least for pre-World War II years and in respect of the period and the countries for which quantitative evidence is available, in the overall capital/output ratio. The trend for the U.S.A., if there is one, is so unpronounced that it is possible for economists to disagree even about its overall direction.[23] In the Soviet Union the capital/output ratio rose modestly (and irregularly) from 1928 to 1961 in constant (1937) prices, but fell, at least until 1950, in current prices.[24] Hoffmann found a marked stability in the German ratio from 1850 to the later 1920s,[25] Matthews modest fluctuations in the constant-price ratio for Britain, 1870 to post-World War II, with no overall trend.[26]

In two periods this long-term stability has been disrupted, however, for most Western countries – in the depression of the 1930s, when the overall capital coefficient was well above trend; and since World War II, when for most countries it has tended to decline. The first deviation is easily explained, since in the great depression output fell rapidly, and capital (like men) stood idle or was used well below capacity. There is no comment to make here except to point out that our statistics usually measure the stock of capital, or capital capacity, *not* – what would be analytically more meaningful in many ways – the flow of capital services or inputs. This is but one way in which statistics generated by accounting conventions or administrative or fiscal necessity are often not well suited, conceptually, to our analytical purposes.

The post-war fall in the capital coefficient is more interesting. Obviously, it reflects the fact that output has been growing more rapidly than the capital stock. This, in turn, is to be explained primarily by the acceleration of that part of growth achieved by technological improvement, or more accurately by factors other than the increase in factor inputs (of which technological progress, in its broadest sense, is often, though perhaps erroneously, thought to be the largest component). The matter is interesting because it bears upon the analytical significance of historical changes in the capital coefficient. Some economists have argued that long-term stability in the capital/output ratio is to be expected; that it is a pronounced upward or downward historical trend which would cause surprise and call for explanation. Cairncross, for example, argued that the magnitude of the capital stock alters by only relatively small annual percentage changes, and further that there are some important elements of the capital stock – inventories, housing, certain types of public capital – which one would expect to be in a roughly constant ratio to total income. Sharp changes in the capital coefficient were therefore not to be expected.[27]

This argument perhaps seemed more convincing when it was first advanced than it does today. We have become accustomed in the last two decades to annual rates of growth of total income of 5 per cent or more, and also to the notion that capital has been 'responsible' for much the smaller part of total growth. It is easy enough therefore to envisage output growing at, say, 2 per cent per annum faster than the capital stock. Two per cent at compound interest doubles the original magnitude every thirty-five years, so that in the circumstances envisaged the capital coefficient would be halved in three and a half decades. This is surely a far cry from long-run stability. The example is of course hypothetical, but it is in fact in some such way that the sharp post-war fall in the capital coefficient from its long-run level, which has occurred in several countries, is to be explained.

This way of looking at it, however, causes puzzlement all the same. For we must agree with Domar that the capital coefficient approaches as a limit the ratio between the propensity to save and the rate of growth of product. If the largest fraction of the rate of growth of product is in fact determined by technological progress, then 'the over-all capital coefficient will emerge as a relatively passive result of the interaction between the propensity to save and the rate of technological progress'.[28] Since it is difficult to see that these two magnitudes should hold a constant ratio to each other, one's expectation would then be for *fluctuations* in the capital coefficient.

To make the point clearer, let us put it in another way: during the long period in which there was apparently no marked trend, in many countries, in the capital coefficient, the capital stock nevertheless grew at a rate substantially in excess of that of the labour force – that is, the capital/labour ratio rose; and in most countries, we might add, the capital/ land ratio rose even more. That much is certain. If *all* growth resulted from the increase of factor inputs, our expectation would then be for product to have risen more slowly than capital, at a rate, indeed, which would be much closer to that of the growth of the labour force, since the latter certainly deserves a greater weighting than capital in the historical aggregate production function, and the stability of the land input would pull overall growth down still further. Hence the capital coefficient would rise. If it stayed put, this could only be because the additional annual increment of product brought about by technological progress, scale factors and the rest, *precisely* – and *fortuitously* – offset this rising trend. This is surely surprising, and one cannot avoid wondering whether the result may not be spurious, arising (for example) from the tendency of estimates of the capital stock in earlier periods to be derived directly or indirectly, and in greater or lesser degree, by capitalizing current incomes.

In the earlier post-war years attention focused for a time on the *incremental* capital/output ratio – the quotient resulting from dividing additions to the capital stock by the increment of income in the same time period. This preoccupation was natural in view of the properties of the Harrod–Domar and similar growth models, and given the shortage of capital in many countries immediately after the war and the consequent desire to secure a growth-optimal allocation of what investible resources were available. More recently, as we shall see, some disillusionment with *ICOR*s has set in, largely no doubt because the *ICOR* has been seen to be volatile, to vary widely from country to country, from sector to sector and through time, and it has proved difficult to discern a systematic relationship between the *ICOR* and rate of growth of product in explaining inter-country differences of growth in the period since World War II.

That *ICOR*s should fluctuate more than the average capital/output ratio is only to be expected. The latter is in fact but the cumulation of the former over the lifetime of capital assets, or in other words the historical movement of the average capital/output ratio is but the trend of the *ICOR* smoothed over the lifetime of capital. Viewing the movement of the two curves over time, the divergence of the *ICOR* from the average capital/output ratio can arise for a number of reasons. One such reason is cyclical variations in the intensity of capital utilization. As we have seen, the overall capital coefficient rose substantially during the great depression of the 1930s as a consequence of the under-utilization of capital. The *ICOR*, however, *rose* in the downswing, since any additions to product arising from new investment were masked by declining output from the existing (much larger) capital stock; while in the subsequent recovery the *ICOR* was very low, the increment of product arising from new investment now being greatly augmented by increases in output achieved by reviving utilization of the existing stock of capital. Hence in the downswing the *ICOR* was well above the average capital/output ratio (and pulling this up to its peak), while in the recovery the *ICOR* was well below the capital coefficient (and pulling this back towards its trend level).

Similar relationships have also emerged, however, when the degree of utilization of capital has changed for reasons which are not, in the normal usage of the word, cyclical in character. For example, capital was much under-utilized in Germany just after World War II, partly (doubtless) because of the general economic dislocation, the shortage of raw materials and demand deficiencies, but also because the capital stock had become 'unbalanced'. Some assets, that is, had become useless because of the destruction of their technological complements: a basically intact railway network was impoverished by the destruction of rolling stock and locomotives – and because many machines and structures were damaged, but not so badly as to be beyond reach of fairly easy restoration. In such circumstances large increases in output could be won by relatively small investments designed to 'balance the stock' or to effect repairs.[29]

This clearly helps to explain, at least in the earlier stages, the rapid growth of product and low *ICOR* which have characterized the West German economy in recent decades. A similar method of securing growth operated in Russia during the N.E.P. period, when substantial increases in product were gained despite a level of investment so low as to permit, according to an official Soviet estimate, only a negligible or even, in the early 1920s, *negative* rate of *net* capital formation.[30] (The exhaustion of growth opportunities through this mechanism was one reason for the lively debate on growth strategy which was mounted by Soviet planners in this period, and for the eventual adoption by Stalin of a 'crash' programme of rapid industrialization via a high rate of forced savings.)

*ICOR*s may vary for other reasons, however, and notably because capital intensity varies substantially from one sector to another and there is a certain tendency for new investment not to be spread evenly over the whole economy, but 'bunched' from time to time in particular areas. In his survey of the U.S. capital/output ratio, Domar for example found that sectoral ratios (in 1929 dollars) for the period of World War II or just after varied from about 0·6 for all manufacturing (1948) to 5·3 for non-farm residential real estate (1939–48). The difference had been even greater in earlier decades, for while the manufacturing coefficient had tended if anything to rise slightly from the later nineteenth to the mid-twentieth century, the coefficients for the sectors of typically high capital intensity, housing and public utilities, had fallen dramatically (for example, the ratio for non-farm residential property was 14·0 in 1889–98, that for steam railroads nearly 16·0 in 1880).[31] Hoffmann's graph shows somewhat similar movements in the various sectors of the German economy.[32]

In view of the magnitude of these differences one would expect bursts of investment in particular sectors to show up in the historical trend of the *ICOR*, or even of the average capital/output ratio. Unfortunately, estimates of historical *ICOR*s are not yet available for sufficiently fine time subdivisions to allow the influence on them of (for example) the British railway booms of the 1830s and 1840s to be assessed, while as for the overall capital coefficient, such investment 'spurts' were perhaps of insufficiently long duration to achieve a clearly noticeable shift. Overall, one would have

131

expected, again, that the appreciable change in the composition of the capital stock of industrial countries would in itself have lowered the level of the capital coefficient from the later nineteenth to the mid-twentieth century, in that the relative importance of railway capital and (to a much lesser extent) buildings has tended to decline, while that of industrial equipment has markedly increased. As yet, however, the influence of this has not been satisfactorily disentangled from that of other factors bearing upon the level of the capital coefficient, though Kuznets has found that for a group of countries for which sufficient historical estimates are available, *intra*-sectoral *ICOR* shifts appear to explain more of the historical variation of aggregate *ICOR*s than does the changing importance of the various sectors.[33]

As has been remarked, the *ICOR* has latterly been thrown into considerable disrepute as an explanatory or predictive tool. Writers as far apart in their outlook as R. C. O. Matthews, Simon Kuznets and Edward Denison have all explicitly criticized the *ICOR* and models which rely heavily on it as an explanatory variable; the last-named subjects the *ICOR* to the ignominy of a footnote reference only.[34] As an expression of the relationship between investment and growth the *ICOR* has, of course, suffered a loss of interest because of the accumulating evidence that the contribution of capital to growth is much smaller than was earlier thought. But in addition, the empirical evidence on the volatility of the *ICOR* has probably contributed to the belief that it can have little value in analyses of the relationship of capital to growth.

It is, of course, perfectly true that the liability of the *ICOR* to very large fluctuations in the course of the trade cycle makes it impossible to adopt it uncritically as a fundamental parameter in explanatory models or planning exercises. But it seems possible that the *ICOR* has been more sinned against than sinning. Its apparent erraticism is to a considerable extent explainable in terms of changing capital utilization – indeed here, of course, the error actually arises not from any lack of determinateness in the relationship between additions to the capital stock and the extra output they generate, but from confounding with these increments to output other increases or decreases achieved by the more or less intensive utilization of the *existing* capital stock – and of changing sectoral allocations of investment. Purged of these disturbances the *ICOR* would still doubtless manifest a tendency to long-run change which would reflect the fact that capital is only *one* of the sources, and possibly even a minor source, of growth; but this characteristic it would share with any other measure of the relation of capital to growth. To the economic historian, at least, there would still seem some sense in a number summarizing the power of new investment to generate output in particular sectors and at particular times. Such a concept has been found useful in explaining accelerations of growth which are associated with changes in the *distribution* rather than the aggregate *rate* of investment, like the British industrial revolution of the late eighteenth and early nineteenth centuries. It certainly helps us, too, to understand the Soviet 'industrialization debate' of the mid-1920s, which turned in large part on investment policy. Finally, the *ICOR*'s very variation from one situation to another would serve as a reminder of the need to go behind aggregate and average measures to the real factors of which they are summaries often serving more to conceal than to reveal the truth.

Investment ratios in theory and history

Much historical and economic discussion of the relationship between capital and growth has been couched in terms neither of the capital stock nor of *ICOR*s, but of investment ratios – that is, the annual value of capital formation, gross or net, national or domestic, expressed as a ratio of the corresponding measure of product. This is understandable. The investment ratio is the magnitude which the policy-maker tries to influence if he seeks to accelerate growth by increasing the contribution of capital. It is the measure of capital most readily comparable with savings proportions and analysable in terms of the sources of capital. And estimates of the national income attempted from the expenditure side naturally throw up values of investment expenditures which thus lie readily to hand for the analyst. However, some writers have criticized the preoccupation of growth analysts and planners with the investment ratio. Denison, for example, is only a degree less severe on the investment ratio than on the *ICOR*. He argues that gross investment ratios have little value for analysing the relationship between capital and growth, and advances four points in justification of this view:

1. relative differences in the prices of capital goods and of output in general have to be allowed for in inter-temporal or inter-country comparisons of growth rates and investment ratios;
2. even if such comparisons yield a significant positive correlation, the causation may run from growth to investment, rather than vice versa;
3. capital is only one source of growth;
4. in so far as capital is a source of growth, it is the growth of the *stock* of capital which is relevant, and this is neither measured nor determined by the investment ratio.[35]

Of these points, the first is completely valid, as we have already seen: most exercises to date relating investment to growth have failed to make the adjustment to 'real' terms called for, and their results cannot, in consequence, be regarded with confidence. The third point is also already familiar to us, but of course it should not deter us unduly, for it can with equal truth be said of every other factor that it 'is only one source of growth'. The second point, again, is perfectly valid but merely expresses a shortcoming of any simple correlation, that it does nothing to establish the direction or indeed the existence of any *direct* causal relationship. The economic historian does not need to be persuaded of the inadequacy of mere tests of correlation in establishing the pattern of historical causation.

The fourth point is the only one which is new to us. Since it is at first sight surprising, and since it seems to imply, if valid, that theory makes empirical investigation of the relationship between rates of investment and of product growth unnecessary, some elaboration of the point is called for. All that can be offered here, however, is a highly-simplified summary of a difficult and warmly debated issue.[36] The line of argument lying behind Denison's comment is roughly this: If (as is usual in modern investigations of the sources of economic growth) we assume a production function in which output is determined by the volume of factor inputs weighted according to their contribution to output multiplied by a constant representing the contribution of 'technology' (i.e. aggregate factor productivity), then a given change in any factor input will generate a change of like sign, but of less than proportionate magnitude, in output. Specifically, an increase in capital inputs alone will indeed generate an increase in output, but not a proportionate one, the extra capital not being accompanied (by assumption) by any change in other factor inputs.

An increase in the investment ratio, by causing an increase in the rate of growth of the stock of capital, will therefore lead to an increase, but a less-than-proportionate increase, in the growth rate of the economy. This disproportion implies that the capital/output ratio must rise, and this rise, in turn, gradually offsets the effect on output of the higher rate of capital inputs and in doing so causes the growth rate to fall back towards its original level. It can be demonstrated that with the type of production function assumed, the rate of growth of output gradually falls back to the same level as before the investment ratio was increased. Similarly, the rise in the average capital/output ratio continues to the point where its new (higher) level precisely offsets the effect of the higher investment ratio, and the rate of growth of the *stock* of capital thus falls back to its original level (which, in equilibrium and supposing an unchanging investment ratio, is necessarily equal to the rate of growth of output). Thus in the long run the equilibrium rate of growth of both output and capital stock is insensitive to differences in the investment ratio.

To leap from this conclusion to the belief that historical

investigation of investment ratios is unnecessary is, however, an unwarranted step. In the first place, the process of adjustment – the process by which rates of growth of output and capital stock fall back to the long-term equilibrium – may be very slow, allowing a very long interval during which the increase in investment *does* generate an appreciable (though always diminishing) increment to growth rates. Since in historical fact investment ratios do *not* remain unchanged for sufficiently long, we should expect their upward and downward movements to show some correlation with output trends in the ensuing period. Specifically, for example, it is entirely possible that the sharp increase in capital formation proportions in most European countries since World War II should have contributed, and still be contributing, to the faster growth rates which these same countries are experiencing.

Secondly, it must be stressed that it is only the *proportionate* rate of growth which is insensitive, in the long run, to changes in the investment ratio; an increase in that ratio lifts output to a higher absolute level and permanently generates larger *absolute* increases in output (and in the capital stock) than would otherwise occur. This may be easier to grasp if one envisages two parallel, upward-sloping lines on a semilogarithmic graph, such as lines AA' and BB' in the sketch below. These lines depict two growth paths, each character-

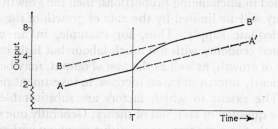

ized by the same proportionate rate of increase, but the path BB' representing a higher (absolute) level of income at every point of time than AA'. The effect of a sudden (and permanent) increase of the investment ratio, say at time T, is to shift the economy from one growth path to the other, like a railway locomotive moving across the points from one track to a parallel one (i.e. following the path *AB'*). *After* it has completed its manœuvre, the economy will move in the same direction (i.e. grow at the same rate) as before, but on a permanently higher growth *path*. And *during* the manœuvre the *rate* of growth will indeed be higher. The theory of the growth-significance of investment ratios just sketched has therefore nothing to urge against the policy-maker who aspires to raise real income by bringing about an increase in investment ratios, nor against the economic historian who thinks he sees a correlation between past investment ratios and levels of real income. Nor, indeed, need we expect to find a lack of correlation between changes in the investment ratio and in the rate of growth either of the capital stock or of output in a 'short' run which may turn out to last a very long time. The only person doomed to disappointment, according to this theory, is the policy-maker who hopes to induce a *permanent* increase in the rate of growth by promoting a higher ratio of savings and investment.

Thirdly, all of the above is in any event dependent on the assumption of perfect substitutability of one factor of production for another. If instead of a production function assuming such substitutability, the economy is actually characterized by a production function in which factors can only be combined in unchanging proportions, then the growth of the economy will be limited by the rate of growth of the factor in inadequate supply. Thus, for example, in an under-developed economy with too much labour but little capital, the *rate* of growth, as well as the *level* of output, may be more permanently improved by an increase in investment propor-tions. The extent to which factors are substitutable is of course a question of fact, not of theory. Generally one would suppose that in a modern, competitive economy with sophis-ticated skills and a wide range of technological possibilities open to it, there must be a very high degree of substitutability in the not-very-long run. But as we move away from such societies in either space or time, the assumption of a very high elasticity of substitution even in the longer run may be less in accord with reality. To whatever extent and over whatever period (and for whatever reason) factor proportions are inflexible, the theory just summarized may be inapplicable, and it may be that (if capital is in relatively short supply) a more *permanent* relationship between growth rates and investment ratios is to be looked for.

Denison's arguments, therefore, do not dispose of the issue as conveniently as might be thought and some discussion of the historical evidence, such as it is, cannot be avoided. And here a mild criticism may be permitted. It is that some economists who have wrangled in a very sophisticated manner over the theoretical issues have displayed far laxer standards when it comes to empirical tests of their theories. Even Denison cannot be entirely absolved from this criticism, for he offers an empirical comparison of the growth rates of the *stock* of non-residential structures and equipment and of the rate of investment in such assets in his nine countries and comments: 'there is hardly any correspondence between the two measures'. In fact, the Spearman rank-correlation coefficient between the two equals $+0.73$, and is significant at the 5 per cent level – a result scarcely justifying Denison's comment.

The historical evidence is very difficult to interpret, for reasons which should become somewhat clearer in the following pages. It is right at once to concede, however, that so far as the relationship between growth and investment ratios is concerned, the evidence, ill-attuned to the purpose as it is, suggests no more than a quite moderate association. Take, for example, the estimates offered by Kuznets (reproduced in Table 3.2) of the rates of growth of output and the investment ratio for a series of pre-World War I years (ten countries) and late-nineteenth and twentieth century years (twelve countries). (We are not concerned in this context to make all the revisions to these estimates which more recent work would have called for, some of which have been discussed in Chapter 1.) For convenience, the countries are arranged in each case in descending order of the investment ratio.

TABLE 3.2 *Growth of output and investment ratios, two long periods, selected countries*

Mid-nineteenth century to World War I				Late nineteenth and twentieth centuries			
Country	$\dfrac{\text{N.D.C.F.}}{\text{N.D.P.}}$	Growth of output	Rank	Country	$\dfrac{\text{N.D.C.F.}}{\text{N.D.P.}}$	Growth of output	Rank
U.S.A.	13·1	4·22	1	South Africa	17·8	4·70	1
Germany	12·9	2·69	2	Norway	14·4	2·82	2
Canada	10·8	3·66	3	Japan	14·1	4·51	3½
Australia	10·4	3·59	4	Australia	14·1	2·81	3½
Norway	8·2	2·04	5	Argentina	14·0	3·31	5
Denmark	7·7	3·27	6½	Germany	12·7	3·31	6
Sweden	7·7	2·95	6½	Sweden	11·8	3·31	7
U.K.	7·3	2·22	8	Italy	10·1	3·01	8½
Italy	6·5	1·23	9	Canada	10·1	3·63	8½
Japan	6·0	3·71	10	Denmark	9·4	3·34	10
				U.S.A.	8·4	3·10	11
				U.K.	6·0	1·67	12

Source: Kuznets (1961), Table 1, p. 5, and Table 5, pp. 17–18.
Note: Where, in either period, two or more countries show the same value for either measure, the mean of the ranks has been allotted to each.

It can be seen at a glance that the relationship between the two measures is not particularly strong: the Spearman rank correlation coefficient is +0·34 for the earlier period and +0·36 for the later. However, the rank correlation coefficient is not necessarily a good measure of association in a case like this (though as Kuznets says, more elaborate correlation analysis seems out of place here 'because the number of cases is small and the variance in the universe far from normal') since it is liable to be unduly influenced by one or two bad misfits. In the case of the pre-war comparison, Japan alone is responsible for a substantial fraction of the apparent divergence, for she is in tenth place in the investment ranking, but in second place in the growth table. I Japan is omitted the coefficient jumps to about 0·7. We may well wonder whether Japan should be permitted to exert quite so much influence in so far as the recent tendency has been to think that the Rosovsky–Ohkawa estimates which Kuznets uses probably substantially overstate the rate of growth of Meiji Japan.[37] If the rate of growth shown for Japan pre-World War I were to be reduced by a third, as some would wish, the correlation would be significantly improved.

In the case of the later period comparison, the coefficient is, again, seriously damaged by the case of Norway, which is in second place as regards its investment ratio but no better than tenth in its growth achievement. It is well established that Norway has unusually high capital requirements in all periods (a feature partly associated, no doubt, with the country's difficult topography and climate and exceptionally costly requirements in social overhead capital). Still, one cannot go too far in excluding inconvenient cases, however plausible the reasons for doing so may seem. Another feature of the later period comparison which renders a rank correlation test somewhat inappropriate is the marked 'bunching' of growth rates in the middle of the range: six of the twelve countries are shown as having growth rates lying between 3·34 and 3·01 per cent. Even if the estimates were subject to no error at all, ranking these countries in positions from 4 to

9 would overstate the importance of the difference between the two values mentioned. As it is, the difference of one-third of 1 per cent between Denmark (ranked fourth) and Italy (ranked ninth) is in all probability well within the margin of error of the estimates, so that these countries could be re-ranked, to the benefit of the correlation coefficient, without doing any real violence to the data.

Quite apart from these points, however, the data used by Kuznets have limitations which would disincline us to place too much reliance on the results. They are drawn, naturally, from various country studies which, whatever their individual merits, incorporate varying techniques for measuring both output and capital, differences which render them on a strict view incomparable. The periods covered by the capital and the output series are not exactly the same from one country to another, nor do they even precisely coincide, in some cases, for the same country. In some instances, too, certain years, notably the world war years, are excluded, whereas in others they are included. In view of the well-known differences between the war experiences of different countries, this seriously reduces comparability. Finally, in most (but not all) cases the investment proportions are measured in current national prices, which as we have seen tends to reduce both inter-temporal and inter-country comparability. (It should be added that there is no intention, in reciting these points, to disparage Kuznets' studies, which have made such an enormous contribution to our understanding of economic growth. The quarrying of conceptually-appropriate historical data is so time-consuming a process that any scholar attempting synthesis must do his best with whatever materials lie reasonably conveniently to hand.)

A similar comparison for more recent years can be made by putting together two tables presented by Angus Maddison in his study, *Economic Growth in the West* (Table 3.3). (It may be noted that these figures have been processed by O.E.E.C. and should have been purged of many of the slight differences of construction which mar the single-country estimates used by Kuznets.) The rank correlation coefficient between the two series here is $+0.66$, which is significant at the 1 per cent level. Again Norway, with its abnormally high capital intensity, does more than any other country to lower the coefficient which for the other ten alone rises to 0.71.

TABLE 3.3   *Growth of output and investment ratios, eleven countries, 1950–60*

Country	G.D.C.F. / G.N.P.	Rank	Growth of output	Rank
Norway	26·4	1	3·5	6
Canada	24·8	2	3·9	5
Netherlands	24·2	3	4·9	3
Germany	24·0	4	7·6	1
Sweden	21·3	5	3·3	7½
Italy	20·8	6	5·9	2
France	19·1	7½	4·4	4
U.S.A.	19·1	7½	3·2	9
Denmark	18·1	9	3·3	7½
Belgium	16·5	10	2·9	10
U.K.	15·4	11	2·6	11

Source: Maddison (1964), Tables I–1, p. 28, and III–1, p. 76.
Note: As for Table 3.2.

These two sets of figures thus seem, given data deficiencies which one would expect to lead to randomness and a lack of association, to provide a moderate degree of support for the proposition that the rate of investment is positively related with the rate of growth of product. Most certainly they do not *disprove* that proposition. But let us be clear as to the very modest significance of any measure of correlation in a case like this. Let us suppose, by way of hypothesis, that the growth of output is determined by a combination of improved technology 'embodied' in new equipment and installations and by capital 'deepening' (the addition of more capital of unchanged technological characteristics to the stock of capital per head), and that investment is divided in the same proportions between these two uses in all countries. Then there will be a perfect correlation between the ranking of countries by

F

rate of growth of product and by investment ratio, and, further, the former will be directly proportional to the latter – *even though* 'embodied' technological progress may be responsible for much the greater contribution to growth. Hence we could not infer, even from a perfect correlation between the two values, that capital was responsible for the whole or even a substantial fraction of growth.

It is also possible, of course, that (as Denison insists) the causation may be working in the opposite direction, that is from growth to investment. Certainly there are some forms of investment, notably inventories, which are undertaken because production increases, rather than vice versa, while an important part of capital formation consists of assets called into existence by the growth of private or public expenditures, such as housing and certain public buildings, and is more naturally explained as the *result* rather than the *cause* of growth. It deserves to be stressed, however, that the differences in the rates of investment, especially in the net ratios shown in the Kuznets tables, are very substantial, and that even if capital is responsible for only a small fraction of growth, appreciable differences in growth rates would arise from the varying investment proportions shown. This conclusion is strengthened, of course, to whatever extent technology is 'embodied', that is to say, that gains from technical progress are proportional to the rate of formation of the capital which is their indispensable 'carrier'.

Investment: the key to the 'industrial revolution'?

We now retrace our steps and return to the question: *does* the historical evidence support a Lewis–Rostow view that a sharp rise in the rate of capital formation accompanies, and is indispensable to, 'take-off'? The reader, accustomed by now to the fact that economic history (like any scientific inquiry) raises more problems than it answers, will be steeled for the reply: the evidence is uncertain, and the matter seems more complicated than appeared at first sight. In at least two major industrial countries, Britain and Japan, there does not seem to have been a sharp increase in the rate of investment of the order postulated by Lewis or Rostow during the early decades of industrialization. The argument by Deane and Cole that the rate of capital formation in Britain rose only sluggishly between about the 1770s and the 1830s, and that the first substantial increase came only with the railway investment booms of the fourth and fifth decades of the nineteenth century, has become classic, and is the evidence most frequently called upon by writers opposed to the Lewis–Rostow view.[38] In the case of Japan, capital formation proportions seem to have been at about the same modest level in 1907–16 and in 1887–96, and to have 'sagged' in the intervening decade, especially if military investments are excluded.[39] In the Scandinavian countries, particularly in Denmark and Norway, and also in Italy, there does seem to have been a marked upturn in investment about the end of the nineteenth century or in the early twentieth century.[40] In Italy this coincides well with the sharp acceleration of growth in 'take-off' from the 1890s to World War I, though the increase in rate of growth of product seems to have been much sharper than in that of investment. Denmark, however, seems to have achieved a respectable rate of growth and to have carried through its well-known agricultural transformation in the last third of the nineteenth century with only a relatively modest, and at best stable, level of net capital formation.

In Germany, on the other hand, the rate of net investment in current prices rose from less than 9 per cent in the 1850s to more than 15 per cent in the decade before World War I; in constant (1913) prices the rise was even steeper, from little over 7 per cent to over 15 per cent.[41] In the U.S.S.R., as we have seen, it makes an even more critical difference whether the measurement is made in current or in constant prices: on the former basis the gross investment share in G.N.P. remained virtually unchanged at 20 per cent in 1928, and 21 per cent in both 1937 and 1950. In 1937 prices, on the other hand, the ratio rose during the first two five-year plans from only 8 per cent in 1928 to 21 per cent in 1937, and thereafter to 22 per cent in 1950 and 31 per cent in 1961.

Net investment rates show a similar sensitivity: 15·1, 17·5 and 16·6 per cent respectively in current prices; 5·8, 17·5, 16·9 and 24·2 per cent respectively in 1937 prices.[42]

Finally, in the regions of recent settlement the course of investment ratios has been different again. The U.S.A. and Australia, particularly the former, already had very high capital formation proportions soon after the middle of the nineteenth century. In Australia gross domestic capital formation rose to about 18·8 per cent of G.D.P. in the investment boom of the 1880s, a level which was not subsequently regained until after World War II.[43] In the United States, almost exactly the same level was registered as early as 1869–78, and has never subsequently been equalled. For the decade mentioned G.D.C.F. was as high (according to Kuznets) as 21·6 per cent of G.N.P. On neither the gross nor the net basis has investment since World War II been nearly as high as in the late nineteenth century. Professor Kuznets' estimates for the U.S.A. do not go further back than 1869–78. Professor Gallman has calculated, however, that there was a very marked upward shift in capital formation proportions over the Civil War interval. He estimates an increase in the ratio of G.D.C.F. to G.D.P. (more accurately, G.N.P. *less* changes in claims against foreigners) of either just over 50 per cent or about 40 per cent as between 1849–58 and 1869–78, according to whether value added in home manufacturing and farm improvements by farm labour are excluded or included. On the former basis there was also a 50 per cent rise between 1834–43 and 1849–58, though there was little change on the latter. If we follow Rostow in placing U.S. 'take-off' in the two decades preceding the Civil War there is therefore less difficulty in fitting the U.S.A. into the Lewis–Rostow specification than if we concentrate our attention on the decades since the Civil War, though it is clear that the U.S.A. had a *relatively* high investment ratio from at least early in the nineteenth century.[44] In Canada the investment boom came later, in the first two decades of the twentieth century; again, the peak values for that period have only barely been recovered after World War II. Though estimates of the investment ratio in Argentina are available only for the twentieth century, that country clearly had far higher capital formation proportions in the early twentieth (and in all probability in the later nineteenth) century than it has ever subsequently recaptured.

Some of these experiences seem to fit the Lewis–Rostow requirements, others do not. Is there any way of narrowing the apparent discrepancies and of explaining those which remain? First, it should be noticed that except where otherwise mentioned the capital formation proportions in the preceding paragraphs have been given in current prices. The cases of Germany and of the Soviet Union indicate that in some instances investment ratios in constant prices might show a more pronounced upward trend in the early stages of accelerated growth. This is because the market for industrial equipment and machinery is at first small and disorganized and the cost of such assets is high. Further, in some cases, such as Germany and Britain, the cost of the chief constructional materials – steel and cast iron respectively – fell relatively as a result of technological innovation in the early stages of industrialization. It is highly probable that a substantial relative fall in the cost of industrial equipment would give a more buoyant trend to constant than to current price capital formation proportions in Britain during the early industrial revolution.

(In the longer run, however, the course of relative prices for capital formation and national product as a whole has been more uncertain, and the former seems more often than not to have become *relatively* more expensive. This is because a very large fraction of capital formation always consists of building and construction, in the cost of which the wage rate for unskilled labour is a large component. In the course of transformation from an agricultural to an industrial society the wages of unskilled labour usually tend to rise relatively, so that building and construction tends to become relatively more expensive as time goes on, particularly since these activities are of their very nature somewhat less prone to dramatic technological improvements than many branches of production. This effect is not always decisive, however, in so far as structures, though always of great importance in capital formation, do tend to decline somewhat in favour of industrial equipment and machinery, which is much more amenable to cost-reducing innovation and less sensitive to the wage rate for unskilled labour. Hence while the relative cost of capital formation has in most cases tended to rise in the more mature stages of industrial growth, this has not always or everywhere been the case.)

To revert to the course of capital formation in early industrial Britain: it has been suggested that this would probably be seen to have risen more in constant prices than in the current prices in which alone estimates are at present available. Beyond this, Deane and Cole's estimates are shaky, as they are the first to admit, and have in fact been seriously challenged by Professor Pollard, who believes that they understate the increase in the capital formation proportions in the early decades of industrialization.[45] However, even Pollard's amendments would not turn Britain into a Lewis–Rostow case, since having excluded capital exports to convert his figures from a national to a domestic basis – as seems appropriate – Pollard's estimates suggest a *gross* investment ratio of only about $9\frac{1}{2}$ per cent for the early 1830s (the net figure would be perhaps a fifth lower). It seems clear that Britain cannot be made quite to fit the Lewis–Rostow specification. But then, need it? After all, the rate of growth was very modest in early industrial Britain – Hoffmann's estimates do not place the growth rate of industrial product above 4 per cent for any sustained period,[46] and the growth of national income was certainly substantially lower – and the rate of Britain's transformation (from a distinctly advanced starting-point, moreover, in the eighteenth century) appeared miraculous only to contemporaries with no previous experience of a similar process. To us, the British 'take-off' was remarkable rather for its smoothness and lack of drama: a sedate piston-engined plane, perhaps, lifting leisurely off the tarmac into a three or four degrees angle of climb, rather than a modern jet accelerating furiously to a critical ground speed three times as high and launching itself noisily into what seems by comparison an almost vertical take-off.

The case of Japan is perhaps a more serious challenge to the Lewis–Rostow view, unless indeed we fall back on what is becoming the one safe generalization of development economics: Japan is *always* an exception; nothing that happens in Japan should be held to disprove propositions which command useful explanatory power in the rest of the world. Perhaps, however, even the Japanese case is not quite as exceptional as it seems at first sight. It is possible that as in Britain a relative decline in the price of capital assets would allow a constant price series to show a more upward trend. It is probable that an error has crept into the investment ratio estimates because the rate of growth in early Meiji Japan has been overestimated. If this is indeed the case, Japan's income in the beginning year (which is the doubtful end of the series) was higher than previously supposed, and capital formation as a proportion of that income therefore lower. Hence the *trend* of capital formation in the early decades would have a more upward slope, and the rate of growth of product with which it was associated a less steep slope, than originally supposed. It is also likely that we should make an adjustment, in making international comparisons, for the low wage rates which were undoubtedly characteristic of Japan throughout the early decades of modernization; this would render building and construction costs, in particular, low in terms of international comparisons and again render a comparison in real terms more favourable to Japanese capital formation.

When all such adjustments have been made, however, it remains almost certain that Japan did enjoy a remarkably low *ICOR* in the pre-World War I decades, permitting her to enjoy large increases in product with relatively low levels of investment. It has indeed been generally agreed in analyses of Japan's economic growth that in respect of capital formation, as in other ways, her development proceeded in a characteristically thrifty fashion.[47] She 'economized' on capital by achieving a substantial fraction of growth in sectors of low capital intensity, notably in agriculture, and by methods making few demands for large-scale investment. She made exceptional use of rural industry, with an extensive network of 'putting-out' industry linked to central factories, thus making use of cheap rural labour (including part-time labour) and minimizing the need for costly factory buildings. By the same token, the particularly heavy expenditures associated with urbanization were minimized, while the configuration of the country with its developed system of coastal shipping reduced the need for early heavy infrastructural investments in transport.

The case of the regions of recent settlement is quite different. Here the characteristic to be explained is an unusually high capital formation proportion in early decades, the all-time peak often having been recorded before World War I. The explanation is fairly obvious: these countries were unusual in the late nineteenth century in experiencing very high rates of population growth, partly or (in some cases) dominantly because of high rates of net immigration, and of geographical expansion of settlement. Capital 'widening' is notoriously extravagant in its use of investible resources; with a (not untypical) capital coefficient of about 5 it would require a capital formation proportion of $12\frac{1}{2}$ per cent merely to equip a population growing at $2\frac{1}{2}$ per cent with an unchanging *per capita* endowment of capital. The actual requirement may have fallen short of this in so far as some items, particularly of infrastructural capital, were notoriously under-utilized in early years and some economies in new capital formation could therefore be achieved by increasing utilization. (Hence the spectacular fall which, as we have seen, occurred in the capital/output ratio for such sectors as railways in the course of the nineteenth century.) On the other hand, so long as the 'frontier' was open and settlement expanding into new areas, additions to social overhead capital were called for which made it impossible to look for much relief from this direction.

The need for investible funds was further aggravated by the generally high relative cost of capital formation in such countries. This arose partly because machinery tended to be costly, being either imported or made domestically in a small, high-cost market – these points would doubtless apply less to the U.S.A. than to the other regions of recent settlement, though even there capital equipment seems to have been generally more expensive than in Britain, at least until the late nineteenth century – and partly because unskilled labour was notoriously expensive (and in inelastic supply), thus inflating the cost of structures. Hence a given monetary investment yielded less real capital (at official exchange rates) than in Europe.

The countries under discussion therefore had exceptionally high capital requirements which they could not meet from their own savings. (The U.S.A., again, is unlike the other areas because its population and wealth were already large when accelerated frontier development began, about the time of the Civil War. The American West *would* fit this pattern, however, if it were possible to bisect the notion and consider the western half as a separate economic entity.) All were therefore major capital importers, as will be seen, and the difference between their *domestic* and *national* capital formations was exceptionally wide. The ratios quoted and comments made in the preceding paragraphs have related whenever possible to *net domestic* capital formation considered, again where possible, in relation to net domestic product. These have seemed the most appropriate measures in considering the relation of capital and growth. But transfer to a *national* basis would not make a great deal of difference for many countries.

In the case of countries like Canada, Argentina and Australia, on the other hand, the reverse is true. In the periods of maximum capital import, such as the 1880s for Australia or the years just before World War I for Canada, the ratio of N.D.C.F. to N.D.P. may have been upwards of three times the ratio of N.N.C.F. to N.N.P. Even over longer periods a disparity of about 2 to 1 was quite usual. The major period of capital import, however, ended with World War I, or for some countries with the depression of the early

1930s. While some of these countries have resumed capital imports since World War II, none of the regions of recent settlement countries today relies on foreign capital to anything like the same extent as in their pioneer past.* Nor is this necessary, for the growth of their own economies and closing of the frontiers have brought capital requirements and domestic savings into much closer relationship. In the case of the U.S.A. the disparity between domestic and national capital formation ratios was nothing like so wide in the nineteenth century, but here the latter has come to exceed the former as the U.S.A. became a capital exporter in the twentieth century. In all these countries, therefore, the trend of investment would look much more 'normal' measured in national rather than in domestic terms, while if the slower growths of population and territorial expansion in recent decades are also borne in mind, the tendency towards increased capital intensity so characteristic of European countries and Japan since World War II does not seem so sharply contrasting an experience.

We shall not attempt to summarize this long discussion of the historical record of investment ratios, except to say that the reader will not have erred if he has interpreted its major import to be that there is really no justification for expecting to find – and certainly we *do* not find – any great measure of consistency from one country to another in respect of the behaviour of the investment ratio over time. Differences of need and of situation as well as *technical* difficulties such as the difference between current and constant price estimates lead, both in expectation and in reality, to divergent experiences. Nevertheless, due allowance made for such points, the record is not as clearly unfavourable to the Lewis–Rostow view as it has sometimes been made to appear. We shall end this part of the chapter by emphasizing two fresh points.

* The comments made in the text have to be modified to an appreciable degree in respect of Canada and Australia, where foreign capital is still helping to explore and bring into production the vast natural resources, hitherto unknown, in the less hospitable regions of these countries.

First, there has been a very widespread rise of investment ratios in the years since World War II. For most European countries, for the Soviet Union and Japan, and for several other countries for which reasonably long-term estimates of capital formation are available (but not for some regions of recent settlement), these ratios have risen in the past quarter-century to levels never previously attained. To refuse to link this fact with the neighbouring fact that in the same countries and the same period growth rates have *also* broken all historical records is surely to carry scholarly caution to an excess of incredulity. Even for sluggish Britain, Matthews has calculated that British growth improved in 1948–62 because of a higher investment rate: the *ICOR* has actually worked in the wrong direction.[48]

Secondly, it deserves emphasis that in speaking of the capital requirements of industrialization we should not lose sight of the fact that even in advanced industrial countries investment in industrial plant and machinery represents only the smaller part of all investment. Only in the 1950s has equipment of all kinds come to exceed a quarter of Germany's capital stock (in 1913 prices).[49] In the U.S.S.R., equipment measured 27·2 per cent of the total in 1962 (1937 prices).[50] *Industrial* equipment and machinery would constitute a still smaller share. In earlier periods the ratio of equipment to total capital was far lower: 5·9 per cent in the Soviet Union in 1928, 13 per cent in Germany as late as 1880. In all advanced countries structures alone comprise something like a half of all reproducible capital. Since the life of structures is generally longer than that of machinery and equipment, a higher proportion of gross investment than of net goes into the latter, but even so it is possible, at an early stage of industrialization, to achieve rapid increases in the stock of industrial plant by only a relatively minor increase in *total* investment, or by only a slight redirection of investment within an unchanging total. Pollard's revised estimates of early capital formation in Britain allot to 'machinery, mill-work, etc.' only 9 per cent of total G.D.C.F., or not much more than one half of one per cent of the national income, *c.* 1770. By 1790–3 the comparable figures were about 13 per cent and seven-eighths of 1 per cent respectively, and these values had barely doubled by the early 1830s.[51] It is population growth and urbanization, social overhead capital and the transport system, which generate the really big demands for capital, and it is necessary to view the relatively modest demands of industrialization proper against this perspective.

Savings and investment in pre-industrial societies

This leads us, of course, to want to look at historical trends of capital formation through the other end of the telescope – from the vantage point of pre-industrial society, that is – and to see what sort of effort was required in the field of savings and investment as societies approached the threshold of industrialization and modernization. Regrettably, lack of knowledge on the writer's part – and perhaps, indeed, the inadequacies of the literature generally – prohibit any satisfactory treatment of this topic. All the same, the question is sufficiently important and intriguing to tempt a few brief comments, drawing largely on the English experience in the full realization, however, that this may be untypical.

The central difficulty is that we do not know precisely what the level of investment was in today's high-income nations before they entered on the phase of sustained secular development; nor, in so far as this can be assumed to have been low, do we know with certainty whether it was low because the capacity or the will to save were absent, or because potential savers and investors were not successfully brought together by the financial market, or because the inducement to invest was lacking. As to the first uncertainty, the data problems which rob the estimates of capital formation proportions in the early industrial period of any quality save that of intelligent but adventurous guesswork are compounded the further back in time we go. For the medieval period, in particular, such accounts as survive rarely permit a reconstruction of investment magnitudes in terms conceptually comparable with modern national accounting notions nor, where they do, is it usually possible to construct any income estimate with which to compare them. The surviving accounts, moreover, are predominantly from larger agricultural estates and the question of their representativeness is thus crucial. The greater part, almost certainly, of income and (less certainly) of investment were non-monetized.

Yet both *a priori* reasoning and qualitative evidence suggest that national investment proportions were low. As to the former, Kuznets has pointed out that if we assume long-term growth rates to have been extremely low in pre-industrial society, as is almost certainly the case, then even a very modest positive rate of *net* capital formation would have accumulated, by the eve of the industrial revolution, to a level of capital stock quite incompatible with either qualitative or quantitative evidence for that period.[52] As to the latter, the far richer array of qualitative evidence about (for example) medieval agricultural techniques[53] and industrial processes convinces us that in general the level of productive capital was quite low. The ubiquity of hand sowing and reaping; the paucity and simplicity of agricultural implements; the prevalence of labour-intensive techniques in the restricted range of industries; the small scale and extent of mining and metallurgy; the chronic inadequacy of roads and almost total lack of any other form of social overhead capital – all of these and many more familiar features of the medieval scene remind us forcibly of low-income peasant societies in the mid-twentieth century.

Perhaps only in three respects did the economy of the middle ages reveal an ability to make investments of any magnitude. First, any agricultural society where the staple food consists of or is made from a crop harvested but once a year must have an average investment equal to 50 per cent of the product of that crop if starvation between harvests is to be avoided (and of course it was *not* always avoided), plus further investment of seed for next year's harvest which, at the low levels of yield then prevailing, might additionally require anything from an eighth to a quarter of the gross yield. Secondly, if industry generally employed few fixed assets, having regard to the prevalence of labour-intensive techniques, by the same token the need for *liquid* capital to finance stocks and work in progress was considerable. It was this need for liquid capital which underlay much of the Mercantilist emphasis on the precious metals, and indeed right through the early decades of the industrial revolution the need for short-term liquid capital continued in most industries to be more exigent than that for long-term loans to finance fixed capital formation. Thirdly, the cathedrals, churches and castles of medieval England remind us that considerable investments *were* possible, where the need was accepted, the institutional mechanism to assemble investible funds was present, and the technological skill to fashion the structures concerned was forthcoming.

This last is an interesting point. It has often been argued that the churches and fortifications (and the wars) and later – when civil peace was sufficiently established for the rich to live in unfortified homes – the palaces and mansions of pre-industrial Europe are counterparts to the pyramids of Egypt or the temples (and the wedding feasts) of the East: testimony to the power of poor societies to finance huge non-consumption expenditures when the ends are socially approved and the means technologically accessible. It is certainly difficult to believe that appreciable savings margins were beyond reach when a small class monopolized a large fraction of income. There are of course today, and were in earlier centuries, societies which were both poor and relatively egalitarian in the distribution of wealth, where no class had a substantial margin above modest consumption needs (though Indian wedding feasts are far from being confined to affluent classes). But in many Asian societies today, and in much of medieval Europe, it is difficult not to believe that there are and were substantial numbers living sufficiently far above the level of subsistence or indeed comfort to make possible considerable savings *if* the will were present and assets were available or capable of being conceived.

It has been said that few studies have been made, even at the 'micro' level, of actual investment levels in the pre-

industrial centuries. For that the deficiencies of the data are
not perhaps entirely to blame. Rather, medieval historians
have not generally oriented their studies in line with modern
thinking about growth or with national accounting concep-
tions, nor have they been equipped to adjust the raw data to
such terms. Economists and growth-oriented economic historians, on the other hand, lack the necessary background
knowledge and diplomatic and linguistic skills – and, be it
added, the time and the patience – to do their own quarrying
in the archival remains of these earlier centuries. That in fact
more evidence has survived which *is* capable, in the right
hands, of yielding information which would reduce the area
of our ignorance about pre-industrial investment is suggested
by the remarkable paper presented by Dr R. H. Hilton to
the second International Conference of Economic History in
1962.[54]

While the data are too fragmentary to permit the construction of any time series or even averages for a number of
years, Dr Hilton's figures suggest that in the fourteenth and
fifteenth centuries, in particular, investment proportions on
the estates of the Earldom of Cornwall may have reached as
high, in some years, as 50 or 60 per cent of gross receipts.
While these were very large and untypical estates, Dr Hilton
is able to adduce evidence also of investment proportions of
20–25 per cent on the estate of a substantial but non-noble
freeholder. All in all the evidence seems to confirm that
where adequate motive existed, the richer classes at least of
medieval society were able to save enough out of income to
undertake substantial acts of investment.

That 'adequate' motive Dr Hilton identifies, in the case of
his fourteenth- and fifteenth-century estates, in the demand
for capital improvements made by tenants whose bargaining
power had been greatly strengthened by the improvement
in the land/population ratio following the plagues and wars
of later medieval England. Landowners, by contrast, do not
seem to have substantially modified their previous attitudes,
which were that income, if not lavished on 'conspicuous
consumption', was to be hoarded, put aside for a rainy day,

rather than productively invested. The general tenor of precepts governing medieval estate management, according to Dr Hilton, was to advocate parsimony in hoarding surpluses and to gear administrative control and book-keeping to the prevention of cheating by subordinates rather than the fostering of productive investment. It was less – the implication seems to be – any absolute lack of investible surplus than a limited entrepreneurial horizon which held back investment on at least the wealthier medieval estates.[55]

In the course of the sixteenth and seventeenth centuries the English economy experienced substantial development, parti-cularly perhaps in its commercial and financial aspects (the two were, of course, intimately related). Over the two centuries as a whole there appears in general to have been a substantial increase in the sophistication of the financial sector and a replacement by domestic sources of the foreign moneylenders on whom the English Crown had so often relied. It may be said that in the seventeenth century, in particular, the rudiments of a capital market evolved. There was a growth of paper money and of inland negotiable instru-ments; a class of financial intermediaries began to form in the persons of (and primitive credit creation was practised by) those antecedents of the eighteenth-century bankers, the goldsmiths and scriveners; insurance developed, joint-stock financing became increasingly familiar, and there was a considerable extension and systematization of mortgage lend-ing; and at the end of the century, the Bank of England was founded and a start made to the funding of the national debt. Above all, the sheer volume of investible liquid funds seems to have grown remarkably, a feature associated undoubtedly with the rise of middle-sized fortunes created in trade, the law and public office. These trends showed themselves most strikingly – it is uncertain however to just what combination of causes this is to be ascribed – in the great secular fall of interest rates from upwards of 10 per cent for first-class risks in the early sixteenth century to 4 per cent or less in the late seventeenth – a fall which an Italian economic historian has referred to as the 'true' economic revolution (as opposed to the so-called 'price revolution') of the early modern centuries.[56]

This dramatic change in the financial sector showed itself in the favourable conditions facing borrowers in the later seventeenth century. Despite the unprecedentedly low borrowing rates there seems to have been little difficulty in raising funds. A £2 million loan floated by the New East India Company – alleged to owe its origin to the dissatisfaction of would-be investors with the 'closed' borrowing policies of its rival – was oversubscribed in three days. There appears to have been no difficulty in mustering resources to make good the ravages of the Great Fire of London in Charles II's reign. Overall, Dr Davies suggests, there was a shortage rather of good investments than of ready money in late seventeenth-century England.[57] Bearing in mind the exceedingly modest sums involved in capital formation in the industrial sector between, say, 1770 and the end of the Napoleonic Wars, it seems impossible to doubt that in terms of overall savings capacity England would have been able to finance the early industrial revolution up to a century before it happened. Whether, though, this investible surplus – held by merchants, 'bankers' and other traders and oriented for preference to overseas commerce, government loans and land mortgages – could have been successfully channelled to the nascent industrial sector, largely separated as it was from London financial circles by geographical, social and economic barriers, is another question. This brings us to the question of the *sources* of growth capital, and to this we must devote separate though brief sections.

(B) THE SOURCES OF CAPITAL

'Direct' financing and intermediation in history

Our interest in the sources of capital must be held firmly in check. The scope of this study extends, by and large, only to the overall contours of modern economic growth and to the more *immediate* determinants of its rate and morphology, such as the supply of factor inputs, natural resources and technology. Behind these more immediate determinants there fans out, of course, an ever more complicated array of remoter causes, the pursuit of which in the case of capital formation proportions would soon lead us, via the factors influencing the propensity to save, deep into the social and psychological characteristics differentiating one human group from another. We are neither equipped nor required to enter this area. But between it and the process of investment interposes a layer of explanation drawing upon characteristics of the capital market and the distribution of wealth; and our examination of the role of capital in economic growth would be unsatisfying if it took the mere *level* of investment as given without saying anything about its determinants – particularly since hints have already been thrown out, towards the end of the last section, that often the severest constraint may have lain not in society's inability to spare an adequate margin of income from consumption needs but in its failure to *mobilize* the potential savings and channel them to those in a position to make productive use of them.

It is evident that if even the rudiments of a capital market are lacking – if no facilities whatever exist, that is to say, for transferring resources from those with surplus incomes to those searching for funds to make investments – capital formation can only be undertaken personally by those enjoying a margin above consumption needs. Quite apart from the *level* of capital formation, we could then say that the allocation of investment would be optimal *only* if the distribution of wealth surplus to consumption needs were exactly symmetrical with the distribution of investment opportunities. This condition, moreover, has to be interpreted not only sectorally – the investible surpluses must occur in the sectors with the best investment opportunities at a particular time – but also in individual terms, that is, the *individuals* with surplus funds must be personally capable of seeing and seizing the most profitable investment openings.

The chance of this condition ever being met completely is doubtless remote. But it is the nemesis of feudal and most other forms of traditional society that their distinguishing features guarantee that it shall not be met at all, for in them the distribution of wealth is based on the accident of birth, on privilege, or on military prowess. In general, wealth is *not* the end product of productive investment; those who possess it have *not* acquired it by sustained success in making such investments in the past; and they do *not* envisage retaining it or increasing it by making them in the future. The vast advantage of capitalist societies, by contrast, is that much – never all, and sometimes not most – wealth *is* the end product of successful investment, and its owners *are* by and large equipped and anxious to augment their fortunes by a continuation of such activity. Even therefore if capitalist societies had not pioneered ways of transferring investible funds from those with surpluses to others seeking them, as of course they have, they would still be far more likely than traditional societies to achieve a marriage between the capacity to invest and investment opportunities. It is here that we find the substantial element of truth underlying theories which would link the development of capitalism with changing psychological attitudes to wealth and saving – the view advanced here holds no support, of course, for those who see the origins of these changes in *religious* movements – and also underlying Professor Lewis' insistence on the rise of profits as the chief cause of the increase of investment proportions, which Lewis sees as the most essential ingredient of the 'industrial revolution'.[58]

We must not allow the dramatic appeal of the contrast just sketched to blind us to the existence of exceptions. If the king or other ruler could establish a sufficiently strong central government to maintain civil peace and restrain the predatory internecine struggles of feudal magnates, some of them might be persuaded to undertake productive investments, particularly if suitably prodded or enticed by the State – as with the noble industries of Tsarist Russia. (But the degree of success of these enterprises was scarcely great enough to make necessary any drastic revision of the argument.) Above all, many large estates in medieval England, both lay, episcopal and monastic, *did* as we have seen undertake substantial investments. On the individual manor, too, the lord owned the few substantial capital assets – the mill, the fulling-mill, the oven and so on – though more with a view to increasing his power of monopolistic exploitation of the peasants than because he had any special appreciation of the economic benefits of such investments.[59] But by and large, the low level and restricted productive impact of medieval capital are more easily explained in terms of the attitudes of its wealthy classes than of any overall deficiency of surplus income – though the restricted range of investment opportunities, a matter not considered further in this context, is perhaps as important an explanation as either.

In sixteenth- and seventeenth-century England change accelerated in this, as in so many aspects of economic life. The change in question was not confined to the growth of new fortunes made in overseas commerce, in the law or in public life, which in conformity with the argument of this section were more apt to generate productive investments than the fortunes of the feudal aristocracy. Changes took place in the ownership of land too, which, impressive as was the rise of the commercial classes, naturally remained the chief source of potential savings well beyond the reign of the last Stuart. During much of the two centuries the land market was extremely active, what with Henry VIII's despoliation of the monastic lands, the huge sales of Crown land made necessary by the fiscal difficulties of the monarch, and the sales and sequestrations of the Civil War period. In the process large numbers of newly-ennobled landowning families came into existence, often with a greater or smaller infusion of capital from commerce or office, and some viewed their estates much more as business enterprises than had their feudal predecessors. Not all, of course; for land was still valued very widely as a source of political power and social standing, and for many its economic potential was subsidiary. Nor did an 'economizing' attitude to one's estate necessarily imply insight into the benefit of productive investments, for the largest landowners often concentrated on 'estate management', meaning thereby questions of leasing policy, land sales and purchases, the perfecting of measures to avoid cheating by subordinates and the like, and left the pioneering of new techniques and the investments occasioned by them to tenants. Still, there is enough left of the argument to justify some emphasis on the contrast often drawn between the English aristocracy, their fingers in a great many economic pies, and their French counterparts, unenthusiastic about commerce and sneering at industry.

The 'Price Revolution' had some responsibility, too, for the fact that the Elizabethan and Stuart aristocracy used their wealth and credit in an increasingly business-like way. Although it is now generally acknowledged that the Price Revolution was not necessarily the graveyard of the fortunes of the landed aristocracy it was once thought to be – for the internal terms of trade moved in favour of, not against, agriculture – it did penalize those who were unwilling or unable to seize the opportunities to increase revenues which the times offered.[60] Hence the Elizabethan and Early Stuart emphasis on increasing rents and entry fines, and the attempt to improve the value of land by enclosures and modifications to farm size. Hence, too, the attempt to supplement rental income by direct farming for the growing London market or by developing other sources of income from the land – especially timber and mineral rights. (The vesting of legal right to minerals in the owner of the soil, save only for the precious metals, gave the English nobleman his opportunities here.) But the economic activities of the Elizabethan aristocracy extended well beyond the land and its fruits. Excited by the prospect of the rich dividends paid by joint-stock privateering and commercial exploits, and using political influence to wring monopolistic concessions from a needy sovereign, noble fortunes found their way into almost every aspect of production and trade[61] – though not always to the benefit of allocative efficiency.

The sixteenth and seventeenth centuries thus saw an appreciable convergence of wealth and investment opportunities brought about partly by new attitudes on the part of landowners, partly by the growth of fortunes based on trade or office, and partly by the pioneering of a rudimentary capital market. It is true, if we can believe the very unsatisfactory evidence which is all we have – but which is supported, as we have seen, by *a priori* reasoning – that these developments did not lead to a permanent and substantial upward shift in capital formation proportions. Perhaps there *was* some increase during the period (1540–1640) which Professor Nef would have us believe witnessed an early 'Industrial Revolution',[62] an increase not sustained into the later seventeenth and early eighteenth centuries – perhaps because of a shortage of investment opportunities falling within the horizon of the owners of wealth? Or perhaps our impressions of the level of capital formation are mistaken, underestimating the investment in enclosures and land improvements underlying an 'agricultural revolution' which some, again, would now wish to place as much in the seventeenth as in the eighteenth century.[63] At all events it is not difficult, as we saw in the last section, to agree with the various authorities from Sir Arthur Lewis to Professor Postan who have argued that as far as the *volume* of investible funds is concerned, England was ready for the industrial revolution at least a century before it happened.[64]

The financing of the 'industrial revolution'

To say this is not to assert, however, that all the problems of mobilization had been solved. The money market, within which there was by the late seventeenth century a reasonable meshing of funds and investment opportunities, seems to have covered roughly the area of government loans, overseas trading and other joint-stock enterprises, insurance and loans on the security of land. In so far as mining and (in the later eighteenth century) the improvements to inland transport needed to carry coal and iron ore were financed by the great landed proprietors or by joint-stock enterprise, these activities may be added. The financial needs of the new metallurgical and factory enterprises of the later eighteenth century, modest though their needs were, were much less well served. Although the sources, and the degree of inadequacy, of the finance available to the early captains of industry are not matters of complete agreement, it *is* generally agreed that many important enterprises were in repeated financial difficulties despite their high profit rates. Some would think with Professor Postan that 'the new enterprises . . . were not much assisted by the fact that England happened to be . . . the richest land in Christendom'.[65] Certainly there is a dramatic contrast between the desperate activity to which Matthew Boulton was reduced in an effort to raise the few thousand pounds needed to keep the engine-making partnership of Boulton and Watt solvent, and the ease with which eighty years earlier a £2 million loan to the new East India Company had been oversubscribed in three days.[66] That such contrasts spring, as Postan asserts, from an imperfection of capital markets which lasted throughout the eighteenth century and beyond is further confirmed by the contrast between the periodic insufficiency of 'blue chip' investments to meet the needs of investors willing to take a 3 or 4 per cent return, and the 15–20 per cent or better profit earned by well-established industrial enterprises.

It is possible, however, to push this argument too far. Factory industry, after all, was unfamiliar, small-scale and speculative, and the collateral it could offer, especially since its greater need was to finance work in progress rather than fixed assets, was not such as to reduce the correspondingly high risk premium. Moreover, the contribution of trade capital in such industries as iron-making and cotton seems to have been far from negligible. Above all, there is another side to the coin: if a capital market dominated by London bankers and traders and by landed proprietors was unresponsive to the needs of industry, it is still true that the *greater* investment needs of the country, for government capital expenditures, social capital, agricultural improvement and enclosure *were* met by it, and to that extent industry could be left free to finance its own development.

This, it is generally agreed, is precisely what industry did. Whatever disagreements there may be about the sources of the *original* capital needed to launch new industrial ventures, historians of the period are unanimous that by far the largest contribution to the funds needed for subsequent expansion came from the reinvestment of profits earned by the firm concerned. Here Lewis' emphasis on the importance of profits to capital accumulation seems fully justified. F. Crouzet has charted the rate of growth of the capital of a number of eighteenth- and early nineteenth-century firms for which he has been able to find comparable figures.[67] The figures range from an average rate of $3\frac{1}{2}$ per cent per annum, sustained over a period of nearly a century and a half by the Darby iron-making enterprise at Coalbrookdale, and also by the London brewery Truman, Hanbury and Brixton over eighty-nine years, to nearly 30 per cent per annum during the quarter-century in which the firm of McConnel and Kennedy rose meteorically to first place among the country's cotton-spinners. More than half of Professor Crouzet's firms achieved growth rates in excess of 10 per cent per annum.

In most cases, the firms concerned expanded chiefly by auto-financing. The high rate of reinvestment was assisted by the high rates of profit, the absence (save during the Napoleonic Wars) of income or company taxation, and the characteristic structure of family firms, which (especially since there were no death duties either) added to business ambitions a more personal motive for accumulation. Further, some importance must be conceded to the simplicity, even asceticism, of the personal style of life and the dedication to their enterprise shown by the early captains of industry, which both contributed to the high rates of profit and permitted the 'plough-back' of a very high proportion of the firm's earnings. It is here, perhaps, that one is readiest to concede a role in the development of capitalism to the personal qualities and values – often, but not always, rooted in the profession of one or other variant of Protestantism – on which some social historians have laid such stress.

Financial intermediation in the industrial era

One way or another the early industrial firms overcame the problems of raising money. Despite the clear evidence of imperfections in the capital market which denied the new enterprises easy or adequate access to the pool of savings created in more traditional areas of economic life, most firms seem to have experienced acute difficulties only in securing short-term accommodation to meet immediate needs; there are few cases of sound ventures foundering for long through an inability to command development capital. (Though in saying that one is conscious that convincing evidence of such failures would have to be sought among the non-existent records of firms which were strangled at birth or in their early years.) But in the course of the nineteenth century new forms of industry emerged which demanded *initial* investments clearly beyond the capacity of the individual entrepreneur or partnership. Of these the railway was in the middle years of the century by far the most important; only in the last third did technological progress and the growth of the market and of (potential) economies of scale generate a demand for very large outlays in other branches of activity. The need was met by modifications to the company laws designed to make the process of incorporation of joint-stock companies easier and cheaper, and to extend the protection of limited liability to the company's shareholders.

Joint-stock ventures had of course been known in Britain since the sixteenth century, having been used to mobilize capital for enterprises where large sums were called for – notably in the longer-distance overseas trade routes and in banking, and (in the eighteenth century) to finance some of the more expensive canals. It has been argued that the company laws were not amended sooner, *not* primarily because of hostility to the principle of limited liability or suspicion of the corporate form, but because outside the areas mentioned capital needs were sufficiently small to be adequately served in other ways.[68] The restricted use made for several decades, outside of railways, of the corporate form other than to provide essentially family enterprises with the shield of limited liability lends some justification to this view.[69] But it is also true that the success of the early railway share floatations not only helped finance activities which could *not* have been financed by other means but also revealed that the growth of middle-range incomes had, by the middle third of the nineteenth century, reached a level at which they constituted an appreciable source of savings which existing investment opportunities and forms of financial intermediation had failed to tap. It is perhaps in this way that we are chiefly to explain the pronounced rise in capital formation proportions, which, if Deane and Cole (1967) are right, manifested itself at the time of the early railway 'manias'. If this is correct, the rise of corporate financing and the changes in company law have an importance which is not diminished by the fact that for several decades they were availed of only by a very restricted range of enterprises.

Details of the amendments to the company laws are well known and need no repetition here; by the 1860s or 1870s all the leading industrial countries – and several others – permitted the easy formation of joint stocks and provided the shelter of limited liability. But corporate enterprise based on 'direct' financing by the sale of shares to the public became of dominating importance only in the United Kingdom and the U.S.A. On the Continent, particularly in Germany, the banking system, particularly the great investment banks, played a bigger role in financing industry. Both total income and income per head were lower in France and Germany than in the U.S.A. or United Kingdom, and the small savings of peasants and the urban self-employed were of relatively greater importance. The scope for tapping a middle range of incomes, which was what the share market did in the English-speaking countries, was therefore narrower, while the small savers were inclined to look for greater safety and liquidity by keeping their assets with the banks. In Britain these small savings were tapped by a variety of intermediaries – savings banks, thrift clubs, friendly societies, insurance schemes. In France and Germany, the intermediation of investment banks channelled large amounts – large in the aggregate, though small of course individually – towards industry.

We might note in passing that these differences in the

sources of industrial finance had an impact on industrial structure, for unlike the situation in Britain, many large German industries depended largely on bank finance, and it has been argued that this was a contributory cause of the greater cartelization of German than of British industry in the period before World War I.[70] Investment bankers do not differ from others of the species in preferring stable and assured profits to higher but riskier and more fluctuating ones, and this led them to wish to promote market control and administered pricing on the part of their client firms, aims which were best achieved by using the financial control over them to engineer an oligopolistic market structure. However, our chief concern here is to point out that this solution to industry's financial needs involved the rise of financial intermediaries and indirect financing (the interposition of an intermediary between the holders of surplus funds and those wishing to borrow to purchase real assets) as opposed to direct financing (when, for example, the individual saver purchases industrial equities).

The rise of financial intermediaries has been a marked feature of capitalist economies in the past century or so. Of course, intermediaries existed earlier in the persons of bill-brokers, goldsmiths, scriveners and others, and in the form of banks. But the range of intermediaries, especially of non-banking intermediaries, has increased greatly in the nineteenth and twentieth centuries, and with it the relative importance of indirect as contrasted with direct financing.[71] From the point of view of the saver, the appeal of the intermediaries is that they offer a more diversified package of financial services – varying combinations of interest and liquidity, pension claims, insurance cover, loan facilities and so on – which increase the chance that the needs of the small saver can be met and thus that otherwise idle balances can be activated. The payments for these financial services are then translated by the intermediary into the purchase of the debt instruments of final borrowers, and here again there is the opportunity to meet special needs which direct or auto-financing might not serve as well, or at all.

It is highly probable that the rise of financial intermediation has both raised the overall level of savings and investment
and also improved the allocative efficiency of the investment
market. However, no measure or indeed completely rigorous
proof of this tendency has yet, apparently, been offered and
it is necessary to fall back on *a priori* reasoning on this point.
Such reasoning is supported, however, by the clear evidence
available for several countries of the relative growth of intermediation and indirect financing as indicated, for example,
by the increasing ratio of the financial assets of the intermediaries to total national financial assets. Evidence is also
forthcoming to substantiate the impression that non-banking
financial intermediaries have latterly grown in importance
compared with the banking system. It is particularly interesting to notice that these trends have been common to several
countries, even of considerably differing economic structures
and systems. For example, David Ott has shown that over
the years 1878–1958 the rise of financial intermediaries in
Japan followed a similar course as in the U.S.A. over a
roughly comparable period of economic development; this
is demonstrated by the similarities in the time paths of some
of the ratios referred to.[72] (A principal, but not unexpected,
difference is that non-banking financial intermediaries have
been distinctly more governmental in orgin in Japan than in
the U.S.A.) This similarity certainly strengthens the presumption that intermediation has met a real and generally-
felt need in the development process, rather than merely
evolved as a species of predatory middleman.

Professor Lance Davis in a number of articles has laid
considerable stress on the rise of intermediation as a contribution to growth in nineteenth-century U.S.A., and has also
suggested that its absence or inadequacy not only impedes
growth, but also can help to explain distinctive features of the
economy which lacks it.[73] He suggests that the capital market
was considerably less adequate in nineteenth-century U.S.A.
than in Great Britain. This was caused less by institutional
shortcomings than by the greater strains placed on the
capacity to mobilize savings and channel them to investment

opportunities in America. The rapid pace of geographical expansion, the profound changes in the composition of industrial output, and the 'bumpiness' of the time structure of the demand for funds caused by the larger absolute size of investment in (for example) some railroads and giant firms, gave rise to spatial, sectoral and temporal discrepancies in the marrying of savings and investment greater than those in Britain. Surprisingly, however, there seem to have been greater restrictions on the freedom to innovate institutional adaptations, too, notably the legal restrictions in the U.S.A. on branch banking and on the investment portfolios of insurance companies. Davis supports these assertions by assembling data on discount rates throughout the U.S.A. grouped in a number of regions. He shows a variation, for the period 1893-7, between 4·854 per cent, the New England average, and 8·990 for the Western states. Rates for individual cities, of course, varied still more, from 3·832 for Boston to 10·000 in Denver.

It is clear that this situation helps to explain, for example, the dependence of American geographical expansion on capital imports: that dependence was not *solely* a question of the overall inadequacy of American savings but stemmed partly from deficiencies in their *mobilization*. (It remains to be seen whether similar imperfections in the capital market help to explain the much greater degree of dependence on capital imports in other regions of recent settlement. That imperfections in the capital market could induce capital imports into areas which were *not*, overall, short of investible funds is shown by the examples quoted by Cameron in his paper on financial institutions in early industrialization: for example, 'In the 1840's and 1850's, German rentiers were purchasing American railway bonds at the same time that French, Belgian, and English entrepreneurs were earning a higher rate of return on mining and metallurgical enterprises in the Rhineland.'[74]) Davis also suggests that the backwardness of the South after the Civil War stems in part from its inability to command Northern capital or to improve the integration of its own capital market. Finally, the imperfections of financial markets in the U.S.A. *vis-à-vis* Great Britain meant that there was greater scope in America for making money through financial manipulation and personal advantage in access to the sources of capital, and Davis offers an alternative explanation of American industrial concentration along these lines. It should be added, however, that while these shortcomings of the American financial market continued to operate in the 1890s, this does not mean that no progress had been made in improving matters during the preceding decades. On the contrary, Davis' charts showing the time paths of regional interest rates indicate a clear narrowing of differentials – though more notably for short-term than for long-term loans – through 1870–1914.

The sources of savings

Improvements in intermediation may both activate hoards and increase the efficiency with which capital is allocated, but there is surely a limit to the extent to which they can actually change *ex ante* savings intentions. The factors which do determine these intentions are beyond our purview, but a few brief comments are in order on the course of personal savings through time. Shortly after World War II some dismay was caused by the observation of a discrepancy between the trend of historical data and the results of cross-sections studies on savings proportions. It was observed that while the latter agreed in portraying the savings ratio as an increasing function of income – the rich saving a larger fraction of their income than the poor – historical data suggested no marked rise in the savings/income ratio accompanying the rise of real income through time. Most contributors to the continuing debate on the determinants of the savings ratio which this discovery inaugurated have accepted the reality of the conflict, and have sought explanations of individuals' behaviour which would fit both sets of data. An example is the 'relative income' hypothesis – that an individual's decisions to spend or to save are a function of his *relative* position in the income distribution at a point in time, rather than of his absolute income.[75] Increases (or decreases) of total personal income through time would therefore not generate changes in the aggregate personal savings/income ratio; the savings behaviour of any given individual would change through time if his relative position in the income distribution moved up or down, but over the whole population such changes in the relative positions of different individuals would naturally cancel each other out.

Only one major attempt has been made to resolve the conflict by denying its reality: Milton Friedman has denounced estimates of the savings ratio based on surveys for single years and has proposed that it is the (unchanging) historical estimate of the consumption function which is the true one.[76] The self-employed and others whose incomes fluctuate considerably from year to year subtract from their income a trend-determined absolute quantity for consumption, so that the balance (which may of course be negative in bad years) is highly correlated with fluctuations in income. Single-year surveys in effect take a snapshot picture of the population of personal savers, some of whom are experiencing a good year and some a bad, and misinterpret the positive correlation thus discovered in viewing it as a relation between savings and *permanent* income differences, whereas in fact it relates the former to *temporary* fluctuations in income.

It is not the intention here to discuss this or any other theory of the consumption function, except perhaps to record that the economic historian, in thinking back over what he knows of the historical behaviour of farmers in good and bad harvest years or of the policy of the early captains of industry, is inclined to see a good deal more attraction in Friedman's hypothesis than many economists seem to have seen in it. The economic historian's reaction to the whole controversy is to be tempted to feel that it is illusory for the *opposite* reason to Friedman's, namely, that the historical trend of personal savings has not been adequately established. The debate was provoked initially by Kuznets' researches in the history of U.S. capital, but it was given added edge by Goldsmith's massive study of U.S. savings, which appeared in 1955.[77] Kuznets' data bore, however, on capital formation proportions rather than on personal savings, while Goldsmith's data cover only the years 1897–1949. There is really nothing very firm to go on for nineteenth-century America and virtually nothing at all for any other major country for any period before World War II. This is a slender base indeed. There is, moreover, strong presumption that *in the very long run* personal savings ratios *have* increased. If personal savings today equal half or more of all savings, as according to some authorities they do,[78] then wherever the *overall* saving and investment ratio has more than doubled, as it appears to have done for most industrial countries in looking back to their pre-industrial pasts, personal savings as a fraction of total income must have increased; and it may be added that since personal income as a fraction of total income has tended to decline, personal savings as a fraction of personal income must have risen still more.

Further, the composition of personal savings has changed through time. Personal saving is taken, broadly, to comprise individuals' savings (the savings of farmers and of non-farm households) *plus* the savings of unincorporated enterprises.[79] Historically, the latter have tended to decline relative to total savings as small businesses have been absorbed or edged out by large concerns – the corner grocery store giving way to the supermarket – and also, in the nineteenth century, since the more successful family firms adopted corporate form in order to gain the shelter of limited liability. Evidence from the U.S.A. and Japan suggests that the savings of unincorporated businesses comprise a large fraction of all personal savings, and also that the savings ratio for such businesses is extremely high – well above the average for other types of personal income.[80] While similar data are not available for early periods, it is reasonable to infer from what has been said about capital formation during the industrial revolution that this second characteristic obtained at that time also. Hence, 'personal saving' has, in all likelihood, been an aggregate whose composition has shifted through time, a systematic loss of elements generated by incomes characterized by higher savings ratios being balanced by an increasing preponderance of those with lower ones. Given that *personal* savings ratios have at worst remained constant through time, there is therefore a strong presumption that *individuals'* savings ratios (that is, the ratios relating to all personal income *less* the income of unincorporated enterprises) have had a pronounced upward trend.

Finally, it is not hard to identify factors which would be expected to have depressed personal savings in the course of the last century or so, and whose operation would therefore tend to reduce one's surprise at the finding that the ratio of personal savings to personal incomes had remained roughly constant, if despite the foregoing arguments that were confirmed to be the case. Notably, income taxes have increased and become more progressive, and there has been some tendency in many countries for income distribution to become more egalitarian. Both trends, on the assumption that at a given time the savings ratio is an increasing function of (disposable) income, would be expected to have pulled the savings ratio down by reducing the fraction of disposable income earned by those with very high savings ratios.

The economic historian, then, finds it hard to get very excited by the great debate over the determinants of the consumption and savings functions. He does not feel that the course of personal savings ratios through time has yet been securely or widely enough charted to allow him to enter usefully into the debate, or to convince him that the conflict alleged between historical and cross-section data is necessarily real; and in view of what has been said about the shifting historical composition of personal incomes and in view of the triviality, until quite recent times, of the distinction between many unincorporated and many corporate enterprises, he does not feel that even a pronounced trend in the average personal savings/income ratio would have a great deal of analytical meaning or interest.

'Involuntary' saving

We have hitherto supposed that saving is the result of a voluntary decision to abstain from consumption. There are, broadly, two major mechanisms of involuntary saving.* One is that the government may tax income which would otherwise have been used for consumption, and use the proceeds to finance public capital formation or make credit available to private investors. The second is that credit may be created and given to investors without any corresponding taxation of consumers, which raises aggregate demand relative to supply and causes inflation. In the first case it is the taxpaying individuals who are forced to make involuntary sacrifices of consumption; in the second, this sacrifice is inflicted on the whole community. To some extent the two processes are alternatives, since governments which do not wish to incur the displeasure of the electorate – particularly if the groups with the greatest untaxed capacity are their own supporters – may be tempted to resort to inflation, the pain caused by which is more widely spread and the responsibility for which is harder to pin down than in the case of a new or increased tax.

The factors which lead to government playing a large role in capital formation are sometimes largely and always partly political. In the extreme case, the governments of socialist economies have almost complete control, directly or indirectly, of the process of saving and investment. But even in market economies the role of government in saving and investment has increased markedly in the twentieth century, for reasons which are as much political as economic. Partly it is that changes in the franchise and party organization have rendered the government increasingly vulnerable to the pressure of particular groups and interests calling for capital expenditures of benefit to themselves; and partly it is a matter of that organic striving to self-perpetuation and growth on the part of government departments which Professor Parkinson immortalized in his famous law. It is not the purpose

---

* Since we are dealing here with savings in modern or modernizing societies, we do not discuss involuntary saving taking the form of the exploitation of one class or race by another, which has historically been doubtless the most important form. It is questionable, of course, whether such exploitation is best handled under the concept of 'forced saving'.

here to attempt any general review of government's role in economic life; we simply need to notice that in addition to the political factors mentioned, there are circumstances in which an economic case for government intervention in the process of capital formation can be made out. Broadly, this arises in one of three ways. It may be desired to raise the overall level of savings and investment, that is to promote accumulation. Or the intention may be to facilitate *mobilization*, if the financial market is insufficiently developed and integrated to achieve the necessary smoothness in the meshing of surplus and deficit spending units. Thirdly, government capital formation may be called for to undertake 'lumpy' investments which are too large for private investment or whose benefits are too widely diffused and difficult to measure for it to be possible for private investors to recoup their expenditure by a user tax.

All three purposes of government activity have played a considerable role in historical growth. The first two have been in evidence chiefly in poorer and less progressive countries in which it was desired to accelerate growth and modernization. Among the leading countries Meiji Japan and Tsarist Russia spring to mind. Their aims were largely similar but their techniques significantly different. In both cases the aims were to raise the level of investment by levying direct taxes on small peasant incomes of which little, in the absence of the tax, might have been saved, together with indirect taxes on articles of widespread consumption, and to use the proceeds to undertake social overhead capital formation and make credit available to new industrial enterprises whose needs the capital market might have been too undeveloped to meet. The chief difference was that in the Russian case nothing was done, or occurred, to cause peasant productivity to rise substantially, so that the taxes depressed an already very modest level of consumption and caused great hardship and opposition. In Japan, on the other hand, agricultural productivity rose quickly, partly because of the government's efforts, and the tax fell largely on the *increments* to income and was, to that extent, much easier to bear. (It may be added that the style of Japanese industrialization also helped, in that it favoured rural industry and thus the perpetuation and indeed growth of opportunities for earning a supplementary income in the countryside. Russian policy even before 1914, on the other hand, was indifferent or even hostile towards peasant industry.)

The other main type of government intervention, that in investments beyond the reach of private capital, finds its most obvious illustration in the field of social overhead capital. This was particularly the case with very large countries like Russia or countries with a low density of population like New Zealand and Australia. Here the provision of railway networks and the like was beyond the capacity of private savings either because of the sheer size of the investments called for or because the opening up of new areas called for simultaneous investments – for example, in a railway and in land development – which it was unlikely that private enterprise would co-ordinate. (It has to be added, though, that political factors, including in the Russian case military considerations, played a large part too in these decisions.) Since in the regions of recent settlement taxation very probably was at the expense, at least in part, of private savings and thus raised aggregate savings ratios little if at all, such activity must be viewed economically as a contribution to mobilization rather than to accumulation. It is for this reason, too, that (as we shall see in the next section) the import of capital was frequently resorted to finance investments of this type.

It is tempting to say nothing about inflation, because there is so little agreement about the nature of its relationship with capital formation and growth, and discussions of its role generate such heat. But one can scarcely avoid reminding the reader that one of the most celebrated explanations of the rise of early capitalism is that it was stimulated by a 'profit inflation' generated by the Price Revolution of the early modern period. The notion, associated with the name of Earl J. Hamilton, is that in the general rise of prices generated by the inflow of precious metals from the New

World wages and rents were left behind, and entrepreneurs enjoyed an increase of profits because prices of inputs rose less than prices of output, thus facilitating accumulation.[81] It is not necessary to consider this argument in detail in the present context, as the question has been much discussed in the literature.[82] Broadly, Hamilton's thesis has declined in acceptance since it was first propounded primarily because it is doubted whether wages and rents did lag all that much behind *relevant* prices: real wages certainly fell, but rents rose far more than Hamilton supposed (and so did some non-factor inputs such as timber), while the prices of manufactured goods rose much less than those of agricultural products (whose increase was the chief reason for the fall in real wages). Further, there is of course no reason why a change in techniques or in productivity should not offset changes in the ratio of input to output prices; the very fact, as some of Hamilton's critics have pointed out, that in several leading countries capital formation proportions in the nineteenth century rose most in periods of *falling* prices, confirms that there is no determinate relationship between changes in the price level and the power to accumulate.

Still, there remains a considerable appeal in the notion that credit creation, even if it causes a little inflation, is good for growth, and there are better reasons for this appeal than that printing money is far easier – and, doubtless, more pleasurable – than any other proposed way of promoting economic growth. Partly it is that a gently-rising price level stimulates business confidence and private capital formation. Partly – and relatedly – it is that inflation gradually erodes the real burden of debt: Keynes' 'euthanasia of the rentier'. But chiefly, credit creation can get funds where they are most needed, which even in advanced societies like post-Civil War U.S.A. other techniques may not be able to do, without being necessarily, if modest in the aggregate, seriously inflationary. Inflation brought on by credit creation in favour of highly productive enterprises is self-liquidating as they generate increments to output to offset the increment to aggregate demand. But whether enterprises called into being by credit creation turn out to be highly productive or not, they need not be particularly inflationary in an economy previously operating with idle reserves of land and labour which can be activated by credit creation. Then credit creation leads to a net addition to productive activity which can partly or wholly offset its inflationary impact.

The historian can add little to these largely theoretical reflections, for the history of credit creation in economic growth has not yet been well studied. All the same, the hints thrown out by modern studies of early banking and finance tend to suggest that in the past we have allowed ourselves to be too easily impressed by orthodox pre-Keynesian monetary theory in making our judgments of credit creation in early industrial and frontier societies. The 'wildcat' banks of the American West and their English counterparts in the new industrial regions doubtless contributed to instability, but they may well have contributed more to growth than the scholars of a generation ago, too much in awe of another breed of bankers, were willing to recognize.[83] The snag, of course, is that growth via credit creation is *too* easy. If there is one thing that governments find harder than to know what to do, it is when (and how) to stop doing it. The government which embarks on a course of growth-via-credit-creation without mastering this secret will soon find itself in the situation of the sorcerer's apprentice.

(c) THE EXPORT OF CAPITAL

The history of capital exports

Long-term transfers of capital between countries, on a scale and of a regularity to make their contribution to economic growth worth discussing, are a phenomenon of the nineteenth and twentieth centuries. International credit was not, of course, unknown in earlier periods. Trade credit was familiar in medieval commerce, and in the later middle ages the bill of exchange was used to tap foreign sources of funds and to evade the usury laws. In the renaissance period great financial houses like the Fuggers and Welsers undertook

extensive international loans to needy rulers. Though essentially short-term accommodation, these were often regularly
renewed and permitted some princes to finance their government on a basis of long-term foreign indebtedness. Nor was
it only the improvidence of the personal ruler which made
recourse to foreign capital necessary; the parliamentary
government of eighteenth-century Britain enjoyed considerable loans from Dutch investors. The contribution of such
borrowing to economic growth is highly dubious, however,
for the financial difficulties of renaissance princes chiefly
arose from war spending, and throughout the eighteenth and
nineteenth centuries the British national debt was almost
entirely a creation of the periods of war, falling in money
terms – and still more as a percentage of the national income
– in years of peace. If the economic benefits of such borrowing
are uncertain, it does nevertheless point to a deficiency of
underdeveloped countries which has formed and still forms
a principal reason for recourse to foreign finance, namely,
the inadequacy of the tax base and of local credit facilities in
such societies to finance government expenditures.

Perhaps more important from the point of view of economic growth was another form of international investment of
the early modern period, namely the creation of fixed capital
assets by expatriates in connection with the conduct of
international trade or the production of the commodities
imported by the metropolitan countries. Examples are the
erection of (sometimes fortified) trading posts in Asia and
Africa by the maritime powers of Western Europe, or the
development of plantations by these same countries such as
those producing sugar in the West Indies and Brazil. Such
investments clearly made an important contribution to trade
between Europe and other continents in the early modern
period. Through this, their impact on the economic life both
of receiving and of lending countries was doubtless very
considerable, though this impact has not been very systematically evaluated from the standpoint of the modern growth
economist. It can be said, however, that from the point of
view of the host economies, and particularly in the case of the

plantations, such investments led to 'enclave' economies,[84] capital and management from the metropolitan country combining with local resources and local (or imported) labour in exploitive activities yielding only minimal benefits to the indigenous population and often inflicting unpleasant side effects on them.

The golden era of foreign investment, however, began only some 150 years ago when British investors, the borrowing needs of their own government curtailed by the ending of the Napoleonic Wars, turned to explore other avenues of investment, abroad as well as at home. The growth of foreign investment in the nineteenth century basically reflected the increase of the savings potential of the more advanced countries brought about by the rise of their incomes. In addition, conditions were such that considerable fractions of these savings were tempted towards investments abroad. The period 1815–1914 was marked by relative political stability and freedom from major destructive wars. International economic conditions such as the fall in ocean freights and the evolution of the gold standard were exceptionally favourable to the growth of overseas trade and thus to a multiplication of opportunities for profitable investments overseas. These were in many cases closely associated, as we have already seen, with the peopling of the regions of recent settlement and the flows of international migration which helped to achieve it. Finally in Britain, much the largest foreign lender before 1914, the London money market was oriented to a remarkable degree towards foreign lending, a circumstance which arose largely because of the unusual prominence of the export of goods and services in the British economy, and because the needs of British industry were met to a high degree by more localized sources of finance and by 'ploughing back' profits.

These circumstances led to a truly remarkable expansion of capital exports. For several decades prior to 1914 each of the major creditor nations invested abroad sums in excess of 1 per cent of their national incomes,[85] the generally-accepted but rarely-attained target for international aid by developed countries in the 1960s. British capital exports rose to over 5 per cent of G.N.P. in the years 1900–14, and in some years exceeded domestic capital formation. After World War I both economic and political conditions became much less propitious and the level of international lending, allowing for changes in the price level, was much lower in the inter-war period, especially in the 1930s, than in the early years of the twentieth century. The U.S.A. replaced the United Kingdom as the major lender in the 1920s, while Germany, in third place (after the United Kingdom and France) as capital exporter before 1914, now borrowed large sums from America. Since World War II rates of lending have increased once again, and annual long-term capital transfers of all types, in real terms, have been two or three times larger than before World War I. A large fraction, however, has been in the form of government-to-government grants or of aid channelled through international agencies; *private* capital exports during the 1950s were probably of the same order of magnitude, in real terms, as before 1914, but as a percentage of the national incomes of the lending countries were certainly substantially lower.[86]

In addition to these fluctuations in the aggregate volume of capital exports there have been marked changes in the composition of the flows both by type of lending and by sectoral distribution of the investments. Prior to 1914 the bulk of capital exports, especially by the United Kingdom, took the form of subscriptions to government bonds or of portfolio investment in securities in the field of social capital such as railway companies or dock undertakings, or of service industries such as banking. *Direct* investment was less common and was chiefly confined to resource-based industries such as mining and plantations. Equity investment in manufacturing was relatively rare, particularly in the case of British capital exports. American lending, however, was characterized from the start by a greater orientation towards direct investment,[87] and partly because of the rise of the U.S.A. and the relative decline of the United Kingdom as supplier of capital this form of capital export became as common as portfolio investment in the inter-war years.[88] Since 1945, *private* capital exports have been dominated by equity investment in resource industries and in domestic manufacturing; portfolio investment and fixed interest bonds have held much less attraction for the capital exporter and the type of lending prominent before 1914 has fallen, by default, to government-to-government grants and aid through international agencies.

Capital imports and growth

Some of the reasons for these changes will be suggested shortly, but we turn now to ask: what contribution have capital imports made to the development of borrowing countries? Obvious though the question is, curiously little searching economic analysis has been devoted to it. The attention of economic theorists has focused chiefly on a succession of specific aspects – capital movements and cycles of various sorts; the 'problem of transfer'; capital movements and the terms of trade – not all of which would be regarded as central to the question of capital exports and growth, and which certainly do not add up to a satisfactory analysis of the relationship. Some writers, it is true, have estimated the average yield on exported capital.[89] But there are many reasons for doubting that this statistic tells us anything worth while about the true economic return on such investment.

Social and *private* rates of return are notoriously liable to diverge in the case of social overhead capital, which was the type of investment so much of the pre-1914 capital imports facilitated. (It has been estimated that nearly 70 per cent of new British portfolio investment overseas in the period 1865–1914 went into S.O.C.[90]) The fact that such a high proportion of overseas capital prior to 1914, and even between the wars, was borrowed by governments at fixed rates of interest (fixed interest bonds are variously estimated at 60–80 per cent of the total pre-1914 capital import) hides from us the rate of return on the investments which it permitted. A mere survey of yields also ignores, of course, other aspects which would have to be considered in a complete appraisal, such as the effect on the balance of payments and on the transfer of technology. But more fundamentally, the growth-promotion effect of capital imports has to be measured with reference to the output generated by the investment *which would have been foregone* in the absence of such imports, and this is not necessarily the same investment as that which the imported capital directly financed, even where the latter can be identified.

There are cases, such as those of the 'enclave' economies – nineteenth-century nitrate mining in Peru, or twentieth-century oil exploitation in the Middle East – where foreign capital has financed activities which fairly clearly would not have been undertaken in its absence, and where the return on that capital may in some sense measure the addition to the level of output generated by it. There are other cases where 'blind' capital has simply searched out profitable assets in a foreign country, 'releasing' domestic capital for other and probably less profitable uses. And there are other cases again – American investments in Canadian resource-based industries in the twentieth century are often held to be a case in point – where the development of new areas of 'autonomous' economic activity has induced an increase in the level of *domestic* savings and investment in other sectors servicing these areas. Clearly, the yield on the foreign capital itself is not an equally good measure of its growth-promoting effect in all these cases.

In default of more sophisticated analysis, one may turn to the historical record and derive a few crude but useful generalizations from a comparative survey of the level and nature of external borrowing by the developed countries of the present day. It is evident, in the first place, that the past experience of these countries in respect of capital transfers has varied enormously. Britain, the first industrial nation, was a net exporter of capital from an early stage – 1815 at the latest – and though her government bonds had attracted some Dutch investment in the eighteenth century, it seems that this was already being repatriated by the time, *c.* 1780, when a marked acceleration in Britain's rate of economic

growth is generally held to have occurred. Most of the other
industrial nations of Western Europe seem to have been
capital importers, at least on a small scale, at an early stage
in their industrial growth, but some, like Germany and
Belgium, became major exporters in their turn at a time
when they were still very much in the throes of industrial
transformation. The U.S.A., on the other hand, remained a
net capital importer until near the end of the nineteenth
century, and was by far the largest borrower overall in the
period 1815–1914. In Japan, capital imports played on the
whole a minor role in the process of modernization, but
reached a significant level in the period 1896–1914 which
was characterized by increased military spending and a
higher rate of investment in S.O.C. and in heavy industry.

One country alone, Russia, provides proof of the fact that
there is no unique relationship between economic growth
and capital imports. The impressive economic growth of the
last quarter-century of Tsarist rule was financed to a very
considerable extent by foreign investors, who owned half
Russia's joint-stock capital and half her national debt in the
early twentieth century. After her economy had been ruined
by war and revolution and a painful recovery to about the
1913 level of *per capita* output had been achieved, she embarked anew in 1929 on a process of massive economic
growth, this time renouncing any help from foreign capital
or indeed from foreign trade. By contrast, some countries in
the regions of recent settlement which are today and probably
always have been among the world's richest countries, notably Australia, Canada and New Zealand, not only depended
on foreign capital in their pre-1914 development, but have
also continued to be, or in Canada's case (after a brief interval
as a capital exporter) have again become, among the world's
greatest capital importers on a *per capita* basis. Finally, this
apparently discouraging lack of correlation between capital
import or export and economic growth would not be
improved if one turned one's attention from those countries
which are rich today to those which are still poor. For one
easily finds examples of poor countries which were histori-

cally heavy importers of capital, like India, and of others, like China, which were not.

A far more encouraging correlation appears – and in doing so gives us a valuable clue to the historical role of foreign capital – if we consider the pattern of capital movements *geographically* and *sectorally* rather than in relation to the relative level or trend of income per head. It is at once apparent that the bulk of capital exported before 1914, and to some extent even after World War I, was absorbed by those regions of recent settlement where geographical expansion of settlement was taking place, often with the direct or indirect aid of an influx of European migrants, in the later nineteenth and early twentieth centuries. Further, the bulk of the capital was channelled directly, or indirectly through overseas borrowing and infrastructural investments by the recipient government, into S.O.C. formation. It is not only countries like Canada, Australia, New Zealand, Argentina and Brazil which exemplify this style of capital import. So does the U.S.A., for foreign capital in America typically entered the transport and resource fields, rather than industry; and so to some extent do the far less obvious cases of India and even Russia (though in the latter there was also a large foreign stake in industrial and mining development).

The reasons why capital exports flowed along such well-marked channels are not quite as obvious as might appear at first sight. It is sometimes suggested that as the advanced nations of Western Europe grew in population and in industrial maturity, they invested abroad in countries apt to become new sources of supply of industrial raw materials and food, and/or new markets for their manufactured exports. This is true enough of *direct* investment in (say) tea or rubber plantations in South Asia, or copper-mining in South America. But such investment accounted for only a smallish fraction of pre-1914, or even pre-1939, capital exports, and in respect of the more typical case the 'new sources of supply and new markets' explanation gives a somewhat misleading impression of the motivations involved. It has to be remembered that the larger part of pre-1914 foreign investment was in government bonds or other fixed interest securities, and that even where the investment was in risk capital, it was typically of a 'portfolio' character. In such circumstances, the European investor was more commonly concerned only with the *security* and the *yield* of his investment; the initiative in determining the sectoral allocation of imported capital lay more with the borrowing than with the lending nation.

In the decisions made by the former, prospective export opportunities undoubtedly played a role; but governments of such countries acted also under the stress of immediate fiscal needs and, particularly, under a strong incentive to find money for improvements to transport and communications. These improvements were often sought because they tended to increase land values – whether because the State was itself the major landowner, depending heavily on sales and leases for its internal revenue (as in New Zealand), or because government was in the hands of great landowners (as in Argentina). It may be, indeed, that the causal sequence *foreign borrowing – S.O.C. investment – increased land prices* provides a major key to understanding the magnitude and direction of international capital flows in the later nineteenth century. Certainly, in such cases as the New Zealand of the 1870s or the Argentina of the 1880s, the 'division of labour' by which foreign capital financed S.O.C. investment while local savings speculated on the booming land market was not only marked, but indeed was carried to dangerous extremes, provoking subsequent crises by neglecting the limits which export prospects set to profitable investment along such lines.

A further factor, inextricably interwoven with the above as both cause and effect, was European migration to the regions of recent settlement. The relative abundance of resources which helped directly or indirectly to attract foreign capital also stimulated an unparalleled inflow of migrants from the crowded and often unpleasant urban environment of early industrial Europe and from over-populated rural areas like Ireland and Southern Italy. The large population increase of which this immigration, in several instances, was the chief cause prompted a demand for S.O.C. investment which local savings were inadequate to finance; the Australian boom of the 1880s, for instance, was based to a large extent on massive urbanization induced by the inflow of migrants. But such investments in turn attracted immigrants by creating buoyant employment conditions, and, in some instances, as in the Vogel era in New Zealand, a substantial proportion of the borrowed capital was used to subsidize immigration directly. Finally, massive immigration encouraged capital imports in another way, namely in that a very high proportion of the political and business leaders of these young countries were expatriates who, when they wanted to borrow money, looked as naturally, or more naturally, to London than to Wellington or Melbourne. The facts that after World War I the frontiers were closed and the stream of inter-continental migration dried up go far to explain the subsequent decline of the pre-1914 type of international lending, though it continued for a time in some favoured areas where these restraints were less inhibiting, as with U.S. investment in Argentina in the 1920s.

One final point is that the well-defined sectoral pattern of lending in the pre-1914 era, dominated by government bonds and railway securities, reproduced in the foreign field the pattern of domestic investment which was familiar to investors of the early and mid-nineteenth century. It has to be remembered that c. 1850, when foreign lending began to assume substantial proportions, the company laws in Britain were still in process of revision, and at this stage neither in that country nor elsewhere were corporate organization and financing at all common outside foreign trade, transport and banking. The investors of the later nineteenth century, in subscribing to foreign government issues and foreign railways, were but replicating abroad the restricted pattern of investment opportunities already familiar at home, a pattern which only in the late nineteenth and early twentieth centuries began to be changed, in the leading industrial nations themselves, by the extension of corporate finance to the fields of manufacturing and service industry.

Whatever the explanation for the dominance of regions of recent settlement as borrowers in the early, classical phase of foreign investment, it is quite clear that this borrowing was used predominantly for 'capital-widening' rather than for 'capital-deepening'; that it was intimately associated with the unique geographical extension of settlement and massive inter-continental migration of the later nineteenth century; and that the borrowing nations were predominantly among the *richest*, rather than the *poorest*, in the world, enjoying in some cases at least levels of *per capita* income and of domestic savings superior to those of the major lending countries. Such considerations naturally lead to the suspicion that some of this capital may have been 'wasted', and this suspicion seems to find at least some support in the adverse judgments which economic historians have passed on, for example, the 'political railways' of New Zealand – unprofitable lines resulting from the political pressure of interested landowners on the construction of which imported capital was lavished. It seems difficult, too, to believe that the extraordinary progress of urbanization in Australia in the last quarter of the nineteenth century was entirely necessary in a country whose wealth still came to such a large extent from living 'off the sheep's back'.

Although searching economic appraisals of the growth record of these countries are rare, Butlin's work seems to suggest that in Australia, at least, the massive immigration and capital imports of the later nineteenth century were associated with a high rate of growth of aggregate output, but a relatively modest rate of growth of real income per head.[91] It seems at the very least arguable that as high a rate of growth of *per capita* incomes could have been achieved with lower rates of immigration and capital import – a situation which would almost certainly have moderated the severity of the crisis of the early 1890s in which the burden of servicing the capital imports of the 1880s played a big part. However, in appraising such an alternative we must also bear in mind the effect of lower rates of migration on the *sending* areas like Ireland and Southern Italy, where even greater rural impoverishment is usually held to have been relieved only by a massive exodus of surplus people.

A further generalization calls for less discussion since it makes good sense and needs only historical illustration rather than argument. It is that generally speaking capital imports have played a *decisive* role only in the economic destinies of smaller countries – smaller, that is, in terms of aggregate incomes, either because their population was small or because their level of *per capita* income was very low. Even the massive capital exports of the years preceding World War I were scarcely large enough, in absolute terms, to allow the lending countries to dominate the economic life of a large borrower. The U.S.A. was by far the largest recipient of gross capital inflows in the century before 1914, but the foreign stake in U.S. reproducible capital in the late nineteenth century is thought to have been only of the order of 10 per cent, and one would not feel inclined to say that the course of U.S. economic development in the later nineteenth century was in any very essential way determined by the foreign owners of assets in America. Indeed, the bulk of capital imports occurred precisely in the period when the U.S.A. shook off the remaining attributes of 'colonial' economic status and blossomed into full economic nationhood and then into world dominance.

In Australia, New Zealand, Canada and Argentina, however, foreign borrowing played a much larger role, financing in the chief periods of capital import a half or more of all capital formation. In 1930, the gross foreign indebtedness of the first three countries mentioned all lay between £120 and £130 per head; in India – a large borrower in aggregate terms – it was only £2·9 per head.[92] Such ratios perhaps overstate the degree of *control* over national economic destinies which seems to be implied, since a large share of the imported capital took the form of foreign purchase of government bonds and other 'portfolio' lending. But even so the economic history of the regions of recent settlement would surely have followed a vastly different course had the export of capital been restricted; indeed, even modest changes in the availability of credit in London could spark off substantial crises, like that in Argentina in 1913–14, in countries where the balance of payments and perhaps the budget had become geared to a rising capital inflow.

In countries less fortunate politically than the 'white' British dominions, foreign capital could exert a profound influence not only on the economy but also on political life. Even in Russia, despite its size, foreign capital won concessions from the Tsarist regime which gave some colour to Lenin's doctrine of economic imperialism; and moreover access to it was manipulated, by the French government at least, to influence Russian decisions in the political and military sphere. But of course it is in the countries which were both small and poor that foreign capital could exert its maximum influence. Although much the larger part of pre-1914 capital exports went to regions of recent settlement, there was some investment of a quite different type in, for example, mining and plantations in much poorer, often tropical countries. From the economic point of view which is our present concern, such investment often led to the creation of economic 'enclaves' which form an interesting, limiting case of one type of economy. As we shall see in the next chapter, what is envisaged is a situation in which the sector penetrated by foreign capital remains an 'enclave', economically isolated in a relatively high degree from the rest of the economy. Such a situation has usually arisen in relatively backward countries, possessing some resource cherished by the more advanced nations. A classic example was South American nitrates. Levin has shown in detail why the interest of the industrial nations in this resource had little general 'growth' effect on the economy of Peru.[93] The foreign country provided to a large extent not only the capital but also management, machinery, even to some degree an imported labour force. Since virtually all the product was exported, and exported in a largely unprocessed form, the economic activity in the enclave sector exercised little 'spill-over' effect into the rest of the economy, whether by way of factor payments, input/output linkages, or in any other way.

The extent of the insulation of the foreign sector in such cases is, of course, a matter of degree. The national government can at least ensure a 'cut' by charging mineral royalties or levying export taxes. This was done in South America: the export tax on nitrates accounted for 43 per cent of Chilean government revenues between 1880 and 1930, rising to a peak of 68 per cent in 1894.[94] In the case of Peruvian guano, a class of native entrepreneurs emerged who participated to some extent in extraction, shipping and selling. The foreign exchange thus gained was unfortunately wasted in financing 'conspicuous consumption' by a politically-dominant minority and in some ill-judged railway construction, and little enduring economic benefit was bequeathed to Peru from the reckless exploitation of a unique resource. It is legitimate to take some encouragement from the fact that in the twentieth century many underdeveloped countries possessing such non-reproducible resources have taken care to wring some enduring benefit out of their exploitation by foreign states. Venezuela, for example, has used its oil revenues purposefully to finance a wide-ranging programme of education and infrastructural investment – 'sowing the oil' – calculated to help it develop its other considerable resources before the oil begins to run out. But the benefits of such programmes are diffuse, long-term and to some extent indeed conjectural, and it is easy to understand the pressures which can develop in such countries, typically dominated by an élite ruling class as they are, for a more prodigal and immediate sharing of the benefits.

Capital exports and the lending country

A complete appraisal of the growth impact of capital exports would naturally require attention to the *lending* as well as to the *borrowing* countries. This, again, is a problem which has not been very often or very exhaustively studied.* Classical

* Important recent exceptions relating to post-war American and British private capital exports are G. C. Hufbauer and F. M. Adler, *Overseas Manufacturing Investment and the Balance of Payments*, Tax Policy Research Study No. 1, U.S. Treasury (1968); W. B. Reddaway *et al.*,

economic theory would create a certain presumption that the capital exports of pre-1914 years, privately and voluntarily undertaken as they were, were profitable to lender as well as to borrower, though the fact that the borrowers were often richer than the lenders might generate doubts as to whether the assumptions underlying this theory corresponded with the facts of the case. There have, certainly, been some who ascribe Britain's industrial retardation of the later nineteenth century to 'capital starvation' induced by the export of such a large fraction of British savings. But this is not the dominant interpretation. It seems difficult to square with the facts that throughout the period in question borrowing rates were relatively low; that established, progressive firms could and did raise capital easily enough when needed; and that there was some under-utilization both of labour and capital in many sectors of the economy. Perhaps the truth is that *if* government and managerial attitudes and policies had changed so as to promote a higher rate of modernization in the British economy, *then* the export of capital might well have been profitably reduced. But in the absence of such modifications it is unconvincing to ascribe Britain's economic difficulties to the appetites of her foreign debtors.

In some other respects Britain's capital exports were more certainly beneficial. They certainly tended to improve the United Kingdom's terms of trade in the long run, by helping develop new sources of imports and by increasing the capacity of the recipient countries to demand British manufactured exports. The terms of trade benefit, however, was shared with

---

Effects of U.K. Direct Investment Overseas: An Interim Report (Cambridge, Cambridge U.P., 1967), and *Final Report* (Cambridge, Cambridge U.P., 1968).

These reports illustrate the great complexity of the issues, the difficulty of finding adequate data, and (in particular) the need for a 'counter-factual' approach. Specifically, the effect of direct investment overseas on the lending country's balance of payments is shown to depend critically on whether, in the absence of such investment by the lending country, comparable investment would or would not have been undertaken by the host country or by some third country. See also Dunning (1970), Ch. 2.

other industrializing countries of Western Europe which exported less, or no, capital, while as the capacity of these countries to compete with British manufactured exports grew, the advantages to British industry also became less marked. By the early twentieth century indeed this relationship was much weaker; Canada in this period borrowed hugely from Britain but spent much of the loans in importing from the U.S.A.

One must remember, too, the implications of capital transfers in the international monetary field. It is generally held that the readiness of the more advanced countries, particularly the United Kingdom, to export capital helped prevent the appearance of major imbalances in the international monetary system before 1914, and in doing so contributed to a mutually-beneficial increase in foreign trade. By contrast, the increasing restrictions put on capital exports, whether directly by governments or by discouragements such as those offered by fluctuating exchange rates and inconvertible currencies, are held to have been partially responsible for the problems of international liquidity and the consequent resort to autarkic policies which characterized the inter-war period and particularly the 1930s. In the period since 1945, the export of capital has frequently been called on to ease the problems of countries in balance of payments difficulties and to promote international liquidity, even to the extent of creating problems for lending countries whose currencies would otherwise be perfectly secure. At the same time the governments of the major lenders have retained controls over capital exports, and applied them with varying severity in accordance with their own balance of payments situation.

The servicing of external debt

The balance of payments aspect is indeed an important facet of capital export which we now explore. Some present-day economists take a 'two-gap' view of the contribution of foreign aid to economic development: it supplements domestic savings if these are inadequate to lift the economy out of some sort of low-income level 'trap', and at the same time covers the trade deficit which a period of more intensive capital formation is likely to provoke, both because of the need to import much capital equipment, and through the 'multiplier' effect wielded by an increase in 'autonomous' investment.[95] Such a view seems at first sight to receive a good deal of confirmation from history, for at various times countries as diverse as New Zealand, Tsarist Russia, Canada and even Japan, an unusually spartan and thrifty developer, have gone through periods of development when an increase in imports induced by higher capital formation rates has made recourse to foreign credit seem inevitable. *Soviet* Russia, indeed, may seem to prove that the word 'inevitable' is too strong, but even here Western trade credit did in fact perform an important though very short-lived function in enabling Russia to buy tractors and similar machinery from abroad while it was building up its own machine-tool industry during the First Five-Year Plan.

This function of foreign investment has, however, been queried on the grounds that the burden of *servicing* foreign capital quickly increases to the point of cancelling the gross inflow of borrowing, and that the major debtor nations in fact derived over the long haul no foreign exchange benefit from their imports of capital in the nineteenth century.[96] It is clear as a matter of simple arithmetic that this is almost inevitable. A constant inflow of capital borrowed at 5 per cent will lead to a servicing outflow equal to that annual inflow in the 21st year; by the 41st year, the cumulated servicing outflow will have equalled the cumulated gross inflow, and thereafter will progressively exceed it. A borrowing country can only ensure a continued cumulative net inward transfer by *increasing* its rate of borrowing geometrically which, even at a modest 5 per cent, would quickly enough involve it in overwhelming indebtedness. Borrowing taking the form of equity investment by foreigners, with its typically higher rate of return, would of course meet these critical periods correspondingly sooner. For the debtor country which aspires to escape from indebtedness, as critics of foreign investment would wish, the matter is even clearer: if the foreign borrowing has yielded any positive rate of return at all the cumulative net transfer *must* be an outflow of foreign exchange, defined as

(Cumulative gross inflow) *minus* (servicing outflow plus capital repatriated).

Simple arithmetic seems to have worked out in history. For in the 'classical' period of capital export before 1914, the net export of capital by the major lenders was barely equal to the interest and dividends they received. For the United Kingdom, the second was nearly 120 per cent of the former in the period 1815–1913;[97] for the three major pre-1914 creditors combined, the two values were approximately equal for the period 1874–1914.[98]

If we ignored the foreign exchange aspect, this would clearly be a totally misconceived criterion of foreign borrowing. It is the rate of return on the capital invested in a given period which we need to compare with the cost of borrowing that capital, not the amount of capital borrowed in some subsequent period. We do not say that a new company which has launched itself by borrowing a large sum on the stock exchange in year one is a failure if in year two it pays its shareholders more in dividends than it needs to borrow in that second year. But the foreign exchange aspect of importing capital does introduce a second criterion in terms of which we have to evaluate that method of raising capital in comparison with others; and this aspect is not trivial. It is in large part because the cost of servicing so soon begins to whittle away the cumulative foreign exchange benefit of foreign borrowing that many economists are sceptical what contribution the present-day programmes of aid to developing countries will make to solving their balance of payments difficulties, unless indeed that aid takes the form of outright gifts or interest-free loans; and it is in part the explanation for the preference expressed by many such countries for 'trade, not aid'. Nor is this attitude new. Partly for this reason, though more perhaps out of considerations of economic nationalism, Japan preferred to carry through its programme of modernization and development with only minimal reliance on foreign capital, and indeed passed laws severely restricting its entry.[99]

The fear of intolerable foreign indebtedness has gained emotional impact from certain much-publicized and well-remembered crises in the history of debtor nations, in which the burden of servicing the external debt was indeed a central factor – the Baring crisis of 1890, the Australian depression of the 1890s, and the difficulties and defaults of many primary-producing countries in the early 1930s. What all such crises had in common was a very high debt service ratio (debt servicing as a percentage of export earnings) arising from a combination of substantial antecedent borrowing and falling or inadequately rising export receipts. The service ratio rose as high as 60 per cent in Argentina in 1890; it was over 38 per cent in Australia even in the late 1880s, before the boom burst; about 25 per cent even in Canada on the eve of World War I, after a period of very successful borrowing and in favourable export conditions; and between 35 and 50 per cent for most primary-producer debtors in the early 1930s.

In some instances these high ratios may have arisen because foreign capital had to be serviced as soon as it was borrowed, whereas the increase in exports followed from the investments gained by it only after a long gestation period. Between 1861–5 and 1886–90, Australian G.N.P. trebled, the visible trade deficit widened from £9·7 millions to £42·1 millions, and external investment servicing rose from £5·3 millions to £50·3 millions; but exports rose only 59 per cent.[100] In the crisis of the 1930s, the situation was more often that the *volume* of the primary producer's exports had risen very rapidly but, pressing against an inelastic demand, had brought about a sharp deterioration of their terms of trade. In both types of case, however, it seems that the additional criterion necessary to judge the efficacy of foreign borrowing, that is, that it should lead, directly or indirectly, to an improvement of the borrower's balance of payments at least equal to the burden of debt service generated, had not been met with.

Before discussing this further, the point should be made that the crises referred to did have another element in common, namely that the antecedent capital inflow had in all cases taken the form, predominantly, of the purchase of fixed interest securities. Moreover this borrowing, as we have seen, coincided with – and may sometimes have caused – a downward trend of prices for the major exports of the borrowing country. It could therefore be argued that the burden of debt service was so onerous in part at least because of the *inflexible* nature of the service payments. Had the foreign investment taken the form, it might be argued, of *equity* capital, this would have shown a greater sensitivity to the earning power of the capital in question, and thus have reduced the foreign exchange burden in times of falling export values.

This, however, may be an over-optimistic view. For one thing, the burden of a fixed interest debt was not necessarily inflexible if the debtor could convert some issues to a lower rate, as some of them took the opportunity to do in the 1930s. Further, the long-term rate of return on equity investment, despite its short-term fluctuations, is usually higher on average than on bond issues. It was partly for this reason that the Japanese preferred to discourage private equity investment in their development programme and to import foreign capital, to the extent that they imported it at all, in the form of subscriptions to government bonds. Moreover, since private overseas lending has been channelled increasingly into the manufacturing field, as it was in the 1930s and particularly since World War II, the assumption that the return on it would fluctuate sympathetically with export values has become increasingly dubious. Indeed where, as in New Zealand, foreign investment is enticed by the offer of protected markets, its profitability may actually be at a maximum in periods of balances of payments crises, which in recent years have typically been caused by fluctuations in the level of domestic activity rather than in export receipts.

We return from this digression to the general question of

the balance of payments aspect of foreign borrowing. It is held, we have seen, that this should promote not merely an acceptable overall rate of return, but improvement to the debtor's balance of payments at least equal to the cost of servicing the debt. It is sometimes held that this implies that the foreign capital should go directly into export or import-replacing production, or at least (as most pre-1914 lending did) into infrastructural development calculated to promote such production. But bearing in mind the earlier contention that the true return on foreign capital is the return on the investment *which would have been foregone in its absence*, even this seems too stringent a requirement; foreign capital in activity seemingly remote from the foreign sector may nevertheless have 'freed' domestic savings for such uses.

As is so often the case, perhaps only a balance of probabilities can be established. It is certainly difficult at one extreme not to find fault, as many commentators did, with the use made of foreign capital by Germany and other countries in the 1920s to build street tramways and the like. At the other extreme, one criticism which *cannot* be levied against foreign investment of the 'enclave' type is that of provoking a servicing problem. Virtually the whole output of foreign nitrate concerns in South America or of rubber plantations in early twentieth-century Malaya was exported. Hence the gross income of such enterprises equalled their export receipts. Since the total of profits, factor payments and other items remitted abroad could not possibly exceed the gross income of the enterprise, if 'profit' is calculated as a residual, the enterprise could not directly *lose* foreign exchange for the host economy. Nor, since the degree of insulation was very high, could a multiplier effect indirectly generate a demand for imports by the non-enclave sector. Hence such enclaves were at worst neutral from a balance of payments viewpoint. Between these two extremes are the much more frequent cases where it is extremely difficult to decide what the net impact of capital import on the borrower's balance of payments has been. But the sceptical view, which relies so heavily on the occasional major payments crises of debtor countries,

THE SERVICING OF EXTERNAL DEBT   199

is surely too selective in its marshalling of the evidence, and
is too overawed by the burden of service payments in years
of *falling* prices – which, if unusually common in the nineteenth century, have been outnumbered by those of rising
prices in the twentieth and, indeed, in the early modern
period as a whole. For many persistent borrowers the burden
of debt servicing has been lower, in relation both to their
national income and to their export earnings, in the period
since 1945 than it was for most of the nineteenth century.

It may be added that the evidence of history appears to
confirm what common sense suggests, that foreign borrowing
is most likely to prove successful if it promotes and is accompanied by an increase in *domestic* savings.[101] This reduces the
danger of inflation which arises if the foreign funds are transmitted through the banking system and used by it to bring
about an expansion of domestic credit: a danger to which
countries on the 'sterling-exchange' standard, for example,
were apt to fall prey; it helps to 'spread' available foreign
exchange over as wide an area of investment as possible; and
it helps guard against the danger that foreign borrowing
becomes an accepted and indispensable element in the normal
financing of consumer imports and government expenditure.
A failure to avert such dangers was perhaps partly responsible for the discomfiture of Argentina in 1890 and of the
southern hemisphere 'white' dominions in the later nineteenth century. By contrast, Canadian domestic savings and
banking policy in the early twentieth century are often held
up as examples of the possibility of 'smoothing the transfer'
of even very large capital imports – though Canada between
1900 and 1913 was much luckier than the other primary
producers in the later nineteenth century in the course which
its export prices took.

Despite the scepticism with which some have viewed
Knapp's strictures on foreign borrowing, it is fair to add that
historical evidence is by no means entirely on the side of the
optimists, for it offers little assurance that large foreign debts
can be easily repaid in normal times. Most of the major
pre-1914 debtors who subsequently got out of the red were

helped to do so by unusual circumstances which one would not wish to repeat – the U.S.A. and India by the exigent needs of belligerents in World Wars I and II respectively, Russia by repudiation of Tsarist debts following the 1917 revolution. Japan in World War I and in the Korean War and Egypt in World War II also reduced or eliminated their international debts by abnormal belligerents' purchases or the expenditures of foreign troops stationed on their soil, as to some extent did countries like New Zealand in World War II. Some 'underdeveloped' debtors defaulted in the 1930s (though prior to 1914, the record of default on foreign loans was generally good, and scarcely justified the normal premium which lending abroad commanded). Other major pre-1914 debtors – Canada, Australia, New Zealand, Argentina – remain debtor/borrowers today. In some of these cases the continuation of external borrowing parallels and may be partly caused by the post-1945 pattern of international migration. But it is not easy to dispel the suspicion that somehow many countries acquire an economic 'character' which renders them prone, in their balance of payments as in other ways, to persistent habits of thrift or of profligacy.

International capital movements and economic growth since 1945

We turn next to examine more systematically aspects of international capital flows since 1945. First, we have said that *private* capital outflows in recent decades have predominantly been of equity investment rather than the purchase of fixed interest securities. For this there have been several reasons. On the supply side, lenders have been little attracted, in a period of substantial and continuing inflation, by fixed interest securities. With the high rates of return on domestic capital in the leading industrial nations, and the political instability and threat of interference or even expropriation which faces it in many underdeveloped countries, *private* capital has been tempted to the latter only by exceptionally high yields, or by the need for supplies of some indispensable resource such as oil. Private capital has been much readier to venture into other advanced and politically stable countries, but in such economies governments have today far better opportunities than before 1914 to finance their expenditures by domestic taxation and borrowing and hence less need to float their loans in London or Paris, as they did before 1914. Countries like the British 'white' dominions and Argentina commonly had 80 or 90 per cent of their public debt overseas before 1914, but this fraction was enormously reduced by World War II at the latest.

The search for additional raw materials to meet ever-growing industrial demand has been responsible for a very substantial outflow of private capital, and to a greater extent than ever before capital export devoted to such ends is becoming indispensable to the economic growth of the capital-exporting countries. The search for oil has been the most urgent, and has lured capital from the advanced countries to wherever in the world the black gold is, or might possibly be, found. But the U.S.A., in particular, shocked by rising raw material costs and by the evidence of the Paley report into the realization that her resources are not only not limitless but are actually in some cases surprisingly close to the limit, has already poured billions of dollars into the proving and exploiting of primary materials outside her own borders. So far, the need for external sources of supply has been sufficiently lacking in urgency to permit a selective search by America; and Canada, close at hand, immensely rich in many mineral and vegetable resources, economically and socially congenial to the American entrepreneur, and tied intimately to America in hemisphere defence, has naturally been by far the largest recipient of American resource-seeking capital. But the need to find other sources can only increase; and at the time of writing these words Australia, as attractive as Canada in most respects save distance and military security, seems to be well on the way to development as a second general reserve for American industrial needs.

Almost certainly the growth of the recipient countries has been accelerated by these trends; but they have not been universally welcomed for all that. Apart from the political and cultural antipathies which a massive foreign stake in one's country naturally provokes, there are after all real economic questions which can legitimately be asked about the merits of growth achieved by selling non-reproducible resources to someone else's industry. But in the Canadian case, in particular, the American stake in domestic manufacturing arouses at least as much soul-searching as does the U.S.A.'s increasing exploitation of Canada's natural wealth. This stake has reached massive proportions. By the late 1950s over two-fifths of Canadian manufacturing output and over half of mining and smelting originated in American-owned firms. Further, while in the nineteenth century ownership figures tended to overstate control because most foreign investment was in bonds and 'portfolio' holdings, the dominance of equity investment in U.S. lending to Canada and the fact that U.S. investment is typically in the largest firms, including some holding companies, imply that at the present time ownership percentages *understate* control.[102] It is quite safe to say that by the late 1950s non-residents, predominantly of course U.S. nationals, controlled substantially more than half of Canadian mining and smelting, oil, and general manufacturing output. This situation has given rise to a wide-ranging debate in Canada whose context extends far beyond the economic sphere, and has led many to believe that economic growth can be too dearly bought when it poses an apparent threat to economic autonomy and even to cultural integrity. While the Canadian case is exceptional in the degree of economic penetration so far achieved, it is quite clear that other advanced countries, Australia perhaps in the lead, are following Canada along the same road.

It has been pointed out that in seeking foreign fields private manufacturing capital has shown a marked preference for advanced, politically-stable countries.[103] For this the promise of security and of reasonable freedom to operate in familiar ways have undoubtedly been partly responsible. But there are other reasons for the geographical selectiveness shown by this type of capital export. Foreign equity investment in the general manufacturing field began to increase in the inter-war years when the rise of tariffs and other impediments to trade made it profitable to set up branches or subsidiaries abroad instead of exporting domestic manufactures. The U.S. stake in Canadian manufacturing received its first big boost after 1932, when the Ottawa agreement on Imperial Preference gave an inducement to U.S. manufacturers to establish branch plants in Canada for export to the United Kingdom under the preferential Empire tariff. The development of customs unions and the like in the last quarter-century has multiplied such incentives to the point where the export of capital to jump tariff or other trading barriers has begun to have a substantial effect on the trade, balance of payments and industrial structure of both capital-exporting and importing countries. Nor have such developments been merely the accidental by-product of commercial policies primarily evolved to achieve other ends. Some governments equipped with the necessary powers, like that of New Zealand which has had a system of direct import controls in continuous operation since before World War II, have wielded these powers to encourage foreign investment in the manufacturing sphere. The usual technique is to threaten to exclude commodities already imported and to promise congenial conditions for the replacement of such imports by the products of branch or subsidiary manufactories at home.

Amongst lower-income countries, only the larger ones have been able to rely on such inducements to effect 'import-replacing' industrialization. Smaller low-income countries have had to try to offer additional inducements to foreign capital – 'industrialization by invitation', as the West Indians engagingly call it – the chief one being the availability of labour at low wage rates. While few countries have experienced industrial development very closely in accord with the model devised by Sir Arthur Lewis,[104] an elastic supply of labour at low rates is of course a very considerable inducement to entrepreneurs struggling with the labour shortages and militant trade unions of high wage rate economies. But that there has not been *more* export of manufacturing to take advantage of such conditions only partly reflects the less attractive political and social environment in such societies. There are, again, more narrowly economic reasons. Labour is only one factor of production; if it is cheap, other factors are often no cheaper or even dearer in low wage economies. The supporting framework of servicing industries is apt to be weak, and transport costs may be considerable for industries which have to export a very high proportion of their output, and may have to import much of their raw material.

Above all, the prime fallacy of the 'industrialization in labour-surplus economies' argument is the assumption that low wage *rates* necessarily mean low wage *costs*. Too often lack of skill, lack of habituation to factory routine and discipline, and a high rate of labour turnover have largely negated the advantage which low wage rates seemed to promise – the mind of the economic historian goes back to the experience of the Soviet Union under its first two Five-Year Plans – and if foreign enterprise through a long process of training contrives to ameliorate these difficulties, trade unions (here unlike the Soviet Union) have surprisingly quickly appeared to lift the rewards and reduce the elasticity of supply of these elite workers. Nevertheless, many under-developed countries have had some success in attracting foreign investment in this way with the aid of inducements such as tax-free holidays, and in a few cases where political or other circumstances have been exceptionally favourable – Hong Kong and Puerto Rico spring to mind – economies have been completely transformed by an enormous injection of foreign capital attracted by the prospect of low-cost export-oriented manufacturing.

If large-scale foreign investment provokes misgivings and hostility even in as rich and politically-advantaged a country as Canada, it can well be understood that such investment is far from unreservedly welcomed in less developed countries, where the economic imbalance between lender and borrower is greater, the social frictions engendered by a different style of life and work are more acute, and xenophobia is a more familiar and less scrupulously exploited platform for political groups. The long and repetitive catalogue of harassments to which foreign capital has been subjected in such environments, from petty bureaucratic annoyances to wholesale expropriation, has convinced many American businessmen that investment in such countries is not worth the effort. But the experience of a few more progressive and patient business corporations, and studies by investigators from the universities and the international agencies, are gradually bringing to light the typical forms and areas of conflict, and suggesting patterns of behaviour by which the outside firm can minimize friction and create conditions in which the very considerable opportunities in some developing countries can be exploited and shared to mutual advantage.[105] Mexico among the larger of such countries, Trinidad and Tobago among the smallest, have shown that very rapid economic growth can be promoted by such techniques in a way compatible with a reasonable degree of political and economic autonomy and the preservation of national self-respect.

But the promise which private investment holds for helping to solve the problems of the underdeveloped nations lies in any event largely in the future. For by and large there is little doubt that since World War II the export of private capital has done more to *widen* than to narrow the gap between rich and poor nations. In 1959 over one-third of U.S. direct investments, and over 40 per cent of all U.S. foreign investment, was in Canada alone. Europe accounted for a further fifth of the total; the whole of Asia and Africa put together, by contrast, accounted for barely 10 per cent.[106] Professor Dunning tells us that by 1965 some two-thirds of the direct foreign assets of the major capital exporters – oil investments apart – were located in developed countries.[107] At a time when many countries in Africa and Asia, with among the lowest real incomes in the world, could attract scarcely a dollar of private capital, about a third of all net capital formation in Canada, usually accounted the world's second richest nation, was being financed by private foreign capital inflows.[108]

H

By default, the provision of general development capital for the poorer countries has devolved upon government aid and loans and grants through the international agencies. It is extremely hard at the present time to know just what the growth-effect of this aid programme has been. Most obviously this is because it is hard to know just what capital transfer there really has been. Foreign aid is a politically touchy subject in the major lending countries, some of which, desirous of appearing magnanimous, include in the total sums which are absorbed in domestic administration, whereas others, with an eye on the reluctant taxpayer, seek ways of hiding the true extent of the programme. There is an intolerable confusion, compounding the conceptual ambiguity which would exist anyway, between 'military' and 'economic' aid. And at the other end the recipient governments, sometimes endowed with only questionable political morality, may be suspected of misusing vast sums to maintain their own power by hand-outs to supporters. Over all hangs the obscuring cloud of political and ideological debate generated by a programme which some think ineffective and wasteful and others selfish and inhumane in its inadequacy for the task.

In any event it is perhaps too early, the first 'development decade' only just ended, to draw many firm conclusions from evidence with such a limited time-span. It is generally agreed that there is a sharp contrast between the brilliant effectiveness of early post-war aid to Western Europe and the more equivocal success of the aid of the later 1950s and the 1960s to the less developed countries. Doubtless this proves nothing more than that there is no unique relationship between any one variable and economic growth, and that aid will be more effective in those societies where other characteristics are well oriented to growth. This is obvious anyway. It is also apparent that the volume of aid per head has varied greatly from one recipient to another. Generally (and relatively) speaking, small countries have got more than large because the total funds are not large enough to give much aid *per capita* to very populous countries, and perhaps also because the United Nations is constructed on the principle 'One country, one vote', not on voting power proportional to population. And countries which are important militarily and politically in the Cold War situation have done better than those more remote, because of the need to 'sell' the programme to the taxpayers in the (predominantly Western) donor countries. Countries which qualify under both heads, like Laos and South Korea, have thus received amounts of aid per head up to scores of times larger than the bigger, less immediately threatened countries like India or moderately large and strategically unimportant ones in Africa. It is exceedingly doubtful that such differences can be justified either on economic or on humanitarian grounds.

Finally, the burden of servicing the loans received is piling up already dangerously high, and some economists foresee that unless the terms of loans become much more generous, or more aid takes the form of outright gifts, the situation will be reached in only a decade or so when the aid programme makes no net contribution at all to the foreign exchange availability of the recipients.[109] But we have seen already that beyond a quite early stage there was often no net transfer of funds, in this sense, in pre-1914 capital export; and the aid would still have done its job if it had effected a substantial improvement to the balance of payments by reducing recipients' imports or developing their exports of goods or services. Much of the third world, however, has such a low level of real income that there are not many consumer goods imports to replace, while imports of capital goods and producers' materials are more likely to increase than to decrease if development really gets under way. On the export side many underdeveloped countries, especially in the tropics, have only a limited range of exports in which, moreover, one country competes with another, so that if one succeeds in boosting its exports it depresses the terms of trade for others.

Perhaps the most disappointing feature is the extent to which the whole question of capital export is today shot through with politics. This is not, indeed, entirely a new

situation. Both the French and German governments inter-
fered a good deal with the outflow of capital before 1914 to
serve their political ends. And in the case of investment by a
major power in small and poor countries, defence of the more
or less legitimate interests of the foreign capital has passed
over all too easily to the wielding of substantial political
influence, even to the extent of making and unmaking
governments, as the history of U.S. investment in Cuba
and in the 'banana republics' of Central America clearly
shows.

But it is surely true that both the extent and the subtlety of
political influence on the migration of capital have increased
since World War II. As we have seen, political considerations
enter hugely into even *private* capital movements, from both
the demand and supply side. But naturally the comment
applies even more to governmental and international aid,
where political considerations show themselves not only in
the *allocation* of aid, but in its terms – 'tying' aid to the
purchase of goods and services produced by the donor, to
the detriment of its economic benefits, and so on.[110] Not only
has such aid to be voted and thus justified in political terms
at the donor end; not only does it help (as many think) to
sustain régimes in the recipient countries of a character politically acceptable to the lenders; but if Russia's economic
strength continues to grow, it will surely become more and
more just one aspect of the Cold War in which decisions
are taken as part of a global strategy of non-military
conflict. Any approximation to an economic optimum will
then be even more a matter of good luck than it has been
hitherto.

But it is certainly possible to be too pessimistic. Overall the
growth record of the poorer nations is generally better than
the more highly-coloured accounts of the Western press
would have one believe. It seems certain that on average they
have achieved higher *per capita* growth rates in the 1950s and
early 1960s than at any previous period in the twentieth or,
probably, earlier centuries, and in quite a lot of cases, higher
than today's developed countries during their emergence

from their pre-industrial pasts.[111] Almost certainly foreign capital has played, on balance, a positive role in achieving this result;[112] almost certainly it would have achieved more but for the major stumbling blocks in the areas of population and trade.

Our final words concern the transfer of technology. This has often been claimed, historically, as a third contribution of capital exports to growth, and the importance of the question is underlined by the general agreement today that technological change, in the broadest sense of the words, rather than an increase of factor inputs, has been the major source of historical growth. Yet it is not easy to agree that until recent years, at least, the diffusion of technology can to any large degree properly be credited to capital exports, though certainly in some cases the two have been closely connected. This is surely sufficiently indicated by the fact that during most of the period in which they were undergoing the basic process of industrialization and technological maturation the major industrial powers of Western Europe were *exporters* of capital, and not for the most part to each other. Japan both up to the wars of the 1930s and again in its astonishing recovery since 1950 has learned from the West through technical agreements, through licences and by sending its young engineers abroad to study, rather than through the importation of techniques alongside foreign capital. The Soviet Union has, of course, depended even less on this method of acquiring 'know-how'.

This should cause no surprise for the period before 1914, since as we have seen the great bulk of foreign capital before that date went into government borrowing and 'portfolio' investment, and such investment normally transfers to the borrower no more than a bare financial claim. Much of what equity investment there was was in 'enclave' economies in which, quite apart from the highly specific nature of the technology involved, there was usually little opportunity for nationals to participate at a level which permitted much transfer of skills. It is of course true that the British built railways, dock installations, and the like in many parts of the world. But the host country paid separately for such help; it was not normally part of a capital export 'package deal'; and was equally available to, and used by, countries which did *not* borrow abroad to finance their railway building, as well as by those which did.

There are, however, some exceptions to this generally negative conclusion. The most important case is perhaps that of Tsarist Russia, which in welcoming foreign capital did attempt, in a tradition stretching back to Peter the Great, to stipulate that foreign owners and managers should train Russians in the techniques of the industry concerned.[113] This is one of many ways in which the story of capital export to pre-revolutionary Russia strangely anticipates features of capital exports in our own day; another, whose economic significance is perhaps barely beginning to be appreciated, is the illustration it offers of the danger of corruption which massive dependence on foreign capital often provokes.

With the growth of equity investment in the 1930s and since World War II, the role of capital export in promoting the diffusion of technology has tended to increase. In Canada, to take an extreme case, there is no questioning the gain from the massive presence of U.S. technology. Where every second industrial worker is employed in an American-owned plant, it requires no developed system of industrial espionage to ensure that 'know-how' gets around. And the Canadian firm which does not learn and use every trick it can will not last long to delay the process. But even where American or European corporations are less thick on the ground and work in an environment less quick to learn than the Canadian, the government of the host country often can and does stipulate that an acceptable contribution to the training of local skills is a condition of their welcome. And, indeed, the more progressive corporations, recognizing this as one of the most sensitive areas from which conflict and interruptions to business may arise, make opportunities available for the local population to master the managerial and technical skills of the enterprise.[114]

Notes

1. MOSES ABRAMOVITZ, 'Resources and Output Trends in the United States since 1870', *American Economic Review, Papers and Proceedings*, XLVI (May 1956), 5–23.

2. The reference is, of course, to JOSEPH A. SCHUMPETER, *Business Cycles*, 2 vols (New York, McGraw-Hill, 1939). Some might quarrel with the phrase 'his finest book', and indeed the *History of Economic Analysis*, though left incomplete by its author, is an extraordinary achievement.

3. NURKSE (1953).

4. LEWIS (1955), 208 and 225–6.

5. ROSTOW (1960), 8.

6. T. S. ASHTON, *The Industrial Revolution, 1760–1830* (London, Oxford U.P., 1948), 11.

7. ROBERT M. SOLOW, 'Technical Change and the Aggregate Production Function', *Review of Economics and Statistics*, XXXIX (August 1957), 12–20.

8. KENDRICK (1961), 79.

9. See the 50th *Annual Report* of the National Bureau of Economic Research (September 1970), 31–2.

10. ODD AUKRUST, 'Investment and Economic Growth', *Productivity Measurement Review*, 16 (February 1959), 35–53.

11. HOFFMANN (1965), 20, 28.

12. R. C. O. MATTHEWS, 'Some Aspects of Post-War Growth in the British Economy in Relation to Historical Experience', *Transactions of the Manchester Statistical Society*, 1964–5, 1–25.

13. DENISON (1967).

14. A. GERSCHENKRON, *A Dollar Index of Soviet Machinery Output, 1927–28 to 1937* (Santa Monica, Calif., Rand Corporation, Report R–197, 1951), Ch. 4.

15. However, in revised estimates of the rate of growth of G.N.P. per head in the United Kingdom in the later nineteenth century, Phyllis Deane finds it necessary to reduce earlier estimates by as much as 44 per cent. The difference turns chiefly on the question of the appropriate price deflator, it being now suggested that previous deflators, based largely on import and export prices, have overestimated the actual fall in the general price level. See DEANE (1968).

16. MOORSTEEN and POWELL (1966), 293, 181.

17. DEANE and COLE (1967), 270.

18. TIBOR BARNA, 'On Measuring Capital', in LUTZ and HAGUE (1961), 92–3.

19. DEANE and COLE (1967), 265, 307.

20. W. MALENBAUM, *East and West in India's Development* (Washington, National Planning Association, 1959), 25.

21. In LUTZ and HAGUE (1961), 95.

22. KUZNETS (1960), 24.

23. See the report of the debate on Domar's paper in LUTZ and HAGUE (1961), 338–50.

24. MOORSTEEN and POWELL (1966), 252–3.

25. HOFFMANN (1965), 23.

26. MATTHEWS, *loc. cit.*, Chart II, 9.

27. CAIRNCROSS (1962), 78–80.

28. In LUTZ and HAGUE (1961), 117.

29. MADDISON (1964), Table III–2, 77 and 82.

30. MOORSTEEN and POWELL (1966), 12.

31. In LUTZ and HAGUE (1961), 103–15.

32. HOFFMANN (1965), Diagram 5, p. 48.

33. KUZNETS (1961), 45.

34. MATTHEWS, *loc. cit.*, 11; KUZNETS (1961), 25; DENISON (1967), fn. 11, 121–2.

35. DENISON (1967), 117.

36. For a recent and very useful summary of the literature to which the discussion in the text owes much, see D. HAMBERG, 'Saving and Economic Growth', *Economic Development and Cultural Change*, 17 (July 1969), 460–82. It should perhaps be added that the overall view to which the discussion in the text tends is one which Professor Hamberg would probably not share.

37. See above, pp. 24–5.

38. DEANE and COLE (1967), 261–3.

39. H. ROSOVSKY, *Capital Formation in Japan 1868–1940* (New York, Free Press of Glencoe, 1961), Table 3, p. 9, and Table 5, p. 15.

40. Comments regarding these and other countries for which no other reference is given are based on the data in KUZNETS (1961), Appendix tables, 58–123.

41. HOFFMANN (1965), Table 36, 104–5.

42. MOORSTEEN and POWELL (1966), Table T–50, 364.

43. Calculated from BUTLIN (1964), Table 1, p. 11.

44. ROBERT E. GALLMAN, 'Gross National Product in the United States, 1834–1909', in N.B.E.R. (1966), Table 3, p. 11.

45. S. POLLARD, 'The Growth and Distribution of Capital in Great Britain, c. 1770–1870', in I.C.E.H. (1965), 335–65.

46. W. HOFFMANN, *British Industry, 1700–1950*, trans. W. O. HENDERSON and W. H. CHALONER (Oxford, Blackwell, 1955), Table 5, p. 31, and Diagram P, 319.

47. cf. G. RANIS, 'The Capital-Output Ratio in Japanese Economic Development', *Review of Economic Studies*, XXVI (October 1958), 23–32.

48. MATTHEWS, *loc. cit.*, 11. As discussed in the text, the rise in the British *ICOR* since the war, as compared with the 1930s, is only to be expected, and more probably reflects changing capital utilization than any decline in the power of new investment to generate increases in output (correction having been made for price trends).

49. HOFFMANN (1965), Table 11, p. 47.

50. MOORSTEEN and POWELL (1966), Table 6–4, 160.

51. POLLARD, *loc. cit.*

52. S. KUZNETS, 'Capital Formation in Modern Economic Growth', in I.C.E.H. (1965), 33–4.

53. For some useful comments on farming capital in early-modern England, see P. J. BOWDEN in J. THIRSK (ed.), *The Agrarian History of England and Wales 1500–1640* (Cambridge, Cambridge U.P., 1967), 655–6.

54. R. H. HILTON, 'Rent and Capital Formation in Feudal Society', in I.C.E.H. (1962), 33–68.

55. On this theme, see also M. M. POSTAN, 'Investment in Medieval Agriculture', *Journal of Economic History*, XXVII (1967), 576–87.

56. CARLO M. CIPOLLA, 'Note sulla storia del saggio d'interesse', *Economia Internazionale*, V (1952), 255–74.

57. K. G. DAVIES, 'Joint-stock Investment in the Later Seventeenth Century', *Economic History Review*, Sec. Ser. IV (1951–2), 283–301.

58. See above, p. 117.

59. E. M. CARUS-WILSON, 'An Industrial Revolution of the Thirteenth Century', *Economic History Review*, XI (1941), 39–60.

60. J. D. GOULD, 'The Price Revolution Reconsidered', *Economic History Review*, Sec. Ser. XVII (December 1964), 249–66.

61. L. STONE, 'The Nobility in Business', *Explorations in Entrepreneurial History*, X (December 1957), 54–61.

62. J. U. NEF, 'The Progress of Technology and the Growth of Large-scale Industry in Great Britain, 1540–1640', *Economic History Review*, V (October 1934), 3–24.

63. E. KERRIDGE, *The Agricultural Revolution* (London, Allen & Unwin, 1967).

64. LEWIS (1955), Ch. V, 2, (b); M. POSTAN, 'Recent Trends in the Accumulation of Capital', *Economic History Review*, VI (October 1935), 1–12.

65. POSTAN, *loc. cit.*, 3.

66. E. ROLL, *An Early Experiment in Industrial Organization* (New York, Kelley Reprints of Economic Classics, 1968), 100–7; K. G. DAVIES, 'Joint-stock Investment in the Later Seventeenth Century', *Economic History Review*, Sec. Ser. IV (1951–2), 288.

67. F. CROUZET, 'La Formation du capital en Grande Bretagne pendant la révolution industrielle', in I.C.E.H. (1962), 622–3.

68. ASHTON (1955), 119.

69. H. A. SHANNON, 'The Limited Companies of 1866–1883', *Economic History Review*, IV (October 1933), 290–316.

70. J. H. CLAPHAM, *The Economic Development of France and Germany 1815–1914*, 4th ed. (Cambridge, Cambridge U.P., 1951), 394.

71. This section owes much to the taxonomy proposed by Gurley and Shaw: see especially J. GURLEY and E. S. SHAW, 'Financial Aspects of Economic Development', *American Economic Review*, XLV (September 1955), 515–38.

72. DAVID J. OTT, 'The Financial Development of Japan 1878–1958', *Journal of Political Economy*, 69 (April 1961), 122–41.

73. A convenient summary is L. DAVIS, 'Capital Immobilities and Finance Capitalism: A Study of Economic Evolution in the United States 1820–1920', *Explorations in Entrepreneurial History*, Sec. Ser. I (1963), 88–105. See also the same author's 'The Investment Market, 1870–1914: The Evolution of a National Market', *Journal of Economic History*, XXV (September 1965), 355–99, and 'The Capital Markets and Industrial Concentration: The U.S. and U.K., a Comparative Study', *Economic History Review*, Sec. Ser. XIX (August 1966), 255–72.

74. RONDO CAMERON, 'Theoretical Bases of a Comparative Study of the Role of Financial Institutions in the Early Stages of Industrialization', in I.C.E.H. (1962), 578.

75. JAMES S. DUESENBERRY, *Income, Saving, and the Theory of Consumer Behaviour* (Cambridge, Mass., Harvard U.P., 1949).

76. MILTON FRIEDMAN, *A Theory of the Consumption Function* (Princeton, N.J., Princeton U.P., 1957).

77. RAYMOND W. GOLDSMITH, *A Study of Saving in the United States*, 3 vols (Princeton, N.J., Princeton U.P., 1955–6).

78. IRWIN FRIEND and I. B. KRAVIS, 'Entrepreneurial Income, Saving and Investment', *American Economic Review*, XLVII (June 1957), 269.

79. Goldsmith includes consumer durables in personal savings, which is one of the reasons why his estimates are higher than those of most other writers.

80. See the article cited in note 78, and also M. SHINOHARA, 'The Structure of Saving and the Consumption Function in Postwar Japan', *Journal of Political Economy*, 67 (December 1959), 589–91.

81. EARL J. HAMILTON, 'American Treasure and the Rise of Capitalism (1500–1700)', *Economica*, IX (November 1929), 338–57.

82. J. D. GOULD, 'The Price Revolution Reconsidered', *Economic History Review*, Sec. Ser. XVII (December 1964), 249–66.

83. CAMERON, *op. cit.*, 586.

84. See pp. 247–51 below.

85. Useful summaries are given in KUZNETS (1966), Table 5.3, 236–9, and in DUNNING (1970), Ch. I.

86. KUZNETS (1966), 329.

87. DUNNING (1970), 18.

88. UNITED NATIONS (1949), 28 ff.

89. e.g. A. K. CAIRNCROSS, *Home and Foreign Investment 1870–1913* (Cambridge, Cambridge U.P., 1953), Ch. IX; J. F. RIPPY, *British Investments in Latin America* (New York, Doubleday, 1959), *passim*.

90. M. SIMON, *The Pattern of New British Portfolio Foreign Investment, 1865–1914*, in HALL (1968), 23.

91. BUTLIN (1964), 12–15.

92. ISLAM (1960), 43.

93. LEVIN (1960), Part One.

94. RIPPY, *op. cit.*, 227, fn. 22.

95. The seminal article is 'Foreign Assistance and Economic Development', by HOLLIS B. CHENERY and ALAN M. STROUT, in *American Economic Review*, LVI (September 1966), 679–733.

96. KNAPP (1957).

97. Calculated from data in A. H. IMLAH, *Economic Elements in the Pax Britannica* (Cambridge, Mass., Harvard U.P., 1958), Table 4, 70–5.

98. UNITED NATIONS (1949), 1.

99. S. OKITA and T. MIKI, 'Treatment of Foreign Capital – A Case Study for Japan', in ADLER (1967).

100. J. D. GOULD, 'A Case of Unbalanced Growth', *Economic Record*, XLII (June 1966), 317, drawing on the researches of Noel G. Butlin.

101. ISLAM (1960), 21–2.

102. HUGH G. J. AITKEN, *American Capital and Canadian Resources* (Cambridge, Mass., Harvard U.P., 1961), 50, 69–71.

103. cf. DUNNING (1970), 33.

104. LEWIS (1954); see further below, pp. 406–7.

105. There is an excellent summary by W. BAER and M. H. SIMONSEN, 'American Capital and Brazilian Nationalism', *Yale Review*, LIII (December 1963), 192–8, excerpted in BERNSTEIN, 1966. See also PEARSON (1969), Ch. 5.

106. ADLER (1967), 190.

107. DUNNING (1970), 32.

108. JOHN J. DEUTSCH in HUGH G. J. AITKEN *et al.*, *The American Economic Impact on Canada* (Durham, N.C., Duke U.P. and Cambridge, Cambridge U.P., 1959), 46.

109. PEARSON (1969), Ch. 8.

110. MYRDAL (1968), 634–7.

111. PAUL BAIROCH, *Diagnostic de l'évolution économique du Tiers-Monde 1900–1966* (Paris, Gauthier-Villars, 1967), 193; B. BALASSA, 'The First Half of the Development Decade: Growth, Trade and the Balance of Payments of the Developing Countries, 1960–65', *Banca Nazionale del Lavoro Quarterly Review*, 21 (December 1968), 332–59; PEARSON (1969), 27–8.

112. An unusually articulate, though not very closely argued, denial of this view is to be found in P. T. BAUER, 'Dissent on Development', *Scottish Journal of Political Economy*, XVI (February 1969), 75–94.

113. O. CRISP, 'French Investment in Russian Joint-Stock Companies, 1894–1914', *Business History*, 2 (June 1960), 75–90.

114. See JOHN F. GALLAGHER, 'The Sears, Roebuck and Company Venture in Latin America', in BERNSTEIN, 1966.

4　Foreign Trade and Economic Growth

Trade, State and economy in early modern times

The role of foreign trade in economic growth, like that of agriculture, has been the subject of considerable disagreement among theorists. Trade has differed from agriculture, however, in having been the subject also of continuous and detailed government intervention for many centuries. For this there are several reasons.

One is fiscal. Rulers in countries at an early stage of economic and political development commonly experience great difficulty in raising an adequate revenue, and foreign trade has some outstanding attractions as a target for the tax gatherer. Such societies generate a high proportion of their income in the countryside, either from peasants whose output is too meagre and insufficiently channelled through the market place to be taxable, or from large landowners with sufficient political influence to resist taxation. The administrative machine, moreover, is rarely capable either of assessing wealth and income with accuracy or of enforcing tax collection with vigour, the more so as income-generating activity is spread more evenly and thinly over the whole area of the State than in countries with geographically-concentrated areas of industrial activity. Foreign trade, by contrast, is almost always monetized; it is carried on by a class which, though often individually wealthy, is not commonly as influential politically as the landowners and, being dependent on State support (for example in bargaining with foreign powers), cannot resist a tax *quid pro quo*; and it is physically channelled through a relatively small number of locations, making it relatively easy to mulct. Moreover, some share of the burden of taxes on trade can normally be passed on to the foreigner, from whose customs duties one is likely to suffer some reciprocal damage; so that to some extent trade taxes can be 'wrapped up in the flag' and rationalized by appeals to patriotism.

Though for such reasons as these taxes on foreign trade are a particularly attractive type of revenue in low-income and politically backward countries, they have also generated an important fraction of revenue in some more advanced societies. A case in point is that of federal States where the different levels of government compete for sources of revenue. Geography – some of the constituent units may have no common boundary with foreign countries – and the close relationship between political and economic unity alike suggest that the regulation of foreign trade must fall to the central government. In the later nineteenth century the German Empire and the United States of America were major countries in which trade taxes yielded a substantial part of the revenue of the central government.

Fiscal considerations were not, however, the only ones which made foreign trade a matter of persistent government concern in earlier centuries. The State's need for revenue and its power to regulate trade, and the merchant's need for State support, combined to make it probable that State control would be manipulated to favour particular interests, the more so since trading groups naturally possess greater cohesion and can more clearly formulate and campaign for their common ends than, for example, peasants or small retailers. The English overseas trading companies during the reigns of Elizabeth the First and the early Stuarts exemplify these relationships particularly clearly. Finally, the frequent use of trade as an instrument of diplomacy and the close connection between merchant shipping and sea power provided another reason for State concern with foreign commerce, especially in the early modern centuries when the intensity of national rivalries was greater than the capacity to maintain standing armies and navies.

Historical examples abound. Every schoolboy knows that the Lord Chancellor of England sits on a wool-sack, testimony to not only the economic but (through Parliament's claim to a control over taxation) the constitutional significance of wool exports in the life of medieval England. But it was in the early modern centuries that the interest in foreign trade, on the part both of government and of writers on economic topics, reached its apogee. The name bestowed by Adam Smith on the economic policy of the eighteenth and earlier centuries – the *Mercantile System* – reflects the central importance of foreign trade in its aims and assumptions.

The rise in the importance of the foreign sector owed its origins to the great voyages of discovery which helped to bring the Middle Ages to an end. The exploration of the west coast of Africa, the opening of an all-sea route to the spice islands of the East, and the discovery of the Americas ushered in a new age of oceanic commerce and of European colonization and conquest in other continents. They brought, too, an intense commercial rivalry among the maritime powers of Western Europe for control of the lucrative *entrepôt* trade in spices, in sugar, in tobacco, in Indian cotton cloths, and for a share in the flood of New World silver with which Spain paid for her armies and her armadas and for Spanish rule in the Low Countries. In the process the map of European commerce was substantially redrawn; the Indian Ocean, the archipelagos and peninsulas of South-east Asia, and the Atlantic were added to and in some measure even replaced the medieval commercial routes in Europe's sheltered inland seas, and Portugal, France, Holland and above all England – the last so much on the periphery of European economic life during the Middle Ages – now found themselves strategically placed to exploit the commercial possibilities of the new ocean routes and thus thrust into the centre of economic activity.

The importance of these new trading opportunities to

general economic development prior to the industrial revolution is hard to assess. It would be easy, in contemplating the romantic and colourful exploits of early modern traders and colonizers, to allow one's sense of proportion to become dulled. England, for example, was still dominantly an agricultural nation in 1700, with probably two-thirds or more of her population primarily tillers of the soil. None of the new commercial fortunes could compare with the wealth of the greatest landed estates. The trade (imports plus domestic exports)/income ratio, according to Gregory King's estimates, was something like 15 per cent about 1688, a figure which had doubled by the early nineteenth century and trebled by the 1870s.[1] And the majority of England's trade was still with Europe throughout the pre-industrial period, though Europe's dominance was declining to the advantage of trade with the East and West Indies and with the American mainland colonies.[2]

On the other hand, foreign trade had undoubtedly increased more rapidly during the sixteenth and seventeenth centuries than either population or income,* and the growth of long-distance trade, in particular, had brought with it important innovations in shipbuilding, marine insurance, company organization and financial institutions and expertise. While, of course, developments in the field of money and credit had other origins than foreign trade, especially those connected with the financial exigencies of the State and of the great landed estates, it is impossible

---

* There has been little attempt to synthesize our knowledge of the quantitative development of England's foreign trade in the early modern centuries. Exports and imports may have roughly balanced at somewhere in the region of a quarter of a million pounds sterling each early in Henry VII's reign. In the closing years of the seventeenth century (domestic) exports were worth about £4½ million and imports £6 million. Trade had therefore increased in value, even excluding re-exports, by a factor of about 20. Allowing for a four-fold rise in prices, which is almost certainly over-generous for internationally-traded goods, the expansion in volume terms would have been at least five-fold. Population is unlikely to have more than doubled and *per capita* incomes may well have fallen rather than risen on average (see Chapter 1).

to deny the foreign sector a substantial share of the responsibility.

It is an open question, again, just how to apportion responsibility for the fall of the rate of interest from the 10 to 14 per cent which was common in early Tudor times to the 4 or 5 per cent at which, so some experts believe, credit was going begging in the late seventeenth century.[3] The rise of financial intermediaries and the associated developments in institutions and knowledge of business and accounting, which were partly but only partly linked with the growth of the foreign sector, were responsible in some measure. The increase in monetary stocks which the cumulative favourable balance of trade, in line with mercantilist aspirations, had brought about doubtless also contributed to this great secular fall in borrowing rates – a fall which a leading Italian historian has singled out, in contrast with the more widely-discussed inflation of the same period, as the *true* economic revolution of the early modern centuries.[4] Finally, of course, some advantage – it is again questionable just how much – accrued to England from her growing colonial empire, which constituted both a protected market for her growing variety of manufactured exports and a monopsonistically-exploited source of imports to feed the important *entrepôt* trade and the substantial commercial and industrial (processing) activity which it generated in England.

On the whole, it is probably fair to generalize that the 'commercial revolution' of the seventeenth century has survived the iconoclastic scepticism of modern historical research better than either the 'industrial revolution', for which it is supposed to have been a condition, or the 'agricultural revolution', which acted as a second prologue. But the example of Holland, which surpassed England in commercial and financial development for most of the seventeenth century but lacked her advantages in the resource field, shows that it was not a *sufficient* condition for sustained general economic growth. The example of England's continental imitators, on the other hand, suggests that it was not a *necessary* condition either. The implication

that there have historically been not one but several alternative paths of economic growth, resembling each other
only at a very high level of macro-economic aggregation (if
at all), is an idea which is forced much more often on the
student of economic history than on the student of theoretical
growth models. It should be added that the foregoing
summary points to the 'spin-off' benefits of trade, rather
than to the normal 'gains from trade' of classical analysis, as
perhaps the most important contribution of the foreign
sector to general economic development in the early modern
period.

This perhaps goes some way to explain the apparent
paradox that while the Mercantilists held seemingly narrow
and (in the estimate of most later economists) largely
erroneous views on the economics of international trade, they
nevertheless accorded the latter a central, indeed dominating, role in promoting economic growth; whereas the British
classical economists of the nineteenth century, who provided
new and superior insights into the effects of foreign trade on
real income, accorded it a much less prominent role. The
paradox is the more remarkable in that, as we have already
seen, Britain's trade/income ratio was undoubtedly substantially higher during the heyday of classical economics
than in Mercantilist times. The greater relative importance
of the 'spin-off' effects and lesser importance of the orthodox
'gains from trade' (which are, in fact, a *narrower* concept of
the growth-promoting effects of trade) would help to explain
and justify the peculiarities of Mercantilist thought.

It is clear, of course, that comparative advantage in the
classical sense did play a smaller part in generating trade
flows in the medieval and early modern centuries, when
many important items of international commerce – salt, dye
materials, wheat, fine wool, spices, sugar, timber – were
resource-based, than in more recent times. The frequently-
criticized Mercantilist views that total commercial activity
was limited in extent, that the objective of trade policy
should be to grasp as large a fraction of this total as possible
for one's country, and that one country's gain was another's

loss, were not perhaps entirely misconceived, given the basis of trade in absolute rather than comparative advantage and the great importance of the colonial and carrying trades in seventeenth-century commercial life. It was precisely, however, in the seventeenth century that new opportunities for international specialization were beginning to emerge with the growth of competition between alternative sources of supply and between competing products. These changes posed problems for the English textile industries, which encountered increasing competition in their export markets in the first half of the seventeenth century and (in the form of the new Indian 'calicoes') in the domestic market too at the end of that century.

It was in this crucible of competitive experience that new theories of the economics of trade were fashioned. A remarkable forerunner of Adam Smith, discussing the challenge posed to economic policy by the competition of the calicoes, argued that it was to England's advantage to import rather than produce at home whenever the labour cost was less (more strictly, the labour time was shorter) abroad. He went on to argue that

> To imploy to make Manufactures here, more Hands than are necessary to procure the like things from the *East-Indies*, is not only to imploy so many to no profit, it is also to lose the labour of so many Hands which might be imploy'd to the profit of the Kingdom . . . as long as *England* is not built, beautify'd, and improv'd to the utmost Perfection . . .

To this primitive perception of the notion of opportunity cost, the writer adds the reflection that the competition resulting from free imports would stimulate 'the invention of Arts, and Mills, and Engines' and promote the division of labour, in both cases with beneficial effects on productivity, and would cause a redistribution of capital tending to equalize marginal yields in all uses.[5]

It is true that this remarkable pamphlet was tendentious, being clearly written by a well-wisher of the East India Company, and also that it was unsuccessful in its aim of averting the imposition of import restrictions. Neither of these circumstances is relevant, of course, to an appraisal of its analytical contributions. Further, other writers in the first three-quarters of the eighteenth century produced arguments conflicting with other Mercantilist tenets, so that Adam Smith's critique of the 'Mercantile System', imposing though it was in its cumulative effect, was not particularly novel and, indeed, was perhaps less penetrating analytically than several earlier commentaries in more occasional vein. Few of the 'spin-offs' of foreign trade in the early modern centuries were as important as the contribution made by the 'occasional' literature which it engendered to the development of economic analysis.

Do trade ratios decline?

It has been mentioned that England's trade/income ratio undoubtedly rose from the late seventeenth to the late nineteenth century, and it is virtually certain that it had also risen substantially over the two preceding centuries at least. Is this rising trend universally characteristic of the relationship between trade and economic development? Some years ago two American scholars rejuvenated an argument going back at least to Torrens that the normal accompaniment to economic growth is a *declining* trade ratio.[6] They buttressed this claim by presenting statistics, drawn largely from the publications of international organizations, permitting calculations of the trade/income ratio for fourteen predominantly industrialized countries for four benchmark years from 1928 to 1957, and for eleven such countries from 1913 to 1957. They also collected estimates for a smaller number of countries from much earlier periods.

Their evidence, however, is far from justifying the confident assertion of any 'law' relating economic growth to a declining foreign trade share. For eight out of Deutsch and Eckstein's fourteen countries the export/income ratio was lower in 1957 than in 1928; in six cases it was higher. The import/income ratio split evenly, seven up and seven down. The 1913/57 comparison looks slightly more convincing, seven out of the eleven showing a smaller trade (export plus import)/income ratio in the later than in the earlier year. But the economic historian is quick to recognize that a comparison between 1928 (or 1913) and 1957 incorporates the effects of the world-wide impediments to trade offered by the great depression of the early 1930s, the autarkic policies which it provoked (which are even today far from completely abandoned), and the world wars. The fact that for almost all of the countries studied the trough value of the trade/income ratio came in 1938, or in 1945 or 1946, suggests that these world-wide influences, rather than any influence arising out of the structural relationship between income and trade in the individual economy, dominate the Deutsch and Eckstein statistics. Another pointer in the same direction is that in almost all cases where estimates for a starting year earlier than 1913 are available, the trade/income ratio is seen to have risen appreciably in the decades before World War I, and in most cases the post-World War II ratio is higher than that for the starting year.

Two further limitations of the Deutsch–Eckstein material combine to strengthen the view that history does not support the 'law of declining trade' which they propose. First, their data are presented in current prices. But a detailed study of U.S. trade has shown that when current-price income and foreign trade values for that country are suitably deflated, the resulting constant-price series completely eliminates the fall in the U.S. trade/income ratio from the 1880s to 1958/60.[7] The reason is that domestic prices and the prices of internationally-traded goods have diverged, probably because of the tariff and other trade-destroying measures and because of the growing relative importance of goods and services which cannot be traded and which therefore tend to become dearer relative to goods whose price is restrained by international competition. Kuznets, who is somewhat sceptical about the 'law of declining foreign trade', presents current – and constant – price evidence for eleven high-income countries (including Japan) over varying periods from their respective 'Early Phases' to the 1950s. For six of the eleven, the trade/income ratio in current prices shows a higher end-year than beginning-year value; but in *constant* prices, rises outnumber falls by 9 to 1, only the U.S.A. ratio falling slightly between the two terminal dates.[8]

The second limitation on both the Deutsch–Eckstein and other similar comparisons is that they include merchandise trade only in the numerator of the trade/income ratio, while including (of course) the full range of economic activity in the income measure used as the denominator. Since in the later stages of development the share of services in the national income usually tends to rise, a downward tendency is thus automatically built into the trade/income ratio. A possible solution would be to include the export and import of services in addition to merchandise trade, but this requirement would reduce the range of evidence at present available, since balance of payments estimates (including 'invisibles') are available, as one moves back through time, for a much smaller number of countries than statistics of merchandise trade alone. It is clear, however, that the proposed amendment would yield analytically more meaningful ratios. It is also clear that it would change the picture substantially in some cases. In the United Kingdom's case, for example, the rise in the trade/income ratio would continue through to World War I on the 'goods and services' basis, instead of stagnating, as it does on the basis of merchandise trade alone, from about the 1880s. For Norway, with its important exports of shipping services, the total trade/income ratio would be substantially higher at all times than the already high merchandise trade/income ratio, and the upward slope of the historical trend would probably be increased.

Actually, one wonders in any event what significance to attach to the changes over time of the trade/income ratio, however measured. For a little theoretical reflection suggests that there is not likely to be any simple functional relationship, invariant over time, between trade and income levels. Rather one can hypothesize a considerable number of possible relationships, some determined by changing technological linkages, some by changes in the pattern of expenditure, some by variations in the resource/income or resource/population ratio, through which changes over time in levels of real income and population might be expected to exert influence, sometimes positive and sometimes negative, on the propensity to export or import particular types of goods and services.

Professor Kindleberger has drawn up an interesting table which schematically presents the likely direction of the influence on trade of factors conditioning economic growth at various stages of development.[9] Thus, for example, during the 'Commercial Revolution', which is said to end the phase of stagnation, resource-based exports increase due to increasing integration in the market; in 'take-off' rising incomes lead to increased imports of consumer goods, and increasing capital formation, with domestic investment exceeding savings, calls for borrowing abroad and increased imports of capital goods; in 'maturity' the development of product differentiation tends to increase exports and decrease imports; in 'decline' the depletion of resources brings decreasing exports and increasing imports of raw materials. Overall, expansionary influences outnumber contractionary influences 4 to nil during 'Commercial Revolution', 8 to 2 during 'take-off', and 7 to 5 during 'maturity', while the latter outnumber the former 3 to 2 during 'decline'. As Kindleberger points out, 'the schema is highly general as well as purely qualitative' (that is, the strength of the various influences is not quantified and one cannot add them together to get a net outcome), but Kindleberger, a guarded believer in the law of declining foreign trade, could claim that at least the relative numbers of positive and negative influences at the various stages fit the historical movements of trade ratios reasonably well.

There is always a danger, however, in constructing analytical schema of this type where the answer is known in advance, and certainly Kindleberger's selection omits some factors which have historically been of the greatest importance in influencing trade ratios, though admittedly they have not been systematically related – or not obviously so – to economic development: tariffs, import controls, the subsidizing of import-replacing activity (e.g. agriculture in countries of the European Common Market). Again, some of Kindleberger's influences seem, analytically, to promise increases in trade *relative* to income, others only absolute increases (which could at times be *declines relative to income*). Finally, there is every reason for thinking that the strength of the various influences will vary widely for different countries at similar income levels. The 'scale of production' effects will surely depend on population as well as on level of *per capita* income; the onset and relative importance of resource depletion will vary according to the resource/population ratio, and so on. Therefore there is every reason for thinking that even at similar stages of development the net outcome will vary from country to country.

This conclusion does not add up to a recommendation to abandon the search for meaningful uniformities in the relationship of growth and trade, but merely to the belief that such meaning, analytically, will be found to reside on a more disaggregated level than the overall trade/income ratio. It has not been proved that the 'central tendency' (that is, the trend of the summation of the various individual influences for a given country) has any analytical interest or meaning *in itself*, even where it appears to persist for a considerable period. It is entirely possible that the limited degree of similarity which certainly exists in the historical shape of the 'central tendency' for various countries arises from world-wide influences such as the succession of wars, depressions and recoveries; whereas the influence of the analytically-meaningful relations between growth and trade varies, in net outcome, from country to country and shows up in the degree of *dis*similarity in those same historical shapes.

Inter-country differences in trade ratios

If the degree to which individual countries have experienced similar changes in their trade/income ratio through time is uncertain both as to its extent and still more as to its analytical significance, inter-country differences in the level of the trade/income ratio appear to be more firmly established and more meaningful. Kuznets' list shows trade (merchandise exports plus imports)/G.N.P. ratios for post-World War II years ranging from 7·3 per cent for the U.S.A. to 157·0 per cent for Luxembourg.[10] Although the opportunity to effect inter-country comparisons for more remote dates is of course limited to a much smaller number of countries, the evidence is that substantial and consistent differences are of long standing, though they have almost certainly tended to widen, rather than to narrow, through time. The degree of reliance on foreign trade thus appears to differ more widely and more consistently between countries than it does for individual countries at different times, which in turn suggests that permanent or very slowly-changing features of the various economies are more meaningfully related to their trade participation levels than are the stages of economic development they pass through. This proposition is of course entirely consistent with the sceptical conclusion reached above about the 'law of declining trade'.

The most-frequently cited of the more permanent characteristics explaining inter-country differences in trade/income ratios is size. Several statistical tests have confirmed the commonsense judgment that other things being equal, small countries are likely to have bigger trade ratios than large.[11] The relationships between size and trade are several, and can be classified according to criterion adopted for judging 'size'. Countries of small extent are likely to have less varied mineral resources and to embrace less varied climatic regions and soil types than large ones, thus necessitating higher trade specialization for a given level of income. (The correlation is far from perfect, of course: Chile is only half the size of Indonesia, but it stretches through about 38 degrees of latitude from the tropics to sub-Antarctic regions, whereas Indonesia is tropical in climate and vegetation throughout.)

Physically larger countries are also likely to have relatively large areas where foreign trade is discouraged by high transport costs to the frontier. This consideration was more important in earlier times when transport costs were relatively higher. Before the advent of the railway the interiors of the great continents were virtually inaccessible from the point of view of the international economy, save for the precious metals; for centuries its European conquerors brought little save gold and silver from any part of the New World more than a score or two miles from navigable water. Even after railways were built the incorporation of countries like Brazil or even Australia into the international economy was spatially piecemeal, limited hinterlands being linked by radial railway nets with the chief ports, facilitating the export of essentially local resources but doing nothing to integrate the national economy.

Indeed the style of trade specialization referred to has bequeathed a legacy of regional differences which has coloured both the economic and political development of such countries. This effect was particularly marked where, as in the two large countries named, the local railway systems were built to different gauges in accordance with the local terrain. Even in Australia, where regional differences are muted as in all high-income countries, it is only a few years since it first became possible to ship freight by rail between Sydney and Melbourne, the two largest cities, without a break of gauge. Moreover, even railroads permit only a limited radius of economic penetration for bulky commodities; in 1937 it was estimated that in normal times iron ore and phosphates for export could only be worked to about 60 miles from the coast, and that of the base metals which could bear very long land transport, only copper and tin were important.[12] The remarkable growth of international trade in resource- and climate-based specializations from the mid-nineteenth century through to the depression of the 1930s was, geographically-speaking, extremely 'spotty'; even where it stimulated growth *on average* it did little to foster national economic integration and in many countries probably accentuated rather than mitigated regional inequalities.

Smallness in the sense of a small population is significant

to trade, if at all, in rather different ways. It is usually argued that countries small in population are at a disadvantage in many branches of manufacturing because their markets are inadequate to permit the capture of all available economies of scale. There is certainly some truth in this. Few if any countries of less than 5 million inhabitants have a genuine automobile industry (as opposed to assembling knocked-down imports); few if any of less than 10 million make more than the occasional hand-built aeroplane. In modern 'science-based' industries where research and development costs are very high the market counts for even more; Europe is struggling, collectively, to deny the U.S.A. a free-world monopoly of the making of computers, and Britain and France, two fairly large and wealthy countries, have probably overtaxed their resources in trying jointly to pioneer the supersonic airliner.

But computers and supersonic airliners do not exhaust the list of possible industrial specializations. Switzerland, Denmark, Sweden, Belgium and Israel among others prove that there is ample opportunity for small countries to build relatively large export trades in manufactures. Fundamentally this is because economies of scale are not nearly so important in many manufactures as is commonly supposed. Small population may also be offset by high *per capita* income for products in income-elastic demand, and while most manufacturers like to claim that a big home demand is essential as a secure base for developing an export trade, the element of self-interested deception in this claim is revealed by the example of Switzerland, which exports between 75 and 95 per cent of the output of its distinctive manufactures. A small home population need not, therefore, mean a correspondingly small market for manufactures.

It is sometimes argued, too, that there are compensations in small size; that the small country finds it easier to 'find a niche' for itself in world trade than the large, and can specialize very completely along the lines of its comparative advantage without turning the terms of trade against itself, as the large country cannot: 'the importance of being unimportant'.[13] There is perhaps a confusion here between the size of the exporting country and its share of the world market for particular commodities, which are not the same thing: Switzerland used to command a large fraction of the world market for wrist-watches as New Zealand still does for lamb. But perhaps there is something to it: among the countries of industrial Europe which Kindleberger studied, it was three small exporters of manufactures, Sweden, Switzerland and Belgium, which enjoyed the most favourable development of their terms of trade over the interval 1913–52.[14] The advantage of a large home market in industries of rapidly advancing technology is substantial, however, and as we shall see an important and growing share of world trade consists of the export by a few large countries of products on the technological frontier which they have pioneered. Nor is this entirely a matter of recouping 'R and D' costs over a large output, for the days of the sole inventor are not past[15] – one man dreamed up the jet engine, one man discovered penicillin – and other things being equal, it is surely likely that a country of 200 million people will come up with more sole inventors than a country of 5 million.

The importance of domestic market size in the period before World War II can only be the subject of generalized argument since there has been surprisingly little study of the magnitude of economies of scale for any but recent times. One remarkable exception must be mentioned, G. T. Jones' study, *Increasing Return*.[16] The book is remarkable both for the precocity of its theme and methodology, considering its date of completion, and for the range of technological insight and econometric ingenuity shown by an author still in his early twenties. Unfortunately, the aim to measure the magnitude of scale effects by calculating the rate of increase of total productivity for industries which were *not* experiencing major technological improvements fails in its purpose because, as the author rightly points out, a significant element in raising productivity is a host of *minor*, often unnoticed, mechanical and organizational improvements, many of which could have been achieved even without any increase in scale.[17] Jones' estimate of 'scale effects' proper in his five industries must therefore represent an upper limit, particularly since, as he tells us, 'all arbitrary decisions upon questions of technique have been such as to exaggerate the tendency to increasing return'. These shortcomings, however, actually strengthen the thesis advanced here, since Jones' estimates are in any event quite low, and the upshot is therefore to suggest an extremely modest role for scale effects in the period covered, that is roughly 1850–1920.

Though Jones' argument might not carry full conviction in itself, his conclusion is consistent with more general evidence bearing on most nineteenth-century industry. It is well known, for example, that in most industries plant size remained very small in the leading industrial nations at least until the very end of the nineteenth century, and that relatively little use was made of the company laws in most manufacturing industries, except to gain for small family firms the protection of limited liability. The first returns of Britain's factory inspectors recorded 1,154 cotton mills in 1834; the number passed the 2,000 mark early in the second half of the nineteenth century and hovered around the 2,600 level for at least two decades after the 'cotton famine' had ended.[18] Both the large number of mills and the upward trend suggest that no firm had the ability to oust its rivals by lower-cost production, and that internal economies of scale must have become insignificant at quite a modest level of output. Hence it is difficult to believe that the size of the domestic market was a severe restriction on the capacity to industrialize, at least in certain industries, for most nineteenth-century nations, and it is worth notice that though both the U.S.A. and Germany pleaded the need for tariffs to enable them to industrialize against Britain's early lead, both countries exceeded Great Britain in total population, and one at least in aggregate income, during the high tariff period beginning in the last quarter of the nineteenth century.

However, it seems likely that the scope for economies of scale became larger in the late nineteenth century both because new processes and products emerged in which the downward slope of the average cost curve was greater, and because some of the disadvantages of large-scale production were reduced by the fall of transport costs and the innovation of new managerial techniques. It is therefore likely that before World War I the size of the domestic market had begun to exert some influence on the ability to develop a wide spectrum of competitive manufacturing activity, though inability to cover the whole range of manufactures would not of course prevent the production and indeed export of some, as such examples as Belgium and Switzerland were already showing.

The preceding discussion is confined in part, however, to economies of scale *internal* to the individual firm. It is possible that in the nineteenth century, in many industries, *external* economies such as facilities for servicing and repairing machinery were more important. The pronounced tendency towards the spatial concentration of particular industries suggests the presence of such external economies, especially where other reasons (such as the location of raw material deposits) seem to be lacking. In many unindustrialized countries the absence or inadequacy of such facilities may conceivably have been a more serious difficulty than inadequate market size. Until further research has been done, little can be said for or against this hypothesis.

'Vertical' specialization before World War I

We have discussed two factors which seem to be correlated with inter-country differences in trade/income ratios: physical size (as a proxy, largely, for size and variety of resource endowment) and population. The former seems to be a more important aspect of 'size' than the latter in this context. In the late nineteenth century, however, it was the relationship *between* these two measurements of size which in some cases became particularly important – that is, the *density of population*. International trade from about the middle of the nineteenth century to World War I or even later was characterized to an unusual extent by what one might term a 'vertical' specialization between primary-producing and manufacturing areas, most trade consisting of an exchange of food and raw materials against manufactures and services, with relatively little balancing of primary products against primary products or of manufactures against manufactures. The facts that trade in primary products is estimated to have been fairly consistently about two-thirds of all commodity trade in this period, and that there was *some* exchange of manufactures against manufactures, may seem difficult to square with the notion of vertical balance, for it may seem to follow as a matter of arithmetical necessity that there should have been a very considerable exchange of primary products against primary products. There was indeed *some*, as when Britain exported coal or re-exported tea to countries from which she imported meat or wool. But the arithmetic was squared chiefly by a huge exchange of primary products against 'invisibles'. European countries, in particular, enjoyed large import surpluses of food and raw materials which were paid for by the export of shipping and other services, by the servicing of Europe's long-term capital exports, and by remittances from emigrants to friends and relatives in European countries.

Many factors contributed to the unique growth of this particular style of international trade in the late nineteenth century. On the supply side, huge areas of fertile land were opened up for the first time as the geographical expansion of settlement accelerated. It had taken roughly two and a half centuries for the North American frontier to expand from the first permanent settlements on the East Coast to the Great Rivers, roughly half the area of the continental U.S.A. (excluding Alaska). The frontier conquered the other half in about three decades. Across the Pacific, New Zealand had lain neglected for a century and a quarter after Tasman's first sighting in 1642. European and American contacts increased but slowly following Cook's rediscovery in 1769, and it was not until 1840 that the British government declared a somewhat reluctant annexation. Thereafter, however, it took only seventy years for immigrants to settle the country, the area of occupied farm land reaching over 90 per cent of its all-time peak by 1911.

There were many reasons for this acceleration in the rate of settlement, which was paralleled also in Canada, in Australia, in southern Africa and in several South American countries. Chief among them were the increased rate of population growth in these regions of recent settlement, brought about partly by higher rates of natural increase but (in some cases) chiefly by the unique swarm of inter-continental migration in the nineteenth century, and the equally unique transfers of long-term capital. This last made possible a far more rapid provision of infrastructural invest-ments than the savings of the new regions themselves could have permitted, and in particular financed the building of the railways and dock installations which made it possible to market the products of new farmland. The consequent expansion of farming was sustained by favourable develop-ments on the demand side, shortly to be mentioned. Finally, the successful farming of the newly-settled land was facili-tated by a host of technological innovations in farm machinery, in food-processing plant, and above all of course in transportation. In regard to this last it was not merely the fall in land and sea freight rates caused by the railroad and the steamship which was important, but also the greater reliability and punctuality of these newer forms of transport and the invention of special facilities such as the refrigerated railroad wagon or ship. These last-mentioned facilitated the rise of meat-packing in the American Mid-west and the de-velopment of such trades as the export of frozen meat and dairy produce from southern hemisphere producers or of bananas from Central America and the West Indian islands.[19]

By a fortunate coincidence developments on the demand side were favourable. The growth of population, income and industry in Europe and in the North-eastern United States provided a growing market for the vast increase in exportable surpluses of temperate farm products and of tropical foods, old and new, like coffee and bananas. In some instances, notably that of wheat, the supply curve seems to have shifted more rapidly than the demand curve, so that a sharp fall in prices ensued, but even so the effect on the farmer in the new lands was muted by the fall in transport costs. (In the rather extreme case of New Zealand – extreme because of the distance involved – the terms of trade improved sharply *vis-à-vis* Britain at the same time as the latter's terms of trade were also improving.) Where Europe's consumption was just beginning to outstrip its own production, imports would of course rise more rapidly than the former; where Europe's production was actually declining, the rate of expansion of imports would be even greater. Wheat illustrates the first of these cases. Wool is an example of the second, for in industrial Europe much land was becoming too valuable to sustain sheep-farming and sheep numbers declined absolutely in favour of more intensive forms of land use.

The dramatic fall in shipping freights favoured long-distance trades more than short, and bulky products more than those with a higher value/bulk ratio. This of course helps to explain the particular emphasis on distant regions of recent settlement and their distinctive products. But other bulky commodities, mineral as well as animal and vegetable, were favoured. Again good fortune played a hand. European farmers, profiting from the teaching of the new science of agricultural chemistry (and from experience) were beginning from about the middle of the nineteenth century to use increasing amounts of nitrogenous fertilizer. European industry was rapidly exhausting the continent's relatively exiguous reserves of some of the base metals, especially copper, of which over 60 per cent of Europe's needs were produced at home in the first half of the nineteenth century, but less than 30 per cent in the second half. Both were bulky products, and in both cases the fall in freights permitted distant suppliers, especially in South America, to meet the growing need for imports.

We began this discussion of the structure of late nineteenth-century trade by suggesting that of all the ways in which 'size' may be interpreted, that relating population to area – that is, density of population – was perhaps most important at that time. For the majority of these new trades were based on a comparative advantage rooted, *essentially*, in cheap land. This of course does not apply to the mineral exports – one can always try to grow wheat, but not to grow copper – nor, indeed, to climatically-demanding plants like the banana. But the most important of the new trades – wheat, meat, wool, dairy produce – involved commodities in which not only was the farmer in the areas of recent settlement in competition with his European counterpart, but he was far from being in a position of marked absolute advantage. The American wheat whose competition so distressed Old World agriculture came off at only about half the number of bushels per acre which European farmers achieved. In New Zealand, and still more in Australia, the number of sheep per acre was far below the level at which sheep-farming was becoming uneconomic in Europe. What enabled the new areas to compete was simply the devising of new agricultural techniques, of new patterns of factor inputs, designed to extract maximum benefit from their one crucial advantage, *cheap land*. It was cheap land which secured for these countries their vital niche in the pattern of world trade, and their low population/land ratio, by comparison with Europe, which made the land cheap.

It should be pointed out that in the case of the U.S.A. the pattern of 'vertical' specialization which we have been discussing resulted in inter-regional even more than in international trade. Though the U.S.A. was a great world exporter of wheat and of meat, as well as of the older staples, cotton and tobacco, the greater part of the farm output of the newly-settled Mid-west and Western States was sold in the vast, growing urban markets of the North-east. America shared, equally with New Zealand and the United Kingdom, in the gains from trade made possible by the exploitation of cheap virgin land; but she was large and diverse enough to capture these gains to a substantial degree by inter-regional trade rather than by international trade, and her (international) trade/income ratio was correspondingly lower. This should not hide from us the fact that the economic benefits (and costs) of the inter-regional trade between Mid-west and New England were in principle and probably in magnitude – proper adjustment made for population size – about the same as those of the international trade between New Zealand and Great Britain.

The expansion of trade in primary products can plausibly be interpreted as the prime mover in the whole remarkable growth of world trade between 1850 and 1914. According to the estimates of a well-known League of Nations study, the volume of world trade in primary products increased from 1876–80 to 1926–9 at a compound growth rate of 2·6 per cent per annum, slightly faster than trade in manufactures (2·4 per cent). Extending the comparison to 1936–8, the lead of primary products trade is greater, because of divergent trends during the world depression: 2·3 per cent against 1·8 per cent.[20] All these rates are, of course, substantially in excess of the growth rate of world population during the same period. In value terms, the two series moved closely together, the difference in rates of volume increase representing an improvement in the terms of trade of manufactures, and trade in primary products approximated two-thirds of all trade. Not only was trade in primary products the largest single component of late nineteenth-century trade, however; it seems reasonable to accord the developing pattern of 'vertical' international specialization a particularly prominent position in the whole – admittedly interdependent – network of economic processes which gives the period 1850–1914 its distinctive flavour. It seems reasonable to do this, despite the essentially interacting relationship between migration, capital movements, technological change and the rest, if only because the massive geographical expansion which was at the heart of the whole process is unrepeatable, there being no new comparable frontiers, at least on Earth, to conquer.

Trade as an 'engine of growth'

Historians and economists of our own day, like the statesmen and business leaders of the years after World War I, have looked back on the half-century or so ending in 1913 as a golden era. In respect of the international economy Sir Dennis Robertson aptly summarized the view of the period which many have taken when he suggested that during it foreign trade was an 'engine of growth' – a role which (writing in 1938) he did not envisage trade being likely to play so well in the future.[21] More recently Ragnar Nurkse has revived and elaborated this theme, voicing in doing so the misgivings and frustrations which many trade-dependent low-income countries have felt in recent years.[22] Nurkse drew a sombre contrast. Before 1913 the rapid growth of world trade in food and primary products ensured that small size and 'skewed' resources were not an impediment to a country's finding an opportunity to develop a growth-inducing specialization; since World War II, on the other hand, the less rapid growth of such trade has reduced the opportunities to achieve growth through this mechanism at a time when the more rapid increase of population in low-income countries and the challenge of closing the gap between them and the rich industrial world call rather for an *acceleration* of their growth rates.

Some qualifications to the 'engine of growth' view of the late nineteenth-century trade will be made in the paragraphs immediately following, and the validity of Nurkse's characterization of post-1945 trade will be discussed later in this chapter. But it is right first to underline the considerable element of truth in the Robertson–Nurkse view of the period from about the mid-nineteenth century to the outbreak of World War I. Thanks to a fortunate – though not, of course, entirely fortuitous – conjuncture of favourable circumstances, that period did offer a quite remarkable, probably unique, opportunity for countries not only to exploit comparative advantage to the full, maximizing the potential contributions of foreign trade to real income at a given moment of time, but, thanks to the rapid expansion of world trade, to achieve on-going growth through such specialization. Nor was this opportunity confined to a mere handful of countries, for rising incomes, more sophisticated tastes, and increasingly

inadequate resources in the industrial countries, together with
the march of technology demanding ever more new raw
materials, created opportunities to specialize in one or more
of a widening range of animal, vegetable and mineral
products. It is a clear fact of nineteenth-century economic
history that the number of countries becoming integrated
into the expanding international economy at one point or
another greatly increased. It is true that technological
progress and sometimes the rise of real incomes can destroy
demand for particular products as well as create it, and there
were occasional examples of such trade-destroying effects
even in the nineteenth century. (The damage done by
synthetic dye-stuffs to India's madder growers is a case in
point.) But the challenge to natural materials from synthetics
has become widespread and serious only in the mid-twentieth
century. In the period before World War I it is impossible
not to conclude that on balance technological change, as
well as the rise of incomes in industrial countries, was highly
favourable to the prospects of less developed countries seeking
opportunities for profitable international specialization.

These facts do justify a very favourable verdict in appraising the opportunities for export-led growth in the later
nineteenth and early twentieth centuries. However, it is
important also to bear in mind some qualifications and
reservations. In the first place, of course, one should stress
that the 'growth' we are speaking of is not well documented
by modern statistical research. Only a handful of industrial
countries boast estimates of national product reaching back
much before the end of the nineteenth century, and even they
are subject to considerable margins of error. For few if any
other primary producers are there estimates as detailed and
as scholarly as those of Butlin for Australia. The strong
impression of growth which leads us to speculate about
'export-led growth' may well turn out to derive, if and when
the statistical estimates are made, primarily from the clear
facts of geographical expansion of settlement and rapid
growth of population in these countries. The growth of real
income *per head* may well have been very much more modest.

This possibility finds some confirmation in Butlin's researches, for while Australian real G.D.P. rose overall at a rate of 5·0 per cent per annum from 1860 to 1889 – the dominant decades of pastoral farming in the nineteenth century – G.D.P. *per head* rose only at an annual rate of 1·4 per cent. If, to take proper account of the cost of servicing the foreign capital which played such a vital part in Australian expansion, we measure growth in terms of gross *national* rather than gross *domestic* product, the *per capita* growth rate falls to 1·2 per cent. Growth of output per head of the work force was higher, 2·3 per cent, which is quite high in terms of international comparisons for the nineteenth century.[23] But it is still true that the growth we refer to is primarily a matter of the growth of *total* income, combined with high population growth and rapid geographical expansion, rather than of a particularly remarkable growth of income per head.

The question might then be asked whether the increase of exports on which the process of growth was based *necessitated* so high a rate of growth of population, or whether society chose, so to speak, to 'spread' the available increase in export revenue over a rising population, to the (possible) benefit of growth of total income but to the detriment of income per head. The extraordinary growth of urbanization in Australia in the three decades cited, a growth for which it is extremely difficult to see complete justification in a society still living to a large extent 'off the sheep's back', would tend to give at least some support to the latter point of view. This interpretation could be sustained even more confidently in the case of New Zealand, where a hectic programme of government-subsidized immigration in the 1870s had little effect in accelerating the progress of farm formation, and contributed rather to a sharp fall in the *per capita* value of exports and to the emergence of a problem of urban unemployment. This last was sufficiently severe to induce many of the migrants who could afford the fare to leave, bringing about a period of net *emigration* – the first and one of the only three so far in New Zealand's history – in the later 1880s.

If this line of argument were sustained, it would permit us still to award very high marks for growth promotion to international trade, for the relative modesty of the rate of growth of *per capita* incomes would then appear as a consequence of society's 'choice' as to the way of sharing out, as between *per capita* increases and the increase of numbers, the total growth which trade, so to say, made available. In any event it is right also to record one's *impression* – an impression validated by the statistical estimates, where available – that in several countries which were able to share very extensively in the 'vertical' international specialization of the late nineteenth century the average *level* of real income was relatively high, whatever the relative rate of growth of that income. Canada, Australia and New Zealand, so far as we can judge, were among the world's highest-income countries a century ago,[24] as they are today, while in the heyday of her specialization as a primary producer Argentina enjoyed a very substantial lead over her South American neighbours.

Even in the case of these more fortunate countries, however, the process of international specialization promoted economic growth only in a limited sense, for that process might well be judged inimical rather than favourable to *development*, in the sense in which that word was defined in the first chapter. The mere fact of such specialization tended, of course, to retain a high share in national product for the favoured sectors. A foreign exchange rate which appropriately reflected the competitive strength of the sector enjoying comparative advantage would give little encouragement to the development of indigenous manufacturing. The cheap backhaul offered by shipping companies providing space to carry the bulky products of the primary producer to their metropolitan market would minimize the artificial protection afforded by distance. In the 1880s some small-scale consumer goods industries did begin to develop in New Zealand, based on the cheap labour which the over-ambitious immigration programme of the 1870s had provided. But this development was nipped in the bud by the fall of outward freight rates (from England to New Zealand) which was caused by the increased shipping capacity provided on the inward route following the introduction of refrigerated shipping in 1882 and the subsequent rapid growth of a frozen meat export trade.

Reliable indications of changes in the structure of economies over time are of course a by-product of attempts to construct a time series of the growth of national product by sector and, as we have seen, there are as yet few such estimates for the sort of economy we have been discussing. But the qualitative impression of little structural change is, in most cases, a very firm one. The mere fact that the primary sector and the associated transport sector still bulked so large in relative terms at the earliest dates for which we *do* have information suggests the modest degree of structural transformation which had occurred in earlier decades. In the case of Argentina, for example, 39·2 per cent of the active population were still engaged on the land in 1900–4 against 19·8 per cent in manufacturing. By 1925–9 these proportions had changed, respectively, only to 35·9 and 20·8 per cent.[25] Again, Butlin's work provides support, as Table 4.1 shows. The share of manufacturing in Australian G.D.P. did indeed increase sharply between 1861–5 and 1900, but at the

TABLE 4.1   *Sectoral shares in Australian G.D.P., 1861–5 to 1937–8 (constant price basis)*

	1861–5	1900	1937–8
Primary	31·8	31·4	27·7
Agricultural & pastoral	18·1	21·6	25·3
Mining	13·7	9·8	2·4
Secondary	16·1	19·6	22·5
Manufacturing	5·3	12·8	15·9
Construction	10·8	6·8	6·6
Tertiary	42·6	39·2	40·1
House rents	9·5	9·8	9·7
	100·0	100·0	100·0

Source: Calculated from Butlin (1962), Table 269, pp. 460–1.

expense, largely, of mining and of construction rather than of the farm sector. Apart from the continued relative decline of mining there was little further change before World War II.

It is, of course, a question of whether one sees economic development simply in terms of a sustained rise in real income per head, or whether one also – or even alternatively – would regard a given direction of change of industrial structure as an appropriate criterion. Certainly there has been in recent decades a tendency in dominantly agricultural countries – and not only in those which are also relatively poor – to regard a prosperity based essentially on agricultural exports as insecure. For this there have been some good reasons as well as many bad ones. Many have adopted this standpoint primarily because of the relative deterioration in the world market for foodstuffs and agricultural raw materials in recent years. This is the Nurkse–Prebisch position, to be discussed shortly. There has also been an increasing realization of the threat of instability inherent in the high commodity concentration and the high degree of dependence on one trading partner historically characteristic of the exports of the primary producing nations.[26] In addition, reserves of unused but cultivable land being everywhere finite and in many instances close to zero, there is no prospect that the land alone can continue to provide employment for a rapidly-growing population. Finally, the impressive pace of technological advance in modern industry, an advance which in many instances is leading to dramatic increases in the optimum scale of output, convinces many in dominantly land-based economies that they are denying themselves access to the main source of modern economic growth, and that the longer they delay industrialization, the harder will subsequent entry become. From such a viewpoint, the judgment naturally follows that growth, in the sense of increase in real income per head brought about by specialization as an exporter of primary produce, is not the same thing as true economic development and may even be hostile to it. It seems likely, however, that this scepticism is less warranted in appraising the primary exports-led growth of the decades before 1914, when the land/population ratio was much higher than it is in 1970.

'Enclave' economies

If the 'engine of growth' view of pre-1914 trade has to be modified along these lines in respect of even the most favoured of the nations participating in it, a still more qualified verdict is called for in appraising its appositeness in respect of what are sometimes called the 'enclave' economies. The 'enclaves' referred to are the enterprises set up in low-income countries by foreign capital, usually European or American, to exploit some particular resource or climatic characteristic: nitrates in Peru; tea plantations in Ceylon; rubber plantations in the Malay peninsula; ivory-hunting in the Congo. Although the lack of reliable statistical information here is even more disarming than in considering countries like Argentina or New Zealand, it seems perfectly clear that neither in respect of their national incomes nor in promoting structural change was such activity as beneficial to the host economy as the pastoral farming or grain production of the areas of recent settlement. Nor was this because the activity in question constituted a smaller fraction of total income; on the contrary, in some instances such as the sugar islands of the West Indies the 'enclave' formed an even larger part of the host economy than did export pastoralism or grain-production elsewhere. One of the very few good modern quantitative investigations into a nine-teenth-century 'enclave' economy, Mrs Eisner's study of Jamaica, tells us that exports constituted some 20 per cent of the national income of that island in 1870, very close to the value for Australia in the same year (21·6 per cent). (In 1832, the export/income ratio for Jamaica had been c. 44 per cent; it was almost certainly substantially higher for Australia, too, in earlier decades, though Butlin's studies go back only to 1861.[27]) Yet no one would wish to claim that trade was benefiting Jamaica as much as Australia.

The difference in impact arises from those economic characteristics of foreign enterprises in low-income countries which lead to the choice of the word 'enclaves' to describe them. The word is intended to reflect the considerable degree of isolation, economic and sometimes geographical, of the foreign enterprise from the rest of the host economy. The reason for spatial concentration in a particular locality is obvious in the case of mining, and where micro-climate is important, of cropping too (e.g. the highland coffee and tea plantations of Ceylon). This geographical isolation has been important in itself in limiting the growth-promoting effect of foreign enterprise in large low-income countries such as Brazil, where huge distances and the inadequacies of communications have permitted the fostering and perpetuation of chronic regional inequalities and have prevented growth stimuli from spreading easily from the growing points of the economy.

The *economic* isolation of the enclave, however, is the more pervasive difficulty, for it has often deprived such enterprises of any growth-inducing effect even in small host economies. By 'economic isolation' is intended the absence or at any rate relative weakness of influences flowing from the enclave to the rest of the economy *via* input/output linkages or the spending of factors of production in the host economy. Forward linkages were weak because typically the sought-after product was exported in its raw state. Backward linkages were weak because if machinery was used at all in the enterprise – mining machinery, for example – it was imported, the host economy lacking a machine-tool industry of its own. The capital of the enterprise was of course usually supplied entirely by the foreign country, and managerial and technical personnel were expatriates, most of whose spending was on imported goods and whose savings, if any, were normally repatriated. Profits, of course, were also repatriated unless reinvested in the foreign enterprise. The sole influences on the host economy were therefore normally confined to those emanating from (*a*) the wages of unskilled labour supplied by the host country; (*b*) the rent of land; (*c*) any export taxes or royalties which the host government might succeed in persuading the foreign enterprise to pay.

The first of these was generally a very weak influence indeed, for the foreign enterprise was usually able to avoid paying much above a subsistence wage. Nor indeed did this always or even usually accrue to nationals of the host country, since for a variety of reasons even the unskilled labour was often imported from distant countries. A mining enterprise might necessarily be situated in an unpopulated area, or there might be (as with Peruvian guano or Ceylonese tea plantations) differences of altitude and micro-climate between the locale of the enterprise and the chief centres of local population which made natives reluctant to offer their labour. Alternatively, if population density was not too great and opportunities for spending on consumer goods were limited, there might simply be little incentive for a peasant people to seek outside employment, as seems to have been the case with the Malayan rubber plantations and tin mines.

Whenever for one or more of these reasons the supply of indigenous labour was inadequate, the foreign enterprise could still keep labour costs down by importing unskilled workers from outside, usually in the persons of Chinese or Indian indentured labourers. It was this form of recruitment – not always easily distinguishable from slavery (which, historically speaking, it replaced) in either its moral or its economic aspects – which distributed Chinese and Indians around the world, in Malayan tin mines and rubber plantations, in the guano workings in Peru, in the sugar plantations of Trinidad and Fiji, in the gold and diamond mines of South Africa. In many instances a legacy of ethnic and economic problems was bequeathed to the host economy for which the cultural enrichment bestowed by the same process may have seemed inadequate recompense.

The rent of land was a significant item only in the case of land-intensive operations. Here the political régime was important. The British in some cases used political dominion to hold the price of land to the foreign enterprise, for example in the case of the Malayan rubber plantations, down to a nominal level. An autonomous government was in a better position to exact a cut, and at an early stage, for example in the matter of the royalty payable by the guano exploiters in Peru, the sort of hard bargaining so familiar in the recent history of oil companies in the Middle East emerged. But unless the host government could secure a substantial share in this way the foreign enterprise, for the reasons discussed, might make little addition to the income stream or the savings capacity of the host country, or (by the same token) to its foreign exchange accrual. In such circumstances the growth-promoting effect of the foreign enterprise was naturally extremely limited.

However, the isolation of the enclave enterprise was (and is) a matter of degree. In few if any instances was isolation complete. The exploitation of Peruvian guano by outside interests in the mid-nineteenth century began by being something close to a 'pure' example of extreme isolation. But J. V. Levin, whose excellent study *The Export Economies* offers both a penetrating theoretical analysis and a fascinating historical study of 'enclave' economies, shows how the Peruvian government quickly learned to extract a substantial cut from the foreign concessionaries.[28] He also shows that a class of Peruvian entrepreneurs arose who enjoyed some success in breaking the foreign monopoly: a useful reminder that although the profit motive may not be universally effective, it is widespread. Unfortunately, neither of these two means of breaking down the isolation of the enclave and diverting a greater share of the benefits to Peru was very successful in promoting that country's economic development. The government at first squandered most of the royalties in buying political support, then tried to atone for this by some ill-judged railway building. The Peruvian entrepreneurs for their part spent a good proportion of their profits on high living based on imported luxuries in Lima. In neither case was any very worthwhile stimulus given to Peru's development. The example is useful as a reminder that the failure of economic enclaves to promote general growth may reflect the economic, social and political limitations of the host as well as the predatory selfishness of the intruder.

A more positive stimulus was given to the host economy in another case, namely where the economic activity in question could be taken up by native producers. Even leaving aside the regions of recent settlement the production of staple export crops has been organized in a variety of ways. In the Malay peninsula the rubber boom of the early decades of the present century was based largely though not entirely on plantations, which again were largely though not entirely British-owned. In Sumatra, on the other hand, peasant smallholdings were responsible for the bulk of output. Peasant smallholdings were also responsible, in the early years of the trade, for much of the banana production in Jamaica, with plantations making their appearance later, while in the Gold Coast the production of cocoa remained a peasant monopoly. The true 'enclave' economy is, in fact, a limiting case which perhaps never existed in its pure form, and at the other end enclaves shaded off into the less opulent of the regions of recent settlement like Brazil. It deserves to be mentioned – by way perhaps of throwing doubt on a negative association rather than of establishing a positive one – that those countries where foreign-dominated mining or plantation activities have been important at some period since the mid-nineteenth century tend today to be somewhat better off, in terms of real *per capita* incomes and general growth orientation, than others where they have been less in evidence.[29]

Trade in manufactures to 1913
Little has been said so far about international trade in manufactures in the period before 1914. In the early modern centuries manufacturing export industries were often resource-based, like England's woollen and worsted textiles or France's silk. But with the coming of the industrial revolution, productivity in the processing phases became more important than raw material costs, and the greatest manufactured export trade in the first half of the nineteenth century – Britain's export of cotton textiles – was based upon a 100 per cent imported raw material. Nor, of course, did

Britain possess any natural or indeed long-enduring advantage in such industries as cotton and metal manufactures, for it is a platitude that her later economic difficulties were caused in part precisely by the success of other nations in emulating and in some instances overtaking her. Thus the distinctive trades in manufactures of the early industrial era – by 'distinctive' it is intended to exclude such longer-standing but smaller trades as that in French silks – seem to have been built largely on the historical accident of an 'early start' and consequent, but temporary, technological supremacy.

In the second half of the nineteenth century both the commodity composition and the direction of world trade in manufactures began to change fundamentally. Britain's early staples began to encounter increasing competition in their former markets both because of import-replacement and because of competition in third markets from other industrializing nations. They did not (for a long time) decline absolutely, but did decline relatively, and firms averted earlier shrinkage only by switching to new markets, particularly in the British Empire. Here they often enjoyed a degree of protection; commercial and personal contacts gave the British exporter an advantage; and particularly cheap freight rates were available because of the growth of shipping capacity providing for the bulky exports of primary products from these countries.

In the new industries of the later nineteenth century, by contrast, special skills were sometimes important (as in 'science-based' industries such as synthetic dye-stuffs and electrical equipment). Here Britain's 'early start' was not a great advantage; some have argued that it was a disadvantage.[30] As other countries industrialized, they exploited such advantages as geographical proximity (for example, the U.S.A. in the other parts of North America, Germany in Central Europe). In consequence, both the share of the older 'staples' in world trade in manufactures and Britain's share of total world trade declined substantially in the half-century before World War I.

It has often been argued that the slower growth of British exports in the later nineteenth century was responsible for the retardation of Britain's overall growth in that period. J. R. Meyer has used an input/output matrix to calculate that, allowing for the effect on the output of sectors producing inputs to the export industries, the decline in the rate of growth of British exports was in fact of a sufficient magnitude to explain the degree of retardation of the growth of industrial output as a whole.[31] (Meyer does not strictly prove, nor does he claim to have proved, that the deceleration of exports *was* the cause of the overall retardation.) It is worth noting that this viewpoint implies a *stronger* claim for the role of exports in economic growth than does the 'engine of growth' view of trade; for the latter merely asserts that growth can be 'export-led', that is that growing exports is a member of the set of *sufficient* conditions of economic growth, whereas the former seems to imply that a sufficient rate of growth of exports is a *necessary* condition of growth.

This stronger claim for the growth-inducing effects of rising exports has sometimes been made explicitly. Thus Professor North, in elaborating his views on the relation of 'staple' exports to growth, maintains that

> The expanding international economy of the past two centuries has provided the avenue by which one economy after another has accelerated its rate of growth. There are few exceptions to the essential initiating role of a successful export sector in the early stages of accelerated growth of market economies.[32]

The distinguished economist Sir Arthur Lewis adopts a similar standpoint: 'it usually falls to foreign trade to give an economy that upward twist which sets it on the progressive road'.[33] His explanation as to why this is so emphasizes somewhat different mechanisms than those stressed in this chapter or advanced by North. For Lewis, exports take the lead because they face a more elastic demand than production for the home market; they do not depend upon the parallel growth of other sectors of the home economy; and they give 'rise to no competitive struggle at home'.

In the later nineteenth century opportunities for specializing in particular branches of manufacturing multiplied with the enlargement of the number of products and processes generated by technological progress, and the opportunity arose to escape the handicap imposed on later starters by Britain's accidental supremacy in the older manufactures. One is tempted to think that this evolving situation would present opportunities to industrializing countries for 'export-led' growth where the exports in question were manufactures, just as opportunities were being presented to (and seized by) land- and resource-rich countries for 'export-led' growth where the exports in question were primary products. The trade/income ratios appear to confirm that this did in fact occur in several cases, for they exhibit a markedly rising tendency for several countries undergoing substantial economic development in the period from about 1850 to World War I, including France, Italy, Japan and the Scandinavian countries.[34] In two important cases, however – U.S.A. and Germany – the course of the trade ratio appears less compatible with this view. In the U.S.A. the ratio was both low and tending to decline slightly. In Germany, according to Kuznets' estimates, the ratio though relatively high changed little between 1872–9 and 1910–13, while Hoffmann's estimates suggest that it declined somewhat during the decades of most rapid industrialization at the end of the nineteenth century.[35]

In the case of the U.S.A. it is indeed true that international specialization in manufactures played a relatively small role in growth, though while the *overall* export/income ratio fell in the later nineteenth century, the *manufactured* exports/income ratio rose. Basically, of course, the U.S.A. achieved the advantages of specialization *internally*, being both populous and diverse enough to achieve through inter-regional trade what most other countries could only achieve through international trade. In any event, though, the U.S.A.'s pattern of international specialization was basically that of an exporter of primary products until as late as World War I, though exports of manufactures passed the

50 per cent of the total mark during that war, and food, drink and raw materials constituted more than half of total imports as early as the 1870s.

In the case of Germany the overall trade/income ratio is more seriously misleading. Germany, like the United Kingdom, was a substantial net importer of foodstuffs and raw materials, but her imports of some commodities in this class were depressed, perhaps quite seriously, by the tariff protection which Bismarck decided to extend to German farmers when their incomes were threatened by falling world prices. Similarly some branches of German industry, such as steel, developed under an umbrella of tariff protection in the last quarter of the nineteenth century. This tended to depress the overall trade/income ratio both by reducing trade relative to output in quantity terms *and* by raising domestic prices temporarily (as in the case of steel) or permanently (as with many foodstuffs) above world price levels, thus further depressing the *current price* ratio of foreign trade to national income. That this last is an important point is suggested by the substantially different result when the trade/income ratio is computed in *constant* prices. Kuznets offers the following estimates, based on Hoffmann's studies:

TABLE 4.2 *German merchandise trade as percentage of 'net total uses'* (*approx.* = *N.N.P.*)

	Current prices	1914 prices
1872/79	36·7%	26·4%
1910/13	38·3%	38·7%

Source: S. Kuznets, 'Quantitative Aspects of the Economic Growth of Nations. X: Level and Structure of Foreign Trade: Long-Term Trends', *Economic Development and Cultural Change*, 15 (January 1967), Appx. Table 1–3, p. 102.

Further, the tariff helped change the structure of trade in such a way as to mask the relatively very rapid growth of exports of Germany's most distinctive manufactures. Hoffmann's constant price estimates show the export of chemical products growing at a compound annual rate of 8·1 per cent, and of machinery at 11·5 per cent, over the period 1880–1913.[36] These are extremely high rates of growth, and suggest that the export market played a very important role in the growth of Germany's leading sectors in the period of rapid industrialization, as it did for example in British cotton in the first half of the nineteenth century or in Swedish pulp in the period 1894–1914.

The trend towards some international specialization in exports of manufactures helps to explain a phenomenon which belied the expectations of many nineteenth-century economists and has even puzzled some of their more recent successors: namely, the fact that as industrialization spread to more and more countries international trade in manufactures did not decline. We shall see later that in the second half of the twentieth century the 'intra-trade' in manufactures between pairs of industrial countries is in fact the most buoyant part of world trade. This at first sight surprising result is the outcome of several facts. With rising incomes the proportion of income spent on manufactures rises, at least over a considerable range of incomes. Secondly, the high degree of integration of the modern international economy allows great scope for the exploitation of even relatively small and sometimes temporary advantages in one direction or another arising from differences of resource endowment, factor proportions, market size, location or any other cause. It was in the late nineteenth century that the growth of trade in products such as those mentioned in the last paragraph first foreshadowed the possible future of such 'intra-trade' in manufactures.

A perhaps more important reason, however, for the fact that before World War I trade in manufactures grew at about the same pace as trade in primary products is simply that the countries which exported the latter imported the former. Since they continued for the most part to be importers rather than exporters of capital, and since in aggregate their import of new capital very roughly equalled the outflow of interest and dividends on the old, their total imports of goods and services grew about as fast as their exports. Hence there was a built-in tendency for the two classes of trade to keep roughly in step so far as the dominant sector of world trade, that depending on the 'vertical' specialization which we have discussed, was concerned.

The 'engine of growth' reconsidered

In the preceding paragraphs some of the reasons for the rapid growth of world trade between the mid-nineteenth century and World War I have been discussed. It has been shown that many countries of widely differing character found an opportunity in this period to 'latch on' to the growth of world markets by developing some specialism, whether permanent or temporary, rooted in natural or acquired advantage; and that for most countries for which the relevant data are available foreign trade was a sizeable and in most cases growing fraction of total output. These circumstances certainly seem to justify the 'engine of growth' view of world trade in that period to which reference has been made. But how far, and in what ways, was pre-1914 growth *dependent* on foreign trade?

Regrettably, no firm answer can be given to this question. The classical school which dominated British economics for most of the nineteenth century accounted for trade by the principle of comparative advantage, which stated that even if one of a given pair of nations was more efficient than the other in producing *both* of two products, it still paid for each to specialize in the production of that good in which it had the greater relative advantage (or smaller relative disadvantage). In this way the aggregate production of both goods could be raised above the level attainable if each country produced some of each, and a rate of exchange could be found which would permit the exchange of quantities of each good such as to leave each country with more of both goods than if there were no or only partial specialization.

The argument is attractive, but does comparative advantage in fact explain how trade is related to growth? In the first place, it would perhaps not be inaccurate to say that despite voluminous writings, economic theorists have not succeeded in reaching agreement as to how to measure the gains from trade through comparative advantage, or indeed as to whether they can be measured (there is in some quarters a shade more confidence that perhaps *changes* in them can be measured). But even on quite implausibly generous assumptions, the gains from trade *as envisaged by the principle of comparative advantage* would seem incapable, in most instances, of accounting for more than a fairly modest fraction of the total increase in income achieved over a given period. On the eve of World War I imports constituted about 20 per cent of the German net national product, which since 1850 had multiplied more than five-fold in 1913 prices. Let us make the outrageously generous assumption that the 1913 exports of goods and services with which Germany paid for these imports were totally costless, being the product of resources which in the absence of foreign trade would have been wholly unemployed. Let us make the equally outrageous assumption that Germany's imports in 1850 were utterly useless to her. Even on these ridiculous assumptions 1913 imports represented only about one quarter of the amount by which total 1913 income exceeded that of 1850, that is, of the achieved N.N.P. growth 1850–1913. For some countries the answer to the same sum would be higher than for Germany; for others (e.g. the U.S.A.) it would be much smaller. It seems that we must either conclude that trade was responsible only in a minor degree for pre-1914 growth, or that comparative advantage does not adequately explain how trade is related to growth (or both).*

---

* Of course if one takes into account not only the output of the export industries themselves but also that of sectors producing goods and services as inputs to those industries, the total activity generated by export production might be much larger. (This is Meyer's approach in the paper referred to in note 31 below.) It then becomes a question of how far, and at what cost in terms of welfare loss, the factors engaged directly and indirectly in export production would have found alternative employment in the absence of exports.

There is surely little difficulty in agreeing that the second of these conclusions is valid, for there are many other reasons for thinking that comparative advantage alone is an unsatisfactory guide in exploring the relationships between trade and growth. We saw, for example, that the trade/income ratio was about the same in Jamaica as in Australia in 1870, and if the economic structures of the two countries are compared with that of their (common) major trading partner (U.K.) it seems probable that the comparative advantage of Jamaica in sugar was greater than that of Australia in wool. Yet Jamaica was much poorer than Australia and growing much less rapidly. Our discussion of enclave economies has, it is hoped, offered some reasons *why*, even for countries with similar trade/income ratios, the impact of trade on growth may be quite different.

Before going on to explore other ways in which trade may be positively related with growth, it is however necessary to caution against the belief that the record of history in some sense undermines comparative advantage and suggests only a trifling growth-promoting role for the type of 'vertical' international specialization to which it led in the nineteenth century. Not only was the prosperity of the regions of recent settlement clearly bound up with their fortunes as international specialists, it is scarcely too much to say that in some instances these countries owed their very existence to the opportunities for trade specialization which they found. The life of the pioneer, it has been well said, was everywhere hard, but in New Zealand it would have been virtually impossible but for the discovery of a succession of profitable exports – grain and potatoes to victual the Australian gold-fields in the 1850s; gold from New Zealand's own fields in the 1860s; wool, wheat and refrigerated foods thereafter. New Zealand's own resources would have permitted at best a life of meagre subsistence farming and hunting (the life the Maoris had lived before the coming of the Europeans). In the early years, a degree of comfort was achieved only by the import of clothing, furniture and other consumer goods which, in the absence of commensurate exports, generated a (relatively) huge import surplus. This in turn was covered by the funds the migrants brought with them, by the disbursements of the imperial civil service and armed forces, and by the import of capital. But the capital would not have kept flowing nor the migrants continued to arrive, had not New Zealand found some form of international exchange which would permit it to lift the level of its *per capita* product above that of subsistence farming.

Nor was this immediate and direct dependence of the standard of living on trade much reduced when the difficult early decades had been successfully survived. In the 1880s the faltering of the existing staples through the depletion of the goldfields and the fall in world prices of wheat and wool brought about precisely the crisis envisaged: the capital flow virtually dried up and the net flow of migration not only declined but actually went into reverse. The country was rescued from seemingly inevitable decline by a series of technological discoveries headed by the fitting of refrigerating gear to ocean-going ships, which permitted the development of new export industries and found a profitable use for idle resources – shipping lamb carcases to London instead of driving the aged stock over a cliff into the sea, and putting the wet, rich lowlands of the West Coast to the use for which nature seemed to have intended them.

New Zealand was perhaps extreme in the degree of its dependence on trade, in its restricted range of resources, and in the lack of encouragement its small and scattered market offered to indigenous manufacturing activity. But the difference was one of degree, and the income levels and growth rates of other primary producers were also highly susceptible to changes for better or for worse in their trading opportunities. One cannot doubt, then, that trade based on 'vertical' specialization was a powerful determinant of growth in the years before 1914. What the economic historian will query is only whether the principle of comparative advantage completely explains the nature of the relationship of trade and growth. For a 'snapshot picture', so to speak, of New Zealand's trade ratio and trade structure, in, say, 1913 would suggest that, as with the German example, the most generous possible assumptions could not explain the total growth of income since the mid-nineteenth century in terms of New Zealand's share of the gains from trade in 1913.

This is partly because the 'gains from trade' approach is ill-adapted to capture the dynamic interaction between trade and rising productivity – and thus of *changing* comparative advantage – which is at the heart of the relationship we seek to explore. To pursue our analysis of the New Zealand case, the history of the dairy industry – specifically, let us say, of butter-making – illustrates the mechanism envisaged. Before refrigeration made possible the development of an export trade in frozen dairy produce, butter was made in New Zealand on the farm by the same methods as Tess Durbey-field observed at Talbothays – only it was not made as well. The resultant product was so poor that some New Zealanders, the lack of refrigeration notwithstanding, preferred to buy imported Irish butter which had survived a four- to six-month voyage, including crossing the Equator! The advent of refrigeration, however, prompted an attempt to establish a butter export trade, an endeavour which would clearly fail unless the problem of low and inconsistent quality could be solved.

The transfer of production to dairy factories, the adoption of the best-proved technical processes and machinery from Scandinavia and Wisconsin, and a compulsory inspection and grading scheme overcame these difficulties. At the same time agricultural extension work, and livestock and pasture research in which New Zealand played the role of a pioneer rather than an imitator, raised productivity on the farm by increasing carrying capacity and raising the output of milk per cow and the butterfat content of the milk. Induced improvements in rail and road transport, which of course yielded a 'spin-off' benefit to other producers and consumers in the locality, enlarged the radius within which the collection of cream from the farm was possible and thus permitted the capture of substantial economies of scale by the building of larger factories. By the mid-1930s the value of butter exported, which had only begun to be reported in the trade statistics less than half a century earlier, was equal to about 10 per cent of gross domestic product. In the process social capital which would be shared with other sectors had been called into being, new towns had been built to service the dairying areas, and the capital investment and consumer expenditures of dairy farmers and factories had created market opportunities for a wide range of manufacturing and service activities.[37]

It is of course true that these developments were not costless, though so far as the land was concerned they were largely achieved by calling an unused or grossly under-utilized resource into productive activity. But almost all investigations into the relationship between the rate of growth of output and the rate of growth of productivity in a particular sector have revealed a strong positive association. Among the reasons for this are the facts that the rapidly growing sector elicits a high rate of technological improvement, can more quickly exploit technological advances because of the high rate of new investment, has a low average age of capital stock and therefore enjoys the advantage of the most up-to-date equipment, and can most readily adjust to the optimum scale of plant size.* It is perhaps in such ways that we should seek to explain the success of New Zealand's dairy industry, 1895–1935, of Germany's synthetic dye-stuffs or electrical equipment in the late nineteenth century, of England's cotton manufacture from 1780 to 1850, or of the general field of synthetics and plastics in our own day. Such beneficial influences can of course come from rapid expansion oriented primarily to the domestic market, but for smaller countries particularly an elastic

---

* The reasons mentioned in the text all lie on the supply side. Often the correlation noted will arise because rising productivity permits relative price reductions which, if demand is price-elastic, bring about a rapid increase in sales. The relationship has something of the character of a 'chicken or the egg?' situation.

and expanding foreign market has often been a tremendous stimulus.

In discussing the import surplus of the early decades of British settlement of New Zealand, stress was laid on the need to find some 'staple' export in order to generate a sufficient increase of foreign exchange accrual. This points to another bearing of foreign trade on growth which historically has been of great importance in many cases. We have seen that while the long-term trend of the ratio between trade and income is a matter of some uncertainty, a rise in that ratio, particularly when measured in constant prices, is well-established for most countries during the early stages of industrialization. So far we have considered chiefly the interrelationships of *exports* and growth; now it must be stressed that the *capacity to import* may also be a major determinant of the attainable rate of growth.

As incomes rise, imports will tend to rise in absolute terms and possibly as a proportion of income. Unless the country concerned is exceptionally well endowed (or, of course, takes measures such as tariffs to achieve a different result) the trade-destroying effect of the growth of import-substituting production is unlikely fully to offset the trade-creating effect of the growth of domestic demand. If the country concerned is at a level of income where marginal income-elasticities of demand, say, for imported consumer durables are high, imports may in the absence of countervailing measures rise not only absolutely but as a fraction of total consumer expenditures. In so far as imports consist of consumer goods, they can be reduced, for example by the imposition of a tariff, without necessarily hampering growth, though of course at some welfare cost. But imports of producers' goods – capital equipment, semi-finished manufactures, raw materials and fuel – are likely not only to rise with growth but to be more indispensable to it. True, imports, say of some raw material or machinery specific to a particular industry, can be eliminated by abandoning that industry and substituting some other activity, but producers' materials used 'across the board' of economic activity – such as transport equipment, steel castings and mouldings, or fuels – are indispensable if the whole process is not to be brought to a halt.

The degree of dependence of growth on imported products will vary with the demands thrown up by the developing pattern of economic activity and with the capacity of the domestic economy to meet those demands. In the regions of recent settlement the crucial role of geographical expansion of settlement and of the ability to move bulky products cheaply threw a special emphasis on infrastructural invest-ment and particularly on the transport system. Since countries like Argentina and New Zealand did not have competitive steel or heavy engineering industries, railway materials and rolling-stock and the like had to be imported and the capacity to finance these imports was essential to growth. We have seen that in fact capital imports were heavily used for just this purpose, but this was equivalent to financing these investments by the proceeds of exports only at one remove, since the ability to service these capital imports and thus to maintain credit-worthy status was dependent on an appropriate growth of export earnings. Fuel perhaps was less important in the later nineteenth century owing to the fairly widespread availability of coal; with the rise of oil-powered machinery and oil-fired heaters in the twentieth century, ability to finance imports of petroleum products has become essential to industry. Natural endow-ment will clearly help determine the extent of the need for imports of materials other than fuels; countries like Japan and New Zealand have been more dependent than Australia or Canada, though until recently – and even today – the full extent of the resources of such large countries has been far from adequately explored, and many materials have been imported which in fact were available at home. Finally, countries at an early stage of development are deficient, almost by definition, in heavy engineering capacity and have needed to import much machinery and transport and con-structional equipment. This need has not been confined to small countries only; despite its size and impressive industrial growth beginning about 1890, Russia lacked a heavy engineering sector right up to the Revolution or, indeed, to the First Five-Year Plan.

Trade-constrained growth before 1913

It is widely argued today that the level of 'importing capacity' made possible by export earnings and capital imports determines the maximum rate of growth which developing countries can realistically aim at. In a well-known article H. B. Chenery and A. M. Strout have constructed a model showing the minimum needs for savings and for foreign exchange of a developing country pursuing a given growth path. They envisage a series of 'phases' in which the most serious constraints on growth are successively the difficulty of achieving an adequate savings rate and the difficulty of earning enough foreign exchange: 'savings-constrained' growth and 'trade-constrained' growth. In an empirical section studying the performance of thirty-one developing countries over the years 1957–62, Chenery and Strout showed that twelve countries met both the savings and trade criteria which the target rate of growth implied, six met the savings criterion but not the trade one, three trade but not savings, and ten met neither. In this classification, moreover, ten of the twelve countries in the most favoured group had export growth rates of 6 per cent or more, and the authors comment that 'One of the most suggestive features . . . is the predominant role played by exports'. A series of projections undertaken in the same paper forecast an even more striking predominance of the trade limit over the savings limit in the future.[38] It may be added that both the 1957–62 calculations and the projections cover only low-income countries; but there is ample evidence that some high-income countries, like New Zealand, have also been in a phase of 'trade-constrained growth' for most of the period since World War II.

Some novel factors which have thrown the 'trade gap' into greater prominence in recent decades will be discussed shortly, but we may first pause to ask how often growth was 'trade-constrained' in the period before 1914? It may seem that in so far as we have endorsed the view of trade as an 'engine of growth' in that period the question is otiose: trains run at the same speed as the engine pulling them, neither faster nor slower, and if the foreign sector really had been the sole area of 'autonomous' economic activity it is tempting to suppose that it must have determined simultaneously both the upper and lower limits of the range of potential growth. However, exports and production financed by capital imports came close to being the only 'autonomous' sectors only in the pure enclave economies. In relatively favoured export economies such as Australia, it is possible to envisage that the rate of foreign exchange accruals may have imposed a 'ceiling' on the rate of growth in certain periods, such as the 1890s, while in other periods the upper limit may have been set by other, domestic, factors. Where the impetus to growth came from other sources such as government policy, as in Russia, foreign exchange earnings may have been the most stringent limitation on more frequent occasions. It could be argued that it is still difficult to admit this possibility in the case of countries which imported substantial quantities of consumer goods, as the more highly specialized primary producers did, for here there was scope, one might think, for 'economizing' foreign exchange by restricting imports of non-essentials and concentrating on the import of more 'growth-strategic' commodities.

Perhaps, however, this is a rather unhistorical assessment, for while policies of this type occur naturally to the growth-conscious economist of the 1970s they would have been in a sense anachronistic in the 1870s. Moreover, the major capital importers could not risk tarnishing their credit-worthy image in London, and too violent a departure from *laissez-faire* ideals might have been dangerous in this regard. However, some countries, notably New Zealand and Victoria, did in fact impose modest tariffs in the late nineteenth century. Their aims were primarily fiscal and employment-protecting but they may possibly have served in a minor degree to divert foreign expenditures away from consumer imports capable of being replaced by domestic production, thus helping to avert collision with a trade-ceiling on growth.

The more important mechanism through which export earnings may have imposed an upper limit on growth is, however, via capital imports, credit conditions and government investments. As we have seen, financing infrastructural investment by importing capital is like financing it out of export earnings at one remove, in that the latter determines the borrower's ability to service his debts, float new loans, and redeem or convert old ones as they reach maturity. Further, under the gold or gold-(or sterling-)exchange standard under which these countries operated, credit conditions in the private sector were primarily determined by the foreign asset position of the commercial banks. One may therefore reasonably envisage a considerable influence on the rate of investment, and through this on the growth rate, which would set a trade-determined upper limit on the latter over and above the usual effect of the foreign trade multiplier, it being understood however that this assumes the impossibility of more drastic policy shifts such as those adopted by 'trade-constrained' countries today.

Two other cases deserve special mention as illustrating quite different experiences. Japan was extremely fortunate in finding good opportunities for export expansion, and admirably self-restrained (as always) in refraining from frittering away her earnings on non-essentials. Notwithstanding the absence of tariff protection until the twentieth century, she was able to finance the imports needed for her rapid rate of growth without undue balance of payments strains or recourse to heavy foreign borrowing, except perhaps to a very minor degree from 1896 to 1914, and it would not occur to the historian to regard Japan's growth as 'trade-constrained' at any period before World War II – if, indeed, one could regard so admirable a growth record as constrained by any factor whatsoever. Russia, on the other hand, engaged in a desperate struggle to boost her exports even at great welfare cost: 'We may starve but we shall export.' It is true that Russia's need of foreign exchange was unduly enlarged by the lavish expenditure of her upper classes on imported luxuries and on foreign travel, but prior to the 1917 revolution this was a politically unassailable component of consumer expenditure which had to be added, in determining minimum foreign exchange requirements, to the cost of imported machinery, transport equipment and other inputs and to the cost of servicing the huge foreign debt. This was a heavy task, not made lighter by Russia's ill luck in encountering falling world prices for her staple grain exports during the early decades of development. Nor was the problem entirely averted by the Revolution, though of course luxury imports could be eliminated and the Tsarist foreign debt was repudiated. Changes in the agrarian sector made the resumption of pre-1913 levels of grain exports impossible, while unfavourable world market conditions would in any event have spelled increasing difficulty for export-led growth in the later 1920s. Though it is not suggested that foreign exchange earnings were at any time the *sole* constraint on the rate of Russian economic growth, it is conceivable that this was the constraint which was operating with greatest severity in much of the late Tsarist period, and certainly economic policy was fashioned to a considerable degree towards lightening this restraint.

The terms of trade of primary producers

We may therefore conclude that in the years before 1914 export opportunities acted in many instances as a stimulus to growth, but also in some sense and in some cases as a 'ceiling' – though only perhaps if we assume certain more drastic refashionings of the pattern of production and expenditure to have been economically or politically impracticable. The evidence for 'trade-constrained growth', as we have seen, is more clear-cut for recent years. However, the inter-war years gave an early warning of emerging problems for economies whose growth was dependent on increasing exports of primary produce. A number of factors interacted to shift the balance of supply and demand against primary producers. The shift was most dramatic in those cases where there had been a particularly rapid expansion of supply in the years just before or during World War I, especially in the case of crops where the threat of over-supply is masked for a time by a 'technological' lag between the decision to expand output and its outcome: rubber and coffee are perhaps the outstanding examples. But the major exports of temperate-zone agriculture – wool, grain, meat, dairy produce – also encountered relatively unfavourable conditions as markets reached saturation point.

The slower growth of European (and industrial North American) population, the first hints of the mid-twentieth-century science-based improvement in agricultural productivity, and the heightened protection which several industrial nations had offered to their own farm sectors during World War I and continued in some measure afterwards, were factors in this unsatisfactory market experience. Some writers, notably Sir Arthur Lewis, have pointed to the marketing difficulties of the primary producers as one of the major causes of world economic difficulties leading up to the crisis of 1929–33. How far these difficulties are to be counted among the causes of that crisis may perhaps be queried, but there is no question that the depression and the measures taken by the great powers to combat it in turn aggravated them. The fall in incomes and in the level of industrial activity directly influenced demand for food and raw materials. As envisaged by economic theory, the prices of food and primary products, whose supply is relatively inelastic, fell in the depression more than those of manufactured commodities, the output of which can be cut back more expeditiously and which are in some instances subject to 'administered' pricing. Hence within the industrial countries (as well as internationally) the terms of trade turned sharply against primary producers. This in turn led to a demand for measures to support the incomes of their own farm sectors which the governments of the industrial countries were politically unable to resist. They did this either by further tightening the screw against imports,

K

as on the continent of Europe, or by direct subsidies, as in Britain and America. In either event a barrier to trade in commodities competing with the products of home farms was erected which further worsened the prospects of the primary produce exporters; and this barrier, as was entirely to be expected, proved much easier to erect than to dismantle.

Before World War II the writing was therefore already on the wall, warning that the period of export-led growth based on 'vertical' international specialization might be drawing to a close. But the message was for a time obscured, and some thought it was perhaps falsified, by World War II. In the manner of such events, this revived economic activity, increased demand for many raw materials and, by causing the loss of some sources of world supply, enhanced the opportunities of others. The continuation of a high level of economic activity after the end of the war (to the surprise of many) prolonged the resultant improvement in the terms of trade of primary producers. A further sharp rise in demand caused by stock-piling during the Korean War then lifted these on to a new high level in 1950–1. However, the quick collapse of the Korean boom and 20 years of worsening terms of trade for most primary producers since then have reinforced more pessimistic views of long-term secular deterioration in their trade opportunities.

Some writers have presented estimates of the long-run terms of trade of primary producing countries as evidence of this secular deterioration.[39] Ironically, it was the United Kingdom which first invoked the terms of trade in the years immediately following World War II to explain – and excuse – the balance of payments difficulties of that country. But it was spokesmen for the primary producers, especially of Latin America, who took up the concept after the collapse of the Korean raw materials boom and used it to underline the foreign exchange problems of low-income countries. The long-term experience of the terms of trade has since been widely and warmly debated. No general consensus has emerged, save perhaps on two points. The historical terms of trade of primary producers were not a mirror image of those of the United Kingdom, especially before 1913, since falling transport costs could permit an increased (f.o.b.) price to the primary-producing country at the same time that the landed (c.i.f.) price of a given commodity imported to the United Kingdom was falling.[40] Secondly, the experiences of different primary producers have diverged sharply, as have those of different industrial nations.

That this variety of experience from case to case is more striking than any central tendency resulting from averaging the experiences of different collections of countries or commodities was one of the major findings of Charles P. Kindleberger's full-scale study of the terms of trade of industrial Europe.[41] Nevertheless, Kindleberger did note some historical tendency for the terms of trade of underdeveloped countries to deteriorate as against industrial nations (though not of primary products as against manufactures), and it is fair to add that if the experience of more recent years were added to his data – which end in 1952, rather uncomfortably close to the Korean boom to allow much confidence of 'normalcy' – his conclusions might be thought biased on the side of optimism.[42] It is also fair to add that it makes a great deal of difference to the whole appraisal of the trading situation of primary producers in recent years whether one includes the oil producers or not. The case for doing so, doubtless, is that if one takes care to exclude from any particular set all the success stories, one is bound to be left with a dismal average. The case for excluding the oil producers is partly that oil has been so important in world trade in recent decades as to merit separate consideration; that the major oil producers are a mere handful of countries aggregating only a tiny fraction of the population of all low-income countries; and that having oil is a matter of mere luck. (It might be added that thanks to this luck, the oil producers are not all low-income countries anyway: it is no longer a classroom novelty to remind one's students that not the U.S.A. but Kuwait has the highest income per head in the world.)

New trends in twentieth-century trade

The precise movement of the terms of trade of primary products as against manufactures is less important, however, than the fact that the *shares* of the two groups in world trade have changed places, and that the share of the latter has shown far the more buoyant trend since World War II. We have seen that before 1913, in the generally received opinion, the shares of primary products and of manufactures in total value of world trade were running fairly constantly at about 62 and 38 per cent of the total respectively. During the inter-war period many primary products encountered adverse markets, and the gap began to narrow. In the post-Korean surge of trade in manufactures the latter rapidly caught up, and first surpassed primary products in value, according to GATT estimates, in 1957. By 1968 manufactures accounted for some 64·2 per cent of the total value of world trade, and primary products for only 35·8 per cent.[43] Whether in terms of *unit* value primary products just held their own in world trade *vis-à-vis* manufactures or failed to do so by a narrow margin, it is clear that in *total* value they grew much less rapidly, and it is also plain that their relative decline has occurred chiefly since World War II, or even more specifically since the Korean War.

Moreover, it should be added that both the number of countries seeking to accelerate growth and relying mainly on primary products for their export revenue, and also the total population of these countries, absolutely and as a proportion of the world total, are far larger than before 1913, so that there is correspondingly more difficulty in 'finding a niche' for oneself in the map of world commerce. The 'importance of being unimportant' argument loses its appeal when the unimportant are so relatively numerous. The less buoyant trading opportunities which primary producers are encountering are therefore correspondingly more serious and reduce still further the prospects for 'export-led' growth on pre-1914 lines.

As already noted, Ragnar Nurkse used the mid-twentieth-century changes in the composition of world trade as the cornerstone of an argument designed to demonstrate that (and to explain why) trade could no longer be relied on as an 'engine of growth' as in the period before 1914. Nurkse's ideas were admirably presented in the Wicksell lectures which he delivered in Stockholm in 1959 shortly before his death.[44] The first of the two lectures, in particular, offered a carefully-reasoned contrast between international trade in the late-nineteenth and the mid-twentieth centuries, showing why, in Nurkse's view, the relative decline of the share of primary products in world trade was to be interpreted not as a fortuitous and temporary accident, but as the consequence of secular changes in industrial technology and the pattern of consumer expenditure which there was every reason to think would continue.

Nurkse argued that in the nineteenth century the process of industrial growth in the advanced economies transmitted a proportional (or in some cases better than proportional) demand for raw materials to other parts of the world; the fact that for much of the nineteenth century a large proportion of industrial growth occurred in Britain, which had only a modest and declining resource endowment and which was committed to free trade, was partly responsible for this outcome. In the twentieth century a greater proportion of industrial growth has occurred in the U.S.A. and Russia, both countries possessing a wider and ampler range of resources and pursuing commercial policies of greater autarky. However, there were in Nurkse's view more specific and subtle reasons for the declining ratio between output in industrial economies and demand for imported materials. He listed them as:

1. a shift in the composition of industrial output in advanced countries towards 'heavy' industries with a smaller ratio of raw material input to final value;

2. the rising share of services in the output of advanced countries;

3. the low-income elasticity of consumer demand for many agricultural products;

4. the protection of agriculture in advanced countries;

5. economies in raw material use (e.g. scrap steel);

6. synthetic substitutes for natural materials.

This is an imposing list, and several items are so familiar as to make it almost intuitively convincing. Yet Nurkse's interpretation did not go unchallenged. A. K. Cairncross, an economist with a special interest in trade and development who had also done distinguished research in economic history, offered some thoughtful criticisms of Nurkse's scheme.[45] Specifically, for example, he pointed out that points (3) and (4) operate to the disadvantage of *temperate* zone primary producers like Canada, Australia and New Zealand, rather than to that of the tropical low-income countries on which Nurkse's theme clearly intended to focus. Nurkse had, in fact, himself anticipated this criticism in commenting on point (4), and it would now be fairly generally agreed that it is these richer temperate zone countries, whose primary exports are more directly competitive with the output of European and U.S. agriculture, which have been particularly disadvantaged by the agricultural protection policies of the industrial countries. Maizels, for example, shows in his study of the trade and growth of Sterling Area countries that it is Australia which has suffered by far the greatest loss from unfavourable terms of trade in the post-World War II period.[46] Cairncross also pointed out that some of Nurkse's factors operated also before 1914, at least to some extent. Most interestingly and more generally, he suggested that Nurkse tended to overlook the importance of price movements; that in some cases industrial countries were moved, for example, to develop synthetic or domestically-produced substitutes because of the high cost of the imported natural product, which in turn sprang from an undue emphasis on import-replacing industrialization and neglect of the export sector in the primary-producing countries.

Without doubt there is some truth in this: Argentina's failure to capitalize on the favourable trend of demand for imported beef since World War II seems to have been very much her own fault. But Cairncross surely overdoes his argument. Maizels tested the regression of the 1937–8 and 1955 export shares of world trade in certain primary products on the rate of industrial growth for a number of semi-industrial (industrializing) countries; the outcome was a weak *positive* association. He also compared the exports of primary products by industrializing and non-industrial countries, showing that while the latter had enjoyed marked export success in products *not* competitive with those of the former, in the case of products which *were* competitive they had performed about equally well (or badly).[47] Both tests suggest that poor export performance in primary products arose chiefly from *demand* rather than *supply* deficiency, or if the latter, that it was not caused by undue concern with import-competing and neglect of export activities.

Further confirmation of this interpretation is to be found in changes in the composition of world trade and in the terms of trade since the time of the Nurkse–Cairncross debate. As we have seen, the course of the terms of trade between primary products and manufactures has run in favour of the latter *despite* a much more rapid growth of trade in them than in the former. As to the shares of advanced and 'underdeveloped' countries in world trade, the changes mentioned in commodity-composition and relative prices of world trade have of course led to a rapid increase of the share of the advanced (manufactures-exporting) nations. Table 4.3 reproduces Nurkse's figures on the distribution of world trade in 1928 by broad country groupings, together with similar figures for 1958 and 1968 calculated from GATT data. It is abundantly clear that the scepticism which Cairncross expressed as to whether the figures really justified Nurkse's case can no longer be sustained, for the relative fall in the exports of the non-industrial countries, both to the industrial nations and to each other, is striking. (In interpreting the figures it should be borne in mind that South Africa, Australia and New Zealand are included with the non-industrial group. These countries deserve this placing, if at all, only by virtue of the commodity structure of their exports, for both their industrial structures and the level of *per capita* incomes would suggest classifying them among the industrial countries. The matter is not trivial, for the three countries mentioned accounted for nearly 15 per cent of all 'non-industrial' countries' trade in 1968.)

TABLE 4.3   *Direction of world exports, 1928–68*
         (communist bloc excluded)

Countries	1928	1958	1968
		Percentages	
Industrial to industrial		41·8	58·1
	66·2		
Industrial to non-industrial		26·0	18·6
Non-industrial to industrial		22·1	17·8
	33·8		
Non-industrial to non-industrial		10·1	5·5

Sources:
1928: Nurkse (1961), 180.
1958, 1968: calculated from data in GATT, *International Trade 1957–58* (Geneva, July 1959) and *International Trade 1968* (Geneva, 1969).
Note: To provide consistency, I have calculated the 1958 and 1968 shares from GATT data to one place of decimals. In Nurkse's table the later percentages related to 1957 and were shown only to the nearest whole number.

Two points deserve emphasis before leaving this discussion of Nurkse's views on the opportunities for trade-induced growth in the second half of the twentieth century. First, substantial endorsement of Nurkse's arguments as applied to the recent past does not necessarily require pessimism as to the future course of exports from primary-producing countries. At some stage one thinks that the demand for the temperate-zone foodstuffs of New Zealand and Argentina must increase in a world of limited agricultural land and of growing population and incomes, and in view of the accelerating westernization of diets in Asian countries such as Japan. As for raw materials (or, where substantial weight-losing is involved, semi-processed materials), the alarming depletion of non-reproducible minerals and even of slowly-regenerating resources like forests is already creating enormous new trade opportunities for the lucky or prudent guardians of diminishing world reserves. Everyone knows that the U.S.A. imports huge quantities of pulp and news-print from Canada; it is not so generally known that in 1968 she imported nearly a sixth of her steel usage, a considerable fraction from Japan. Further, of course, present-day primary producers are not condemned to an eternally unchanging pattern of exports, and the extraordinary growth of world import of manufactures since World War II, which we shall shortly discuss, has presented an opportunity to industrializing as well as to industrialized countries – an opportunity of which not only 'special cases' like Hong Kong and Puerto Rico, but for example India, have taken advantage.

Secondly, it deserves to be stressed that we have drawn in the preceding paragraphs chiefly on the more generalized arguments of the various writers. It must be added that perhaps all of the scholars concerned would agree on the considerable *diversity* of experience from case to case. Our own exposition has noted in passing the differing departures from the 'underdeveloped average' shown by the oil-producing countries on the one hand and the rich, temperate-zone agricultural specialists like New Zealand on the other. Low-cost export-oriented manufactures have turned Hong Kong, Puerto Rico and a few others into quite special cases, while mineral (other than oil) producers have fared differently from tropical foodstuffs producers. As in Kindleberger's study of the terms of trade, one's conclusion might well be that dispersion around the trend is more striking than the trend itself. It is timely to recall, perhaps, that both in recent economic history and in development theory the limits of useful generalization are constraining. The world is indeed more complicated than before 1914, when a crude two- or three-fold classification of economies sufficed to permit tolerably realistic generalizations by the international economist.

Patterns of trade since World War II

Nurkse's analysis focused on factors affecting the level and rate of growth of world trade in primary products. But the *share* of such commodities in total world trade has of course been depressed by the extraordinary upsurge of trade in manufactures in the last twenty years. This phenomenon has perhaps received less attention than the trading problems of low-income countries, but in the perspective of the economic historian it is perhaps the most remarkable feature of the international economy in recent decades. Since 1950 world trade in manufactures has grown at a rate substantially in excess of the growth of production of them. In the earlier post-war years it seemed plausible to explain this in terms of recovery to a more 'normal' trade/production level after the trade-destroying experiences of depression and war. But it has long been evident that this explanation is inadequate, and that more persistent factors are at work. Some importance, certainly, is to be attributed to the lowering of trade barriers, a process which began at the very end of the depression with the passing of the Reciprocal Trade Agreements Act in the U.S.A. (1934) and which has owed something to the erosion of specific duties by inflation, and more to the very considerable success of the GATT in negotiating reductions of tariffs on manufactures. (GATT's much more modest record in bringing down barriers on trade in agricultural products helps to explain the change in the composition of world trade which we have noted.)

But fairly clearly, there is more to it than this. There is surely a relationship between the very high overall rates of economic growth achieved by industrial countries since World War II and the rapid growth of trade in manufactures. This assertion might cause surprise if one adopted the standpoint, assumed by many nineteenth-century commentators, that industrialization would *reduce* trade in manufactures by causing import substitution. The classic

League of Nations report, *Industrialization and Foreign Trade*, revealed the fallacy in this view more than a quarter of a century ago. It showed that even in the later nineteenth century, despite tariffs and a good deal of import-replacing industrialization behind their shelter, trade in manufactures increased. The mechanism can be conveniently represented in simple algebraic terms.[48] Let S_t be total 'supplies' of manufactures in a given industrializing country in a given year, and m_t the import content of those supplies in the same year. Then over time the change in imports of manufactures will be given by the difference between the products of total supplies and the import share in each of the years concerned,

$$dM = m_1 S_1 - m_0 S_0.$$

This subdivides into

$$dM = S_1(m_1 - m_0) + m_0 (S_1 - S_0).$$

In this equation the first term on the right-hand side represents gross import substitution, and its value will be negative whenever import substitution is taking place (that is, when $m_0 > m_1$). The second term on the right-hand side represents the change in imports due to the change in home demand, and will be positive whenever growth is taking place ($S_1 > S_0$). Overall, then, imports of manufactures will increase whenever the growth effect exceeds the substitution effect. This was so, apparently, even in the later nineteenth century; and even in the U.S.A. where import substitution, one would think, was particularly strong, imports of manufactures increased substantially in absolute value, though they declined as a proportion of the national income.

Since 1950 not only has the growth effect led to an increase in demand for manufactured imports in the industrial countries; it has been *reinforced* (not counteracted) by the tendency for import substitution to be reversed (that is, the value of $(m_1 - m_0)$ has been positive). This reflects the fact that such tendency as there has been towards further import substitution in these more mature industrial nations during the 1950s was more than offset by new opportunities for international specialization in manufactures which appeared

TABLE 4.4   *Effects of import-substitution and of expansion in demand on imports of manufactures, 1913–59*

$ billion, f.o.b. at 1955 prices

	Industrial countries			Semi-industrial countries		
	Import substitution	Expansion in demand[a]	Total	Import substitution	Expansion in demand[a]	Total
	$[S_1(m_1-m_0)]$	$[m_0(S_1-S_0)]$	$[S_1-S_0]$	$[S_1(m_1-m_0)]$	$[m_0(S_1-S_0)]$	$[S_1-S_0]$
1913–29	−2·2	+4·5	+2·3	−1·9	+3·0	+1·1
1929–37	−5·1	+1·9	−3·2	−1·8	+1·1	−0·7
1937–50	−2·0	+4·1	+2·1	−2·1	+3·7	+1·5
1950–59	+6·1	+6·3	+12·4	−3·1	+3·9	+0·8
Total	−3·1	+16·8	+13·7	−8·9	+11·6	+2·7

[a] Including export demand.
Source: Maizels (1963), 153.

in that decade. In the 'semi-industrialized' (industrializing) countries, on the other hand, a process of import replace-ment, often consciously pursued, has been under way which has progressively reduced the previous high share of imports in total supplies of manufactures (the value of (m_0-m_1) is high), so that even though the growth rate has also been high, *imports* of manufactures have not grown very rapidly or have even declined. These features are quantified in Table 4.4, taken from Maizels' work, in which the magni-tudes of import-substitution and of demand-expansion for groups of 'industrial' and 'semi-industrial' countries are set forth.

We shall see shortly that these differing experiences in respect of demand for manufactured imports help to explain the differing success in promoting exports experienced by the old-established manufacturing nations. Our immediate in-terest, however, is to point out that they also help to explain the relative decline of 'vertical' international specialization along pre-1914 lines and the increasingly dominant role in total world trade of the 'intra-trade' in manufactured com-modities amongst the industrial countries. For of course the depressing of their import shares by import replacement on the part of the industrializing countries reduces 'vertical' exchange, while the fast growth of import demand by countries already heavily industrialized increases what might be called the 'horizontal' specialization of the intra-trade in manufactures.

This, in turn, helps to explain another important and novel feature of recent world trade, namely that in sharp contrast with all pre-World War II experience, the rapid growth of trade in manufactures in recent decades has been associated with an *increase* in unit value. Before 1939, on the other hand, there had been a marked *inverse* correlation between volume of trade in manufactures and their unit value.[49] While the coincidence of increasing volume and rising prices is of course partly fortuitous, arising from the accident that the expansion of trade has taken place in a period of general inflation, the fact that the prices of inter-nationally-traded primary products have risen less or have actually declined, despite a smaller rate of volume increase, suggests that other factors are at work. It appears likely that the rising trends both of prices and of volume for manu-factures reflect an exceptionally favourable demand situation arising from the rapid growth rate of the industrial countries, now the major importers of manufactures, as well as from the rapid multiplication by technological progress of new products in which it has been possible to create *new* trade, thus avoiding the depressing effect which saturated markets have so often, sooner or later, exerted on the price of older staple goods.

This last point is of considerable importance. We saw that in the early nineteenth century the most rapidly growing items in world trade, Britain's exports of cotton textiles and metal manufactures, were based on the accident of Britain's 'early start'. A substantial part of today's intra-trade in manufactures between industrial nations is based in exactly similar fashion on a 'technological gap' between the pioneer of a new product and its 'imitators'. In a fascinating case study of international trade in synthetic materials,[50] Pro-fessor Hufbauer has shown how trade in the *newer* synthetic materials is dominated by this 'technological gap' trade – the

lead of the favoured country, needless to say, being maintained as long as possible by impeding the export of the
technological knowledge, exploiting the often considerable
scope for economies of scale by vigorous export promotion
and protection of the home market, developing 'tied' retail
outlets and the like. In all this there is no doubt that the
scales are heavily biased in favour of large countries because
of the high level of R and D expenditures and the significance
of economies of scale: Hufbauer claims that of 68 innovations
in synthetic fibres, 29 were made in the U.S.A., 22 in
Germany, 4 in Britain, 3 in France, 5 in Italy, and only 5 in
the rest of the world. Eventually, however, knowledge of
new processes gets abroad by independent research, licensing,
or foreign subsidiaries (or by industrial espionage). Then
'technological gap' exports may decline and low-wage
economies may be able to generate some trade in the older
products *in the reverse direction*. Hence the phenomenon that
the world's major exporters of synthetic materials are at the
same time large *importers* of them.

This, however, is only an apparent paradox, which has
been a familiar feature of the world trading scene for a long
time; as early as 1925 countries with substantial engineering
industries of their own took over 55 per cent of world
imports of machinery. Today this *intra-trade* is much more
nearly 'horizontal' than ever before. Sometimes this arises
from the peculiarities of 'technological gap' trade as out-
lined in the last paragraph. Sometimes imports cater to an
'unrepresentative demand' which domestic industries, geared
to mass production, do not find it economic to cater for, as
with U.S. imports of sports cars and small cars from Europe
and Japan. Sometimes foreign subsidiaries import from the
parent company components or materials which their
competitors manufacture in the host country. And where
tariffs are not prohibitive and transport costs are very low,
having regard to the value/bulk ratio of the product, even a
modest range of consumer preferences will permit both the
home-produced and the imported article to enjoy a fraction
of the market by practising product differentiation. Thus we

find, for example, that in 1968 more than one-sixth of all world trade consisted of the exchange of engineering products to each other by the industrial nations. This 'horizontal' specialization is even more strikingly exemplified in comparing the pattern of imports and exports for some individual countries: for example in 1968 again, the Federal Republic of Germany was at the same time the world's largest importer and the world's largest exporter of synthetic yarn and staple.*

The various changes in the composition and direction of world trade which we have discussed have had differing implications for the leading trading countries, according to their patterns of commodity and area specialization. In a pathbreaking paper twenty years ago,[51] H. Tyszynski sought to separate out the extent to which the leading traders' shares in world export of manufactures had on the one hand benefited (or suffered) as a result of changes in the composition of trade which favoured (or disfavoured) their pattern of industrial specialization, or had on the other hand risen or fallen as a consequence of a change in that country's competitive power *within* each separate classification. The results suggested, for example, that France and the United Kingdom had both suffered to some extent from the 'changing composition' effect, but that their major loss of position was to a greater extent due to declining competitive power

---

* The fact that the most rapidly growing part of world trade consists of the mutual exchange of similar types of product between countries of broadly similar structure has led the Swedish economist Linder to propose a novel theory according to which it is *similarity* in patterns of output and demand, not *dissimilarity*, which gives rise to international trade. The theory seems not to apply to the continuing exchange of a 'vertical' type, which is growing absolutely though not relative to total trade, and which may well accelerate again as resource depletion becomes more critical in industrial countries. It also pays inadequate regard to the existence of widely differing production functions for many manufactures, between which countries of differing factor proportions can choose. But Linder's theory has a decided appeal, and to the extent that it correctly identifies the *future* basis for international trade, it bodes no good for the low-income countries. See Staffan B. Linder, *An Essay on Trade and Transformation* (New York, Wiley, 1961), Ch. III.

in almost all groups. The impressive gains of Japan and Canada in world manufacturing trade, on the other hand, were largely due to these countries' increasing competitiveness, Japan losing marginally and Canada gaining marginally through the composition effect. The U.S.A., in contrast, owed much of its impressive gains to the good fortune of an industrial pattern well attuned to take advantage of compositional changes, though its increase in competitive strength was also appreciable.

The significance of Tyszynski's results may be questioned, partly because changes in composition *within* his broad categories may have been important (particularly in view of the trend to increasingly 'horizontal' specialization which we have noted), and partly because one might legitimately expect advanced countries to have some capacity to adjust to changing situations, and thus be inclined to blame them and not the situation if they fail to achieve this. This is an important general point, which alone suffices to make it difficult to know how much significance to attach to trade, or indeed to any one factor, in 'explaining' growth performance. But even the most demanding critic must agree that inherited patterns of industrial specialization have a considerable momentum arising from the deadweight of existing fixed capital and the pattern of labour skills and training facilities, as well as from more permanent influences such as resource-endowment and geographical situation – which even today have a considerably greater importance, even in manufactures, than is generally realized. We must therefore acknowledge *some* possibility of sheer good or bad luck in these matters.

More recently the work of Maizels has made plain that changes in the distribution of imports of manufactures by type of importing country have also influenced the fortunes of particular exporting countries. We have seen that much the most rapidly-growing share of world imports of manufactures is that taken by the advanced industrial nations themselves, whereas the *industrializing* (semi-industrialized) countries' imports have stagnated because their rapid growth of consumption has been offset by equally rapid import-substitution. The major exporters have been differently affected by these divergent trends. The countries of Northern and Western continental Europe have benefited because *intra*-European trade has long been of great importance to them, and geographical propinquity combined with exceptionally rapid trade liberalization have enabled them to take maximum advantage of recent trends. Britain, on the other hand, has historically oriented her manufactured exports to a greater extent to her overseas empire and to the other continents. She has therefore been vulnerable to a far greater degree to recent import substitution in some of the more important semi-industrial countries, India and Argentina in the 1930s and the 'Southern Dominions' since World War II.[52] In respect therefore both of commodity and area changes in the composition of world trade in manufactures, Britain has found herself holding the short end of the stick.

It is hard – not just for the reason mentioned in the second-last paragraph – to know how far foreign trade has promoted or retarded the economic growth of the rapidly-growing industrial countries in recent decades. The *fact* of a close correlation between overall economic growth and the rate of growth of exports is well established, and there have always been some writers who have pointed to the latter as a major determinant of the former.[53] However, the closest possible correlation between two variables tells us nothing as to the direction, or even the existence, of any direct causal link between them. If output and exports have grown in parallel fashion it may be that the second has 'caused' the first, but it may equally well be that the first has 'caused' the second; it is perhaps more plausible still, in this instance, to suppose that a third factor, rising productivity, has simultaneously determined both.

This latter view gains some plausibility from the case of the U.S.A. The U.S.A. (because of the size of its internal market) is unique among industrial nations outside the Communist world in exporting only a small fraction of its output of manufactures. But as Maizels shows, for the U.S.A.,

equally with other industrial countries, fluctuations in manufacturing output have been highly correlated in the years
since World War II with fluctuations in exports of manufactures.[54] In view of the low trade/output ratio it is scarcely
credible that the second should have caused the first, and not
much more plausible that the first should have caused the
second, for in this case one would have expected the 'over-
spill' of exports to have fluctuated much more violently than
the level of output, which was not the case. It is more
plausible that changes in productivity underlay both
changes in the level of output and also the competitive
strength, and thus the level, of U.S. exports.

But it is hard not to believe that there has been a substantial direct dependence, also, of growth on trade, and
since the influences envisaged here may be expected to have
been more important for smaller than for larger countries,
any argument to the contrary from the case of the U.S.A. is
not conclusive. Notably, the enormous burden of R and D
costs for many products in 'science-based' industries has to be
spread over as large an output as possible. (The Anglo-
French *Concorde* project, if it goes ahead, will certainly have
been wildly uneconomic unless the initiative of the two
countries succeeds in winning for them a very large 'technological gap' trade in supersonic airliners, and possibly so
even in that event.) Economies of scale, which have certainly
been of growing importance in many industries of rapid
technological progress, point of course in the same direction.
More generally, there is little doubt that keeping or increasing one's share in the highly competitive world of manufactured exports has a beneficial, galvanizing effect on the
quality of management, the search for higher productivity,
the streamlining of sales methods, and the like. A recent
GATT report, surveying world trade in the 1960s, underlines
some of these points and argues strongly for a large dependence of industrial investments on exports.[55] It points out
that not only does the trade/G.N.P. ratio understate the
share of exports in *manufacturing* production, but that when
trade in manufactures is rising faster than output (as has

been true since the middle of the century), *average* ratios will understate the *incremental* dependence of new investment on the export markets. Thus a typical overall trade/income ratio of, say, 15 per cent would translate into an incremental trade/output ratio for manufactures of at least one-third, and in some cases much more.

Trade and growth: some concluding remarks

It is impossible to conclude a chapter on trade and growth without posing the 64-dollar question, does trade promote growth or not? For at the very time when the rate of growth both of trade and of output began to accelerate and when statesmen, heeding the advocacy of theorists, were demolishing Mercantilist barriers to give free rein to international commerce, other voices were raised urging the merits of protection as a recipe for growth. And as a matter of history, the number of countries which have achieved substantial growth behind tariff barriers probably exceeds that of those who have become rich with the aid of free trade.

It may seem strange that such a crucial issue should have been left to the very end of a long chapter. But indeed this postponement has been undertaken deliberately, in the hope that by this point the reader's mind will be well disposed to accept the suggestion that the question, as formulated, is not capable of being answered with a simple yes or no. For, as has surely become apparent, the relationship between trade and the rate of growth is not unique. With the clarity of exposition we have come to expect of him, Professor Kindleberger has sketched for us three models of the relationship of growth to trade: trade as a leading, as a balancing and as a lagging sector, concluding that 'The impact of foreign trade on growth is then indeterminate over a wide range'.[56] Everything in this chapter suggests the justice of this view.

Moreover, trade is sometimes said to have been detrimental to growth when what is meant is that it was detrimental to *development*, as that word was defined in Chapter 1. It is in this sense that some might say that a *reduction* in their trade participation ratios might have helped promote the 'growth' (meaning, structural change) of, say, New Zealand or Argentina just before and just after World War I. That exchange rates geared to the comparative productivity of the exporting industries, cheap freight 'backhauls', an orientation of credit, transport facilities and technology towards the sectors favoured by comparative advantage, could and did stamp some economies with a particular industrial structure which some would call 'underdeveloped' is undoubtedly true; the tendency for this structure to change as soon as some adventitious event, such as the world wars, offered a temporary 'protection' from trade is clear. In some other instances we see that increasing integration into the international economy and specialization on an export staple drew resources away from and ultimately destroyed the traditional manufactures of a peasant society.[57]

It was open to anyone to argue that the increase in real income which this form of specialization won, at least in the short run, was too dearly bought, and to advocate a degree of 'trade-off' between real income and structural change. The latter might be favoured for its own sake: there are those who would prefer relative poverty in the city to relative affluence in the countryside. Or a degree of diversification might be sought as a shield against externally-induced fluctuations or against the threat (which history has shown to be not imaginary) which technological progress always hangs over the head of specialists in primary products, or for the sake of gaining access to the areas of most rapid technological advance, or for some other more or less valid economic reason. In this event, if industrialization cannot get under way so long as imports from established low-cost manufactures are left free, then some resort to protection is indicated.

How far the tariffs imposed in the later nineteenth century under the guise of such arguments were responsible for promoting industrial growth is difficult to know. (It is not suggested, incidentally, that these arguments were ever, politically speaking, the chief *reason* for imposing tariffs. The desire to make concessions to politically-important interests, the need for revenue, and in some cases the desire for autarky based on military considerations were probably more important. And in the case of the leading nations of Western Europe the tariff in any event benefited the farmer as much as the manufacturer and preserved for agriculture a much larger share, at least in employment, than would have been the case under a free trade régime.) There has been surprisingly little historical work on the effect of tariffs on industrial structure. Perhaps this is because to assess the effects of a tariff – how would the U.S. steel industry have grown in the later nineteenth century if the protective duty had not been imposed? – is an exercise in 'counterfactual history', a mode of analysis which has only recently become fashionable. The effects of a tariff would be difficult to disentangle, moreover, from those of other influences working in the same direction. Tugan-Baranowsky was inclined to depreciate the role of the tariff in promoting Russian industrialization in the late nineteenth century, but he employed no rigorous technique for separating its effects from those of the government contracts and purchases, monopolies formed with government connivance, and similar devices employed to achieve the same end.[58]

Whatever the efficacy of import tariffs, they worked – directly, at least – against imports, and particular imports at that, rather than against trade in general. Russia, which had perhaps the highest import duties in the world in the twenty years before World War I, coupled with its tariff policy draconian measures to increase exports, if need be at the cost of substantial welfare loss. The Russian position, as we have seen, was that industrialization generated import needs which exceeded the country's equilibrium foreign exchange earnings and that measures to 'ration' imports, promote exports, and encourage capital inflow were all necessary. The position of present-day protectionists like Prebisch is essentially similar. It is a complete misunderstanding of their views to assert that they are hostile to trade as such or believe that developing countries would fare better without it. Rather, their complaint is that these countries *cannot get enough trade*; that structural features of the growth and import demands of the industrial countries make it impossible for the primary-producing world as a whole to achieve a rate of export growth sufficient to meet its foreign exchange requirements, and that import duties or controls to 'ration' scarce foreign exchange and give priority to growth-strategic areas thus become necessary. These measures thus simultaneously serve both a balance of payments and a development aim.

But it would be a mistake to characterize such policies as implying a *denial* of the growth-promoting value of trade, and it would equally be a mistake to think that they lead to a decline in the level of importing of the country concerned. There is every likelihood that countries pursuing import-replacement policies – and these include rich temperate zone producers like New Zealand as well as low-income countries in the tropical world – will spend every dollar of foreign exchange they can lay their hands on. To say this is not to deny that these policies sometimes, perhaps always, involve some degree of damage to the export industries by raising internal costs and distorting the domestic allocation of resources, and it may be that in some cases a significantly lower degree of protection and correspondingly greater emphasis on improving the performance of the export industries would have been preferable. But the room for manoeuvre has become dangerously constrained for such countries thanks to the deceleration in world import demand for primary products and the acceleration of their own population growth.

Notes

1. DEANE and COLE (1967), 309–10.

2. R. DAVIS, 'English Foreign Trade, 1700–1774', *Economic History Review*, Sec. Ser. XV (December 1962), 285–303.

3. K. G. DAVIES, 'Joint-Stock Investment in the Later Seven-

teenth Century', *Economic History Review*, Sec. Ser. IV (1951–2), 283–301.

4. CARLO M. CIPOLLA, 'Note sulla storia del saggio d'interesse', *Economia Internazionale*, V (1952), 255–74.

5. *Considerations on the East-India Trade* (London, 1701), Chs. X, XII, XIII; reprinted in J. R. MCCULLOCH (ed.), *Early English Tracts on Commerce* (Cambridge, Cambridge U.P., 1954).

6. KARL W. DEUTSCH and ALEXANDER ECKSTEIN, 'National Industrialization and the Declining Share of the International Economic Sector, 1890–1959', *World Politics*, XIII (January 1961), 267–99.

7. R. E. LIPSEY, *Price and Quantity Trends in the Foreign Trade of the United States* (Princeton, N.J., Princeton U.P., 1963), 40–5.

8. KUZNETS (1966), Table 6.4, 312–14. (Australia is not included in the constant-price comparison.)

9. KINDLEBERGER (1962), 178.

10. KUZNETS (1966), 301.

11. KINDLEBERGER (1962), 32–7; P. LLOYD, *International Trade Problems of Small Nations* (Durham, N.C., Duke U.P., 1968), 24–5.

12. LEAGUE OF NATIONS (1945), 46.

13. LLOYD, *op. cit.*, 75, 92 ff.

14. C. P. KINDLEBERGER, 'Industrial Europe's Terms of Trade on Current Account', *Economic Journal*, LXV (March 1955), 27.

15. See further Ch. 5 below.

16. G. T. JONES, *Increasing Return* (Cambridge, Cambridge U.P., 1933).

17. See further below, pp. 356–60.

18. M. BLAUG, 'The Productivity of Capital in the Lancashire Cotton Industry during the Nineteenth Century', *Economic History Review*, Sec. Ser. XIII (April 1961), 379–80.

19. D. C. NORTH, 'Ocean Freight Rates and Economic Development 1750–1913', *Journal of Economic History*, XVIII (December 1958), 537–55. For an interesting study of the early banana trade, see DOUGLAS HALL, *Ideas and Illustrations in Economic History* (New York, Holt, Rinehart and Winston, 1964), Ch. 4.

20. LEAGUE OF NATIONS (1945), 14.

21. D. H. ROBERTSON, 'The Future of International Trade', *Economic Journal*, XLVIII (March 1938), 1–14.

22. NURKSE (1961).

23. NOEL G. BUTLIN, *Investment in Australian Economic Development 1861–1900* (Cambridge, Cambridge U.P., 1964), 9, 13. An Argentinian estimate is for a growth of real income per head somewhat in excess of 1 per cent, 1860–1929, compared with a growth of total income at four or five times that rate: ALDO FERRER, *The Argentine Economy*, trans. M. M. URQUIDI (Berkeley, Calif., U. of California Press, 1967), 123.

24. See above, pp. 33–4.

25. UNITED NATIONS, E.C.L.A., *El Desarrollo Económico de la Argentina* (Mexico, 1959), Table 39, p. 37.

26. KINDLEBERGER (1962), 31, 143–6.

27. G. EISNER, *Jamaica, 1830–1930: A Study in Economic Growth* (Manchester, Manchester U.P., 1961), 62, 25.

28. JONATHAN V. LEVIN, *The Export Economies* (Cambridge, Mass., Harvard U.P., 1960), Ch. 2, *passim*.

29. See, for example, MYRDAL (1968), Vol. I, 446, and Ch. 11.

30. For a summary, see C. P. KINDLEBERGER, 'Obsolescence and Technical Change', *Bulletin of the Oxford Institute of Economics and Statistics*, XXIII (August 1961), 281–97.

31. JOHN R. MEYER, 'An Input-Output Approach to Evaluating the Influence of Exports on British Industrial Production in the late 19th Century', *Explorations in Entrepreneurial History*, VIII (October 1955), 12–34.

32. D. C. NORTH, *The Economic Growth of the United States 1790–1860* (New York, Prentice-Hall, 1961), 1–2.

33. LEWIS (1955), 280.

34. KUZNETS (1966), Table 6.4, 312–14.

35. HOFFMANN (1965), Table 65, p. 151.

36. *ibid.*, Table 69, p. 157.

37. W. M. HAMILTON, *The Dairy Industry of New Zealand* (Wellington, Government Printer, 1944).

38. H. B. CHENERY and A. M. STROUT, 'Foreign Assistance and Economic Development', *American Economic Review*, LVI (September 1966), 679–733. For a forceful statement of the

case 'that the ability to maintain adequate levels of imports is as critical for economic growth as, say, it is to raise capacity by maintaining appropriate investment levels', see LORETO M. DOMINGUEZ, 'Economic Growth and Import Requirements', *Journal of Development Studies*, VI (April 1970), 283–99.

39. See especially, UNITED NATIONS, E.C.L.A., *The Economic Development of Latin America and its Principal Problems* (New York, 1950), 8–10.

40. For some striking illustrations, see C. M. WRIGHT, 'Convertibility and Triangular Trade as Safeguards against Economic Depression', *Economic Journal*, LXV (September 1955), 426.

41. CHARLES P. KINDLEBERGER, *The Terms of Trade: A European Case Study* (Cambridge, Mass., Technology Press, M.I.T. and New York, Wiley, 1956).

42. A convenient presentation of recent experience is T. WILSON, R. P. SINHA and J. R. CASTREE, 'The Income Terms of Trade of Developed and Developing Countries', *Economic Journal*, LXXIX (December 1969), 813–32.

43. GATT, *International Trade 1968* (Geneva, 1969), Table 1, 1.

44. NURKSE (1961).

45. CAIRNCROSS (1962), Ch. 12.

46. A. MAIZELS, *Exports and Economic Growth of Developing Countries* (Cambridge, Cambridge U.P., 1968), 11.

47. MAIZELS (1963), 127, 130.

48. The notation is borrowed from MAIZELS (1963), 151.

49. MAIZELS (1963), 109.

50. G. C. HUFBAUER, *Synthetic Materials and the Theory of International Trade* (London, Duckworth, 1966).

51. H. TYSZYNSKI, 'World Trade in Manufactured Commodities, 1899–1950', *Manchester School of Economics and Social Studies*, XIX (September 1951), 272–304.

52. MAIZELS (1963), 224–31.

53. e.g. H. DENIS, 'Croissance industrielle et commerce extérieure', *Revue d'economie politique*, 71 (March/April 1961), 165–88.

54. MAIZELS (1963), 223–4.

55. GATT, *International Trade 1968* (Geneva, 1969), 11–12.

56. KINDLEBERGER (1962), Ch. 12.

57. STEPHEN A. RESNICK, 'The Decline of Rural Industry Under Export Expansion: A Comparison among Burma, Philippines, and Thailand, 1870–1938', *Journal of Economic History*, XXX (March 1970), 51–73.

58. M. TUGAN-BARANOWSKY, *Geschichte der russischen Fabrik* (Berlin, Emil Felber, 1900), 403 ff.

5 Technology and the 'Residual'

The 'residual' in economic growth

We saw in Chapter 1 that macro-economic investigations of the sources of economic growth in recent times have usually concluded that the increase of aggregate inputs is able to explain only a small part of the measured growth of output which has accrued, and that the bulk – in one investigation as much as seven-eighths – of that growth has to be explained by 'residual' factors. Since the mode of analysis adopted has been based on the concept of the 'production function', and since the production function is an expression summarizing the ranges of possible outputs which given collections of inputs can generate, *given* the state of technology available at the time, it seems natural to think of this 'residual' as a measurement of the increase of the ratio of output to input arising from the historical development of technology, constantly pushing out the production possibility frontier.

In theory, the growth equation *could* be specified in such a way that the 'residual', the remainder left by subtracting the rate of growth of measured inputs from that of measured outputs, would represent the contribution to growth of technological advance (interpreting this last phrase in a perhaps rather old-fashioned way to mean product and process changes resulting in an improvement in aggregate productivity). But in our present state of knowledge this is an ambitious aim to attempt, and in practice the large majority of estimated 'residuals' do not in fact measure the contribution of technical change with even approximate accuracy, other perhaps than by accident. This is partly, of course, because the residual *is* a residual; whatever errors creep into the estimation of output and of aggregate input are bundled together with all other influences collectively referred to as 'the residual'. There are, however, subtler difficulties, and difficulties less likely to cancel each other out by offsetting, than errors arising from data deficiencies or like causes.

In the first place, indices of inputs of labour and capital are often compiled by some process of mere 'counting' which fails to take account of changes in the *quality* of these inputs. For example, there is much reason to believe that an improvement in the educational level of the labour force exerts in general a beneficial effect on output; a labour-input index compiled merely by counting heads omits to measure this effect directly and instead leaves it to be picked up as part of the residual, where it may then be mistakenly interpreted as part of the contribution of technical change. Similarly, there is reason to think that many indices of capital input are downward-biased through failing adequately to capture the secular improvement which has been wrought in the quality of investment goods. This is particularly likely in the case of capital inputs which are difficult to measure *directly*, and which are estimated in terms of the cost of producing them, such as construction. The effect of this procedure is to fail to credit productivity improvements in construction to the construction industry, where they belong, and to leave them instead to become part of the residual of the industries which use the outputs of the construction industry as inputs. In view of the generally very large share of construction in capital formation, this is a serious disadvantage, which only fortuitously is somewhat mitigated by the fact that construction is not characteristically an industry of rapid productivity improvement. In general, the measurement of capital inputs, which often proceeds by the deflation of current-price estimates of capital formation by a price index, is hampered by the paucity and unreliability of input price indices. As Griliches points out, the latter are by way of being 'orphans in the world of social statistics', not commanding the public importance – nor, therefore, the public funds – of indices of, say, consumer goods prices or land values.[1]

Apart from such sources of downward bias in the measurement of inputs included in the production function, other inputs may be omitted altogether. For example, farm output may be expected to respond *ceteris paribus* to changes in the volume of fertilizer used; so that if fertilizer is not included as an input in the production function and farm output is measured gross of fertilizer use, the effect on output will be consigned to the residual.

A different point is that the production function traces out alternative outputs which *could* be produced if, given the inputs and the technology available, the economy in question functioned at maximum efficiency. But for a variety of reasons economies, like motor-car engines, often do not function at maximum efficiency, and sometimes they may function far below it. In comparing output in two different periods, therefore, allowance must be made for any change in the extent to which output is improved or impaired by movement during the interval in question towards or away from the production possibility frontier. Failing this, such output changes will once again be consigned to the residual and become confused with the results of technological progress.

Finally, the type of production function customarily used in analysis of the sources of growth assumes constant returns to scale. In short-period exercises this doubtless is not usually a severe deficiency; but in estimates of the long-run rate of historical growth one cannot so readily assume this consideration to be of negligible importance.

These are perhaps the most important reasons why the residual, as usually estimated, does not correctly measure the contribution of technological progress to economic growth. But even if appropriate corrections were made under each of these headings, the residual would still be a composite including, along with the contribution of technology

in its narrower, 'engineering' sense, improvements of what
we might term a 'managerial' kind – incentive pay schemes,
the benefits of time-and-motion studies, improvements to
factory layout and work flow, and the like. Further, improvements in technology may be subdivided to distinguish
the benefits of newly-won knowledge applied by the most
advanced plant working 'on the technological frontier' from
changes in the relative lag of the average behind this 'best-
practice' plant – a lag which may, of course, vary between
industries, between countries, and over time – and also to
distinguish major inventions from gradual, piecemeal
improvements, and innovations which involve scientific
novelty from those which do not. A 'family tree' of the
origins of economic growth, in fact, looks something like that
depicted in fig. 5.1. It can be seen that there is no justification
for equating the 'residual' (B_2) with technological change
(D_1), still less with just those changes in the technique of
production which involve scientific novelty $(G_1 + G_3)$.

Thanks to the widespread effort devoted in recent years
to the macro-economic study of the sources of growth, these
points are now far better appreciated than they were even
fifteen or twenty years ago, when such study was in its
infancy. Still, we do not as yet have many careful investigations yielding evidence as to the relative sizes of the contributions to growth of the various factors mentioned as
forming part of the residual. There is every reason, however,
to believe that, at least for the advanced countries whose
growth records we have discussed in this book, the combined influence on growth of residual factors *other* than
technological advance has been positive. This is so because
while none of these factors appears to be systematically
unfavourable to growth, some are known or believed to have
made significant positive contributions to it. Thus, for
example, in most advanced countries the quality of the
labour force in recent historical times, as determined by
level of educational attainment and also – a widely ignored
factor – by physical health and strength, has surely trended
upwards. Adjustment of labour inputs for qualitative change

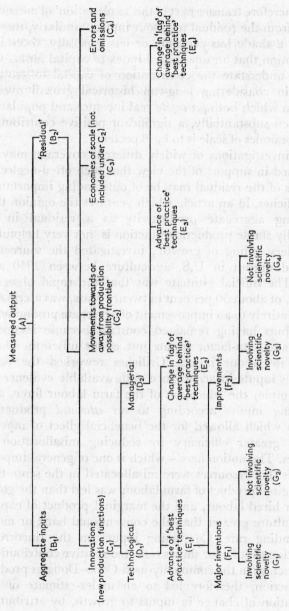

FIGURE 5.1 The sources of increase in (measured) output

would therefore transfer part of the 'explanation' of measured growth from the residual to labour inputs. Similarly, though perhaps a shade less certainly or less generally, there is a presumption that an unadjusted index of capital inputs will tend to understate the contribution of capital to growth. Again, in considering long-run historical growth over a period in which both *per capita* real incomes and population have risen substantially, a significant positive contribution from economies of scale is to be expected.

Two investigations of widely different coverage may be mentioned in support of the view that such often-neglected elements of the residual may be of outstanding importance. Zvi Griliches, in an article which ventures the opinion that estimating aggregate productivity as a residual in an assumedly stable production function is 'not very helpful to the understanding of growth', investigated the sources of increased output in U.S. agriculture between 1940 and 1960.[2] The official estimate was that the rapid observed increase, of about 50 per cent in twenty years, was ascribable almost entirely to an improvement of aggregate productivity, total inputs having remained constant because increased capital and non-factor inputs just about offset the sharp decline in labour inputs. Griliches reworked the data, adjusting inputs in accordance with available evidence on (for example) the education of the farm labour force, and combining inputs according to an *estimated* production function which allowed for the beneficial effect of moving towards greater efficiency by reducing misallocation of resources. The notion here – which is one of general import- ance – is that resources were misallocated in the sense that the marginal product of farm labour was less than the going wage for hired labour, and the marginal product of capital in agriculture greater than the conventional bank or mort- gage lending rate. Combining inputs on the (incorrect) assumption that factor shares reflected relative contributions to product, as in the commonly-used Cobb–Douglas produc- tion function, therefore led to an under-estimate of the contribution of change in inputs to growth, by attributing too large a power to contribute to output to the declining input (labour), and too small an output-generating power to the increasing inputs. Growth which should have been attributed to changes in aggregate inputs was therefore consigned to the residual and misinterpreted as the fruits of technological advance.

Overall, Griliches found that the impressive increase in aggregate factor productivity disappeared entirely when inputs were correctly measured and proper allowance made for economies of scale with increasing average farm size. Roughly one-third of the increase of output, Griliches claimed, could be accounted for by improvements in the quality of inputs, notably better education, and one-quarter to one-sixth by improved allocation of resources; the remainder was explained by economies of scale.*

An investigation on a much more ambitious scale, but based upon similar concepts, is Edward Denison's outstanding study, *Why Growth Rates Differ*.[3] Faced by the sharp contrast between rapid growth in Western Europe and the sluggish performance of the U.S. (and the United Kingdom) economies after World War II, Denison was reluctant to accept the finding of simpler investigations which seemed to suggest that the greater part of this discrepancy was due to more rapid technical progress in continental Europe. Rather, Denison essayed a multi-variate analysis of the sources of growth, the result of which was to suggest that a large part of Europe's rapid growth, and of the superiority of its post-war growth achievement over that of America, could be attributed to less familiar factors. Prominent among these were the following sources of growth:

(a) improved allocation of resources, principally by the transfer of labour from agriculture and the self-employed in other sectors (small shopkeepers, for example) into more highly-productive employment (C_2 in fig. 5.1);

* Somewhat embarrassingly, the remainder was actually *rather more than* accounted for, leaving a small negative residual suggesting technological retrogression – which seems most unlikely.

L

   (b) a reduction in the lag of the application of knowledge behind U.S.A. (principally $E_2 + E_4$);

   (c) economies of scale (C_3).

For North-west Europe as a whole, Denison estimates advances in knowledge to have been responsible for only one-quarter of the rise in aggregate productivity over the years 1950–62, and in fact less important than the third factor mentioned above (C_3) and not very much more important than the first two factors.[4] Moreover, 'advances in knowledge' is here to be construed comprehensively, as comprising both technological and managerial knowledge $(E_1 + E_3)$. Further, Denison feels justified in setting the contribution to growth of advances in knowledge $(E_1 + E_3)$ at the same value in all nine countries, thus denying this factor any part in the explanation of differences in growth rates. This implies, of course, that the advance in knowledge is judged to have played a more prominent proportionate role in the U.S.A.'s relatively slower post-war growth, but even there was responsible for only a shade more than one half of the rise of aggregate productivity over the same period.

While Denison's procedure here may well be called in question, the two outstanding studies we have mentioned find in other, less comprehensive, studies support for their conclusion that the advance of the frontier of technical 'know-how' can easily (and substantially) be over-rated as a source of economic growth. It is necessary to add, however, that the role of technological progress might be redeemed somewhat if we could estimate its contribution to welfare rather than to measured output. This is by no means certain, for one would then need to bring into the reckoning social costs such as despoliation of the environment about which so much is heard nowadays, and for which modern technology is held responsible. The justification for the conjecture, however, lies in the belief that as a measure of welfare the index of measured output also has a downward bias because it fails to capture the benefits of increasing consumer choice and improvements in the quality of consumer goods. Since most of these can be credited to technological progress it might be argued that the latter makes a bigger proportionate contribution to the increase of welfare than to the rise of measured income.

Allocation of resources

The chief finding of the studies discussed so far, that technological progress plays a more modest role than the earlier estimates of the residual were thought to imply, clearly demands and doubtless will provoke careful reappraisal of the impact on growth of some of the other factors mentioned. In default of such reappraisals, however, little can at the moment be said with any confidence. The idea, for example, that the reduction of disequilibria through improved allocation of resources could rival technological progress as a source of growth, even over a short period, has not been easily and generally accepted, and indeed is (implicitly) denied by some. Harvey Leibenstein has summarized the results of some empirical studies which seem to suggest only a trifling welfare loss – less than 1 per cent of G.N.P. in all cases, and only a small fraction of 1 per cent in most – arising from departures from optimal resource allocation.[5] Each study is concerned, however, with only *one* source of allocative inefficiency, arising from either tariffs or monopoly, and none deals with the probably much larger loss of potential output arising from failure to equalize marginal productivities in different sectors and regions of large and complex economies. The extent of this type of loss has also, however, been queried, for example by Arnold Harberger, who shows by assuming certain hypothetical values for the measure of sectoral misallocation that it is difficult to account for an improvement of as much as 10 per cent of G.N.P. by a move to optimal allocation.[6] This demonstration is given substantive content by Harberger's claim that the degree of misallocation represented by the hypothetical values chosen is substantially greater than obtained in Chile, a country with whose structure he was well acquainted and which might on general grounds have been expected to be more subject to such distortions than many.

On the other hand this scepticism runs counter to Denison's finding that improved allocation of resources – largely, as has been mentioned, the contraction of the labour force in agriculture and in non-agricultural self-employment – was responsible for a substantial part of economic growth in North-west Europe as a whole in the period 1950–62. Specifically, it is suggested that this source alone generated an average of 0·68 per cent points per annum to growth of real income in the seven countries concerned; in Germany and in France the contribution was a little over and a little under 1 per cent per annum respectively. In Italy (not included in the North-west Europe average) the comparable figure was almost $1\frac{1}{2}$ per cent, not a surprising contrast in view of the clearly greater scope for improved allocation in that country. Thus in Italy the total growth from improved allocation over the years 1950–62, according to Denison's estimate, was substantially larger than the maximum Harberger thought conceivable. By contrast, neither the U.S.A. nor the United Kingdom is judged to have gained much from this source, a finding which (relative to that for the other countries) might plausibly be explained by reference to the generally highly competitive and mobile economy of the former country and the uniquely small place of agriculture in the employment structure of the latter. So far as agricultural contraction is concerned, Denison's calculations appear to find support in the report of a group of O.E.C.D. experts on the role of agriculture in the economic growth of a group of European and North American countries over the years 1950–60.[7]

As yet, however, there is relatively little evidence elsewhere from carefully conducted analyses bearing on the belief that reallocation may often be a major source of growth. The example of Soviet Russia springs to mind: it is generally acknowledged that this country has depended on increased inputs to an unusual degree for its achieved growth, and especially under the first two Five-Year Plans the massive transfer of labour from agriculture to other sectors was a major source of growth. But it is not clear what studies Professor Postan had in mind when he referred to 'the generally accepted historical generalization that all past increases in national *per capita* incomes were primarily due to transfers of labour from agriculture to industry', and one must also conclude that there is some exaggeration – though also support for Denison – in his subsequent assertion that 'for most European countries the historical generalization . . . still hold(s) good'.

Postan does, however, make a valid and valuable point when (following Kindleberger, who has stressed the contribution of labour transfers to European growth in the 1950s) he goes on to suggest that as far as Western Europe is concerned, this source of growth may nearly have run dry by the mid-1960s as a consequence of the shift in the allocation of labour having brought labour productivity in agriculture much closer to that in other sectors.[8] This provides a timely reminder that at any point of time the scope for increasing output by improving allocation, though it may be large, must nevertheless be finite. One cannot after all better optimal allocation. Hence, speaking rather vaguely, one could say that improved allocation could in some cases be responsible for a major contribution to growth over a fairly short time-span, or for a small positive contribution over a long period. The cases of Russia under the early five-year plans and of post-World War II Europe clearly fall in the first category, imperfections in resource allocation which had endured for several generations, or in the Russian case perhaps for centuries, moving very rapidly towards the optimum under the stimulus of high investment rates, full employment and a high and sustained level of demand. Such major improvements cannot, in the nature of things, be expected to continue indefinitely or even for very long. But it is necessary to add that while departure of resource allocation from any given optimum offers scope only for finite, if perhaps large, improvement, the optimum *itself* is not static, but constantly shifts as technology changes and relative marginal products alter. The 'ceiling' performance of which a given economy is theoretically capable therefore constantly moves, and actual allocation chases an ever-shifting target. It is not to be wondered at, the economic historian's tools and data being what they are, that there is as yet little information as to how much of the growth of output achieved over any given period is to be ascribed to an improvement in technology moving the ceiling of optimum performance, and how much to a movement of the economy *towards* the equilibrium allocation as it might have been conceived at some particular point of time.

'Human capital' and growth

In respect of the role of education in economic growth, again there has so far been little in the way of attempts to apply the methods of recent economic investigations to the historical course of growth. Education has of course assumed a place of some prominence in the pre-occupations of economists during recent years, under the guise of 'investment in human capital'.[9] Their investigations have proceeded from the everyday observation that level of educational attainment and earnings are positively correlated, and the focus of attention has been on the rate of return to 'investment' in education conceived as the ratio of the discounted stream of earnings differentials to the costs, direct and indirect (earnings foregone during years of schooling), of attaining a given level of education. Clearly a mere comparison of average incomes or income ranges for each level of educational attainment is apt to overstate the responsibility of the educational difference for the earnings difference, since there are other factors – intelligence, capacity for effort, father's occupation, educational background of parents – which are known, or may plausibly be assumed, to be positively correlated both with educational attainment and with earnings. This would tend to lead to a higher-than-average level of income for those who in fact attain a higher-than-average level of education, even were the differences in educational level eliminated.

There are, of course, other factors too which help to determine the level of individual earnings in a given country, notably age and sex. It is possible to hold the latter characteristics constant, at least for the U.S.A. where it is feasible to achieve a breakdown of incomes by sex, age and length of schooling. But correcting for the autocorrelation between length of education and other income-producing characteristics is far more difficult. In his two major contributions to the study of the sources of growth, Denison assumed that three-fifths of the differences in income between groups with varying years of formal education (correction for sex and age having been made first) was *caused* by these educational differences, the remainder being due to other characteristics which correlate with educational experience. In *The Sources of Economic Growth* this assumption was acknowledged to lack statistical foundation; when *Why Growth Rates Differ* was written, some modest support for it had been forthcoming,[10] but Denison would certainly not wish to suggest that the evidence here is as convincing as one would like, given the importance of the assumption made for the attribution of achieved growth to its 'true' causes. That the matter *is* important is sufficiently suggested by the results of the first of the two studies just mentioned, which claims that in the U.S.A. the increase in education was responsible for 23 per cent of the rate of growth of national product over the years 1929–57, or of as much as 42 per cent of the increase of *per capita* product.[11] This, moreover, relates only to the *direct* effect of increased education on the quality of the labour force. It makes no allowance for indirect benefits such as a possible favourable influence on the rate of increase of technical knowledge.

These findings are not entirely unexpected, given first that the 'human capital' studies have tended to show a very high rate of return on educational investment and secondly that educational provision has in fact increased markedly in the twentieth century. An academic author writing for a doubt-less predominantly academic audience has every incentive to endorse findings which attribute so large a material return to educational improvement. Unfortunately, the argument is not at the present time completely convincing. There are indeed those who remain sceptical of the whole approach to estimating the rate of return on 'investment in human capital' by working from observed differences in earnings. It may, for instance, be held that the market for those with high education – or rather markets, for engineering graduates are not part of the supply offered to the legal profession nor the dentist's skills readily transferable to agricultural extension – is not perfectly competitive; in some advanced countries certain professions, medicine or the law, are to some extent 'closed shops', and there are those who believe that the average earnings of the members of such professions in consequence overstate their contribution to real product. Similar misgivings attend the assumption of equality of earnings and marginal product in the case of many public servants, where substantial political factors enter into the determining of the level of employment and salaries.* Further, it seems highly improbable that the 'spin-off' effects of war and space research are anything like large enough to compensate for the diversion of skills from consumer-oriented economic activity to these areas.

This is perhaps not the most serious difficulty, however. Due allowance made for departures of the market from perfect competition, the earnings of a particular type of labour at a particular point of time represent the interaction of its supply and demand curves. But one cannot infer the shapes of those curves at a particular time, nor their displacement through time, from a single observation of their intersection. Hence it is illegitimate to infer from the fact that at a particular time the return on 'investment in human capital' is some particular (relatively high) value, that a *very large* increment in such investment would be, *ceteris paribus*, profitable – as illegitimate as it would be to advocate a *huge*

---

* In default of any other measure, the *income received* by tertiary workers is sometimes used as the measure of their output. In this event earnings and contribution to measured output are equal by definition, and one's misgiving is rather whether *measured* output correctly represents *real* output.

increase of investment in glasshouses because today's tomato growers are making a good living.

It would be an odd coincidence if the contribution of a given quantum of educational improvement to growth of product had remained constant over time, and there is in fact no more reason for expecting it to have done so than for expecting that the capital/output ratio should be always – or everywhere – the same. This analogy points to a further difficulty, namely that in default of other means of assessment educational 'investment' is measured merely by number of years schooling – which is neither a measure sensitive to differences in the output-generating power of different types of schooling, nor one capable of reflecting the changing average quality of education over time. There has, of course, been a huge increase in educational provision in advanced countries within the past hundred years. There has also been a great increase in demand for highly-educated people: the increasing economic importance of science and technology, the increase in scale of enterprise and the associated rise in managerial and accounting skills, the growth of the professions, and the expansion of the public service, are among the more obvious sources of this. It is not perhaps certain whether supply has tended to outstrip demand, or vice versa; but there is reason to believe that professional incomes have tended to fall relative to average incomes through time[12] (the higher ratio of professional to average incomes in underdeveloped than in developed countries supports this, though weakly), and since professional occupations generally call for a high level of education one might be tempted to infer from this that supply has tended to outstrip demand. If so, and if one could believe that earnings differentials really measure the contribution of education to product, the use of *present-day* differentials would understate the 'true' contribution of improved education to growth.

To the economic historian scanning a longer time-horizon it perhaps seems questionable whether any simple scheme of counting increments of schooling and relating these to the growth of product by a crude formula really meets the complexity of the case. It seems clear that not only has the importance of education for economic performance on average, so to say, changed over time, but also the demand for different types and levels of education has grown at different speeds, so that one must pay some attention to the changing composition of educational provision. The first industrial revolution beginning in Britain in the late eighteenth century was achieved, so the orthodox account would suggest, without the aid of any satisfactory or systematic facilities for education. It is true that recent researches have somewhat modified this account by documenting the considerable, though unsystematized and informal, opportunities for adult acquisition of technical knowledge – such as it then was – in some of the industrial districts, and by suggesting that by the 1830s, at least, spending on school education in Britain reached a level comparable, as a percentage of G.N.P., to that of the years between the two world wars.[13] The impression remains that the early industrial revolution was successful in spite of, rather than because of, the educational facilities on which it could draw. If we can accept as correct the tentative indications that earnings differentials for a given margin of educational superiority were wider in those days than at the present time, this would imply that a Denison-type analysis would attribute a greater growth-promoting effect then than now to a given quantum of educational improvement. But this differential was determined proximately by professional and public service earnings, and more fundamentally perhaps by class-generated imperfections in the labour market, to a far greater extent than by any advantage which higher education conferred on the entrepreneur, the workman or the farmer. Indeed it is questionable whether the multiplication of places in English grammar schools and universities of the period would have had the slightest relevance for British performance in the early industrial revolution.*

* The adjective *English* is important, for the statement would be less true of *Scottish* education, which may be one reason for the disproportionate contribution of Scotsmen to the industrial revolution in England.

It is possible that by the middle of the nineteenth century English educational facilities were even less satisfactory, in relation to the total population, than in the late eighteenth or early decades of the nineteenth centuries; almost certainly they were more inadequate to the needs of industry and commerce, which had grown substantially both in size and complexity. By that time the *relative* inferiority of English education, at least viewed from the standpoint of the needs of the economy, was becoming widely known. A British expert had commented on the superiority of German scientific education well before the middle of the century,[14] while in the 1850s British observers of the industrial scene in America were struck by the 'superior education and intelligence' which seemed to them to explain America's ability quickly to absorb and diffuse the most advanced European techniques and her precocity in improving on them.[15]

In the later nineteenth century the economic importance of education began to increase markedly as changes in industrial structure and the composition of output both made greater demands on highly-educated manpower. The relative rise in new 'science-based' industries, notably in the chemical and electrical fields, widened the scope for the employment of scientists both in research and development and in production control, while the widespread growth of large-scale enterprise provoked the emergence of 'scientific management', with its proliferation of wholly new professions such as those of the cost accountant or the time-and-motion engineer. In this period it is widely believed that the inappropriate orientation of her grammar schools and universities, with their emphasis on the classics and mathematics, constituted part of the reason for England's increasing industrial discomfiture, and particularly for her failure to follow up her enviable tally of scientific discoveries and inventions as successfully as her major competitors. Germany, by contrast, is deemed to have owed her exceptional prowess in chemicals to the excellence of her scientific education and its stress on learning through laboratory experience rather than merely from textbooks.

These same developments in industrial structure, however, had a different implication for the skills required of shop-floor workers. The older crafts became relatively – in some instances even absolutely – less important, while the ever-greater subdivision of the productive process, and technological developments such as more general use of interchangeable parts and assembly-line processes, multiplied the number of simple repetitive tasks requiring only a low level of skill. The relevance of formal education to the efficiency of those performing these tasks has been and is questioned. Some – having regard both to the nature of the work involved and to the fact that in some instances, for example on the assembly-line, operatives must in any event work at the speed of the machine – have denied that education can improve labour productivity. The success of some large American corporations in the later nineteenth century in using immigrants of the 'New Immigration', innocent alike of industrial experience and of the English language, suggests that this is not necessarily an over-cynical view, and in the labour-hungry factories of post-war Western Europe, Australia or New Zealand (not to mention, for example, the mines of South Africa) there have been and are many eagerly sought-after immigrant workers who are functionally illiterate in the language of the country concerned, or in some cases even in any language.

The effect of the developments in question may therefore have been to 'polarize' demand for skills, greatly increasing the demand for highly-trained scientists, engineers, managers, accountants and lawyers at the one extreme, and at a somewhat lower level their supporting staff of technicians and clerks, and at the other the demand for workers capable of carrying out routine, repetitive tasks or tasks involving physical effort with only the minimum of skill, capable of being quickly acquired on the spot. It is sometimes suggested that in such industries primary education is of little value in itself and is needed only as a basis for the more advanced training of white-collar workers and to facilitate the selection of those most capable of receiving that training.

It should be emphasized that it is not suggested that the picture which has been painted is a faithful representation of all, or even most economic activity, and if the picture be thought unusually repulsive it might be recalled that education is being considered only in respect of one of its benefits, a benefit which many will think not the most important. To the extent, however, that the preceding historical analysis is valid, it has two relevant implications. In the first place, it seems questionable to propose to evaluate the contributions of extended education to growth in the periods discussed by a formula which counts a given addition to schooling-years as generating an equal increase in output whatever the content of the education or the occupation of the person receiving it. It seems improbable, for instance, that an extra graduate in theology with three years university study would have added as much to growth in the Britain of the late nineteenth century as an extra graduate in chemistry with the same length of training.

More importantly, the question is provoked whether it is legitimate to proceed on the assumption that 'contributions' of education and of, say, investment in new industrial equipment can be separately evaluated on a *ceteris paribus* basis. It is surely certain that the increase in secondary and tertiary education which has occurred in Western countries in the last century would have provoked a drastic decline in returns to investment in education had there not been the concomitant changes in industry, in technology, in public service occupations and in the professions which have so increased demand for the products of high schools and universities. But equally, these technological and managerial developments underlying recent increases in productivity and the appearance of whole new industries would have been quite impossible but for the changes which have taken place in the provision of education. Measuring the separate 'contributions' of each is rather like measuring the 'contributions' of iron ore and of coal to a given increase in the production of pig-iron. A statement of the relative costs of the inputs is possible, but substantial variation in the ratio of their volumes is not.

Denison on the 'partitioning' of growth

To date, then, there has been only limited progress towards satisfactory assessment of the role in economic history of some long-neglected sources of growth such as those concerned with the quality of inputs (B_1), or the various possibilities of improvement envisaged under (C_2) and (C_3). This is regrettable not only because these are in themselves interesting subjects for speculation and possibly important sources of growth, but also because as yet no means has been discovered of measuring *directly* the contribution to growth of innovations proper. Whether of a so-to-say physical and engineering (D_1), or of an organizational and managerial (D_2) character, these still have to be estimated *residually*. Any improvement that can be made to specifying more fully and measuring more accurately *other* sources of growth therefore promotes a consequential improvement in the measure of the contribution of technological change in its most comprehensive sense. It should be noted, moreover, that this residual (C_1) is still far from being a single, homogeneous 'source of growth': notably, it includes (as just stated) innovations both of a technological and of a managerial kind $(D_1$ and $D_2)$; and further, each of these is to be subdivided into advances of 'best practice' techniques $(E_1$ and $E_3)$ – i.e. at the 'innovational frontier' – and changes in the lag of average behind 'best practice' techniques $(E_2$ and $E_4)$.*

It is therefore necessary to attempt to dismember this complicated, though logically well-enough articulated, collection of truly 'residual' factors. One of the tasks, for example, is to distinguish the contribution of advances in

---

* In logic, it might appear preferable to regard such lags as forming part of the explanation why economies operate *within* rather than *on* their production possibility frontier, though the point is debatable. Such lags are located in our diagram at E_2 and E_4 because in practice they are estimated *residually*, along with E_1 and E_3. Provided the matter be understood it matters little where they are placed in the scheme.

the 'frontier' of technological knowledge from changes in the lag of average practice behind that of the most efficient firms. Edward Denison, to whose pathbreaking studies this book, like every empirical study of growth, owes so much, has proposed a simple but extremely ingenious solution to this problem.[16] His technique involves two bold assumptions: first, that in respect of technological and managerial 'know-how' the U.S.A. operates close to the 'best-practice' frontier and has not discernibly approached closer to, or retreated from, that frontier during the period covered by his studies; and secondly, that 'know-how' is readily importable and that all nine countries covered in his second study have therefore had equal access to it.

On the basis of these assumptions he then proceeds as follows. First, the estimated U.S. 'residual' (growth rate of measured output less that of measured (adjusted) inputs and all other identified sources of growth) is credited entirely to the advance of the frontier of 'know-how', it being assumed that there is no change here in the (small) lag in the application of knowledge. This 'residual' equals 0·76 percentage points of growth. The second assumption is then brought into play: the contribution of advances in knowledge is set at the same value – 0·76 percentage points – for all other countries, and is *subtracted* from their several calculated residuals to yield the value of the contribution to their growth of changes in the 'lag' of their productive techniques behind the 'best-practice' frontier. Since this subtraction results in a positive remainder in all eight countries, the suggestion is that in all cases the 'lag' in question was reduced, thus imparting a positive impetus to output, over the interval 1950–62. Over North-west Europe as a whole, as we have seen, this narrowing of the gap between the average and the most advanced techniques was responsible for a contribution to growth not much smaller than that of the advance of the technical frontier; in France it made virtually the same contribution and in Germany (and also in Italy) a larger one. Denison's procedure has a seductive appeal. It appears to solve an intriguing problem which we are very anxious to solve; it generates results which seem intuitively plausible; it helps to explain the remarkable growth achievement of post-war Europe's fastest-growing economies. Unfortunately, both of the assumptions on which it rests seem to be just a little *too* strong, so that we cannot really regard the result as more than suggestive.

Take first the assumption that the gap between 'best-practice' and 'average' techniques has not changed appreciably in the U.S.A. over the period of Denison's studies. This assumption receives its strongest support from the belief that American firms are compelled by the force of competition to operate *consistently* close to the technological frontier, and that there is no reason to suppose that *changes* in whatever lag this mechanism may have allowed have been of an order of magnitude to make a significant addition to, or subtraction from, the measured growth of the U.S. economy. This *may* be so; but it is not certain that competition prescribes technological modernity throughout U.S. industry as effectively as popular opinion suggests. Salter, for example, offers, in his important book *Productivity and Technical Change*, evidence on the range of outputs per man-hour for individual enterprises in certain U.S. and United Kingdom industries, and this evidence suggests no substantial difference between the ratios of the best-practice to average or best-practice to worst-practice performance in the two countries. In any event the gap seems to be, or to have been, quite wide in some U.S. industries. For example, output of pig-iron per man-hour in best-practice U.S. plants was consistently about twice as high as the industry-wide average over the years 1911–26, and while average labour productivity in the industry more than doubled over the fifteen years in question, average output per man-hour in 1926 was still lower than that which had already been attained in the best-practice plants of 1911.[17] It is also shown that the range of outputs per man-hour covered a differential of about 3·5 to 1 in U.S. cement-making in 1935, or 3 to 1 in beet sugar – differentials which are higher than some, although lower than other, differentials quoted for certain United Kingdom industries.[18]

The nature of the industries concerned makes it seem unlikely that much of the differentials quoted can be explained by differences in the quality of the outputs of the plants concerned.

This evidence is not *compelling*, since it relates only to labour productivity, which is not the same as the aggregate productivity which is relevant to a firm's competitive performance. The below-average labour productivity plants may have been located in low-wage areas (e.g. in the American South) and have represented a rational adjustment to relative factor prices. The same possibility also holds, however, for the United Kingdom plants with which comparison is involved. Further, Salter goes on to offer, in respect of the cement and beet-sugar industries, evidence which suggests that inter-plant differences in labour productivity may have been generated primarily by differences in the date of construction, and thereby the 'technological vintage' of the plants concerned.[19] While acceptance of this conclusion would not, of course, prove that average U.S. productivity *has* been altered by a change in the distribution of inter-plant productivities, it would open the door to that possibility, and in doing so weaken the foundation for an argument that changes in best-practice/average 'lags' cannot add to or detract from U.S. growth because such lags are always sufficiently close to zero for it to be safe to disregard them.

Denison's second assumption, that the contribution of knowledge to growth was the same for all his countries 'Because knowledge is an international commodity',[20] can also be questioned. It involves, of course, the whole problem of the *diffusion* of technology – a problem whose importance has been, in all probability, gravely underestimated and which at all events has been little studied. A few comments on this problem will be reserved for later in this chapter, but here the validity of Denison's assumption may be queried by pointing to the implausibility of some of its implications.

It may be conceded, first, that the assumption is less difficult to accept in respect of the nine countries which form the object of Denison's second study than it would be if it were postulated in respect of a comparison between the U.S.A. and a group of low-income countries. In *that* comparison, the assumption would run counter to a widespread body of opinion that technological advances generated in advanced industrial countries are in some degree inappropriate to the economies of less developed countries, being fashioned for a different output-mix and different factor proportions than those which obtain in the latter, and relying on the existence of entrepreneurial talent and skilled labour and an environment of ancillary services which do not in fact obtain there. While the relevant disparities are certainly less critical in a comparison between the U.S.A. and Europe, they are not necessarily negligible in that case, especially in so far as concerns small and rather specialized economies like those of Norway or Belgium or the somewhat special case of Italy. The pattern of international trade provides support for this more agnostic position since, as we have seen, a substantial and *in all probability a growing* share of international trade in manufactures has consisted, in recent decades, of the export of commodities in the production of which the exporter's advantage consists largely if not wholly in his possession of technical knowledge of which he is able to prevent the dissemination.[21] Further important segments of such trade arise from considerations of market size, such as trade in computers.

So far as *technical* knowledge is concerned, Denison's assumption would seem to imply that allotting resources to research and development, at least beyond the cost of hiring, stealing or otherwise acquiring knowledge from others, is a waste of money. Such a conclusion is also implied for firms as well as for countries, and on this level it is very difficult to reconcile with known correlations between rate of growth of output and R and D expenditures. Moreover, we should also remind ourselves that the 'lag' in application of technological know-how of which we are speaking relates to 'know-how' *in its widest sense*, including, that is, not only engineering but managerial knowledge $(D_1 + D_2)$. Denison's assumption would have us believe, then, that not only engineering but

managerial knowledge is equally available (or, more precisely, grows at equal rates) for all his nine countries. While
it is conceptually, not to mention practically, difficult here to
distinguish the non-availability of knowledge from failure to
apply it, the tendency for managerial and organizational
techniques to be much more deeply rooted in the social and
legal systems of individual countries, as compared with
technical knowledge which in principle at least can be
merely 'looked up', does suggest the unreality of assuming
that advances in such techniques occurring in one country
are immediately and easily transferable to others. Finally,
Denison's assumption also implies that no technology
originates in Europe which is not either independently
discovered or immediately imported by the U.S.A., which
is a surprising belief to hold.

Let us summarize the major conclusions so far. Estimates
of the sources of economic growth in terms of the growth of
factor inputs and of a residual have typically suggested that
the latter has been responsible for a substantial fraction of
growth, in some cases for much the larger part. The easy
inference that the 'residual' represents wholly or largely
a technologically-induced rise of aggregate productivity
should, however, be resisted. More complete specification of
inputs, and especially making appropriate allowance for
improvement in the quality of inputs, may reduce the size of
the 'residual' appreciably. Further, even this diminished
residual measures, along with the effects of increasing 'know-
how', several other influences, notably improvements in the
allocation of resources, the effects of economies of scale, and
errors and omissions. In so far as these items can be separately
estimated and allowed for the remaining residual, so to say,
approximates more and more to the true value of the contribution of 'know-how'. In the case of the fast-growing
economies of Western Europe since about 1950, required
adjustments to inputs and allowance for factors other than
technological advance substantially reduce the size of the
'residual', making the contribution of technology, at about
one-quarter of the measured increase in output per unit of

input over the years 1950–62, much smaller than it would have appeared in a first approximation.

There is reason to believe, however, that increases in output generated by better allocation of resources and the rising quality of inputs have been unusually great in post-war Europe: and it is a plausible inference that since the scope for at least some of these improvements is finite, the advance of 'know-how' has been of greater significance in the long-term perspective of history. Even so, such advances are still a complicated matter, concerning 'know-how' of both an engineering and a managerial kind, and including both advances of the frontier of knowledge and changes in the lag of average behind best-practice techniques in both these fields. A valiant attempt by Denison to separate out, for his nine countries, this movement of the frontier from changes in the lag cannot be regarded as entirely convincing, but one broad implication of his analysis does seem acceptable, namely that post-war Europe is indebted for an unusually large increment of growth to a quick reduction of the lag in its application of 'know-how' behind that of the U.S.A. Since the scope for narrowing this lag is of course once again finite, the view is strengthened that Western Europe's recent 'super-growth' contains an unrepeatable element; that (other things being equal) it will slow up when these finite sources of improvement are exhausted; and (more conjecturally) that in the long haul of history the less familiar sources of improvement have made a relatively smaller, and the advance of the technological frontier a relatively larger, contribution to the growth of aggregate productivity. We now turn, therefore, to these 'truly' residual elements in longer-term growth, and first to technical (as opposed to managerial) know-how, and to its growth at the frontier, rather than its rate of diffusion within and between countries.

The role of technological change

There is perhaps a widespread belief, one which was fashioned by economic historians before it was adopted by economists, that the role in economic history of technical advance (in its narrower sense) has been not only large but also increasing. This belief was doubtless fostered, unconsciously at first, by the success of economic and industrial historians in uncovering more important inventions and changes in productive techniques for the late eighteenth and later centuries than for earlier centuries. In so far as the growth of income per head is to be interpreted as arising from technical advance, the general acceleration of the former in modern times is consistent with the belief that the latter has also accelerated, though of course from our present standpoint this is circular reasoning. More independent but still circumstantial evidence is that numbers of scientists and engineers, both absolutely and relatively, have undoubtedly risen in recent times to record heights.

More relevantly and more subtly, it is interesting to note the acceleration in the increase of the maximum speed of movement of which man is capable. The speed of a man running was overtaken by that of man on horseback only as late as seventeen centuries or thereabouts before the birth of Christ. The horse, in turn, remained the fastest means of locomotion for some three and a half millennia until the superiority of the steam railroad engine was proved at the Rainhill trials in 1829. The railway in turn enjoyed only a century or so of pre-eminence before it was overtaken, in quick succession, by racing cars and then by the aeroplane. The speed of the latter climbed through the sub-sonic range in a few decades, and first military and now civilian aircraft are flying at speeds several times that of sound. Meanwhile a few men have already travelled on predetermined routes at much larger speeds in rocket-propelled craft.

It comes then as something of a surprise that a trend for which there is so much circumstantial evidence, and which is so much taken for granted in popular discussion of a 'technological age', should in fact largely have escaped *direct* measurement; and even more that such measures as there have been *do not* unequivocally corroborate the thesis of a perpetually-increasing rate of technological progress. Economists, indeed, might well have been prepared for this fact had they recalled that it is only a decade or two since some of their number espoused, as an explanation of the chronic underemployment which then plagued the capitalist world, a doctrine of 'secular stagnation' – a doctrine based, in part, on the belief that the stock of commercially-significant inventions was finite and that diminishing returns to inventive activity had in fact set in, reducing the scope for new investment below the rising level of *ex ante* savings. In the event most economists, like the popular imagination, have succumbed in recent years to the heady euphoria induced by recent technological developments and have seen man's future welfare threatened, if at all, by dangers other than a possible drying-up of the investment opportunities which apparently rampant science and technology generate year by year.

The evidence of patent statistics

Yet such measures as we have do not fully justify this optimism. The number of patents issued annually in the U.S.A. rose from an average of 28 in the 1790s to over 36,000 in the first quarter of the present century. Since then, however, there has been a further rise only to 43,000 during the 1950s. Proportional to population, or still more to real national income, the annual average tally of patents has on the whole declined in twentieth-century America, after rising sharply in the nineteenth century. If the patent statistics were converted to some sort of 'inventive index', by measuring annual patents against the cumulated total of previous inventions still in use, the impression of a twentieth-century decline would undoubtedly be even more marked.

This rather perverse finding provokes, of course, the question of the validity of patent statistics as a measure of inventive output. It has long been doubted that patent statistics do accurately reflect the rate and direction of inventive activity; but they continue to be used because they are readily accessible, already classified in some degree, and quantitative, and they are the only source of information on inventive activity which possesses any one of these characteristics, let alone all three. Thus Professor Ashton, the greatest historian of the first industrial revolution, documents the rise of invention in eighteenth-century England with patent statistics whose validity for the purpose he nevertheless seems to doubt: 'If (as is very doubtful) [he writes] the number of patents may be used as an index, inventive fertility increased rapidly.'[22] A later historian of the same period spells out the reasons for her misgivings about patents more explicitly, concluding that 'The number of inventions patented is unfortunately a very weak index of the number of new processes becoming available to British entrepreneurs, still less of the productive significance of these new inventions' – a conclusion which does not, however, deter her from presenting a table showing the numbers of English patents by decades and invoking the figures as a broad indication of trends.[23]

Attitudes of similar ambivalence are characteristic of economists concerned with the technology of more recent times, but here the aptness of patent data for statistical and econometric handling has proved irresistible to some. The best-known advocate of their use was perhaps the late Jacob Schmookler. Though Professor Schmookler was convinced that this great body of data could not be ignored, and performed, with encouraging results, several tests designed to establish the reliability of patent statistics in comparison with other data, he was far from an uncritical defender, coming close at times to regarding his source as a *pis aller*: 'No one will dispute that accurate measures of a thing are always better than an uncertain *index* of it. There is just one difficulty. While we have the uncertain index, we do not have accurate measures.'[24]

Unfortunately for anyone interested in the broad sweep of economic change, the likelihood is that patents are least unreliable when short-term fluctuations and individual industries are the focus of attention, and progressively more misleading as the time horizon is lengthened or the area of economic activity under scrutiny broadened. Some of the reasons for this are quite clear. Over the long haul changes in

patent law, administrative changes in handling and approv-
ing applications, and changes in the locus of inventive
activity and in industrial organization, are all liable to
provoke changes in the ratio of patents to inventive activity.

Schmookler himself, indeed, believed that for some of
these reasons patents have borne a declining ratio to inventive activity in recent decades in the U.S.A. Public hostility
to patents dating from the New Deal era; greater delays in
processing since World War II; the increasing tendency for
large corporations to rely on secrecy and market dominance
rather than on patents to capture the rewards of inventive
activity; and the continuing trend away from the individual
inventor – relying on patent protection for his reward –
towards the large research laboratory: all of these help to
explain a tendency for patents to fail by an increasing margin
to reflect the full range of inventive activity. To these must
be added a tendency, as more and more inventions originate
in corporate research laboratories, for new products and
processes to be more fully tested and appraised before being
patented, and (relatedly) for standards of patentability to
rise, so that the average content of effective inventive output
per patent has probably tended to increase.[25]

It can well be imagined that these and similar sources of
indeterminacy in the relationship of patenting to inventive
output are even more discouraging in long-run comparisons,
and also in inter-country comparisons, than when considering the course of invention in one country since the 1930s.
In any event, from the historian's point of view patents,
though a voluminous source, have not an unlimited chronological span. The English initiative of 1624 (the Statute of
Monopolies) was followed, prior to the last decade of the
eighteenth century, only by some of the American colonies.
The U.S.A. enacted its first patent law in 1790, followed by
revolutionary France in the following year. The adoption of
a patent system spread over much of continental Europe in
the quarter century following the fall of Napoleon, and
through Latin America in the early decades of inde-
pendence. Most other parts of the world have followed only

at later dates, if at all. At best, therefore, patent statistics shed some light on inventive activity over only a limited area of modern history.

The reasons mentioned for rejecting an invariant relationship between patenting and inventing are interesting in that they relieve us of the necessity of believing the conclusion to which patent statistics seem to point, namely that inventiveness has declined in the past thirty or forty years: it may well be only a decline in *patenting*, rather than in inventing, which is in question. But we cannot banish the latter possibility as easily as all that, for an alternative 'direct' method of measuring inventive output also offers some support to this rather than to the conventional view. This alternative is, of course, simply to list and count inventions *seriatim* by studying the technological histories, trade journals and so on of a particular industry or industries. A complete listing would scarcely be possible, because of the numbers involved. (It is a sobering fact, for instance, that from 1852 to 1914 there were some 1,200 patents in the U.S.A. relating to as simple and ancient an object as the horseshoe, as well as more than 850 relating to horseshoe calks.[26]) But counting inventions has the advantage that the counter can make some estimate – necessarily partly subjective – of the *importance* of the invention; failure to distinguish 'important' inventions from 'unimportant' ones, or indeed inventions which are used from those which are not, is one of the many deficiencies of patent statistics.

Schmookler presents statistics of the number of 'important inventions' made annually, and of patents registered annually over the period 1810–1950 in four industries: railroading, petroleum refining, paper-making, and agriculture.[27] Only in the second of these four are the shapes of the important inventions and 'number of patents' curves fairly similar throughout (a fact which of course provides ammunition for the opponents of the use of patent statistics to measure inventive output). But on one point most of the eight curves do agree, namely in suggesting a decline of inventive activity in the twentieth century. Only three of the eight curves –

petroleum refining (both curves) and paper-making (patents granted only) – lie higher *c.* 1950 than *c.* 1900, and even in these cases the curve reaches a maximum before 1930 (petroleum and paper-making, patents granted) or during the 1930s (petroleum, important inventions) and thereafter declines. Transformed to an index of the rate of increase of inventions (that is, dividing each year's inventions by the cumulated total of previous inventions) the downward trend characteristic of the twentieth century would of course be far more marked.

Before leaving these graphs it may be pointed out that they offer no support at all for the conclusion to which the discussion of a few pages back seemed to point, namely that the ratio of patenting to invention has declined. On the contrary, in all four cases the curve of patents granted has a steeper upward or more gently downward slope than that of important inventions over the period 1850–1950 as a whole, and also in almost all major subdivisions of it. This unexpected and disconcerting feature must merely reinforce our distrust of patent data for establishing long-term trends, for it is difficult to believe that the careful investigation of trade journals and the like by Schmookler's assistants left uncovered more important inventions of recent years than of the remoter past.

Schmookler's graphs may quite likely be highly misleading if interpreted as evidence of the course of inventive activity in the economy as a whole in the twentieth century, for they deal only with four industries, only one of which – petroleum refining – might perhaps be thought of as technologically dynamic in recent decades. Similar graphs, say, for electronics or petro-chemicals would surely show greater buoyancy in recent times. Taken in conjunction with the course of total patents granted, however, they do suggest the need for caution in accepting the popular concept of continued acceleration in technological progress. Particularly for the U.S.A., which is so much closer to the 'technological frontier' than most countries and has less of a backlog of investment in *already-known* techniques to make good, the question might well be pondered whether the rate of invention of new products and new processes would prove rapid enough to generate a demand for investment equal to *ex ante* savings, *if* the immense allocation of resources to war and space research and investment were to be substantially reduced.

The technological revolution?

It is in a *longer* historical perspective – in considering the last three or four centuries, or better the last three or four millennia, *rather* than the last few decades – that the idea of a 'technological explosion' is most convincing. In this connection it is interesting to reproduce two graphs (see fig. 5.2) presented by S. Lilley in his book, *Men, Machines and History*, which plot the 'relative invention rate' for mechanical inventions from 5500 B.C. until the present time.[28] The basis for these graphs is a list of important inventions compiled by Lilley, to each of which he attaches a 'score' or weight reflecting the relative importance of the invention. The weighted inventions are then added up to yield a cumulative total of available inventions, and the 'relative invention rate' is calculated as the value of a moving average of weighted inventions divided by the cumulated total of (weighted) inventions. It plots, that is to say, neither the cumulated total of mechanical inventions nor the absolute increase of that total within each interval of time, but the percentage *rate* of increase.

There are three chief features which deserve comment. First, the period before the onset (say *c*. A.D. 1700) of modern economic growth was marked neither by complete technological stagnation nor by a very slow but steady increase in technological knowledge. Rather, these millennia were characterized by very substantial *fluctuations* in inventiveness, long centuries of virtual stagnation being punctuated by periods of considerable advance, notably during the great agricultural riverine civilizations, in the periods of Athenian culture and Hellenistic expansion, and in the later middle ages. It would be quite impossible here to attempt to

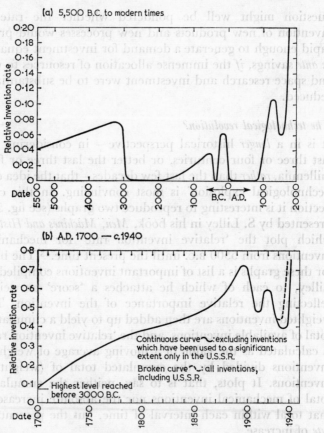

(a) 5,500 B.C. to modern times

(b) A.D. 1700 — c.1940

Continuous curve ⌣: excluding inventions which have been used to a significant extent only in the U.S.S.R.

Broken curve ⌣: all inventions, including U.S.S.R.

Highest level reached before 3000 B.C.

FIGURE 5.2 The 'relative invention' rate, 5500 B.C. to modern times (after LILLEY, 1965, by kind permission).

appraise the validity and significance of this broad chronology of inventiveness proposed by Lilley, but it is interesting to note the similarity of the general finding – pronounced secular fluctuations rather than stagnation or a steady upward trend *before* c. 1700 – to that suggested by Phelps Brown and Hopkins regarding the course of real wages in pre-industrial times.[29] Within the much shorter time-span covered by the latter study, one is tempted to note as a topic deserving of reflection the rough coincidences between

Lilley's peak of inventiveness in the later middle ages and the high level of real wages in the later fourteenth and fifteenth centuries, and again between the decline of inventiveness (at a time of rising population) and the dramatic fall of real wages in the early modern centuries.

Secondly, Lilley's graphs strongly confirm the general historical impression that there has been a massive upturn of inventive activity in the last two and a half centuries, the relative invention rate reaching *c.* 1890 a level about ten times as high as the highest value attained before 3000 B.C. When we bear in mind the immense increase in the cumulated total of invention (which forms the denominator in the expression to which the relative invention rate is equal), this represents an enormous increase in inventive output. But thirdly, Lilley's second figure suggests a marked (though not continuous) decline in relative inventiveness from a peak about 1890 until the beginning of World War II, when a steep recovery occurs (and Lilley's series comes to a stop). The late-nineteenth-century peak and subsequent decline are quite consistent, as we have seen, with the evidence of patent statistics and with some more detailed counts of important inventions.

A number of reservations must be made which qualify the degree of confidence which it may be appropriate to place in Dr Lilley's findings. First, as the author himself properly acknowledges, the scope of his study is immense and it is impossible that any one man should have been able to safeguard against the overlooking of some, even very important, inventions. Nor, of course, have some periods yet been adequately explored from the technological point of view by historians or archaeologists. There is also inevitably a very large subjective element in the *weighting* of inventions; the principles on which this has been carried out are only roughly stated, and not very convincingly justified, by the author. It seems impossible to know what sort of bias may have been imparted to the graphs by any of these factors.

Secondly, Dr Lilley's book is ostensibly about 'tools and machines', but this phrase is interpreted extremely broadly to include e.g. metal-making and -working processes, and even many inventions in the electrical and electronic field which would not normally be thought of as 'mechanical', such as the thermionic valve. On the other hand the chemical industry and its offshoots, including the whole range of synthetics, plastics and petrochemicals which bulks so large in today's consumer goods, is almost entirely excluded. Since such products are very much the creation of the last century, their inclusion would undoubtedly tilt upwards the right-hand side of the graphs, that is, enhance the contrast between the nineteenth and twentieth centuries and earlier times, and might also (less certainly) mitigate the apparent fall in inventiveness between 1890 and 1940.

Thirdly, it might be asked whether the formula employed to calculate the relative invention rate is appropriate, in so far as its denominator includes *all* past inventions, whether still useful or not. For example, the Newcomen engine continues to be counted even though such engines have been completely superseded by later sources of power. If the assumption that inventions are economically-speaking immortal were thought inappropriate, the conclusion might seem to be that the denominator in Lilley's 'relative invention rate' formula has a systematic upward bias, and the calculated rates therefore a systematic *downward* bias.* Correction for this feature would, therefore, further enhance the claims of the modern period to a relatively more impressive showing.

The sources of invention

There has long been speculation as to the reasons for fluctuations and inter-country differences in inventiveness, and also for changes in the industrial distribution of in-

* A good defence can, however, be made for Lilley's procedure along the following lines. The 'score' awarded to each invention is intended to reflect not its 'absolute' economic importance, but only its improvement over predecessors. The 'absolute' importance of an invention is therefore represented by the cumulated total of scores for itself plus those for all superseded predecessors. The relative invention rate is properly represented by the *increment* of improvement represented by a new invention divided by the *absolute* importance of what it supersedes.

ventions. It is interesting to notice that recent investigators have concerned themselves largely with the same sort of questions which have been asked by earlier generations of historians and sociologists; and it is perhaps a little saddening that though bringing to bear on these issues the familiar modern array of statistical and econometric techniques, they have neither produced many important new insights nor been able to generate a greater degree of agreement on the answers to familiar problems.

Over the generations, opinion has generally moved away from the 'heroic' interpretation, which in the earlier nineteenth century tended to explain the history of technology in the same sort of terms as the 'Great Man' view of history explained the course of political events. Partly, this interpretation has declined in appeal because (as we shall see) 'major' inventions are now thought to have been less important than they were once considered, and innumerable anonymous and often unrecorded minor improvements more important. But also, there is a doctrine, most strongly championed some decades ago by the Chicago school of sociology, which propounded a *social* interpretation of invention, according to which inventions do not appear full-blown from the imagination of some inspired benefactor of mankind, like great symphonies or paintings, but rather are socially-determined processes whose content, timing and direction are to be explained by the same sort of widespread and slow-changing influences which determine, say, population trends. In its most austere form this doctrine asserts that individual inventions are 'inevitable', and the individuals who make them no more, therefore, than the chosen instruments of impersonal social forces. The fact that a considerable number of discoveries, e.g. in the electrical field in the nineteenth century, appear to have been made simultaneously by two or more investigators is proffered as in itself sufficient proof of this.*

* The belief that many inventions have been made independently and nearly simultaneously has had a considerable influence on social science. It stems from an article by W. F. Ogburn and D. S. Thomas, 'Are

This extreme form of the social theory of invention is today not generally accepted, even investigators who are well-disposed in general, like Jacob Schmookler, denying that individual inventions are 'inevitable' and disputing the inferences drawn from, or even the reality of, 'simultaneous' inventions. Certainly there is compelling evidence that despite the twentieth-century growth of corporate and governmental research, the individual inventor is still responsible for a substantial fraction of technological advance, and for a share proportionately larger than the resources at his command. But the view that major variations in the rate and direction of inventive activity, whether carried on by individuals or not, are influenced in a substantial degree by broad social forces is widely held and is common ground both to modern econometricians and to most economic historians.

Within this area of agreement, however, there is a considerable difference of opinion between those who favour a 'science-based' and those who favour a 'demand-induced' view of invention. According to the former new products and processes are generated primarily by the advance of scientific and engineering knowledge. The latter view elaborates the old theme that 'Necessity is the mother of invention', and holds that it is opportunities created by the changing pattern of demand, or by the challenge to cut particular costs or overcome particular shortages eating into profit margins, which determine the size and distribution of inventive activity. Among modern economists, Schmookler has most warmly championed the 'demand-induced' view of invention. He supports this interpretation by two empirical inquiries. First, close examination of lists of important nineteenth- and twentieth-century inventions in the four U.S. industries mentioned earlier uncovered 'no identifiable

---

Inventions Inevitable?', *Political Science Quarterly*, XXXVII (March 1922), which includes a long list of 'duplicate inventions'. Technological historians nowadays might be inclined to question the credentials of a fair proportion of these 'duplicate inventions' either because they were not genuinely equivalent or because they were not in fact discovered independently.

scientific component', or only science twenty years or more old, in the majority of cases.[30] Secondly, in considering patents of inventions in the capital goods industries, statistical analysis both of time series and of inter-industry data reveals a high degree of correlation between number of patents and volume of investment. This correlation is explained by the hypothesis that inventive effort is elicited primarily by expected profitability, which depends in turn upon the volume of capital formation, i.e. on demand.[31]

Schmookler's argument is suggestive, but not fully persuasive. It has been complained, for example, that he defines 'science-based inventions' in too demanding a fashion when he looks for some fairly immediately preceding scientific novelty in such inventions, for this formulation would fail to capture the dependence of invention on the broader secular sweep of scientific advance, or to allow sufficiently for the inevitable lag between advances in 'pure' science and the discovery and bringing to the point of patentable specificity of attractive-seeming commercial applications. The correlation in the field of capital-goods inventions is open, like all such analyses, to the objection that correlation analysis does not of itself prove in which direction the causal influence flows. It would be consistent with the view of some economists to say that the locus of inventions determines the volume of investment, just as much as the volume of investment determines the locus of inventions (though this is an objection which Schmookler foresaw and attempted, with some success, to forestall). More generally, Schmookler is open to the charge that he assumes demand to be exogenous to his scheme of explanation, quite neglecting advertising and 'demand creation' generally. This of course carries the danger that some inventions may be wrongly labelled as 'demand-induced' when the demand in question is, in fact, deliberately generated in order to promote the sale of some new product made possible by scientific advance.

The more obvious difficulty about Schmookler's argument is that of the four industries which he studies closely and in a convincingly empirical fashion, only one at the most would

M

be thought of as occupying an area of rapid scientific progress. It may be for this reason that another American economist specializing on the economics of invention, Richard R. Nelson, rates the importance of scientific advance as a generator of inventions considerably more highly, for Nelson's researches have involved to a greater extent the study of such 'science-based' industries as synthetic fibres and electronics.[32] A point to notice here, however, is that some of the larger and more adventurous industrial laboratories of the twentieth century have encouraged some of their staff to carry out basic research in 'pure' science with perhaps only a qualified hope of commercially valuable results, and certainly with no specific, defined market product in mind at the outset.

A case in point was the scientifically novel work on the theory of semi-conductors carried on in the Bell Telephone laboratories. This work was initially not directed towards any obvious commercial applications, but was sanctioned by the company partly because the general field was one which had a whiff of commercial possibilities about it, and partly because of the enthusiasm for this field of some first-rate scientists in their employment, some of whom at least were more concerned with advancing knowledge than with devising marketable products. In the event the work was to lead to an 'invention' of capital importance, the transistor; but while this is from one point of view undoubtedly a 'science-based' invention, the commercial direction and financing of the basic research involved scarcely allows us to view it as a pure example of this genus. On the other hand it certainly cannot be called a 'demand-induced' invention either, though its inherent possibilities and vigorous commercial exploitation quickly enough generated plenty of demand for it. The truth is that simple classificatory schemes like 'science-based' and 'demand-induced' are fashioned with an eye to promoting statistical manipulation of the data, and do a violence to complex reality which is ultimately unacceptable and which rebounds to rob the techniques of analysis they are intended to permit of much of their power.

It is not necessary to expound in great detail the views of researchers like Schmookler and Nelson, for they are readily accessible in books enjoying wide circulation. Rather, we now point out that the dichotomy of 'science-based' and 'demand-induced' inventions is not entirely a newly-invented classification introduced only to facilitate the analysis of the origins of recent technological advance. Economic historians have long debated the respective roles of similar factors in generating the classic inventions of the eighteenth and nineteenth centuries. It is easy, on the one hand, to identify a host of important inventions of the period which were consciously sought in order to meet a particular need. Thus techniques permitting the use of coke rather than charcoal in smelting and working iron were devised to combat the growing shortage and therefore costliness of suitable timber in the eighteenth century. Several inventions in the field of textile machinery were intended to improve labour productivity in one particular process which had fallen behind others in a sequential series of processes. Vulcanizing was an eagerly sought-after process intended to rid an otherwise very attractive material of its one serious defect. The Gilchrist–Thomas 'basic' process of steelmaking, whose announcement has been described as an 'international incident', adapted the Bessemer furnace and the Siemens open-hearth so as to enable these revolutionary processes of steelmaking to use ore rich in phosphorus, inability to cope with which had been their one crippling inadequacy. On the other hand, the electrical and chemical fields throughout the nineteenth century provide many instances, from the telegraph to synthetic dye-stuffs, of new products which, for all that they were quickly integrated into the pattern of demand, are more realistically viewed as 'knowledge-induced' than as 'demand-induced'.

It is perhaps fairly generally agreed that if we confine our attention to the period of the early industrial revolution, say to c. 1830, the role of science was not a large one. Most 'inventions' incorporated little scientific novelty, except perhaps in the sense of mechanical contrivances novel in design and assembly but the *elements* of which had long been familiar; and in some of those which could claim such novelty it was the inventions which led to the basic science, rather than the other way round.* Even this generally accepted interpretation has been challenged, however, in particular by two British economic historians, A. E. Musson and E. Robinson, who have argued for a considerably greater role of science even during the 'first' industrial revolution.[33] Leaving aside the need for a possible revision here – and Musson and Robinson have not fully convinced their colleagues of much more than that there was more personal and intellectual contact between scientists, industrialists and inventors than is usually thought – one might be tempted to say that the role of basic science in technological progress has tended to increase through time.

Until perhaps the late nineteenth century this is probably true, but before one could accept the relationship as a monotonic increasing one throughout time one would need to weigh another consideration which in a sense tells in the other direction. This is the point made by Schmookler when he writes that 'society has now, and probably has had for a long time, a highly flexible, multipurpose knowledge base amenable to development at virtually all points.'[34] The contention here is that the stock of scientific and engineering knowledge is (and has for some time been) large enough to permit new products and processes to be 'invented' whenever demand presses hard enough and the returns to inventive activity therefore promise to be great enough. In such a situation, inventions may clearly be said to be 'science-based' in one sense, and 'demand-induced' in another. Again, the scheme of classification does violence to reality; but the point here is that one may need to be careful of the sense in which his words are intended in making such a statement as 'the role of science in invention has increased through time.'

* The classic instance here is, of course, the steam-engine, which prompted theoretical investigation into thermo-dynamics, rather than vice versa.

Before leaving this topic one other point of a terminological character should perhaps be made. It is tempting to say that the whole tedious question of 'science-based' and 'demand-induced' inventions can be avoided by recognizing that all inventions actually made are both: that they represent the intersection of the sets of (scientifically) *possible* and (economically) *desired* inventions. But this really neither removes the problem nor helps greatly to solve it, for the changes in the content of this common sub-set may still arise predominantly from the growth of the set of 'possible' inventions and its increasing overlap with the set of 'desirable' inventions, or from changes in the set of 'desirable' inventions resulting in a changing overlap with the set of 'possible' ones. We cannot, by positing the tautology mentioned, evade the need to analyse the determinants of the 'possible' and of the 'desired', any more than we can escape the need to analyse demand and supply functions by observing that in competitive equilibrium market price always represents the intersection of the two.

Private and corporate invention

A second feature of the inventive process which has been much studied in recent years is the changing *locus* of inventive activity. Here, fortunately, there is more common ground. There is no disputing that in the present century the proportion of inventions made by individual inventors has declined. For example, in 1900 about 80 per cent of U.S. patents were granted to individuals; by 1957 the corresponding figure was about 40 per cent.[35] Even this probably overstates the share of individuals in the number of *inventions* (as opposed to *patents*), since the individual must normally patent his invention if he is to reap any reward, whereas (for reasons already discussed) inventions made by large corporations or government research agencies are increasingly often (as it seems) *not* patented.

Individual inventing has declined relatively, of course, because of the great expansion of industrial and governmental research laboratories in which much inventive activity is concentrated. (In most countries university research is *quantitatively* less important and tends to be more distinctively oriented to 'pure' research.) Corporate research is entirely a growth of the last one hundred years: the first industrial research laboratory in the U.S.A. is usually considered to have been that established by the Bell Telephone Company in 1876.[36] The same is broadly true of governmental research. Yet the patent data quoted, and much other evidence, indicates that the individual inventor still plays a surprisingly important role in technological advance. His claims to recognition have been very fully documented and warmly championed in *The Sources of Invention* by John Jewkes and co-authors, a book which offers a very useful summary of information about a wide spectrum of inventors and inventions of the present century.[37] Moreover, if instead of merely *counting* inventions (or patents) we try to allow for the relative importance of different inventions, the claim of the individual inventor may well be higher still, for there is some evidence and a good deal of expert opinion in favour of the view that the individual inventor, as compared with the corporate research laboratory, contributes disproportionately to the more important or fundamental inventions.

That the individual inventor should be able to make such a contribution when so many cards are stacked against him – he is debarred from many areas of inventive activity by the mere cost of the equipment needed – arises, in the view of some experts, from the enormous importance in inventing of the uncommitted mind open to the consideration of novel ways of doing things. There *are* advantages, evidently, in knowing a lot about one's field, but there are disadvantages too, which in some cases may more than offset the gains. Knowing a lot about a particular field involves intensive specialization, but invention often consists essentially of the *combination* of elements – sometimes quite simple ones – from several fields. The education and experience which bring great knowledge of a particular field may involve subtle indoctrination in a traditional way of looking at problems which inhibits the capacity to envisage novel approaches. And the awareness of previous – unsuccessful – attempts to solve outstanding problems which formally-acquired knowledge of a field brings may be psychologically daunting: many inventors, like the Rust brothers who developed mechanical cotton-picking, have testified that 'if they had studied this long history of disappointments they would have been so discouraged, that they would never have got as far as they have'.[38]

It is in such ways as these that the importance of the individual inventor is explained by Jewkes and his associates. But evidence as to his importance, particularly in the more fundamental inventions, is not confined to the case studies assembled by these writers, which if well-documented have been thought by some to be interpreted in a somewhat partisan fashion. The historian of invention and innovation in petroleum refining has shown that invention in this industry became institutionalized only *after* the major technological advances of the modern industry had been achieved, and further that the most 'heroic' of these advances, the first practical catalytic cracking process, was pioneered by an independent engineer-inventor, Eugene Houdry, not originally connected with the petroleum industry.[39] A scholar of a quite different cast of mind, S. C. Gilfillan, a product of the Chicago school of sociology and author of two remarkable books on invention first published between the great wars, stated in discussing the origins of 'revolutionary' invention that 'as to the ship . . . the striking innovations of known . . . origin have all been made by men not professional sea-farers nor owners, nor even builders nor designers of ships, tho they often were led by their inventions to become such'.[40] Gilfillan regards this as but an instance of a general principle that 'revolutionary' inventions are 'due to men outside the occupation affected, and the minor, perfective inventions to insiders'. He attributes the first half of this principle to the fact that for any one industry there are far more outsiders than insiders, and that these outsiders have the crucial advantage of 'freedom from custom'. This latter, however, is doubtless also responsible for the tendency, noted by Gilfillan in his scrutiny of patents relating to ships, for outsiders to generate, along with a notable number of 'revolutionary' inventions, a far higher proportion of impractical and foolish ones.

Individual inventors and 'outsiders' have made many well-known contributions throughout the history of modern technology. Every first-year student of the economic history of the industrial revolution knows that the basic process of steelmaking, so important that its announcement was 'an international incident', was discovered by a London police-court clerk with no previous knowledge of the iron industry, who was helped by a cousin employed as a chemist at a South Wales ironworks, only in testing his idea. Professor Landes, the historian of nineteenth-century technology, points out that although the 'solution was a simple one, founded on a widely known principle', it 'had engaged the attention of some of Europe's most highly trained engineers for years'. Professor Landes comments further, 'Success lay in the ingenuity of the practical arrangements – the combination of basic flux and lining – and it is probably no coincidence that the idea came to an amateur who approached the problem with an open mind'.[41] Another well-known example of early invention by a rank outsider was the pioneering of the power loom by Edmund Cartwright, a clergyman-poet with no previous connection whatever with the textile industry. Even James Watt, though he had previous scientific training and was to become the leading steam-engineer of his age, made his greatest contribution to the new form of power, the separate condenser, at the very beginning of his acquaintance with these machines when he had no practical experience of them.

Such examples are, however, selective, and there are also a great many well-known instances of invention by 'insiders'. There have been few attempts to calculate the relative contributions of the two groups comparable to Gilfillan's work on the ship, and of course the statistic would in any event be of little significance considering that the ratio of all 'outsiders' to all 'insiders', whether inventing or not, varies from industry to industry and from time to time. Indeed in the case of a quite new industry everyone is an 'outsider' at first, which is one good reason why such people contribute disproportionately to the 'fundamental' inventions which give rise to new industries. There is however plenty of evidence, both historical and recent, that 'insiders', and specifically in the twentieth century the corporate research and development laboratory, contribute by far the greater part of the *development* of promising new processes and also of the slow, piecemeal improvement of existing products and processes which, as we shall see shortly, is often unduly ignored as a source of productivity improvement. This is natural, since development and improvement call for practical, on-the-job experiment and physical proximity to the actual productive process, and are motivated, as invention is not of necessity, by the expectation of profit to the actual firm in whose plant the work is going forward. This is yet another reason why the sole inventor contributes disproportionately to major inventions: neither opportunity nor financial incentive exist for him to play a corresponding part in development and in minor inventions and improvements.

Their role in these directions has to be borne in mind in assessing the performance of research and development departments. A widespread criticism of the first edition of the book by Jewkes, Sawers and Stillerman was that it exaggerated the contribution of the individual inventor by neglecting the frequent need for a substantial and costly process of 'development' lying between the devising of a patentable invention and its readiness for commercial exploitation. It is estimated that in 1964 more than three-quarters of all industrial R and D funds in the United States of America went to development, about 4 per cent being devoted to basic research and one-fifth of the total to applied research.[42] We do not have comparable figures for earlier periods, but a modest acquaintance with technological history suffices to suggest many instances in which the development and improvement to the point of commercial feasibility of a basically good invention have given more trouble than the invention itself: consider, for example, the decades of work which were required to iron out the problems of Cartwright's power loom.

For all that, comparison of the rates of return to inventive activity on the part of individual inventors and of research and development laboratories provokes intriguing speculations. Such comparisons are difficult to make, for rates of return to invention have attracted curiously little attention from economists. This is surprising, not only because one would have thought such rates interesting in themselves but also because knowledge of them would seem necessary to facilitate both rational resource allocation and the analysis of the sources of growth. From the standpoint of the present book, this last is the more important point. We have seen that when Abramovitz presented estimates of the sources of U.S. growth since about 1870 which indicated that the 'residual' was a far more important source than increase in factor inputs, he regarded this result as 'sobering, if not discouraging, to students of economic growth'.[43] He took this view because it seemed to remove the greater part of the sources of growth from the purview of the economist into an area whose contribution to growth was not subject to economic laws and therefore not amenable to economic prediction and explanation. This frustration would be removed, however, if it were discovered that there is some systematic – not necessarily simple – relationship between the input of inventive effort on the one hand and growth-promoting technological change on the other, for then one could detach that part of the 'residual' which actually represents the fruits of technological progress and measure it instead as the return on inputs of inventive effort and investment in education, just as one does with capital or labour inputs.

The growth analyst is in fact far indeed from being able to measure the contribution of inventive activity in this way. Attempts to measure returns on such activity have been few and confined to recent times. They have not so far converged on even a range of 'normal' rates of return, and indeed the prevailing view is that industrial research is an area inherently subject to such extremely wide margins of uncertainty that there are no grounds for expecting that a consensus on a typical range of returns will emerge from even a much larger number of studies. It is true that several investigations, like those of Griliches on hybrid corn or of Enos on petroleum refining, seem to point to extremely high returns on investment in research as compared with investment in fixed capital,[44] but these estimates and others suffer (from our point of view) from the disadvantage that they relate to the rate of return on the *successful* inventive effort only, whereas our interest would be in the (lower) rate of return on *all* effort directed towards the end in question, whether successful or not. Finally, such work as has been done in this area relates predominantly to recent times, being based chiefly on estimates of R and D expenditures available only for recent years and for one or two leading industrial countries. Movement backwards into the period when inventing was predominantly the work of individuals would make the task of estimating the volume of inventive activity progressively more difficult. The conclusion must be, therefore, that the prospects are not bright for improving estimates of the sources of long-term economic growth by transforming the technological component of the 'residual' into estimated returns on inputs of inventive effort.

Despite these gaps in our knowledge and the lack of determinateness in the relationship between inventive effort and output which may be suspected, one cannot easily resist the intriguing, and disturbing, hypothesis that the institutionalization of industrial research may have served to *decrease* rather than *increase* the ratio of technological output to inventive input. Even allowing for large expenditures of effort on unsuccessful and unrecorded research and also for the (often much higher) costs of subsequent development, the results achieved by individuals working with an absolute minimum of resources are in many cases astonishing. The fact that so many individual inventors have often died poor is not inconsistent with this statement, for a survey of the history of inventions leaves no doubt that by and large society has been clumsy and uncharitable in its treatment of the individual inventor, though not all have encountered quite the degree of 'neglect, discouragement, or active obstruction'[45] which met Frank Whittle of jet-engine fame. When an individual inventor's work has proved commercially acceptable, all too often history has demonstrated the accuracy of Gilfillan's judgment that patent rights prove a precarious safeguard 'when a small firm or an isolated inventor attempts to extract a fitting sum from a great or monopolistic corporation'.[46] Thus the unimpressive private rate of return to so many individual inventors is no indication of the *social* return to their work; and, indeed, it may prove that Enos' conclusion with respect to invention and innovation in petroleum refining, that if anything returns to inventor and to innovator have been *negatively* rather than positively correlated,[47] is generally valid.

Nor can one dispose of the disturbing hypothesis under discussion by maintaining that if private inventors really produced greater results from a given input of inventive effort, large companies would buy the ideas from such inventors rather than produce their own. This is partly, but not chiefly, because the circumstances we have discussed preclude the possibility of rational calculation. (The often wildly inaccurate estimates of development costs, let alone of research costs, which are becoming an almost daily feature of the western Press endorse this apparently cynical view.) More importantly, large firms carry out their own research *primarily* in order to deny technological superiority to competitors, to offer the most attractive development prospects to individuals or small firms with an idea to sell, and to attempt to internalize the return which might otherwise accrue to the private inventor, none of which aims they could otherwise be sure of achieving. (It must be remembered that on average development absorbs a much larger fraction of total R and D budgets than does research.)

The hypothesis under discussion is consistent with such evidence as that of Mueller, who in reviewing the history of Du Pont's major new products and processes from 1920 to 1950 demonstrates that of the eighteen new products, the Du Pont laboratories themselves – outstandingly enlightened and well-equipped though they were – discovered only five, and shared in the discovery of a sixth.[48] They were more successful, however, in *process* (as opposed to product) innovations, confirming the generalization that large-scale corporate R and D has a comparative advantage in development and improvement and the individual inventor (or small laboratory) in fundamental invention. Mueller also shows that the expansion in Du Pont's research budget over the period was *not* matched by a comparable increase in the output of 'important' inventions.[49] It seems on the face of it likely that similar conclusions may hold for government-backed research, but here evaluation is even more difficult because the research is intended to serve larger national ends rather than make profits. This is not to say, however, that it should not be organized and controlled rationally, and details released (or prized out) from time to time indicate that even in terms of its ostensible ends much weapons research is extremely wasteful. From a shorter-run economic-optimizing standpoint, most military (and space) research constitutes, of course, a colossal misallocation of resources.

Invention, innovation and lags in technological advance

We now turn from the *advance* of the technological frontier to various 'lags' in the application of knowledge. Newly-won knowledge of (potential) commercial value is sometimes not at once applied anywhere, and when it is it is not applied everywhere simultaneously. At any one time countries – and individual industries and plants – differ in the extent to which they have applied the most recent technical (or managerial) knowledge available; we have seen that if Edward Denison's analysis is to be believed, changes in the 'lag' of one country behind another in this respect may account for a significant share of the difference between their rates of economic growth.

There are several types of lag and many reasons why countries and plants do not all rush to apply the latest techniques available over the whole front of their economic activity. Prominent among these is that it would certainly not be profitable to do so, since it is uneconomic to scrap plants, however obsolete technologically, as long as operating costs fall short of price, and this replacement point will vary in accordance, e.g., with differing factor prices from one country or plant to another. Here our concern is not with such general principles but with more specific and historical influences on the rate of adoption of new techniques.

First, an invention may prove stillborn in that the pattern of demand offers it insufficient profitable space. Neoprene was discovered in the depths of the depression of the early 1930s, at a time when natural rubber was selling at 5 cents a pound; and though it quickly proved to be an excellent material with many industrial uses it made only relatively modest headway until the demands of war and the loss of South-east Asian natural rubber to the Japanese completely changed the market situation.

Or secondly, it may prove unsuited to relative factor supplies and thus fail to appeal to producers, or even arouse their hostility. There is a long history of Luddism arising from the opposition of workers to labour-saving machinery, and in a paternalist State government may support workers. William Lee, the English clergyman who invented the stocking frame in the reign of Elizabeth the First, received discouragement both from that monarch and from her successor and eventually sought refuge in France; but he fared better than his contemporary, the Polish inventor of the ribbon loom, who was secretly strangled on the orders of the Dantzig city council because of the threat his device posed to poor weavers in the town. The King of England attempted by proclamation to forbid the importation of this loom, after it had been re-invented in Holland half a century later.

More frequently, technological improvements have proved stillborn because though sound in design the level of engineering skill or the quality of materials available have not matched the concept. The advantages of higher pressures and of compounding in improving the thermal efficiency and increasing the power of the steam engine were understood well before the advent of cheap steel permitted really effective exploitation of them. Charles Babbage designed in the mid-nineteenth century an 'analytical machine' which was a brilliant forerunner of the modern computer, but the engineering skills of the day were not equal to producing it at a cost and within physical dimensions such as to make it a commercial proposition. (It was also ahead of its time demand-wise, no doubt.)

Even inventions for which there is a potential demand and which are practicable given the factor supply, skills and materials available may still fail of application through simple lack of perception on the part of entrepreneurs – the rebuffs suffered by Whittle, inventor of the jet engine, spring to mind – or perhaps because of the threat posed to the profitability of existing installations (it has been said that an electric light bulb of virtually indefinite life has long been technically feasible). Finally, of course, in all of this we have ignored the need for a period of *development* before even a good and thoroughly practical invention can be placed in readiness for commercial production.

It is therefore not to be wondered at that there should be an interval, and sometimes a substantial one, between the devising of a worthwhile invention and its appearance on the market. It has sometimes been asserted that on average this lag has been diminishing through time, and if so this would constitute one minor explanation of the modern acceleration of economic growth – society has been catching up, so to say, on the inventions at its disposal. Such a shortening of the lag would not be difficult to explain. Higher real incomes and modern advertising surely make it easier to squeeze a new product into the pattern of final demand, while higher rates of capital formation permit a similarly speedier exploitation of new producers' equipment and processes. One would imagine that the wider array of available materials and superior assortment of engineering skills would have reduced the practical barriers to new concepts. And modern R and D facilities ought, one would think, to permit a foreshortening of the development period.

Despite its plausibility, the hypothesis that the interval between invention and innovation is becoming shorter rests on remarkably little evidence, and what there is is scarcely convincing. Enos, for example, has compiled a list of thirty-five product and process inventions of the eighteenth, nineteenth and twentieth centuries showing the time interval between invention and innovation in each case. The lags average out as follows:

Date of invention	Number of inventions	Average interval (years)
to 1800	5	6·4
1801–1900	9	30·0
1901–onwards	21	8·3

Source: Calculated from Enos, N.B.E.R. (1962), Table 2, pp. 307–8.

Certainly the expected acceleration appears in the twentieth century, but it is disturbing that the average interval between invention and innovation seems to have been shorter in the eighteenth century than in either the nineteenth or the twentieth, and also that the high average for the nineteenth century is caused largely by the inclusion of three inventions with intervals of upwards of fifty years before innovation – inventions which, if they had been made in the present century, could not have been included in the table as they would not have been innovated before the date of its compilation.

Another frequently-quoted source is the study of twenty major innovations of the last century by Frank Lynn, whose chief findings are summarized below:

Period of development of selected technological innovations (in years)

Date of beginning of commercial development	Average incubation period (a)	Development (b)	Total
1885–1919	30	7	37
1920–1944	16	8	24
1945–1964	9	5	14

(a) = from basic discovery to start of commercial development
(b) = from start of commercial development to introduction as commercial product or process.
Source: Frank Lynn, 'An Investigation of the Rate of Development and Diffusion of Technology in Our Modern Industrial Society', *Report of the National Commission on Technology, Automation, and Economic Progress* (Washington, D.C., 1966), quoted in Mansfield, *Economics of Technological Change*, p. 102.

This investigation is worth quoting for the (perhaps unexpected) suggestion that it is through speedier decisions to develop inventions commercially, rather than through quicker development, that the lag between invention and commercial appearance has been shortened. But not much weight can be placed on either of these sets of data, since the inventions included are hand-picked and not necessarily representative, and also since in both exercises the number of cases chosen seems far too small, bearing in mind the wide dispersion of time intervals indicated by Enos' data.

A second type of lag is the interval between the first introduction of a new product or process in a given country or industry and its adoption by all interested producers. The historical evidence again suggests that this lag may sometimes be very long. Salter, as we have already seen, offers evidence indicating that even in two very advanced countries, the U.S.A. and the United Kingdom, there are industries in which plants of substantially different technological vintage coexist.[50] Griliches' classic study of the diffusion of hybrid corn in the U.S.A. revealed that in Iowa, the most progressive State in this respect, it took only four years for the share of corn acreage planted with hybrid varieties to rise from 10 to 90 per cent; but in Alabama the 10 per cent level was not crossed until twelve years later (1948), and in 1956, at the end of the study, the 90 per cent level had still not been reached.[51]

It is easy to misinterpret such findings. On the one hand, the technological lags mentioned would show up in differing *partial* productivities among the plants or States concerned. Salter's newer-vintage firms had (as we have seen) very substantially higher outputs per man-hour, and Iowa produced more corn per acre than Alabama. Such differences are sometimes proffered as explanations of varying levels of real income per head or as evidence of relative backwardness or progressiveness. In reality, of course, it is total productivity which counts: a fully depreciated, technically-obsolete plant will still be competitive if its variable costs are less than price; the *costs* of innovating and diffusing hybrid corn will be higher in a marginal corn State such as Alabama and may more than absorb the more modest gains of introducing it in such areas. Transport costs and raw material supplies will be relevant in some instances: the Urals iron-masters were able to persevere with charcoal-iron in their timber-rich but coal-deficient region of Russia well after up-to-date, highly-integrated steelmills had begun production in the South.

Inter-country lags

Perhaps the most important 'lags' for us – the ones which feature largely in Denison's study – are lags *between countries*. Actually, these can of course be regarded simply as inter-country instances of the two sorts of lag already discussed; the less developed economy is retarded technologically in the sense of not having adopted the most advanced techniques relevant to its structure and/or by having a distribution of plants by technological vintage skewed towards the obsolete end. Inter-country differences deserve a few separate comments, however, both because of their evident interest for the student of comparative economic growth and because they invoke new dimensions in explaining lags which are not present, or are markedly less important, in comparisons between sectors or regions within a single economy. Above all, it deserves to be stressed that while much discussion in this chapter has so far concerned the movement of the technological frontier wherever in the world that has existed, most countries have grown, historically speaking, by *importing* the bulk of their technology. This applies not only to small countries like New Zealand or Switzerland, whose technological parasitism is easy to explain, but also, until recent years at least, to 'late' industrializers like Japan and Russia and even, in considerable measure, to larger European countries like Italy and France.

That countries should have been able to grow by importing technical know-how is not at first sight surprising, and we have seen that Denison is prepared to make the extreme assumption that new technological knowledge is available on equal terms, and with equal growth-promoting capability, to all nine of his European countries. We have already queried, however, the validity of Denison's assumption here even as between the small group of predominantly high-income countries with which he is concerned, while hinting that it would be even less defensible if it were extended to other countries of sharply differing structure and degree of development (see pp. 317–19). The problem involves the whole question of technological diffusion, and this is an area which has been very much under-researched both by historians and by economists.

Despite this neglect a few points can be made. Chapter 2 has already pointed out that agricultural technology is often not exportable because it is sensitive to even relatively slight differences in soil and climate over which man has virtually no control. This is true not only on a broad scale, say as between temperate and tropical agriculture, but when considering the cultivation of a single crop, say wheat, the spread of whose cultivation in the nineteenth century from 'old' farming areas to newly-settled regions such as the prairie belt of North America, South Australia, or the Canterbury

Plains of New Zealand, required in each case subtle (or not-so-subtle) modifications to seed varieties, cultivation techniques, farming calendar, agricultural machinery and the like. One interesting facet of Griliches' paper on hybrid corn is its indication that the new corn was 'not a single innovation immediately adaptable everywhere'; rather, the researching of new hybrid strains had to be undertaken afresh for each separate climatic zone.[52] It can well be understood that *a fortiori* agricultural techniques are often even less immediately transmissible from one country to another, and that an analysis of growth founded on the assumption that an extension of the frontier of agricultural technology anywhere in the world implies an equal immediate increase in output potential all over the world is based on false premises.

Considerations of this sort extend well beyond the agricultural sector, indeed to any sector where the conditions imposed by nature ineluctably affect production possibilities and techniques – to mining, forestry, the sources of power, transportation. However, it is usually claimed that *industrial* technology is no respecter of place: a steel mill is a steel mill wherever it may be. Even here we have to except newly-won knowledge which is closely guarded by firms using it to achieve market dominance; we have seen that a major component of modern international trade in manufactures is based on precisely this sort of 'technological gap'. But one would think that a very large reservoir of industrial technology of less recent vintage remains which *can* be freely tapped by a developing nation, as a concert pianist can still draw on a huge classical repertoire if he wants to avoid paying royalties to composers still alive or to the beneficiaries of those recently deceased.

The economic historian and the perceptive traveller know that most countries, most of the time, have *not* tapped this reservoir very effectively. Interpretation, again, is difficult, for nations may abjure an available technology for perfectly rational reasons – because it does not suit their pattern of demand or of factor and resource availability; or because it requires for profitable operation a larger market than they can offer. Such impediments to the diffusion of technology are not, of course, new; but it is plausible to argue that they have tended to *increase* through time, as a consequence of the fact that conditions in technologically advanced and in less developed countries have become, in many instances, *more* unlike rather than *less*. The 'conditions' in mind here include both the technologies themselves, which differ more as between most advanced and most backward than was the case a couple of centuries ago; market conditions (e.g. levels of real *per capita* incomes, patterns of expenditure); the supportive framework of financial and other services on which modern industry depends; and the 'lumpiness' of investment in capital-intensive industrial plants which puts them out of reach of the unaided savings potential of many poor countries. In this sort of way modern technology has probably become less readily exportable from advanced to less advanced countries over the past century or two. History confirms that this trend is not of extremely recent origins. Professor Landes, the leading historian of nineteenth-century technology, notes that for just such reasons as those listed above the countries of Western continental Europe found that 'emulation of Britain was probably harder after Waterloo than before', and tells us that in the years following the Napoleonic Wars 'The bulk of the entrepreneurs of France, Belgium and Germany did not take advantage of their opportunity to install the latest equipment and surpass the British in productivity.'[53]

In this sense diffusion of technology, at least as between countries towards opposite ends of the continuum of development, may have become more difficult in recent centuries. But viewing the matter in more institutional terms – having regard (that is) to the actual mechanism or channel of transmission of know-how – the tendency has been just the opposite: technological diffusion has become easier, rather than harder. Consider the situation in the medieval and early modern centuries. Technical knowledge was traditional, transmitted orally and by on-the-job training from master to apprentice, from father to son. Printed literature on mining began to appear in the sixteenth century and on agriculture in the seventeenth, but there is no evidence that it acted as an important vehicle for the diffusion of technical knowledge, least of all internationally, and much of it in any event purveyed more error than truth. Nor was there on any significant scale anything comparable to the modern international company of international equity investment to act as a vehicle of diffusion of the industrial arts (though there was in *finance*, and significantly, international diffusion of such techniques as double-entry book-keeping or arbitrage was much more thoroughly and earlier accomplished than was that of industrial and mining techniques). In consequence the international transmission of know-how typically involved the *migration* of skilled workers; and in the conditions of the day this often implied *permanent* migration. Only in the area of foreign trade and of finance were international contacts sufficiently regular to make such transmission possible without at least semi-permanent migration.

Consider the case of England in the Tudor and Stuart period. During these centuries England developed, technologically speaking, from a backwater on the periphery of a more advanced Europe to a position in the forefront of nations and on the verge of becoming the leading pioneer of advances in the productive arts. Yet virtually the whole of this improvement was achieved by importing technological knowledge through the international movement of people and the face-to-face learning of their skills. New crops and new skills in textile manufacture were brought in in two waves of Protestant immigration from the Low Countries during the period of Reformation and Counter-Reformation. The French Huguenots, fleeing from persecution in France in the following century, brought in an even wider range of industrial techniques. Queen Elizabeth sought to make the country more self-sufficient and stronger militarily by fostering mining and metallurgy, for which purpose she granted charters giving concessions to German miners and engineers. The same monarch sought to encourage other new industrial arts also: some of the more worthwhile of her patents of monopoly, before they degenerated into a mere fiscal device, sought to encourage Italian and other experts to settle in England and establish such industries as glass-making and salt manufacture. In the following century the draining of the Fens was begun under Dutch contractors, while following the restoration of Charles II Royalist *émigrés* returned to their English estates, there to pioneer the new techniques, crops and rotations which they had learned during the years of exile in the Low Countries.

By the late eighteenth and early nineteenth centuries it was Britain's turn to be able to give something in exchange, and the contribution of British engineers to the early stages of industrial development on the Continent is well known. At first, the *personal* transmission of skills, sometimes accompanying some minor export of British capital, was important, notwithstanding the law prohibiting the emigration of skilled workmen. (This law, not repealed until 1825 though largely ineffective, testifies to contemporary recognition of the essential role of migration in the diffusion of technology.) In the early nineteenth century, however, rising incomes, cheaper and quicker travel and communications, the development of trade journals and scientific literature, the extension of patent systems, and growing awareness of the significance of the industrial changes taking place in England and desire to emulate them, all led to the situation in which the transfer of technological knowledge across national boundaries no longer required its embodiment in the skills of a migrant worker. By the middle decades of the century major inventions such as the fundamental discoveries establishing the modern steel industry were quickly adopted by several leading industrial nations under licensing arrangements.

In the later nineteenth century the export of capital, though at first predominantly *not* equity capital, pioneered new channels of technological diffusion through the international firms and the formation of foreign subsidiaries. Russia was the first major country to launch a 'take off' on the basis of know-how imported alongside foreign capital. Japan, more resistant to the threat of foreign domination, accomplished the same thing largely by licensing arrangements and by sending her young people to foreign schools and universities. In the twentieth century it is of course these methods, aided especially since World War II by the upsurge of foreign 'direct' investment amongst the leading industrial nations, which have led to technical knowledge being so much more readily diffused than in the past that Denison's assumption is not obviously outrageous.

All the same, the acquisition of technological knowledge by such means is not costless even today. Many large firms have sought to guard their secrets more jealously than ever to counter the changed conditions which make their escape more likely. Industrial espionage would not have risen to the extensive profession that it is were not the secrets in which it trades not only valuable but closely kept. Even in one industry and one country large corporations will seek to 'invent around' new processes which their competitors have innovated, rather than try to hire them or steal them.[54] Since it is easier to keep such secrets from foreigners than from fellow-nationals, especially where differences in economic and educational background are great and the language different, we should not be led by the prevalence of international firms and foreign subsidiaries to believe that host countries can easily learn much more than the head office in the metropolitan country wants them to know. We have seen in the section on the export of capital that from the Russian industrialization drive of the 1890s onwards, host countries have been concerned to devise formulae to ensure that there is in fact what they regard as an adequate 'spin-off' of technological knowledge from the foreign firm in their midst. All the same, it cannot be doubted that conditions today are very much more favourable to technological diffusion than they were a couple of centuries, or still more five centuries, ago.

Technical 'improvements'

We turn from this discussion of major technical changes and their diffusion to make a few comments on 'improvements'

(F²). Evidently, the line between the two is arbitrary; but it seems desirable to have a scheme of classification reflecting the difference between, say, the Bessemer converter as a completely novel successor to the 'puddling' process on the one hand, and later minor improvements to the system of air ducts feeding the converter on the other. There is a substantial body of evidence that minor and often anonymous improvements have been responsible, historically, for a substantial fraction of the improvement in productivity due to technological progress. Thus Professor Landes states firmly that 'in iron as in textiles, small anonymous gains were probably more important in the long run than the major inventions that have been remembered in the history books'. For example, in the South Wales iron industry between 1791 and 1830 'changes in the blast and in the shape and size of the furnace' (but excluding any really fundamental single innovation) reduced coal consumption per ton of pig-iron produced from about 8 to $3\frac{1}{2}$ tons. Later in the nineteenth century, many machine-using industries improved productivity at little cost by greater attention to proper lubrication.[55] Tungsten steel permitted higher speeds in cutting machinery – and so on.

While quantitatively rigorous comparisons of the effect of major inventions and of 'improvements' on productivity are few, a well-known exercise of this type, John L. Enos' study of invention and innovation in petroleum refining, unequivocally supports the view put forward here. Basing his conclusion on estimates of changes in input/output ratios and in factor proportions induced on the one hand by the change-over from one major cracking process to the next, and on the other hand during the intervals of more gradual improvement to each such process before it was superseded by the next, Enos is able to state firmly that 'in terms of almost any measure other than originality – reduction of costs, saving of resources, expansion of output – the improvements made in the processes subsequent to their initial application were as significant as the innovations themselves'.[56] This conclusion, actually, is not all that surprising, for in a competitive system a substantially new process will be introduced when, but only when, it promises a discernible reduction in total costs below those of existing (improved) processes. This process, however, will then be 'worked over' and adapted wherever possible to effect cost reductions until it, in turn, is just overtaken by a successor. Unless major inventions come thick and fast, which is often unlikely from the very nature of the scientific field in question, it is probable that a substantial part of overall productivity gain will come from the gradual improvements going on continuously between the discrete major innovations.[57]

One well-informed writer on technological change, S. C. Gilfillan, comes close to *equating* that process with piecemeal improvement: he writes, 'The great truth, the essential process, of invention and technic progress, is reflected under the head of general efficiency, not of major inventions.'[58] This is surely going too far, for clearly there *have* been major inventions, such as, say, the series which made possible the modern steel industry, which the prescription does not fit. Gilfillan was undoubtedly influenced by the character of the particular industry he happened to have specialized in, ship designing, which – doubtless because of its exceptionally long history and world-wide nature – has indeed been singularly *evolutionary*, rather than revolutionary, in its progress. But there is an important element of truth in Gilfillan's remark, even beyond what has already been said about the cumulative importance of minor improvements, and that is that often – not always – that which for expository convenience we choose to call a 'fundamental invention' is in fact a composite bringing together a great many elements, some new but most old, in a novel way. As Gilfillan goes on to say, 'The multitudinous little turnings-up not only overbalance the big in importance, but include the big and compose them. For what we call a major invention, like an efficient fore-and-aft rig (9 centuries in the making), rudder, steering wheel, steamship, or a propeller or oil engine worth using, is composed of at least a dozen minor inventions and usually of thousands . . .'

One may be too easily persuaded by this line of argument, which is very typical of what one might term the Chicago 'gradualist' or 'general equilibrium' reaction against the 'heroic' interpretation of history, an interpretation which lionized *Great Inventions* as it lionized *Great Men*. (It is interesting to note that Gilfillan anticipated, in respect of shipping, the conclusion which twenty-nine years later another Chicago teacher, Robert Fogel, reached by more laborious methods in respect of railways. 'The careless thinker [Gilfillan wrote] . . . sees steamships carrying over every sea an immense international commerce . . . and concludes that the invention of the steamer did it . . . [in fact the] windjammer has been so constantly and greatly improved that she could carry all the world's freight, with no great loss.'[59]) The reaction can go too far: not *every* major invention can be decomposed into a host of minor ones and not *every* industry is like shipbuilding. But minor improvements have still other claims on our attention, aside from their great and neglected importance, because of their qualitative difference from major inventions, and of some of the consequences flowing from this.

The difference referred to is that because of their very nature improvements virtually have to be conceived *on the job* – in the light of experience with particular machinery, of the indications of production and accounting data relating to a particular plant, to combat shortages or seek to reduce waste actually experienced in production, and so on. This feature of improvements has a number of implications which are extremely important for us. It strengthens, in the first place, the 'demand-induced' rather than the 'science-based' explanation of the rate and direction of inventive activity. For 'improvements' are often simple changes lacking scientific or other novelty – there is no *new* vision in taking advantage of stronger materials to build bigger furnaces or distilling vats, for example – and even when this is not so it is normally the desire to cut costs or some similar consideration which suggests the locus and nature of the change. (It is curious that Schmookler, though fully convinced of the high importance of 'improvements' relative to fundamental inventions, did not make very great use of this point to buttress his advocacy of the 'demand-induced' explanation of technological change.)

Secondly, the fact that improvements are often in some degree specific to a particular plant or to a pattern of factor and resource availability peculiar to a particular region means that they often cannot be transmitted, as basic techniques can, from one environment to another. This implies a major qualification to the remarks made earlier about the international mobility of technological knowledge. A less developed country with little industrial experience and poorly-endowed with engineers and technologists may be at a disadvantage even if presented with a free gift of a plant of the most recent technological vintage, through its relative inability to make subsequent improvements. The admiration expressed by British observers for the American factory worker and manager and for their ability to devise minor improvements suggests that an inter-country difference of this type was present and acknowledged early in the nineteenth century, and there is little doubt that it is a real factor in the ability of many present-day under-developed countries to profit from the opportunity to borrow technology from more advanced countries. But it has to be confessed that the historical significance of this point remains largely unexplored.

Factor proportions and technical change

Thirdly, and perhaps most intriguingly, it has been suggested that one function of the 'improvement' period of a process may be to allow it to be adapted to the prevailing local pattern of factor availability, and that it is *in the improvement stage*, rather than in the basic invention which the improvements modify, that the capital- or labour-saving bias of such inventions is introduced. Again, it is Enos' excellent paper which advances the idea, supporting it by close analysis of changes in factor proportions (and prices) during the introduction and subsequent improvement of successive innovations in petroleum refining.[60]

The hypothesis is one which certainly ought to be tested by economic historians, for like economic theorists they have been considerably interested by the notion that one dimension of technological change is its responsiveness to the relative factor scarcities characterizing particular economies and particular periods. There was a tendency, for example, for earlier historians of the industrial revolution in England to stress the labour-saving character of much technical change, a feature which seemed easy to explain given rising wage rates and a low rate of interest. Professor Ashton repeatedly sought to disabuse this simplistic notion, claiming (quite correctly) that some inventions were intended to save particular scarce resources – timber or water (for water power) or, on occasion, capital; and also pointing out that some inventions were *not* fashioned primarily with *particular* factor substitutions in mind, but rather took their character from their scientific content and justified themselves by their ability to economize on several or all factors simultaneously.[61]

The most celebrated discussion of factor-saving bias in technical change has revolved around the thesis propounded by H. J. Habakkuk in his book, *American and British Technology in the Nineteenth Century*.[62] Habakkuk argues that American entrepreneurs adopted more capital-intensive methods than the British because the ratio of American wage rates to British wage rates was higher than the ratio of the product of the cost of capital goods times the rate of interest in America to that of the corresponding product in Britain. Further, the American labour supply was not only dearer but less elastic. Both features arose because of the availability of cheap land in the U.S.A., which set a floor price to wage rates there. The relatively lower ratio of capital costs arose because of America's ability to import machinery, and in any event the hazy notion of capital costs which was all entrepreneurs had in the earlier nineteenth century meant that decisions tended to be taken on the basis of wage costs alone. Habakkuk argues perhaps *chiefly* in terms of the choice made between alternative (existing) factor combinations, but also for a bias in American invention (and improvement) towards labour-saving devices.

His thesis, broadly considered, is not new, but it was argued with both theoretical and historical sophistication and has provoked a series of specialist studies which have considerably enlarged our knowledge of nineteenth-century technology and managerial practice. Perhaps inevitably, there has been a considerable erosion of the thesis as these have progressed, but its appeal has by no means been completely undermined. Perhaps the most fundamental criticism is that which disputes its essential premise, that the price of labour relative to that of capital was sufficiently higher in America to lead to the alleged bias.[63] There is certainly a difficulty here, as it is clear that wage rates varied very substantially indeed within as well as between countries: for example, a high-to-low spread of daily wage rates of more than 3 : 1 as between the industrialized and non-industrialized parts of the country is revealed by a recent examination of Scottish wage data relating to the last decade of the eighteenth century.[64]

Nevertheless, contrasts both in wage rates and in choice of productive technique similar to those between Britain and America seem to be present during the nineteenth century as between Britain on the one hand and Australia and New Zealand on the other. It is highly probable that comparative studies of these other regions of recent settlement and of the United Kingdom would provide strong support for every major aspect of the Habakkuk thesis, including the (traditional) view that it was the cheap land which caused the wages floor to be so high. More important still, both these economies (unlike that of the U.S.A.) had far smaller markets than that of Britain, so that an alternative hypothesis, which proposes to explain capital-intensity of techniques in terms of market size, is obviously false here. The scope for helping to resolve this particular historical debate by enlarging the area of comparison to include other 'new' countries is very great.

The point more immediately at issue, however, is that

America's array of capital-intensive techniques may have been acquired as much in the 'improvement' stages as in the original choice of technique. Certainly this was not always so; an excellent article by Lars Sandberg has analysed the reasons for the technical development and rapid adoption of ring spinning in the U.S. cotton industry in the later nineteenth century, and for its much slower diffusion in Britain.[65] The article reveals that the choice between mules and rings was not a simple one – the advantages of the two processes varied critically with the count of the yarn being spun, for example – but Habakkuk's thesis receives some support in that it is shown that respective costs of labour were certainly a critical factor, and that entrepreneurs in both countries made *rational* choices in the light of this and other considerations. In some other industries, however, the basic techniques employed were the same in both countries, but rational adjustments to suit differing factor prices were achieved by the choice of different scales of production, minor improvements to economize on scarce factors, and the like. One outstanding case in point is the U.S. steel industry, which, though inventing no really major new technique to suit its own circumstances, *modified* the techniques which were common to all producing countries by (for example) adopting very large-scale production, mechanizing handling of ore and other raw materials to save labour, and similar devices. It is in such cases that the notion of factor-bias in *improvements* rather than in fundamental invention seems a useful concept to bring to the historical data.[66]

'Managerial' improvements and productivity

In conclusion, a few comments must be made on 'managerial' improvements as a source of increased productivity. By this term is intended such functions of management as promoting the motivation on the part of workers to seek high productivity; planning factory layout, the logistics of materials flow, and the integration of sequential processes to minimize delays; intra-firm allocation of resources and selection of output-mix to maximize profits, and the like. There is no question but that big differences in output can emerge from success or failure in discharging these responsibilities. A useful summary of some relevant studies is to be found in Harvey Leibenstein's already-quoted paper, where the magnitude of some reported increases in productivity stemming from changes of this type is seen to contrast very favourably with the apparently small loss of output associated with such impediments to optimal macro-economic allocation as tariffs or monopoly. Increases of labour productivity of upwards of 100 per cent in some cases have been reported by I.L.O. productivity teams following advice given in developing countries. Even in highly developed countries improvements in the range of 40–70 per cent in output per man have frequently been reported following major change in one of the areas mentioned.[67]

From the point of view of the economic historian these studies are deficient in a number of respects. First, they have a restricted historical range, relating only to recent decades. Secondly, they relate, in general, only to particular plants, or indeed to a particular department in a plant, and do not add up to a measure of the contribution of this factor to the growth of the whole economy. Most frequently, too, the effect of a given change has been measured in terms of *labour* productivity rather than of *aggregate* productivity. And a good many studies emanate from industrial psychologists or sociologists and do not report results in the manner which economists or economic historians would find most useful. Nor, unfortunately, has any way yet been found in macro-economic investigations to isolate the effect on growth of managerial changes; even the ingenious Denison has been unable to propose a solution to this problem, and in his studies 'technological' (D_1) are not differentiated from 'managerial' (D_2) contributions, the sum of the two being estimated as the final residual.

Our ignorance is in one way even greater than this, for it is not even clear whether, for a given state of technical knowledge and array of factor inputs, the potential gain from managerial improvements is finite or not. In the case, for example, of misallocation of resources the extent of the improvement to be looked for from moving towards equilibrium is clearly finite; one cannot – as has been stated already – better optimal allocation. But is managerial inefficiency to be regarded analogously as a source of *finite* loss of output which can in theory be completely eliminated by a move to 'optimal' management? ('Optimal' management being defined, presumably, as that sort of management which facilitates achievement of the 'ceiling' level of output determined by the volume of inputs and the state of technical knowledge.) The notion that potential gains to improved management are infinite is difficult to accept, yet the very large increases in output secured in some instances warns us at least against assuming that this is necessarily a quickly-exhausted source of productivity improvement. Finally, the line between 'technological' and 'managerial' change, and indeed between these two and fixed capital formation, is a fuzzy one indeed: it is conceptually unclear, for example, how to allocate an increase in output brought about by the introduction of conveyor-belt assembly.

Despite these uncertainties, it seems fairly clear that whatever contribution to increased output has emanated from improved management has come largely within the last century or even half-century, though of course the slave and military societies of pre-industrial civilizations have to their credit not a few extraordinary logistical feats such as the building of the pyramids. But a conscious search for appropriate methods of factory organization and managerial leadership with a free labour force seems to have been provoked only by the industrial changes beginning in late eighteenth-century England. The captains of industry of that era then had to pioneer solutions to the logistical and other problems which larger-scale enterprise posed. With no inherited background of knowledge on which to draw, they necessarily tackled the problems they encountered in a pragmatic way; though there seems to have been a degree of sharing of managerial experience between some of the leading industrialists. In the best of the few cases of which we

N

have detailed knowledge, such as the engine-works of the firm of Boulton and Watt, solutions of remarkable ingenuity were achieved. Though struggling with novel problems and unaided by any guide from experience or hint from the general body of organized knowledge, these pioneers at least managed factories which were sufficiently small for it to be possible for one man to gain an overall, integrated view by personal observation, and the owner-managers of those days were often dedicated and extraordinarily hard-working men. There is every likelihood, however, that the few firms of whose practices detailed evidence has survived, such as the Coalbrookdale iron-masters, the Darbys; the engine-makers Boulton and Watt; and Wedgwood of pottery fame[68] were untypical, and that as Professor Pollard has contended there was neither any very widespread systematization of managerial practice, nor even any general recognition of a managerial problem, during the early industrial revolution.[69]

Moreover, even the most enlightened managers of the day were not uniformly successful. Accounting, especially those aspects of the profession concerned with providing a financial check on the efficiency of the firm and with the costing of production, proved a particular stumbling block, for here conceptual problems are involved which are *not* capable of being reasonably adequately resolved, as is for example the problem of optimal factory layout, by careful observation and the application of common sense. It is fascinating to see a Josiah Wedgwood floundering in the midst of a liquidity crisis and struggling to understand the reasons for it. Notwithstanding some partial successes in the leading firms, overall the judgment of Professor Pollard seems apt, that 'entrepreneurship in the industrial revolution did not develop to any significant extent the use of accounts in guiding management decisions'.[70]

In a different area it seems probable that an increase in productivity was achieved unintentionally, and against the opposition of the majority of managers, that is by the success of the movement to limit maximum hours of work. Though no conclusive proof has yet been offered, it appears very

possible, in the light of subsequent investigations of the
relationship between daily hours of work and output, that
the limitations imposed by new laws in early Victorian
Britain should have increased total output per man, and
extremely probable that they increased output per man-
hour. This indeed was claimed by some contemporaries to
have been the effect of the British Ten Hours Act of 1847,
and Robert Owen had testified to a Parliamentary Committee as early as 1818 that reducing the working day from
fourteen to twelve hours in his New Lanark factory had
brought about an increase in total output. The legislation in
question was pushed through Parliament, however, more
particularly on humanitarian grounds, and had to contend
with vigorous opposition in which prominent use was
made of the argument that 'all the profit is made in the last
hour'; moreover, the prevailing, though not universal and
sometimes implicit, assumption of contemporary classical
economists as well as of factory owners was that output
would fall proportionately to the reduction in hours.[71]

Some outstanding exceptions acknowledged, however, it
was not until the late nineteenth century that managerial
problems became the subject of scientific study and that
standard solutions capable of being widely diffused and
applied were evolved. There were, doubtless, a number of
reasons for the timing of this development, but almost
certainly the major one was that it was only in the last
couple of decades of the nineteenth century that really large-
scale enterprises became sufficiently numerous for it to be
worth while innovating solutions to their managerial
problems, or indeed possible to discern that such problems
existed widely. There is an impressive convergence of
evidence pointing to the 1880s and 1890s as the critical
decades. Frederick Winslow ('Speedy') Taylor directed his
famous experiment in loading pig-iron, often regarded as the
birth of time-and-motion study, about the turn of the century
while 'Consulting Engineer in Management' to the Bethle-
hem Steel Company, but his experiments along these lines
go back to the mid-1880s. He delivered his first paper on

management to the American Society of Mechanical Engineers in 1895. Slater Lewis' book, perhaps the first modern text on factory organization, appeared the following year, 1896. The pioneer books on factory cost accounting were published in the 1880s. Serious attention to plant layout as a major source of higher productivity seems to have been pioneered in such firms as the Carnegie steelworks at Pittsburgh during the same decades. The most dramatic (though not the first) demonstration of the conveyor-belt assembly line came from Henry Ford at Detroit in the early 1900s. Above all, it was towards the end of the nineteenth century that such advances began to be widely discussed and to cohere into an organized and transmissible body of knowledge: the Wharton School of Finance and Commerce was established at the University of Pennsylvania in 1881; Chicago and California followed with similar schools in 1898.[72]

However, it would be easy to overstate the rapidity with which the new teachings were actually applied; in 1911 'Taylor claimed no more than that at least 50,000 people were employed under scientific management in the U.S.A.'[73] and outside North America progress was undoubtedly slower even than this. Moreover, these early advances were unhelpful or even harmful in one critical area, motivation, because they were the product of a somewhat dehumanized view of workmen which looked on the problem of labour efficiency as essentially the same as that of achieving the maximum mechanical efficiency in designing factory machinery. The inadequacy of this view was strikingly demonstrated in the famous experiments in labour productivity carried out at the Hawthorne works of the General Electric Company in Chicago in the mid-1920s.[74] The significance of these experiments, for which Elton Mayo, a professor in the Harvard Graduate School of Business, was responsible, was to demonstrate that good morale and motivation could easily be more important than the orthodox 'objective' working conditions (lighting, heating, system of rest breaks and so on) as influences on labour productivity, and that morale and motivation in turn were improved, at first unintentionally, simply because the research being carried out gave the workers the feeling that their problems were not being ignored. This was demonstrated most dramatically when, following a series of successive improvements in 'objective' conditions and 'conventional' inducements – better rest breaks, piece rates and so on – all improvements were taken away and the original, least favourable, conditions restored: output, which had already been increased by almost all of the successive individual improvements, *now went up again* to its highest level ever!

The Hawthorne experiments were of great significance to social science generally, since they demonstrated the importance of the fact that human beings are not mere passive elements in an experimental situation, like hydrogen atoms whose characteristics can reasonably be assumed to be unchanged by the fact that they are under scrutiny, but rather are active agents whose attitudes and behaviour are liable to be altered by their very awareness of being observed. (It is curious and unfortunate that economics, in so many ways the most highly developed of the social sciences, has been perhaps least able to come to terms with this reality.) For management, the Hawthorne results inaugurated a new era in which attention was directed to an important area of determinants of productivity neglected by the early phase of 'Scientific Management'.

The overall situation, then, is that while important principles of progressive modern management began to be explored in the late nineteenth century, they were probably not widely implemented even in the U.S.A. until the 1920s, and moreover some important sources of productivity improvement were not uncovered until that decade. Outside America progress was probably even slower. The Soviet Union in the person of Stakhanov rediscovered 'Taylorism' during its Second Five-Year Plan, fifty years after Taylor. The major contribution of improved management to higher productivity in Western Europe has probably come in the years since World War II, and indeed this contribution may constitute a substantial fraction of the 'catching up' element to which, as we have seen, Denison ascribes such a large share of the disparity between European and American rates of growth since World War II. Changes in the recruitment and training of managers, well summarized by Professor Postan, would seem on the whole to reinforce this supposition.[75] However, the 'contribution' in question has yet to be measured either in macro- or in micro-economic analysis, and at present one can do no more than hazard the inference from this brief survey of the chronology of managerial innovation that the chief impact of managerial changes on productivity has come in the last half-century, rather than in earlier decades of the modern industrial era.

Pitfalls and possibilities in the historical analysis of productivity change

As we have seen in the foregoing pages, the 'residual' is something of a rag-bag of items, difficult to sort out and classify, and defying easy valuation. It is partly for this reason that research has so far failed to produce a really satisfactory analysis of the extent to which, and the ways in which, the various factors which it comprises have combined to generate the increase in aggregate productivity to which most studies have ascribed a large fraction of modern economic growth.

But some writers have discerned another and in some ways more fundamental deficiency of the manner in which the problem has been tackled. We have already seen that Zvi Griliches, himself the author of excellent studies on productivity, has criticized the general approach to the study of technological change *via* the aggregate production function.[76] This has been developed into a more pointed criticism by Edward Ames and Nathan Rosenberg, who have used a specific case – the establishment of the British Government Arsenal at Enfield in the mid-nineteenth century – to argue that the macro-economic approach is fundamentally unsuited to the analysis of the historical course of productivity.[77] If the authors making this claim were themselves economic historians of a more traditional mould, innocent of any claim to econometric expertise, one might be suspicious of their competence to make such a judgment or indeed of their motives for publicizing it. But this is manifestly not the case, for both authors – and of course Griliches too – are fully-equipped modern economists who cannot be suspected of any shabby intent to denigrate a mode of analysis in which they lack competence.

The charge undoubtedly has to be taken seriously, and indeed there can be little question that Ames' and Rosenberg's criticism is completely valid, as far as it goes. Their complaint, at bottom, is that the macro-economic approach to productivity involves the jettisoning of much historical evidence and the distorting of the rest in an effort to comprehend it within the restricted range of variables which is all a highly aggregated production function can handle. They show that in fact the establishment of the Arsenal involved the supersession of one type of product, the 'handicraft' gun, by another, the gun with interchangeable parts, and also of old types of labour and machinery by new. They urge that both output and inputs were, in fact, heterogeneous, and that the bull-dozing of the historical facts which justify this contention into the confines of a production function with homogeneous outputs, and with inputs of homogeneous labour and of homogeneous capital, is unwarranted.

In the present problem [they comment] it appears that the characteristics of individual machines and their outputs are essential parts of the subject matter under discussion. If this is so, then the use of drastically aggregated input hypotheses is apt to be misleading. . . . The working historian will naturally wish to keep his explanation as simple as he can . . . but on historical and analytical grounds he knows that every time he suppresses a variable a part of his record becomes irrelevant.[78]

Nor is it only part of the *record* which becomes irrelevant: the vast body of non-econometric economic history already written loses much of its value in the strait-jacket of a highly-aggregated macro-economic approach. Here the writer of these words can testify with some feeling, for in the preparation of this book by far the most difficult problem has been that of achieving, at relevant points, some sort of integration or even comparison between macro-economic and econometric studies on the one hand, and the huge mass of more traditional economic historiography on the other. At the risk of seeming to wish to find an excuse for what the reader may judge to be a clear failure in this respect, one might add that the difficulty was compounded by the fact that of all the problems which were encountered, this was the one where least guidance was found in the existing literature.

One feels intuitively that despite its shortcomings for the purpose in question, the aggregative and econometric approach cannot be abjured, as might appear to follow from the logic of Ames' and Rosenberg's case (though, perhaps significantly, they do not explicitly recommend this course). The internal consistency of its results and the readiness with which they can be integrated with overall growth analysis, and its indispensability as a basis for judging the relative performance of different sectors of a growing economy, make it difficult to envisage a satisfactory analysis of economic growth without the aid of some such framework. Even less should one be ready to contemplate the jettisoning of the fruits of more traditional types of research into economic history. One may well feel, then, that a major task in the immediate future is to attempt a synthesis between these two approaches.

That such a task, if difficult, is not impossible is shown by a number of modern studies which have accomplished it with considerable success. To mention only three, all of which have already been referred to in this chapter, one may instance Griliches' own classic paper on the diffusion of hybrid corn, Sandberg's study of the adoption of ring spinning in Britain and the U.S.A., and that of Enos on invention and innovation in the petroleum-refining industry.[79] It is characteristic of all three that they adopt a rigorous quantitative-analytical approach, and frame their conclusions in a way which permits ready comparisons with other studies and throws light on problems of general concern to the growth analyst, while at the same time refusing to distort or overlook facts which complicate the analysis. Griliches, for example, not only accommodates in his study, but both explains and shows the consequences of, such 'institutional' information as that in the Corn Belt hybrid varieties are offered to the farmer by door-to-door salesmen, whereas in the South the farmer has to find them for himself at such country stores as stock them. Sandberg makes clear that the *lack* of homogeneity in the output of his industry in respect of the differing yarn 'counts' was precisely one of the critical features explaining the differing response of American and British entrepreneurs to the invention of the ring spindle. Enos pays close attention both to the technical details of the processes under study and of the personal circumstances of their inventors.

Such studies are as yet rare, partly because few economic historians have received a widely-based education in all disciplines relevant to their subject, and most approach it in the spirit of the discipline in which they have received their major training. One may hope that today's widespread conscious attempt to avoid too narrow a base in university courses and the increasingly general recognition that economic history is a many-sided discipline, the approaches to which are essentially complementary rather than competitive, will lead in future to more such studies. In them seems to lie the best hope of building a bridge between the vast mass of 'traditional' economic history on the one hand and the economist-dominated aggregative analysis of growth and its constituents on the other, and by doing so of averting the onset of diminishing returns which otherwise might soon afflict each several activity.

Notes

1. *International Encyclopedia of the Social Sciences* (New York, Macmillan and Free Press, 1968), Vol. 1, 243, *s.v.* 'Agriculture: Productivity and Technology'.

2. ZVI GRILICHES, 'The Sources of Measured Productivity Growth: United States Agriculture, 1940–60', *Journal of Political Economy*, 71 (August 1963), 331–46.

3. DENISON (1967).

4. The data in this paragraph are taken from Tables 21–2 (p. 299) and 21–4 (p. 301).

5. HARVEY LEIBENSTEIN, 'Allocative Efficiency vs. "X-Efficiency"', *American Economic Review*, LVI (June 1966), 392–415.

6. ARNOLD C. HARBERGER, 'Using the Resources at Hand More Effectively', *American Economic Review (Papers and Proceedings)*, XLIX (May 1959), 134–46.

7. *Agriculture and Economic Growth* (Paris, O.E.C.D., 1965), Table 8, p. 43.

8. POSTAN (1967), 177; CHARLES P. KINDLEBERGER, *Europe's Postwar Growth: The Role of Labour Supply* (Cambridge, Mass., Harvard U.P., 1967).

9. For a useful summary of findings, see D. COCHRANE, 'The Cost of University Education', *Economic Record*, 44 (June 1968), 137–53.

10. EDWARD F. DENISON, *The Sources of Economic Growth in the United States and the Alternatives Before Us* (New York, Committee for Economic Development, 1962), 69–70; DENISON (1967), 84.

11. DENISON, *The Sources . . .*, 73.

12. TIBOR SCITOVSKY, 'An International Comparison of the Trend of Professional Earnings', *American Economic Review*, LVI (March 1966), 25–42.

13. A. E. MUSSON and E. ROBINSON, 'Science and Industry in the Late Eighteenth Century', *Economic History Review*, Sec. Ser. XIII (December 1960), 222–44; E. G. WEST, 'Resource Allocation and Growth in Early Nineteenth-Century British Education', *ibid.*, XXIII (April 1970), 68–95.

14. Quoted in J. H. CLAPHAM, *The Economic Development of France and Germany 1815–1914*, 4th ed. (Cambridge, Cambridge U.P., 1936), 101–3.

15. H. J. HABAKKUK, *American and British Technology in the Nineteenth Century* (Cambridge, Cambridge U.P., 1962), 6, quoting Joseph Whitworth.

16. DENISON (1967), 286–7.

17. SALTER (1960), Table 1, p. 6.

18. *ibid.*, Appx. to Ch. VII, 95–9.

19. *ibid.*, Table 9, 96.

20. DENISON (1967), 282.

21. See pp. 281–3 above.

22. ASHTON (1955), 107.

23. PHYLLIS DEANE, *The First Industrial Revolution* (Cambridge, Cambridge U.P., 1967), 128.

24. N.B.E.R. (1962), 78. For an excellent summary of his views, see SCHMOOKLER (1966), published shortly before the author's death.

25. SCHMOOKLER (1966), Ch. II. For a view highly sceptical of the value of patents, see B. S. SANDERS in N.B.E.R. (1962), 68–75.

26. SCHMOOKLER (1966), Table A–3, 227.

27. *ibid.*, Table A–1, A–2, 218–26, and Figures 4–7, 76–9.

28. LILLEY (1948), 187, 193.

29. See above, pp. 37–9, and fig. 1.2.

30. SCHMOOKLER (1966), 67. For an excellent review of the literature on invention until the late 1950s, see NELSON (1959).

31. *ibid.*, Chs. VI, VII.

32. cf. N.B.E.R. (1962), 13–14.

33. A. E. MUSSON and E. ROBINSON, *Science and Technology in the Industrial Revolution* (Manchester, Manchester U.P., 1969).

34. SCHMOOKLER (1966), 173.

35. EDWIN MANSFIELD, *The Economics of Technological Change* (Harlow, Longmans, 1968), 91.

36. *ibid.*, 44.

37. JOHN JEWKES, DAVID SAWERS and RICHARD STILLER-MAN, *The Sources of Invention*, 2nd ed. (London, Macmillan, 1969).

38. *ibid.*, 244–5.

39. JOHN L. ENOS, 'Invention and Innovation in the Petroleum Refining Industry', N.B.E.R. (1962), 303.

40. GILFILLAN (1963), 88–9.

41. HABAKKUK and POSTAN (1965), 486.

42. MANSFIELD, *op. cit.*, 59.

43. See above, p. 115.

44. cf. MANSFIELD, *op. cit.*, 65–8.

45. JEWKES *et al.*, *op. cit.*, 187.

46. GILFILLAN (1963), 55.

47. ENOS, *op. cit.*, 310.

48. WILLARD F. MUELLER, 'The Origins of the Basic Inventions Underlying Du Pont's Major Product and Process Innovations, 1920 to 1950', N.B.E.R. (1962), 342.

49. *ibid.*, 344.

50. See above, pp. 316–17.

51. GRILICHES (1957), Figure 1, 502.

52. *ibid.*, 502.

53. HABAKKUK and POSTAN (1965), 376.

54. See, for example, ENOS in N.B.E.R. (1962), 303.

55. HABAKKUK and POSTAN (1965), 321, 322, 525–6.

56. N.B.E.R. (1962), 302, Table 5, 318.

57. For further well-informed opinion in favour of the importance of 'improvements', see SALTER (1960), 5; SCHMOOKLER (1966), 18–19.

58. GILFILLAN (1963), 21.

59. *ibid.*, 140–1.

60. N.B.E.R. (1962), 313 ff.

61. ASHTON (1955), 108–13.

62. H. J. HABAKKUK, *American and British Technology in the Nineteenth Century* (Cambridge, Cambridge U.P., 1962).

63. For example, DONALD R. ADAMS, JR, 'Some Evidence on English and American Wage Rates, 1790–1830', *Journal of Economic History*, XXX (September 1970), 499–520.

64. VALERIE MORGAN, 'Agricultural Wage Rates in late Eighteenth-Century Scotland', *Economic History Review*, Sec. Ser. XXIV (May 1971), Figure 1, 185.

65. L. SANDBERG, 'American Rings and English Mules: The Role of Economic Rationality', in SAUL (1970), 120–40.

66. The point was, however, foreseen, like most other relevant points, by HABAKKUK; see the extract printed in SAUL (1970), 42.

67. H. LEIBENSTEIN, *American Economic Review*, LVI (June 1966), 399 ff.

68. See, respectively, ARTHUR RAISTRICK, *Dynasty of Iron Founders: the Darbys and Coalbrookdale* (Harlow, Longmans, 1953); E. ROLL, *An Early Experiment in Industrial Organization* (Augustus M. Kelley Reprints, 1968); N. MCKENDRICK, 'Josiah Wedgwood: an Eighteenth-Century Entrepreneur in Salesmanship and Marketing Techniques', *Economic History Review*, Sec. Ser. XII (April 1960), 408–33, and 'Josiah Wedgwood and Cost Accounting in the Industrial Revolution', *ibid.*, XXIII (April 1970), 45–67.

69. SIDNEY POLLARD, *The Genesis of Modern Management* (London, Edward Arnold, 1965), *passim*.

70. *ibid.*, 248. McKendrick's 1970 article, however, makes a more favourable claim for Wedgwood's accounting methods, suggesting that amongst other things they uncovered the prevalence of dishonesty in his subordinates: 'Wedgwood and Cost Accounting', 61, 65.

71. cf. MARK BLAUG, 'The Classical Economists and the Factory Acts', in A. W. COATS (ed.), *The Classical Economists and Economic Policy* (London, Methuen, 1971), 104–22.

72. On some of these points see LELAND H. JENKS, 'Early Phases of the Management Movement', *Administrative Science Quarterly*, V (1960–1), 421–47.

73. ASHWORTH (1962), 84.

74. For a brief but interesting summary and discussion, see J. A. C. BROWN, *The Social Psychology of Industry* (Harmondsworth, Penguin, 1954), Ch. 3.

75. POSTAN (1967), Ch. 11.

76. See above, p. 300.

77. EDWARD AMES and NATHAN ROSENBERG, 'The Enfield Arsenal in Theory and History', in SAUL (1970), 99–119.

78. *ibid.*, 117–19.

79. See above, pp. 349–50, 357 and 363.

6 Some Theories of Growth and Development

Patterns and the unique event in history

The methods of economics, like those of any other science, are predicated on the belief that in the universe of events and processes which is the subject matter of the discipline, there exist certain regularities, certain patterns, generated by the causal linkages which bind the system together. While it is one of the tasks of the economist to describe this universe, his more essential (and more difficult) task is to identify these regularities and to explain them in terms of a consistent and mutually-supportive hierarchy of causal 'laws' which, once discovered, serve as a basis for 'explaining' past events and 'predicting' the future. By contrast, an influential and until recently dominant belief among the writers of history has been that their discipline concerns itself with events whose leading characteristic is their *uniqueness*, their unrepeatability (the Germans have the somewhat better word *Einmaligkeit*). Since it does not seem possible for unique events to be the stuff of 'patterns', it is said that it is the character, the origins and the implications of the individual event – not the discovery and explanations of patterns – to which historians address themselves.

This is not the place to embark on a systematic discussion of the philosophy of the social sciences, but it is necessary to point out that the economic historian is perilously placed at the point at which these two opposing views confront each other, and that his writings have reflected – and do reflect – some of the qualities of each. That the two views *are* opposed is clear enough. The subject matter of economic history is the economy of past societies. It cannot be true both that an economy is orderly and lawlike when scrutinized by social scientists who live in it, but anarchistic when analysed by the historian of a later period. The nature and degree of determinateness of the relationships between the constituent 'events' of an historical period are objective facts, like the events themselves, and cannot be changed after the event, however much our subsequent interpretations of them may be selective, subjective, 'culture-bound'. Thus the economic historian cannot, without inconsistency, espouse simultaneously the viewpoints both of the 'idealist' philosopher of history and of the positivist social scientist.

Even a modest acquaintance with the literature of economic history suffices to show that the mixed parentage of the discipline has imbued it with something of a split personality. As a very broad generalization, European economic historians tend more often than not to have been trained as, or in the company of, historians, and to be closer to the position associated with that upbringing, whereas North American economic historians – though here generalization is even more risky – have more often taken a social scientist's view of their profession. However, these differences of philosophy are perhaps more closely correlated with differences of time than of space, for in all countries the last few decades have seen the viewpoints of economic historian and of economist come closer together. The reasons for this convergence – it is not only economic historians who have changed their stance – need not be discussed here, except to say that an increasing common interest in the process of economic growth is one of the chief of them.

This change of position over time has happened so quickly and so easily that one needs to re-read some of the literature of a generation or two ago to convince oneself how substantial it has been, and indeed to some extent new ways of thought have been perhaps unconsciously adopted by scholars reared in earlier traditions. In the Preface to the first edition of his splendid short history of the international economy, Professor W. Ashworth committed himself to a fairly sceptical position: '. . . I have made no attempt to develop or employ any theoretical system into which the whole course of world economic history in my period might be fitted. I do not believe that such a system exists, either actually or potentially.'[1] When the book went into its second edition ten years later, the original Preface was not reprinted, and this frank statement of philosophy was not included in its successor; the major change in the text of the second edition was the addition of a new chapter making adept use of recent additions to quantitative knowledge of comparative economic growth, and deploying such concepts as investment ratios and capital/output ratios in an attempt to 'explain' observed differences and similarities in rates of growth and levels of *per capita* income.

Those who have troubled to read this book are far more likely to be sympathetic to the position of the social scientist than to that of the idealist philosopher of history, and it seems otiose to offer evidence – easy though that would be – of the substantial element of orderliness and lawlikeness in the world the economist studies. Rather, we must seize the opportunity to emphasize that there is an important element of truth also in the opposite direction. If we consider two economies, both developing but at different 'stages' of development, the mere chronological difference betwen them, were there no other consideration, suffices to ensure that their development *cannot* follow precisely similar paths. For country B does not reach until, say, 1875 the equivalent point on its development path to that which country A had already attained in 1825. Now the world environment facing country B in 1875 is substantially different from that confronting A in 1825. New materials like steel, new modes of transport like the railroad and the steamship, have been pioneered and are in the process of replacing their predecessors. Changes in the 'institutional' environment are marked: 1875 is largely a free trade world, 1825 was a protectionist one. Above all, country B in 1875 confronts a world in which other countries are fifty years more advanced than they had been in the environment facing A in 1825, a fact which, for example, changes the foreign trading possibilities facing country B.

If the number of countries which have experienced economic growth were infinitely large, it would be easier to sort out the disruptive influences of differing chronologies and differing resource endowments and to chart and explain any residual underlying pattern. But it is not infinite; it is not even large. Until the decolonization movement got under way after World War II the number of independent political units with an economic history worth considering was well below 100, and the number of such countries whose long-term economic development has been the subject of substantial, scholarly and roughly comparable research is scarcely more than a score or couple of dozen. In such a population it might be thought optimistic to hope to set on one side the *unique* elements in development – unique because generated by circumstances of, e.g., timing or endowment peculiar to each individual country – and uncover common elements in the course of each country's growth path.

The student of economic growth is therefore not in the same position as a scientist conducting experiments to determine the effect of temperature changes on the conductivity of a particular metal, where observations can be repeated as often as is desired and the influence of all factors save the one under scrutiny held constant. He is not even in the position of an economist seeking to 'explain' the price of cabbages, who is likely to find the same restricted range of variables at work in market town A as in market town B ten miles away, or who can normally assume them to interact in much the same way this Tuesday as they did on Tuesday last week. It is doubtless for such reasons as these that economists have not succeeded in devising a theory of growth commanding the same degree of acceptance as, say, the theory of price determination or of consumer behaviour, and capable of being confidently borrowed by the economic historian. There may, in fact, be insufficient similarity in the growth paths followed by countries which have actually achieved economic development to serve as a basis for such a theory.

This is not to say, however, that economic theory has nothing to offer the student of economic growth, or that the working economic historian can cheerfully jettison it. The implication is merely that theory will confer explanatory power at a more disaggregated level, or over a shorter time horizon, than the behaviour of the whole economy throughout a long period of economic development. That is why in the preceding pages we have examined one by one a number of sectoral features of the historical experience of growth, seeking to relate relevant theory to each aspect as we considered it, rather than launch a frontal attack, as it were, on the whole body of evidence about growth in its most aggregated form. Even then, we noticed several times that understanding seemed to be much sharpened if we sought to explain events at a yet lower level of aggregation; for example, the behaviour of the capital/output ratio over time makes far more sense if we consider different types of capital separately than if we try to explain the course of the *average* for the whole economy.

The wish to discover patterns in the behaviour of whole economies over time has nevertheless proved irresistible to many scholars. And, indeed, the extent to which such patterns exist *in fact* is an open one, to be determined by investigating the facts of history rather than by *a priori* speculation; the arguments rehearsed above intend nothing more than to diminish the confidence of those who feel sure that the regularities which provide the basis for economic theory at the micro level obtain also in the experience of whole economies over lengthy periods of time. In the remainder of this chapter we shall therefore discuss some of the elements of similarity and of dissimilarity in the process of modern economic growth, and some of the theories which, at various levels of universality, have been proffered to explain them.

The 'regularities' which one might hope to uncover in considering the historical record of economic growth might concern principally the *morphology* or the *aetiology* of growth. We might, that is to say, find universal trends in economic structure in the course of growth, such as a persistent decline in the share of agriculture in the national product or a persistent rise in the share of wages and salaries in the national income. Or, secondly, we might find similarities over time and between countries in the extent to which, say, increases in factor inputs or improvements in factor productivity respectively 'explain' observed increases in product. We shall consider in this chapter some of the conjectures put forward by a number of scholars touching both types of similarity. But first it is convenient to spell out rather more explicitly some of the reasons for expecting *dis*similarity.

Some limiting factors in historical generalization

In respect of structural changes it seems obvious that we have to expect some substantial *dis*similarities. Both at the present day and in previous centuries there have been obvious differences of economic structure from one country to another. Today's rich countries vary greatly, for example, in both size and population, as do today's poor countries – indeed most tests have revealed virtually no correlation between either area or population and income per head. Rich countries may be large and populous like the U.S.A., large and fairly lightly populated like Canada, small and densely populated like the Netherlands or fairly small and lightly populated like New Zealand. Among poor countries India, Brazil, Ceylon and Paraguay fall in the same four categories respectively. There are also extremely large differences, for example, in trade/income ratios within both groups, and also (though within a narrower range) in the sectoral origins of national product.

While the paucity of quantitative information makes such comparisons harder for earlier periods, it seems certain that there were substantial inter-country differences in many important respects. Clearly this was true of size and population, and also of trade/income ratios: many backward parts of the world had very little foreign trade until the late nineteenth century, whereas Jamaica had an export/income ratio as high as 44 per cent in 1832, according to Mrs Eisner's estimates.[2] The majority of poor countries of the past, it is true, were dominated by agriculture; but there were still big variations in the structure of landholding and, arising from this, in the distribution of income. The big seigniorial estates of Eastern Europe, cultivated by serf labour, yielded a very uneven income distribution, while the peasant proprietorship of parts of Western Europe and of South Asia led to a more egalitarian though still poor society, as did the dominantly hunting economy of, say, the pre-European Maori or as still does the nomadic pastoralism of the East African Masai.

It does not therefore seem easy to conceive of growth as involving, in any very rigorous way, either convergence towards a similar structure (though much has been made in recent years of the possibility that the U.S. and Soviet economies may be 'converging') or divergence from a common base. On the other hand there is more plausibility in the notion that developing countries have followed parallel but not identical paths, that is to say that though both the cluster of starting-points and the cluster of finishing-points are widely scattered, individual countries have tended to occupy similar positions in both of these clusters. Thus, for example, country A's growth may have been accompanied by similar changes in its trade/income ratio as country B's, the ratio having, however, been *consistently higher* for A than for B. Until more work has been done on comparative economic growth it does not seem possible to say more about this hypothesis than that one can think of a good deal of evidence which fits it and of some which does not.

The dissimilarities we have discussed so far arise chiefly from differences of a geographical character such as size, population, resources and location. It has already been mentioned that differences in the timing of development can also lead to differing growth paths. This contention now calls for a little elaboration. There are perhaps three chief reasons why the date at which different countries have embarked on sustained economic growth has helped determine their growth paths. The first is that technology has of course developed extremely rapidly in the past two centuries, making new products and materials available and old ones obsolete, and introducing new techniques of producing familiar commodities. The least important though most obvious implication of this is that industrial structure – 'industrial' in its widest sense, for of course technological change is not confined to manufacturing industry – is likely to be different in countries reaching similar stages of development at different periods. England could not possibly have 'taken off' in the late eighteenth century on the basis of a rapidly expanding electronics industry, and it is unlikely that the later twentieth century will see many successful 'take-offs' based on hand-woven textiles and steam engines.

More important is that modern technology has greatly increased the scope for economies of scale in many traditional industries, so that small countries are at a greater disadvantage than their predecessors when seeking to promote industrial growth. This is of course one reason for the interest shown in recent decades in regional economic groupings designed to enlarge markets as a necessary condition for the cost-reducing adoption of modern production techniques. Finally, and of course closely connected with the last point, capital requirements in most industries for a production unit of optimum size are now enormously larger than a century or two ago. Paul Bairoch, in an excellent study little noticed in the English-speaking world, has shown that capital (including stocks) per head of the industrial labour force was equivalent to about four months' wages in England during the industrial revolution, and to six to eight months' wages in early nineteenth-century France. In the U.S.A. in 1953, notwithstanding the far higher wage rates, the equivalent figure was about twenty-nine months' wages. For a typical underdeveloped country of the present day the level of capital per industrial worker characteristic of the U.S.A. *c*. 1950 would be equivalent to something like three years' wages![3]

Of course, U.S. capital-intensive techniques would not necessarily be appropriate to an underdeveloped country where factor proportions are quite different. Even so, embarking on new industries tends to be harder for today's

low-income countries than for their nineteenth-century predecessors because of the much higher capital costs of entry.
This fact not only has implications for the aggregate savings
and investment ratios but also means that it is far harder for
the individual small trader or artisan to save enough to set
up in business on his own, so that the area of recruitment for
industrial entrepreneurs is correspondingly narrower, with
unfavourable implications for social mobility and the adjustment of talent to role. A further implication is that it is much
harder today than in the past for industrializing countries to
build factory machinery, not so much because this is more
expensive (though comparative advantage works in producing machinery as well as in producing consumer goods, and
imported machinery is likely to have a price advantage over
local products) as because it is far more complicated than the
simple mills, looms and engines of the early industrial revolution, and well beyond the capabilities of native craftsmen.
This means not only that capital formation in industry has
a larger import component than in the past – a fact which
helps to explain the greater importance of the foreign trade
constraint as compared with the savings constraint for today's
industrializing countries[4] – but also that an important means
of technological diffusion is lost. Countries importing the
bulk of their machinery do not get the same opportunity for
developing engineering skills as, say, French and Belgian
firms which built their own factories and machinery under
British supervision in the early nineteenth century.

The second reason why the timing of development affects
the growth path open to a developing country is that the
world environment facing the country in question changes
in other ways, as well as in its stock of technology. Notably,
the levels of income and productivity of other nations will
differ and thus affect the country's trading prospects. We
have discussed at length the arguments of Nurkse and other
writers as to the differences between the pre-1914 and post-
1945 decades in this respect; many of these differences were
of course the consequence of technological developments, but
even had technology remained stagnant the accumulation of

capital, rise of population and depletion of resources in earlier-developed countries would have generated a constantly changing environment for 'later starters'. Indeed, it might of course be argued that in so far as technology is equally available to all (which is not however in any very real sense true), then for countries of roughly similar size and resources changes in trading prospects are a function of the degree of development of a given country in relation to that country's potential trading partners, rather than of the level of (world) technology as such. It was for such reasons that List and similar thinkers argued that tariff protection was needed if later European industrializers were to make headway against Britain's early start, though Britain herself could afford the luxury of free trade. It may be added that rising incomes in the rest of the world imply changes for a developing country in other prospects than those of *merchandise* trade: it would scarcely have been possible even for a Switzerland to contemplate tourism as a 'leading sector' during the nineteenth century, whereas today one is inclined to say that tourism offers the best if not the only hope for some small low-income States to lift themselves out of the rut of poverty and backwardness.

Apart from changes in the levels of productivity and income of the surrounding world, time brings changes too to more strictly international institutions and relationships which also bear upon the prospects for developing countries. The significance of the dramatic relative fall in transport costs throughout the nineteenth century has already been discussed, while of course air travel has been as important as the rise of incomes in generating the twentieth-century tourist revolution just referred to. We have also seen that the availability, in terms both of quantity and of types, of capital exports has varied widely as between the pre-1914, inter-war and post-1945 periods, and this fact again implies that the opportunity to pursue certain growth paths has not been constant through time.

Thirdly and finally, the timing of development is significant in that not merely technological knowledge but *economic* knowledge has made enormous progress in the past century and a half. We all remember the valedictory paragraph in Keynes' *General Theory*, in which he insists on the long-run supremacy of ideas over vested interests:

> . . . the ideas of economists and political philosophers, both when they are right and when they are wrong, are more powerful than is commonly understood. Indeed the world is ruled by little else. . . . I am sure that the power of vested interests is vastly exaggerated compared with the gradual encroachment of ideas.[5]

This is evidently a large thesis, and one we are neither equipped nor required to explore, though to an academic writer and his (doubtless) predominantly academic readers it may seem plausible as well as flattering to subscribe in some measure to Keynes' thesis. In any event, however, one has in mind here not merely the possible influence on events of broad new ways of looking at economic problems – such as those of Adam Smith, of List, of Marx, of the Fabians, of Keynes himself, of the modern econometricians – but also the growth of economic understanding concerning particular sectors and processes of the economy, and of the *information* about the economic system of particular countries and of the world at large which is indispensable if effective policies are to be formulated and implemented. Even in post-revolutionary Russia the sheer lack of knowledge of, e.g., input/output relationships within the economy and the consequent impossibility of formulating consistent plans was one (though only one) of the reasons for the retreat from the wholesale nationalization of the Civil War period and the adoption of the mixed economy of the New Economic Policy; and one of the factors permitting the adoption of the First Five-Year Plan was the gradual increase in technical knowledge of the economy gained in the increasingly adventurous 'planning' exercises of the N.E.P. period.

The much more widespread (if usually less thoroughgoing) adoption of economic planning in many countries since World War II has obviously depended on the enormously increased flow of both national and international economic information characteristic of recent decades, while even countries which would not regard themselves as practising a 'planned' economy normally frame national budgets nowadays against a background of Keynesian or some similar theory of income determination. Finally, the element of example and imitation has to be recognized: it is evident that developing countries are likely to borrow economic concepts as well as technological ones from more highly-developed neighbours, and there has been a strong temptation for several decades for them to borrow from planned rather than, or as well as, from free market economies. In short, one can reasonably say that not only the broad policy implications of the changing dominant modes of economic thought, but the accelerating growth of economic understanding and of stocks and flows of economic information, and the competing merits of the changing collection of economic systems capable of being emulated, constitute together a third type of influence which the *timing* of development may wield on the form that development is likely to take.

It may seem that the case which has been built up in favour of the expectation of *dis*similar growth paths is very strong; but there are reasons too for a contrary expectation, and some evidence that the 'similarity-inducing' factors have in some areas preponderated over their opponents. We now turn to review some of the evidence on *similarities*, and of the hypotheses put forward to explain them.

Hollis B. Chenery's 'patterns of development'
We saw in Chapter 1 that there is only a limited measure of agreement as to how far and why common structural changes occur in the course of economic growth. Following on the pioneer work of Colin Clark and A. G. B. Fisher before World War II, Simon Kuznets has made herculean efforts to systematize and synthesize the growing volume of information in single-country studies on the major aggregates of historical growth. These studies have suggested that the share

of agriculture in national product normally declines with rising incomes, and that the share of industry rises, but only to a plateau which may be reached at a relatively modest level of *per capita* incomes. The share of the tertiary sector, when this is lumped together as (in effect) a residual, follows a less certain course, though with a slight upward tendency especially at higher income levels. It has been suggested already[6] that the behaviour of services would probably appear far more consistent if this sector were subdivided into (a) a 'traditional' sector comprising labour-intensive services and making use of the low opportunity-cost of unskilled labour in low-income countries (petty trading and hawking, hand-laundering, domestic service and the like), and (b) a 'modern' sector comprising trade and communications, the professions, and government administration. The limited statistical evidence tends to confirm *a priori* expectations that both these categories are systematically and strongly related, the former negatively and the latter positively, to rising incomes; the equivocal behaviour of the services sector as commonly defined arises only because these two relationships offset each other when 'traditional' and 'modern' sub-sectors are lumped together.

In a path-breaking article dating from 1960, Hollis B. Chenery argued that the structural characteristics of economies *are* found to be systematically related to a small number of economic variables, notably income per head, and that this relationship can be discerned both in the historical development of growing economies and in cross-country analysis of economies of differing levels of income at one point in time. He hypothesized that this systematic relationship arises from the universal influence of a number of 'similarity-inducing' factors: (a) common technological knowledge; (b) similar human wants; (c) access to the same markets for imports and exports; (d) the accumulation of capital as the level of income increases; (e) the increase of skills, broadly defined, as income increases.[7] These factors, it is true, are specified primarily with a view to explaining a 'pattern' of growth suggested by cross-section analysis; and as Chenery elsewhere recognizes, factors (*a*) and (*c*) would be expected *not* to remain constant in development over time. Chenery is none the less among those who believe that in this area of economics, at least, cross-section data should yield patterns reasonably comparable with those of time series, and though his first paper was based largely on the former, he has sought in a later paper[8] to demonstrate that the 'patterns' suggested by these data may be true historical shapes describing the changes undergone in the course of long-term growth.

An aspect of Chenery's thesis which is immediately appealing to the economic historian is the finding that the 'fit' of his equations is substantially improved when the sample of countries from which data are drawn is subdivided into more nearly homogeneous subsets. Specifically, somewhat differing growth patterns are suggested for (*a*) large countries, (*b*) small industry-oriented countries and (*c*) small primary-oriented countries. The point about the distinction between small and large countries is, of course, that in the former market size poses a greater impediment than in the latter to the development of industries in which economies of scale are important. The division of small countries into 'industry' and 'primary-oriented' allows for the fact that small countries with a strong resource-based comparative advantage in certain primary products, like New Zealand, will tend to specialize in that direction and acquire manufactures by international exchange, whereas those lacking such natural advantages (e.g. Belgium) may specialize in manufactured exports and import primary products. These trade specializations will, of course, be reflected in corresponding differences of internal economic structure.

How far Chenery's curves do in fact portray *historical* changes as well as cross-sectional variations remains something of an open question. One of the few independent attempts to test the historical validity of Chenery's 'patterns', by Peter Temin, compared them with longer-term data for nine countries drawn from the Kuznets studies.[9] Unfortunately, the form of indirect testing adopted in order to

392

Figure 6.1 (1)

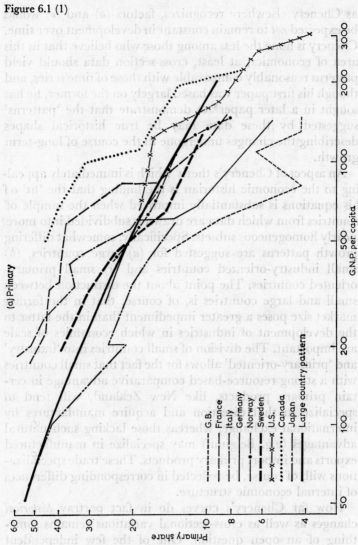

Figure 6.1 (2)

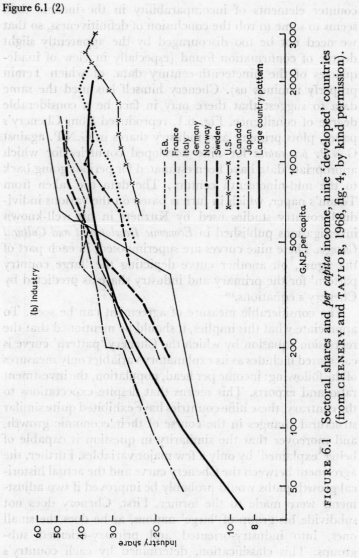

(b) Industry

G.B.
France
Italy
Germany
Norway
Sweden
U.S.
Canada
Japan
Large country pattern

G.N.P. per capita

Industry share

FIGURE 6.1 Sectoral shares and *per capita* income, nine 'developed' countries (from CHENERY and TAYLOR, 1968, fig. 4, by kind permission).

counter elements of incomparability in the income data seems to some to rob the conclusion of definitiveness, so that we need not be too discouraged by the apparently slight degree of confirmation found (especially in view of inadequacies of the nineteenth-century data, of which Temin properly reminds us). Chenery himself has used the same data to suggest that there may in fact be a considerable degree of consilience. Fig. 6.1, reproduced from Chenery's paper, plots primary and industry shares in G.N.P. against G.N.P. *per capita* for nine developed countries for which appropriate data have been estimated for periods going back to the mid-nineteenth century. The data are taken from Temin's paper, which in turn is based on the various individual country studies used by Kuznets in his well-known investigations published in *Economic Development and Cultural Change*. These nine curves are superimposed, in each part of the figure, on another curve depicting the 'large country pattern' for the primary and industry share as predicted by Chenery's equations.[10]

The considerable measure of agreement can be seen. To appreciate what this implies, it should be mentioned that the regression equation by which the Chenery 'pattern' curve is calculated includes as its explanatory variables only measures of the following: income per head, population, the investment ratio and exports. This means that despite expectations to the contrary, these nine countries have exhibited quite similar structural changes in the course of their economic growth, and moreover that the similarity in question is capable of being 'explained' by only a few major variables. Further, the agreement between the Chenery curve and the actual historical growth paths would probably be improved if two adjustments were made to the former. First, Chenery does not subdivide his group of 'large' nations, as he does the small ones, into industry-oriented and primary-oriented subgroups. This classification, determined by each country's pattern of trade, is actually intended as a proxy for resource endowment, of which a suitable direct measure was not to hand. The decision not to make such a subdivision in respect of large countries perhaps reflected a belief that resources are not quite so critical a determinant of the economic prospects of large as of small countries; but doubtless it also had regard to the statistical undesirability of allowing the number of cases in any subdivision to become too small. Nevertheless, the structures of large countries too *are* influenced by their natural resources, and doubtless (for example) the primary shares of countries like the United Kingdom, Japan and West Germany are smaller than they would otherwise be, and those of the U.S.A. and Canada larger, because of this, and contrariwise with the respective shares of manufacturing. *Two* sets of Chenery curves for large countries applicable to resource-rich and resource-poor sub-groups would almost certainly show a better agreement with the historical growth paths, as is indicated by the displacement of the curves for the countries mentioned from the 'Large Country Pattern' curve in fig. 6.1.

Secondly, a feature which Chenery himself notes several times is that the primary share as measured by time series seems in general to fall more rapidly than cross-section data would have led one to expect, and this feature can certainly be seen in the first diagram. While there are several possible reasons for this, a likely one seems to be that conversion of cross-section data at official exchange rates distorts the comparison since, as is well known, these rates tend to *over*-value the currencies of high-income countries relative to those of low-income countries. The range of real *per capita* incomes against which sectoral shares are plotted is therefore artificially extended. Correcting for this distortion would involve, so to say, compressing the horizontal axis on Chenery's cross-section data graphs concertina-wise, so that the curves of primary and industry shares would respectively fall and rise more steeply. It can be seen that somewhat steeper 'Large Country Pattern' curves would fit the historical shapes better, particularly in respect of fig. 6.1a.

Before leaving Chenery's work, it should perhaps be made clear that it is as yet concerned only with 'patterns of growth' in the sense of *change in the relative importance of sectoral subdivisions*. There is no investigation of growth of incomes *not* involving such change, that is to say, of growth proceeding equiproportionally in all sectors; it is the degree of *deviation* from equiproportional growth, that is of structural change, which is the focus of attention. This of course restricts the interest of this type of study to the period of great structural transformation associated with modernization; it would have little to say, even if statistical data were forthcoming, for the long centuries of broadly unchanging structure which preceded the onset of industrialization. And it may be added that in the most advanced countries, whose primary sectors already generate no more than say 10 per cent of G.N.P. and whose industrial share seems to have stabilized or even to be declining slightly, future growth may no longer be accompanied by substantial broadly-interpreted structural change.

We shall return to Chenery's studies later in this chapter in a somewhat different connection, but it is convenient now to refer briefly to some developments of a different sort which have been in evidence in many or all cases of historical growth. These developments will be passed over briefly and in a largely illustrative fashion, for unlike the broad structural similarities with which we have been concerned so far, they do not lend themselves to easy presentation or to testing by statistics. Belief in their widespread importance must either be evoked by appeal to the reader's own historical knowledge or generated by a fairly massive presentation of qualitative evidence; in deference to considerations of space and of readability, and in view of the assumption made throughout this book that readers have a reasonable prior acquaintance with economic history, the first alternative is adopted.

Legal and institutional change in economic development

First, there is a long list of legal changes and institutional developments which bear upon economic history. (The two are bracketed together since so many new institutions, such as the joint-stock limited liability company, have required legislation, sometimes involving considerable legal innovation.) Although few would care to go as far as Professor

Hayek, who once wrote 'There is probably no single factor which has contributed more to the prosperity of the West than the relative certainty of the law which has prevailed here',[11] it is almost certainly true that the importance of a congenial legal framework to economic development has been underestimated, and little understood, by economic historians. This is doubtless because of the layman's proper reluctance to discuss changes which can scarcely be understood or indeed identified without some knowledge of a second and highly specialized discipline (and partly also, perhaps, because of the difficulty of discovering and proving what their influence has been anyway).

Despite these obstacles, one can hardly fail to perceive, in a general way, the importance to a developing market economy of provisions for the peaceful enforcement of contracts or the safeguarding of private property. In early economic societies such organizations as guilds and trading companies derived part of their importance from their attempts to supply the deficiencies of non-commercially minded governments in these respects. The fact that the economically most advanced nation of Western Europe in the seventeenth century, Holland, was about the only one *not* influenced by Mercantilism has sometimes been explained by pointing out that Holland was the only country ruled by a merchant oligarchy, and therefore the only one where the State was fully responsive to the legal needs of the mercantile community. On these and many similar points the reader will find some excellently suggestive passages in Sir John Hicks' essay, *A Theory of Economic History*.[12]

The contribution of the law to economic life is not confined, however, to the enactment of such general measures as those to secure enforcement of contracts or the rights of property – measures which have generally been a condition of earlier, non-industrial development. Specialized legal innovations have conferred more specific advantages in later stages of development also. Two examples must suffice. Patent laws, by securing a proportion of the fruits of an invention to the inventor, provide a financial incentive to apply creative

o

talent to the end of improving productive efficiency. Though the first patent laws date from the late Middle Ages, it was the English Statute of Monopolies of 1624 which served as the most general model – not widely adopted, however, outside of the U.S.A. and France until the first half of the nineteenth century. (We must pass over here the long-standing – and unresolved – debate as to the net economic effects of patent law.) In a quite different field, and at a later date, the innovating of new systems of registering titles to real estate, such as the Torrens system, has cheapened and speeded transfer and improved the defensibility of titles and thus rendered the real estate market more perfectly competitive.

Market imperfections and national economic integration

A second area in which economic development implies – or in some measure, perhaps, is conditional upon – substantial change is even more difficult to define: one may try to identify it by referring to the progressive reduction of market imperfections. In the earliest stage of economic emergence from the traditional society the most important feature here may be simply the increasing monetization of the economy. Later features include, for example, the physical and economic integration of the national market by the construction of an adequate transport network. In turn, this is a condition (but by no means a guarantee) of the reduction of regional inequalities in such matters as *per capita* incomes and the level of unemployment. Such a trend towards national equality of factor returns and employment levels is of course not only of direct significance for welfare, but evidence of progress towards a more nearly optimal allocation of resources. Finally there is the question of the distribution of incomes.

One feels almost intuitively that the reduction of market imperfections, in its broadest connotation, must be of vital importance for economic growth. The feeling is one which comes not only upon the historian reading about economic conditions in medieval times, but upon the traveller who has the opportunity to juxtapose nearly contemporaneous impressions of the economy of a backward peasant society and of a modern industrial State. And we have seen that even in the case of the rich and developed countries of Western Europe Denison claims to have found a major source of recent growth in improved allocation of resources. Yet it is extremely difficult to discuss these features in an acceptably rigorous way, so difficult are they to define, still more to measure, and the economic historian in particular is acutely conscious of the paucity of good historical work in this area.

It is true, for example, that the rise of a money economy was often adduced by older historians to explain economic development – so often, indeed, as to move Professor Postan to begin a sceptical article on the subject with the sentence: 'The "rise of a money economy" is one of the residuary hypotheses of economic history: a *deus ex machina* to be called upon when no other explanation is available.'[13] Postan goes on to assert that if 'the rise of a money economy' means anything at all, it must mean something more than the use of money, which in Europe at least certainly antedated the early economic stirrings for which money economy has been proffered as an explanation. Nor, if the phrase means the increasing preponderance of payments in money rather than in kind or by performance of labour services, was this movement either continuous and progressive or parallel in all spheres of activity at once. Postan points out that there were periodic general backslidings, as during and after the Thirty Years War in Germany, and that increasing monetization in one area was not incompatible with retreat in another – as in fifteenth-century England, when the increase of self-sufficiency and decline in food production for the market were coupled with the widespread commutations of labour services to money rents.

Yet a totally sceptical verdict, viewing the 'rise of a money economy' as but a pale and passive reflection of economic progress induced solely by 'real' factors, is just a little hard to accept. At the very least one must view money transactions as an indispensable channel through which forces of change can be brought to bear on those who might otherwise not respond to economic signals; one thinks of the deliberate use of money taxes to induce the production of cash crops in Tsarist Russia or the offer of labour services in modern Africa. And it is not easy to believe that such exposure to the need to value work or goods in terms of money, whether enforced, as in the instances cited, or occurring more spontaneously as a by-product of market integration, can fail to deposit permanently in the minds of those experiencing it some residual habit of 'economizing'.

In all save the very smallest countries there is an important spatial dimension in economic growth. There is no doubt of the need, if a realistic picture is to be presented, to view the economic history of, say, France or even England in the early modern period in part in regional terms. Broadly speaking, the effect of growth is to diminish regional inequalities; a clear visual illustration of this is given by the 1880–1950 portion of Richard Easterlin's graph charting the course of personal *per capita* incomes in the major regions of the U.S.A. as percentages of the national average.[14] But the degree of regional equality is even less a monotonic function of growth than the rise of a money economy. It may be, that is, that at times economic development is associated with *increasing* rather than with decreasing regional inequality. In the case of the U.S.A. the marked increase in regional inequalities between 1840 and 1880 is chiefly to be explained, it is true, by the effects of the Civil War and its aftermath. But in conjunction with changes in demand or technology, the geographical accident of favourable or unfavourable market access or resource location may well bring about differing regional rates of growth, which can just as well increase as decrease regional disparities. Professor Williamson has indeed argued that there is a *general* tendency for regional inequalities to increase in early stages of growth, and then to decline. This conclusion, however, rests at present on inter-country more than on time-series evidence.[15]

In Great Britain the great industrial changes beginning in the late eighteenth century occurred for the most part in regions which, in the dominantly agricultural past, had been

relatively disfavoured by nature and hence poor and backward. In Germany, on the other hand, and more certainly
in Tsarist Russia, nineteenth-century industry developed
chiefly in regions which were already probably more advanced than others, and thus tended to widen rather than
narrow existing differentials. Even in the U.S.A. the entry
of two non-agricultural, resource-rich regions of high *per
capita* income, Pacific and Mountain, contributes to the
impression of a very wide spread of regional *per capita*
incomes in 1880 and thus of its widening in 1840–80.

Such geographical influences, however, are a matter of
chance, and if one asserts that *generally* development reduces
regional inequalities it is because the economic forces concerned tend to act more systematically and uni-directionally
than do the geographical ones. Basically it is the reduction in
transport costs, promoting the integration of markets and
tending to equalize prices, and the increase of factor mobility
which lead us to expect, and explain, the tendency towards
a reduction of regional inequalities. We have already seen
this process revealed, in so far as concerns capital, in the
studies of Professor Davis.[16] The increasing internal mobility
of labour too is a commonplace of social history. What one
needs to stress here is that although there are obvious
explanations in the increased speed and ease and lesser
relative cost of travel, there have been social and sometimes
legal obstacles to labour mobility too, the existence and
subsequent removal or alleviation of which permit us to view
greater intra-national mobility as a condition and cause, and
not just as a consequence, of economic growth. One thinks
of the severe restrictions on the power of the Russian peasant
to leave the *mir*, even after emancipation, or of the (doubtless) less onerous but still substantial discouragements to the
movement of the English poor under the Settlement Laws
and the Speenhamland system. Less obviously but perhaps
not less importantly, sheer ignorance of geography and of
opportunity must have impeded mobility – until indeed it
was discovered in the nineteenth century that ignorance cuts
both ways, and that it could be turned, through the creation

of false or at any rate exaggerated hopes of utopias in distant
lands, to the profit of colonizers, land sharks and transport
interests. (This discovery itself is in one of its aspects testimony to the spread of economic rationality, though in
another it perhaps reminds us that progress, like ignorance,
is a two-edged weapon.)

Despite the clear evidence that by and large regional
inequalities have been reduced in the process of economic
development (notwithstanding some not infrequent and not
always short-lived backslidings), it is right to recall that even
in the most advanced countries income inequalities and
imperfections in the factor markets are by no means totally
erased. At the present time, average money income in the
wealthiest American States is not far short of two and a half
times that in the poorest; in the United Kingdom unemployment in the less prosperous areas like Northern Ireland has
fluctuated between four and six times the rate in the booming
Midlands during most of the post-1945 period. When one
moves back along the spectrum of development in Italy, least
developed of the E.E.C. communities but still on a world
view by no means a backward country, it is only in the very
last years that the terrible economic and social problems of
the *mezzogiorno* have begun to yield to a combination of dis-
criminatory State action and the inducement of high wages
offered by the labour-hungry industrial areas of the community.

The trend of income distribution

Inequalities of income, viewed occupationally rather than
regionally, are even harder to discuss purposefully. Economic
history has thrown up little relevant evidence, economic
analysis has formulated little relevant theory. The pieces of
evidence which do exist are not free from mutual contra-
diction, and still less the various theories. It is also peculiarly
difficult to disentangle influences which are a function of
time and which to some extent have influenced all economies,
developed and less developed – such as the establishment of
new occupations through organizational, scientific and politi-

cal advance – from those influences which spring from the process of development itself. Finally – and perhaps accounting for most of the existing contradictions – this is an area in which the influences of factors specific to the history of particular countries at particular times have often overwhelmed those of 'universal' factors, whether a function of time *or* of degree of development.

Thus, for example, it is uncertain whether there has commonly been any marked historical trend in the ratio of skilled to unskilled wage rates. It is often assumed that a wide differential is characteristic of underdeveloped countries and that this differential will narrow as development takes place. A well-known paper by Harry Ober in 1948 seemed to offer support for this view in presenting estimates for the U.S.A. for a number of benchmark years over the period 1907–47, which seemed to indicate a progressive reduction of the advantage of the skilled worker.[17] A later study by Robert Ozanne, however, based on the records of only one firm but covering a uniquely long period (1858–1959) and providing full year-by-year coverage, cast doubt on the general validity of the Ober thesis.[18] 1907, Ober's starting year, was seen to be near the peak of a substantial quarter-century rise in the differential in favour of skilled workers, whose rate culminated at about 85 per cent above the rate for 'common labour' in 1908 and 1909.

Looking at Ozanne's series as a whole there appears little long-term trend, certainly not in a downward direction, over the century in question. Equally to the point, the substantial and in some instances quite long-sustained differences between sub-periods may plausibly be explained by influences often quite specific to the U.S.A. and to particular periods – the 'floor' to wage rates provided by the easy availability of cheap land in the mid-nineteenth century; the contrasting but in both instances substantial influences on wage differentials of large-scale immigration, now of skilled, later of unskilled labour; and the shifting impact of unionization (which again, of course, began to influence the skilled and unskilled labour markets at different times). Ober's choice of 1907 as starting-point is seen to be unfortunate since it was close to the end of a period in which several factors chanced to combine to lift the skilled/unskilled differential to a level substantially above that of either the preceding or the following decades: the closing of the frontier and large-scale immigration of unskilled labourers pulling the common labour rate down, the more rapid unionization of skilled workers pulling their rates up.

In the case of Britain, also, the authorities disagree. It seems probable, indeed, that there was very little change in differentials, overall, from about 1860 to 1914; but whereas for the period 1914–50 Knowles and Robertson find a considerable narrowing of differentials, Guy Routh's study suggests that the earnings gap was about the same in 1960 as in 1906, though the experience of various industries differed.[19] The conflict may not be as acute as appears at first sight, partly because the two studies relate to different though overlapping sets of industries, and for the two industries common to both sets there is at least agreement about the direction of change (a narrowing of differentials). Perhaps more importantly, the Routh study relates to *earnings*, but that of Knowles and Robertson to wage *rates*, and it seems likely that the earnings gap should have narrowed less than the rate gap. It is interesting, in any event, to note that most of the narrowing is alleged to have taken place during the inflationary periods between 1914 and 1920 and since 1939, and to have been caused by the practice in such periods of giving similar flat-rate cost-of-living increments to all grades of workers, which of course represent a smaller proportionate addition to higher than to lower earnings. In respect of wartime inflations the British experience was thus both different in itself, and determined by different factors, than that of the U.S.A. Finally, in Germany, so far as somewhat meagre evidence permits us to judge, there may have been some narrowing of differentials between 1871 and 1945, but it appears to have been relatively slight and by no means continuous. As in Britain differentials seem to have narrowed primarily because of the granting of 'across the board' increases in periods of rising prices.[20]

Phelps Brown and Browne demonstrate that the differential was substantially narrower in the early twentieth century in the United Kingdom than in either the U.S.A. or Germany.[21] This finding does not surprise us, so far as the contrast with the former country is concerned, since it could well be explained by the factors already mentioned as affecting the American labour market and by the more advanced unionization of unskilled workers in the United Kingdom at that period. The contrast with Germany, however, is not so obviously explainable in these terms, and it is tempting to record that it is consistent with the hypothesis which views the wage differential as inversely related to degree of development (Germany c. 1905 being viewed as less developed than Britain, on the whole and notwithstanding the precocity of its steel and light chemicals industries, especially in the relevant aspects of the persistence of a relatively large reservoir of low-wage labour in agriculture and self-employment).

The belief that the skilled/unskilled wage differential is inversely related to degree of development is more strongly supported, however, by present-day cross-country comparisons than by historical evidence. It finds apparent theoretical explanation in the facts that in today's underdeveloped countries skilled labour is in short supply, while disguised unemployment in agriculture and self-employment makes unskilled labour cheap and abundant. While these characteristics may obtain fairly widely among today's underdeveloped countries, they have not necessarily prevailed in all historical instances of earlier development, certainly not in the regions of recent settlement which have been characterized by abundant land, labour scarcity and high wage rates. We have in fact encountered another of those areas in which the temptation to pool cross-sectional and historical evidence is strong, but should be resisted.

On this topic it might be pointed out that the same comment probably applies with even greater force to the ratio of professional to manual workers' pay. It is a common-place of present-day development literature that the salaries of professional workers in low-income countries are far higher in comparison with average *per capita* incomes than in developed countries. This is largely, however, because the skills of many professional workers – university professors, doctors, engineers, schoolteachers and nurses – are inter-nationally *portable*; so that to retain and attract such people something approaching an international scale of payment must be offered. Since average *per capita* incomes at realistic exchange conversions have at the very least a ten-fold spread between rich and poor nations, this implies far wider differ-ences of remuneration in low- than in high-income countries. We must beware, however, of assuming too easily that similar differences obtained in the past, both because international average *per capita* incomes were less widely spread and because physical, institutional and psychological impedi-ments to the international movement of this 'migratory *élite*' were greater than at the present day.

'Labour surplus' models

The changing distribution of incomes through time may well seem, in the light of this discussion, to be one feature of economic development which is dominated by 'unique' rather than 'universal' factors. We cannot avoid brief com-ment, however, on one model which is postulated on the contrary assumption. In a well-known paper published in 1954 Sir Arthur Lewis propounded a model which has greatly influenced subsequent thinking about the strategy of economic development in low-income, and especially in densely-populated, countries.[22] The title of the paper, 'Economic Development with Unlimited Supplies of Labour', well indicates its general theme. The contention is that em-ployers in countries of the type envisaged enjoy a highly-elastic supply of labour at or a little above subsistence wages. They are therefore able to expand without the restriction from the side of labour supply which their counterparts in more developed countries face, and without wages eating into the share of profits. Since, as we have seen, Lewis views profits as the chief source of investible funds, this means that the growth of savings and investment is accelerated.

Lewis' model is postulated on the existence of a particular sort of market imperfection and suggests how its reduction may make a major contribution to economic growth. It is therefore unfortunate that while it has been widely discussed from the viewpoint of economic theory, it has been largely neglected so far as a possible tool of analysis in historical inquiry. Strangely enough, the one major attempt to use it for such a purpose has been in Professor Kindleberger's study of rapid economic growth in Europe since World War II.[23] In his introduction Kindleberger tells us that after a period of disenchantment regarding the value of growth models for historical explanation, he came to think that the Lewis model 'had much more explanatory power in history' than he had previously recognized. It may seem paradoxical that a model fashioned to explain development possibilities in countries with large, underemployed agricultural sectors should be found useful in explaining growth in a set of highly-developed industrial economies. But in fact a massive withdrawal of low-wage labour from peasant agriculture has been a feature of several European countries since 1945 (and has been a chief feature explaining the very rapid rise of labour productivity in agriculture itself). Moreover, agriculture is not the only source of labour which may help to keep the supply elastic. Even in advanced countries there is often a considerable reserve of manpower in low-productivity self-employment and service occupations. Further, several European countries were able in the earlier years of post-war recovery to absorb a considerable reservoir of unemployed. And finally not only could the existing labour force be redeployed in these ways but also it has been enlarged by immigration (in West Germany's case, notably of refugees from the East) and by the typically higher rates of natural increase which were characteristic of the early post-war period.

There is little doubt that the achievement in these ways of

both large increases in total employment and substantial sectoral shifts of employment does help to explain the 'super-growth', as Kindleberger calls it, which the leading countries of continental Western Europe have enjoyed in the last twenty years. The absence of similar elasticity in Britain's labour supply may also help to explain the relatively poor post-war performance of that country. But Kindleberger's thesis has not been by any means universally accepted, and conflicts in varying degrees with the results of other investigations. The relevant findings of the most ambitious and systematic of these investigations, Denison's monumental *Why Growth Rates Differ*,[24] are summarized in Table 6.1.

Columns (1) and (6) show, respectively, the annual rates of increase of national income and of national income per person employed for the seven countries. Columns (2), (3) and (4) show respectively the contributions to the rate shown in column (1) of capital inputs, of employment, and of the improved allocation of resources resulting from the contraction of agricultural inputs and of non-agricultural self-employment. Columns (7) and (8) similarly show the contributions of capital and of resource reallocation to the growth of income per person employed (naturally, the growth of employment makes no contribution here). It can be seen from the two remaining columns that some, but limited, support is provided for Kindleberger's thesis. For example, increased employment and resource reallocation together account for between 20 and 35 per cent of total growth, but it is the relatively slowly-growing U.S.A. in which they make the largest contribution, and quickly-growing France in which they make the least. The right-hand side of the table, which is more relevant, provides only slightly greater support for Kindleberger. Improved allocation accounts for between 14 (Netherlands and Belgium) and 24 (Italy) per cent of the growth of national income per person employed in the continental European countries, as against 13 per cent in the U.S.A. and only 6 per cent in the United Kingdom. Even so, far the greater part of the differences remain unexplained. The higher gain from improved allocation, for example,

TABLE 6.1 *Sources of growth of total national income and national income per person employed, 1950–62*

(Contribution to growth rate in percentage points)

Country	Growth of national income	Contribution of:			(3+4) as percentage of (1)	Growth of national income per person employed	Contribution of:		(8) as percentage of (6)
		Capital	Employment	Realloca-tion			Capital	Realloca-tion	
	(1)	(2)	(3)	(4)	(5)	(6)	(7)	(8)	(9)
U.S.A.	3·36	0·83	0·90	0·29	35%	2·19	0·60	0·29	13%
U.K.	2·38	0·51	0·50	0·10	25%	1·72	0·37	0·10	6%
Germany	7·26	1·41	1·49	0·91	33%	5·15	0·93	0·91	18%
Netherlands	4·52	1·04	0·78	0·47	28%	3·44	0·78	0·47	14%
Belgium	3·03	0·41	0·40	0·35	25%	2·47	0·28	0·35	14%
France	4·70	0·79	0·08	0·88	20%	4·58	0·76	0·88	19%
Italy	5·95	0·70	0·42	1·26	28%	5·35	0·57	1·26	24%

Source: cols. (1)–(4) and (6)–(8) – Denison (1967), Tables 21–1 to 20, pp. 298–317.

accounts for less than a quarter of the excess of the rate of growth in Germany over that in the United Kingdom:

$$\frac{0 \cdot 91 - 0 \cdot 10}{5 \cdot 15 - 1 \cdot 72} \times 100\% = 23 \cdot 6\%$$

Reallocation of resources does not, however, fully measure the gains contemplated by Kindleberger's thesis, which is that the greater elasticity of labour supply in Continental countries helped to maintain a higher rate of profits and thus of investment. This is why we have also reproduced, in Table 6.1, Denison's estimates of the contribution of capital to growth. It is hard to know *how much* of the differences in investment rates to credit to this cause. If, however, we make an assumption which is surely far too kind to Kindleberger's case, and allot the *whole* of the difference between the contribution of capital to growth in Germany and the United Kingdom, as shown in Table 6.1, to this cause, we still find three-fifths of the difference in growth rates unexplained:

$$\frac{(0 \cdot 91 - 0 \cdot 10) + (0 \cdot 93 - 0 \cdot 37)}{5 \cdot 15 - 1 \cdot 72} \times 100\% = 40\%$$

Only if we perform a similar operation for the growth of *total* national incomes, and again ascribe the whole of the difference in the contributions of capital to the Lewis–Kindleberger mechanism, can we explain as much as half of the observed difference in growth rates in this fashion:

$$\frac{(1 \cdot 41 - 0 \cdot 51) + (1 \cdot 49 - 0 \cdot 50) + (0 \cdot 91 - 0 \cdot 10)}{7 \cdot 26 - 2 \cdot 38} \times 100\% = 55\%$$

The theory is capable of explaining even less of the differences between the United Kingdom and the other Continental economies than of that between the United Kingdom and Germany. Hence it seems possible to conclude that if Denison's estimates are near to the truth, the Lewis model as applied by Kindleberger is capable of explaining part of post-war Europe's 'supergrowth', and part of the differences between the faster-growing economies of continental Europe on the one hand and the United Kingdom on the other; but that even on outrageously favourable assumptions it still leaves considerably the greater part of the *explicandum* unexplained in almost every case.

The thesis of Kindleberger just reviewed is the only full-scale attempt so far to apply the Lewis model to a historical problem. In the same volume, its author briefly argues that the model helps to explain the contrasts between British and American growth in the first and second halves of the nineteenth century, but his remarks can hardly be viewed as more than suggestions for further research. The view has been put forward, however, that Japanese economic development in the early Meiji period may usefully be interpreted with the aid of one of the several proposed variants and extensions of Lewis' scheme, the Fei–Ranis model.[25] A chief feature distinguishing this model from that of Lewis is the relatively greater emphasis placed on changes *within* the agricultural sector during the period in which marginal product in that sector, though rising, is still below the conventional wage rate. The authors view the resultant increase in productivity as a source of potential savings which can be siphoned off to finance industrial and infrastructural investment. That the taxing of increments of productivity in agriculture for just this purpose was an important feature of Meiji economic development is generally (though not universally) agreed. However, it seems probable that that increase of productivity was achieved as a result of some positive improvements rather than as a by-product of a rising land/man ratio. (A point worth making is that in this instance economic analysis of Japan's historical experience preceded, rather than followed, the formulation of the theory.)[26]

The possible application of the Lewis or Fei–Ranis models to other historical examples remains to be explored. One might have expected development to have followed these lines in Russia, but a quick glance suggests that neither in the late Tsarist nor in the Soviet period did it do so. Before 1914 the policy associated particularly with the name of

Witte did, it is true, involve siphoning an investible surplus from an over-populated rural sector; but so far from appearing spontaneously, this surplus represented only the fruits of draconian taxation. If agricultural productivity rose, and it seems unlikely that it rose much, this was not because of any improvement in the land/man ratio: despite the rapid *proportionate* growth of the non-agricultural sectors these were relatively so small that they by no means absorbed the rural natural increase, and over-population in the countryside grew gradually worse, rather than better. During the early five-year plans, on the other hand, the hectic progress of collectivization and of the mechanization of agriculture did permit an absolute reduction of numbers on the land. But so far from facilitating a rapid industrialization with *stable* wage rates, low productivity and the unsuitability for factory work of this ex-peasant labour forced wage bills up and generated a competition for labour which resulted in large-scale inflation. Finally, in both Tsarist and Soviet periods a feature which strikingly impeded the course of industrialization, 'surplus' labour notwithstanding, was the critical shortage of *skilled* workers. Indeed it has been suggested that a seeming paradox of late Tsarist industry, the characteristic emphasis on large-scale, capital-intensive plants, is to be explained in terms of (skilled) labour shortages and (thanks to foreign investment) a relative abundance of capital.[27]

Patterns of industrial growth: Chenery and Hoffmann

Models like those of Sir Arthur Lewis and of Fei and Ranis seek to illuminate both the sources of economic growth and the structural transformations which accompany it. This is also true of attempts to discover systematic patterns in the process of industrial growth which have been made by several writers. To introduce this topic, let us revert to Chenery's work and discuss one final feature, namely his use of regression equations to chart typical growth paths not merely for the industrial sector as a whole, but for particular industrial groupings. The expectation underlying this investigation is that just as the industrial, agricultural and service sectors as a whole grow at different rates during development, so will individual industries or broad groups of industries. This expectation is grounded fundamentally on the fact that income elasticities of demand are no more uniform for different industrial products than for the products of the three major sectors considered as aggregates. However, as with the more highly aggregated equations other factors, such as scale and resource effects and trading opportunities, help to determine deviations from the 'normal' pattern. Here again the estimation of three sets of patterns, for large, small industry-oriented and small primary-oriented countries respectively, proves helpful in separating out the various influences at work.

It is not necessary to report Chenery's findings with respect to the behaviour of the output of single industries or finer industrial groupings. Particular interest attaches however to his discovery of three typical patterns, describing the relationship to income of the output of 'early', 'middle' and 'late' industries respectively. The former, for example, include such categories as food processing, leather goods, and textiles. Characteristically, demand for such products has a low-income elasticity so that output reaches a maximum at a quite low level of income and then tends to decline relatively – though in small primary-oriented countries the composition of exports gives the output curve for this group a steeper and longer-continuing upward trend. The 'middle' and 'late' industries, as their names imply, make their maximum contributions to the growth of industrial output in the middle and higher ranges of *per capita* income respectively. Here, however, differences between the three types of country are more marked: in particular, both the resource effect and the scale effect retard the development of such industries in small primary-oriented countries, so that the proportionate contribution of the output of such industries to G.N.P. is very small at lower income levels but increases, at an increasingly rapid rate, as income rises. In the small industry-oriented countries scale and resource effects pull in opposite directions and partly cancel each other. In the large countries, on the other hand, the output of middle industries, though growing rapidly at first, levels off asymptotically at medium income levels, and in the higher ranges the continued growth of the industrial sector depends entirely on the still-rising demand for the products of the 'late' industries.

Chenery's findings at this point bear closely upon the debate concerning 'balanced' versus 'unbalanced' growth, and upon the discussion of the role of 'leading sectors' in economic development, which have been a feature of the literature of the past couple of decades. The interest of his argument does not arise solely from the confirmation which it offers that the industrial sector does not advance simultaneously across the whole front, but is spearheaded now by this, now by that group of industries. In addition, the limited number of variables in the estimating equations indicates that a restricted range of 'universal' factors can explain more of the pattern than might be expected, particularly since when the countries studied are divided into three groups an even better 'fit' is achieved. Chenery is leading us here across the dividing line between 'patterns of development' and 'causes of growth'.

This aspect of Chenery's work recalls an earlier attempt to uncover and explain similarities in the pattern of growth, an attempt which has not perhaps received the credit it deserves as a pioneering effort. We have already drawn on the research of Walther G. Hoffmann as principal author of the major study of Germany's modern economic growth. Earlier, however, Hoffmann had made distinguished contributions to British and to comparative industrial history. It is the second of these which is referred to here. *Stadien und Typen der Industrialisierung* was first published as long ago as 1931, and with the advantage of hindsight one confesses to some surprise that this book did not make a greater impact at the time, considering the precocity of the work when viewed against the background of the literature of that period. Perhaps this was partly because of the language barrier, for when the book eventually appeared in 1958 in an English version (under the somewhat less informative title *The Growth of Industrial*

Economies) it at once began to attract reviews and comments disproportionately more numerous than those provoked by its first publication.[28] It was an instance of the unkindness of fate that these notices should be, in some cases, somewhat critical in tone, for their authors had failed to make due allowance for the advances achieved both in statistical techniques, in the study of quantitative economic history, and in economic theory in the twenty-seven years which had elapsed since the German edition appeared.

Hoffmann's aim, as stated in his preface, was to 'understand the process of industrialization' by making 'a systematic examination of its various phases in as many countries as possible'. Specifically, he sought to discover regular patterns in industrial growth by making a series of international comparisons over as long a time-horizon as possible. His aim was therefore identical with that of Chenery, but the method rested on the construction and comparison of time series rather than on cross-sectional analysis of countries of differing income levels. Hoffmann's study is mentioned here because on several points it reaches conclusions similar to those of Chenery – for example, as to the sequential prominence, at increasing levels of income, of different classes of industry. Given that Hoffmann's conclusions are based on *historical* evidence covering a much longer time span than Chenery's (though for fewer countries), this provides welcome confirmation of Chenery's contention that his 'patterns', estimated though they are from post-World War II data alone, are sequences which we may expect to find in historical development too.

While in some ways it is his findings regarding the growth of individual industries or groups of industries which are of greatest interest, the basic similarity of many of these to Chenery's results allows us to pass them over in favour of a brief discussion of Hoffmann's more general interpretative scheme. This is based on the contention that underlying the differing growth paths of individual industries is a more general and systematic structural change, according to which capital goods industries grow at a faster pace than consumer goods industries, which however predominate in all but the later stages of mature industrialization. Over time, therefore, the process of industrialization is marked by a persistent decline in the ratio of consumer to capital goods industries (computed from the added values of their respective outputs). Some examples of these ratios, taken from several of Hoffmann's tables, follow:

Brazil	1919	6·2	*New Zealand*	1906	5·5
	1940	3·0		1916	4·8
				1924	3·4
				1949/50	2·1
Great Britain	1851	4·7	*U.S.A.*	1850	2·4
	1871	3·9		1870	1·7
	1907	1·7		1880	1·8
	1924	1·5		1925	0·8
	1935	1·1		1939	0·7
	1948	0·7		1947	0·7

Source: Hoffman, *The Growth of Industrial Economies*, pp. 68, 71, 79, 83, 89, 92.

Hoffmann's scheme here bears a clear family likeness to Chenery's classification of industries into 'early', 'middle' and 'late' groups. There is a good deal to be said, it is true, in favour of Chenery's alternative, as Hoffmann's classification of industries is open to some question, particularly in its somewhat procrustean treatment of the output of 'intermediate' goods. Equally, it is not surprising that criticisms have been voiced of several of the procedures by which the immense problems of data collection have been tackled. Nevertheless, Hoffmann's enterprise represents an extraordinary achievement, all the more remarkable for being the product of a one-man team, lacking most of the advantages of finance and computerization which at the present day similar investigations usually depend on so heavily.

The consumer/capital industries ratio would have an immediate attraction, were it possible to use it as a possible measurement of 'degree of development'. We have seen that *per capita* income and sectoral shares in output or employment have both been used for such a purpose, but that they fail in many instances to afford intuitively plausible measures of development when applied to historical examples. It may be granted that this is partly due, and could conceivably be wholly due, to the fuzziness inherent in the phrase 'degree of development'. But one feels that there is perhaps something here of which one would like a better measure than either *per capita* income or the sectoral distribution of output. Unfortunately, the Hoffmann ratio does not seem to improve on the other two measures mentioned. While many of the values agree with intuitive impressions of the inter-country differences in level of development at various times in the past, others are more difficult to reconcile with them. For example, it would not be easy to agree with the indication that in the mid-nineteenth century the U.S.A. was very much more advanced in terms of 'degree of development' than Great Britain, or still less that in the following century America lost this lead and was subsequently overtaken or at least rivalled. Moreover, one could not readily accept as plausible the implications of these three ratios, taken from a recent chronological extension of his studies by Hoffmann:[29]

Italy (1966)	0·53
U.S.A. (1966)	0·46
U.K. (1963)	0·4

However, it must be added that in this more recent paper Hoffmann himself warns against using his ratio as a sole indicator of the stage of development: he plots it against income per head, revealing an inverse relationship, as expected, but only a relatively weak one, and explains discrepancies between the two measures in familiar ways (by reference, for example, to differing trade patterns and resource endowments).

There are other ways in which the course of Hoffmann's ratio over time is of some interest, particularly in its implications for international comparisons. For example, when the ratios for various countries are plotted on a semi-logarithmic scale it is apparent that countries industrializing relatively late experienced a more rapid rate of structural transformation than early starters (p. 149). We shall see shortly that Gerschenkron has built around this feature an interesting general hypothesis as to the significance of starting date (or rather, starting-point) for growth.

Its descriptive and suggestive powers apart, one is, however, entitled to ask just what the analytical importance, or indeed meaning, of the Hoffmann ratio is? Hoffmann himself offers some quite familiar (and plausible) explanations for the ratio's persistent decline in terms of the differing capital requirements, degrees of technological complexity and demand elasticities for the products of different types of industry. But one may wonder whether he does not greatly underrate the importance of another explanation of a more definitional character, namely the changing degree of industrial specialization and integration. In domestic industry, or in rudimentary and unspecialized factory production, the whole manufacturing process from raw material purchase to the completion of a finished consumer product may be carried out by the same 'industry' without need to purchase other inputs from other industries. Nor did the introduction of power machinery imply that this at once ceased to be the case: many early Lancashire cotton mills built their own machines, including even steam engines. As the market grew, however, and technology became more advanced, the productive system became more complicated and capital goods and inputs were increasingly 'bought out' from specialized producer and intermediate goods industries. In the light of such circumstances what we choose to call a 'consumer good' industry is a matter of definition and of the prevailing degree of 'vertical integration' in industry.

A recent critic of Hoffmann has argued, along somewhat similar lines, that Hoffmann's ratio does not in reality measure relative changes in the volume of output of capital and consumer goods; this is an illusion which (it is argued) is misleadingly generated by Hoffmann's conceptual scheme.[30] The writer, Armando Lago, attempts to show by the evidence of successive United Kingdom input/output matrices for a series of years from 1907 to 1954 that the ratio of value added generated by industrial sales to capital formation to that generated by industrial sales to household expenditures has *not* increased over time, as would be required by Hoffmann's thesis. On the other hand, a strong similarity is discovered between the course of the Hoffmann ratio over time and the ratio of the output of heavy to light industries, as revealed by time-series data for the U.S.A., Canada and Australia, and also by an international cross-section for the year 1953. It is suggested on the basis of this evidence that what the Hoffmann ratio is really measuring is *not* the changing relative importance of capital and consumer goods industries but that of the products of heavy and light industries.

At the time of writing these words, the debate continues – Hoffmann has already published a rejoinder to his critic[31] – and it is not within the scope of this book to attempt to adjudicate on what appears to be a rather difficult theoretical issue. The matter has been raised, rather, so as to underline the formidable conceptual and analytical problems posed by any attempt to 'understand' economic growth. It is not *merely* a question of quarrying suitable data, difficult enough though that is, and subjecting them to standard statistical tests; rather, it is at the very point at which apparently significant patterns begin to emerge that the real difficulties, of deciding what these patterns mean and what generates them, arise.

We have left until last any mention of one of Hoffmann's central aims, an aim which is adumbrated in the first word of the German title of his book: namely, the desire to identify *stages* in the development of industrial economies. Hoffmann achieves this in the simplest possible way, by marking off arbitrary 'cutting points' on the continuum of his ratio. Thus Stage I economies are those for which the ratio is $5(\pm 1):1$; Stage II economies those with ratios of $2\cdot 5(\pm 1):1$; Stage III; $1(\pm 0\cdot 5):1$; and Stage IV below $0\cdot 5$. It will be noticed that this scheme provides no place for a ratio of more than $6:1$, such as that given for Brazil in 1919, nor for ratios between

3·5 : 1 and 4 : 1, and in his later article, Hoffmann modifies the scheme as follows:

Stage I	2·5/6·5 : 1
Stage II	1·5/2·5 : 1
Stage III	0·5/1·5 : 1
Stage IV	0·3/0·5 : 1

It is apparent that these schemes of classification are purely arbitrary, since no theoretical justification is offered for the second set of cutting-points in preference to the first or vice versa, or for either in preference to some other choice. Hoffmann indeed concedes this in his last paper, admitting that one might just as well have ten divisions as four.

Hoffmann's procedure is not as curious as it may appear, for whenever one is faced with a continuum any proposed division on it is liable to have an arbitrary element: tall men are not sharply and clearly differentiated from short ones, nor rich countries from poor, nor 'A' students from 'B' students. But the economist is not in the position of the pyjama-maker who has to make some of his garments for 'tall' men, some for 'medium', and some for 'short'; or of the university professor who has to grade his students 'A', 'B' or 'C'. Since we are not compelled by any expository necessity to make any subdivisions at all on the continuum of the Hoffmann index, one is entitled to expect that any subdivision which *is* proposed is not going to be completely arbitrary, but is going to highlight certain strategic features of the development process which help to explain the transition from one stage to another, up the ladder of economic development. The criticism to be made of Hoffmann is that his classification *is* purely arbitrary, that no attempt is made to justify the particular choices made in heuristic or even expository terms. This leads Hoffmann into some quite untenable propositions. For example, he claims to have 'shown that countries in the first stage of industrialization have a uniform industrial pattern. . . . The ratio between the consumer-goods industries and the capital-goods industries in countries in the initial stage of industrialization generally falls between six and four' (pp. 76–7). But of course, countries in this first stage have been allotted to it precisely *because* they yield a ratio falling within this particular range; the argument is therefore completely circular and devoid of any substantive significance.

'Stage' theories of growth

It is perhaps not unfair to say that Hoffmann has been unable to resist a typically German preoccupation with taxonomy, for the belief which many scholars have manifested that it is useful to postulate 'stages' in the process of economic growth is of Teutonic origin. Its first important manifestation was in the programme of the German 'Historical School' of the nineteenth century, whose adherents dissented from both the conclusions and the deductive methodology of the dominant British school of classical economics and attempted to pioneer a new inductive science of economics by distilling 'laws' from the facts of economic history.[32] Since they claimed, dissenting from what they took to be the view of the classical economists, that economic 'laws' are relative, culture-bound, limited in application to a particular economic structure and institutional environment, it was natural to seek to classify economies of the past into some series of types or stages.

There is no need here to discuss the works and the fortunes of the Historical School, though the economist who is passing through what Arthur Lewis called 'a phase where he is dissatisfied with the deductive basis of economic theory, and feels sure that a much better insight into economic processes could be obtained by studying the facts of history'[33] would do well to recall the complete failure of *Historismus* to achieve its theoretical intentions, and the enduring damage which the bitter debates between advocates and opponents inflicted on the study of economics in Germany. Our only concern is to notice that the tenets of the Historical School wielded great influence over early economic historiography. Not only were the writings of members of the School among the first major contributions to economic history as a recognized discipline, but the great international reputation of the

German Ph.D. degree in the later nineteenth century offered an outstanding opportunity for the transfer of intellectual styles from Germany to the universities of the English-speaking world, in which most of the early teaching positions in the subject were established. There is in fact, for example, a direct line of descent from the Historical School to the American Institutionalists, through Thorstein Veblen and his protégé, Wesley Mitchell, to the National Bureau of Economic Research and its important series of quantitative investigations in economic history.

We can pass over the writings of the Historical School, however, since with one or two exceptions the study of them falls nowadays to the writer on the history of economic doctrines rather than to the working economic historian. But we can scarcely avoid some comment on the best-known of all examples of stage theory, W. W. Rostow's *The Stages of Economic Growth*.[34] It is very difficult, however, to know what to say about this book, for it has provoked so much discussion that all the obvious comments are already 'old hat', and has generated such an unusual degree of almost emotive response that the climate for temperate discussion has been impaired. We are not required, fortunately, to speculate whether this last is because of the book's astonishing success – it averaged two impressions a year during the first eight years after publication – which may have induced an outlook of sour grapes on the part of some scholars who conceive themselves to have written better but less widely-noticed works; or because of the book's political overtones – the expectations aroused by the subtitle (*A Non-Communist Manifesto*) are belied neither by the style of writing, often somewhat racy and journalistic, nor by the frank involvement in Cold War politics in which the later pages become bogged down; or even, perhaps, because of Rostow's personal political activities. The fact remains that *The Stages of Economic Growth* has given a great many people something for which they have been looking, some putative enlightenment – whether real or not – about matters of widespread concern; enlightenment of the sort which history and even political economy once dispensed to the intelligent lay public, but which in their latter-day specialization and esotericism these disciplines seem to have lost the capacity for offering.

From our point of view the book demands some notice not merely because of its popular success but also because it is after all one of the very few attempts by one who is, on any reckoning, a leading economic historian, to present 'an economic historian's way of generalizing the sweep of modern history'. But advantage may be taken of the book's popularity (and of its brevity and readability) to forego any attempt to offer a brief summary of its main contentions. Readers of the present book will surely know of the five 'stages', from 'traditional society' to 'high mass consumption', into which it is judged 'useful to break down the story of each national economy – and sometimes the story of regions' (p. 1). They will know, too, that it is stage three, 'take-off', which has elicited by far the most notice, a form of partiality which Rostow himself seemed to invite in referring to it as 'the great watershed in the life of modern societies' (p. 7). They may be several degrees more hazy in their recollection of Rostow's claim that his stages 'are not merely descriptive. . . . They have an inner logic and continuity . . . an analytic bone-structure . . .' (pp. 12–13): more hazy because they have been told so often by Rostow's critics that this is just what the stages do *not* have. And they may frankly have forgotten, again because critics have accused Rostow's scheme of procrustean tendencies, that the stages are presented only as 'an arbitrary and limited way of looking at the sequence of modern history . . . designed, in fact, to dramatize not merely the uniformities . . . but also – and equally – the uniqueness of each nation's experience' (p. 1).

The two later stages, 'maturity' and 'high mass consumption', certainly seem to add more in the way of difficulties than of enlightenment. Discussion of them, from the point of view of economic analysis, is frankly sketchy. Above all, they are defined in different terms, stage five (on the whole, and notwithstanding some flirtation with alternative definitions) in terms of real *per capita* income, and stage four in terms of

technology. (Stage four is reached when 'the society has
effectively applied the range of (then) modern technology to
the bulk of its resources' (p. 59).) Clearly these two criteria do
not necessarily lead to the same ordering, as is demonstrated
by the fact that Canada and Australia are shown as entering
the stage of high mass consumption *before* reaching maturity
(Australia enters high mass consumption at the same time as
take-off), whereas Britain reached maturity all but ninety
years before high mass consumption. It was possible, given
the unimpressive production functions of those days, for
Britain to have applied the most advanced technology of the
mid-nineteenth century over a large range of her economy
without being able to achieve a really high level of *per capita*
income. On the other hand, resource-rich countries with
strong comparative advantage in certain sectors could
achieve high levels of real income through specialization and
trade while remaining technologically callow over all save a
restricted area of productive activity.

'Take-off'

However, it is stage three, 'take-off', which has captured the
limelight, not so much (we may think) because of the topical
and seductive metaphor by which the stage is christened, but
because the process of industrialization which it inaugurates
is so widely viewed as a great once-for-all change in the
human condition. Not only policy-makers obsessed by the
problem of achieving a sustained rise in living standards in
low-income, dominantly agricultural countries, but even
historians with a professional penchant for stressing continuity rather than change in social affairs, have urged this
view. Cipolla has it that the onset of industrialization is one
of two great revolutions which have 'created deep breaches
in the continuity of the historical process', each inaugurating
'a new story dramatically and completely alien to the
previous one'.[35] For Hartwell, the industrial revolution
'began one of the great discontinuities of history'.[36] According to Landes, it 'yielded an unprecedented increase in man's
productivity and, with it, a substantial rise in income per

head . . . transformed the balance of political power, within nations, between nations, and between civilizations; revolutionized the social order; and as much changed man's way of thinking as his way of doing'.[37]

In view of this widespread readiness to see the industrial revolution as a unique transformation of outstanding importance in human history, it is perhaps a little surprising that the concept of 'take-off' should have elicited so much criticism. Partly this may be explained by the rider added by the remainder of the title of Rostow's original article on the subject: 'The Take-off into Self-Sustained Growth'.[38] 'Self-sustained growth', certainly, is not an easy concept to grasp. The flight of an aircraft after take-off is surely not self-sustained, as pilot and passengers would quickly discover if the engines failed; and everything we know suggests that however advanced or fortunate a country may be, continued growth is never 'self-sustained' either, in the sense (for example) of not requiring any abstinence from consumption today in order to enjoy higher incomes tomorrow. But to reject the idea of take-off because of a possibly inept description of what it is take-off into does not seem fair criticism.

There is more substance to the complaint that Rostow's claim to some special quality of decisiveness for the first few decades of industrialization – he suggests periods of only eighteen years for the U.S.A. and twenty for Britain – is inadequately substantiated. As Cairncross writes, 'I know of no evidence that growth was more self-sustaining in 1802 than it had been in 1782.'[39] Even this criticism would be more compelling, however, if those who advance it were able to deny the 'inevitability' of growth after take-off by pointing to abortive take-offs, to experiences of growth-quickening and modernization meeting the Rostovian specifications which yet failed to inaugurate a period of sustained growth. Such examples have not been forthcoming. Certainly there have been historical examples of economic retrogression, in parts of early modern Italy or Spain, for example, but it is not at all clear that history has yet produced an example disproving the claim that an economic experience of the type intended by Rostow produces *irreversible* growth. The only possible example that comes to mind is that of Russia between about 1890 and 1914, and if this *was* an abortive take-off, massive and unique political and military explanations of the abort lie readily to hand. Moreover, some criticisms seem a trifle over-confident, such as the claim that there is no sharp change in macro-economic aggregates like rate of growth of output or investment ratio such as would validate the placing of 'take-off' in a particular short, critical period. We have seen that once allowance is made – and Rostow makes this allowance – for the special circumstances of capital-importing regions of recent settlement, the evidence on capital formation proportions, though perhaps never (except in the case of the Soviet Union in the 1930s) quite meeting the Rostow specifications, is still not as far removed from them as economic historians have been ready to suggest.

There is in fact some disagreement among economists as well as among economic historians on the broad issue of continuity *versus* discontinuity in economic change. Moreover, since there is really no question but that over the broad sweep of the centuries there has been decided acceleration in economic change – as measured, say, by rate of growth of output, by investment ratios and by the pace of technological change – it is a question of what degree of acceleration, of change in the rate of change, constitutes discontinuity? There are many today who find it useful to think of some social systems in terms of 'circular causation'. Specifically, the proliferation of models defining on the one hand low-level equilibrium traps and on the other 'Golden Age' growth paths suggests the widespread belief that there may be two systems of macro-economic equilibrium, one of persistent stagnation and the other of continuing growth. Since it is not the characteristic of an equilibrium system to transform itself smoothly and spontaneously into a second equilibrium system one must imagine, for any society which shifts from one system into the other, a more or less sudden jolt, a period of disturbance, of changing parameters and relationships.

'Take-off' is presumably an interval of this sort, and however much one may quarrel with the dates Rostow wishes to attach to his various 'take-offs' or indeed with his specification as to what constitutes a 'take-off', the existence of such a critical period in the past history of presently-developed societies, due allowance made for the rather special circumstances of countries 'born free', is neither theoretically implausible nor clearly at variance with historical fact. One might wish to qualify these last words only by saying that the earlier the date at which a country's modern economic growth began the more gradual and evolutionary its development tended to be. This is one reason for thinking that the special familiarity to so many scholars of the story of British economic development may well have encouraged an unfortunate tendency to generalize from what is in fact, by virtue of its primacy in time and its unique continuity, a highly exceptional case.

The real criticism of Rostow's discussion of the take-off lies perhaps elsewhere: in the looseness with which the characteristics of 'take-off' are specified, in the lack of sophistication and subtlety in the analysis of the economic interrelationships of the society experiencing take-off, and in the impressionistic way in which the proposed take-off dates for the various countries are justified – where an attempt is made to justify them at all. For example, the third part of the tripartite definition of take-off is 'the existence or quick emergence of a political, social and institutional framework which exploits the impulses to expansion in the modern sector and the potential external economy effects of the take-off and gives to growth an on-going character' (p. 39). It is difficult to know just what this means, if it means anything more than that if take-off is to inaugurate sustained growth, then growth must not fizzle out – which may be readily agreed. Again, the requirement of 'the development of one or more substantial manufacturing sectors, with a high rate of growth' (p. 39) lacks specificity because of the imprecision of the adjectives 'substantial' and 'high'; while if these words be interpreted only in a relative sense, then that some portion of a growing economy should grow faster than other portions is implicit in the very definition of structural change.

The limited power of Rostow's discussion to advance our understanding of 'take-off' is apparent when we read a detailed and rigorous attempt to confront one of his proposed identifications with the facts of history. A well-known case in point is R. W. Fogel's 'Railroads and the "Take-Off" Thesis: The American Case'.[40] Fogel tests Rostow's ascription of U.S. 'take-off' to the dates 1843–60 by marshalling the available statistical evidence to test two propositions seemingly implied by the Rostovian requirements: that there was in this period a uniquely rapid (or otherwise significant) process of structural transformation, and that the demand generated by the railway for the output of other industries was a decisive element in their own growth. The evidence – though it is neither abundant nor easy to weigh, and the skill of a Fogel is needed to marshall and interpret it – seems to be against both of these propositions. It is shown that the increase of the manufacturing share in output during the alleged 'take-off', though large, was not uniquely so, and that rather there was a 'more or less continuous increase in the absolute and relative size of manufacturing' covering virtually the whole nineteenth century. Further, while the railways' demand for iron did increase substantially within the period, it averaged only 17 per cent of the output of the iron industry over the years 1840–60, and was little more than 10 per cent of the total in the years 1845–9, in which the largest quinquennial increase in iron production of those decades was recorded. Railway demand was an even less significant item in the output of other industries.

In default of similarly careful studies for other countries, it is impossible for the time being to adjudicate Rostow's other proposed 'take-off' dates. In any event it is by thorough statistical testing of this sort, rather than by *a priori* theorizing, that the validity and helpfulness of explanatory schemes must be gauged. In this connection it is fair to add that Rostow had conceded that his views 'might have been elaborated, in a more conventional treatise, at greater length, in greater

detail, and with greater professional refinement', but went
on to claim that there might 'be some virtue in articulating
new ideas briefly and simply to an intelligent non-professional
audience' (pp. ix–x). The commercial success of *The Stages of
Economic Growth* confirms the justice of this claim; but perhaps
professional reaction might have been more favourable if the
'more conventional treatise' had also subsequently appeared.

Uniformity and diversity again

Rostow's quest in *The Stages of Economic Growth*, like that of
other scholars in this area, is for evidence of and explanations
for the element of unity underlying the evident diversity of
historical experience. By 'diversity' is intended here not just
that some countries have achieved growth while others have
not, or that some have grown faster than others; one envisages
also differences of the type stipulated early in this chapter –
in trade/income ratios, in investment ratios, in industrial
structure, in the assortment of financial institutions or type of
market structure and of course in the extent and nature of
government intervention in economic life. Rostow validates
the claim that his scheme is designed to highlight 'the uniqueness of each nation's experience' (p. 1) as well as underlying
uniformities by pointing, for example, to the variety of industries which have served as leading sector in 'take-off'. Here
the element of uniformity is that there has to be (in Rostow's
view) a 'leading sector', whereas the diversity arises in that
differences of timing, market situation, resource base and so
on confer advantages on different industries from one case to
another.

This sort of approach to 'uniformity within diversity' is one
which has considerable appeal for the historian. Its basic
premise is that it is a condition of economic growth that a
number of economic requirements be fulfilled – for an
adequate level of aggregate demand, for the achievement of
a given level of savings and their channelling into areas of
productive investment and so on – but that the *ways* in which
these requirements are met may vary from case to case in
response to the differing cultural, political, geographical and

P

all other relevant circumstances of each individual country. Obvious analogies suggest themselves. One might think of the many types of vehicle propelled by internal combustion engines; despite their variety, the essential requirements – a combustible mixture, a detonating device, a mechanical system capable of transforming the expansive force of burning gas into forward thrust – are few and simple, and not only provide the unifying element which enable the various examples to be recognized as members of the same species but also permit the engineer to calculate roughly, from a minimum of data such as the volume of the combustion chambers, how much work the engine will be capable of doing. Or one may think a biological analogy more appropriate – the great variety of animal life whose capacity to grow and survive is predicated on meeting, in one or other of a variety of ways, a few basic requirements – for a supply of food, for oxygen, for a mechanism of reproduction. Not only are the 'unifying' requirements common to all members of the genus but also the ways of meeting them, though perhaps numerous, are themselves far from random, being capable of classification and explanation in terms of features of the particular case – the medium (for example) on or through which the vehicle is to move or in which the animal must live.

In the same way one may conceive of a theory of economic growth on a very high level of abstraction, involving the interaction of only a few elements or 'requirements' and of universal application, but not 'explaining' in any detail or exactness the unique features of any particular economy's growth. Below this pinnacle of abstraction, however, one can approach progressively closer to reality by identifying relevant features of each particular case which open or close access for it to particular ways of meeting these basic requirements, just as mention of the element through which a vehicle is to move or in which an animal lives narrows down the possible choices of mode of propulsion or of food-gathering.

A chief appeal of this way of looking at things is that it

effects some reconciliation between the competing views of
the subject matter of economic history discussed at the beginning of this chapter. Experiences of economic growth which
are unique, different in every case one from another, may
yet be capable of explanation within a single framework
consisting of the specification of certain basic determinants
of growth whose actual forms and values vary systematically,
in accordance with 'given' features of each individual case.
The appeal does not rest there, for a method as well as a
philosophy is implied. Economic models at a high level of
abstraction are *necessary* but not *sufficient* to explain the con-
crete detail of historical experience. On the other hand brute
empiricism is not enough either, for the *systematic* nature of
deviations can be apprehended only when the central tendency from which they are deviations is itself recognized and
measured. Failing this the empiricist is obliged to treat each
case as completely *sui generis*, and the possibility of a gradual
accretion of understanding through the progressive accommodation of explanatory scheme to fact is remote.

There is of course nothing novel in all this; the views
expounded are the common property of most research in
today's social sciences. In the area of economic development
Chenery's work is an outstanding case in point, with its
initial assumption of 'universal' and 'particular' factors, and
the successive adaptations to the equations to achieve better
'fits' by allowing for the influence of factors, like resource
endowment, which are not equal in every case but which
generate *predictable* deviations from the central tendency. Yet
so far this approach has not perhaps been *consciously* adopted
by more than a minority of the economists and historians
working on problems of long-term growth. A case where it
has is that of the 'relative backwardness' hypothesis propounded by the *doyen* of American economic historians,
Alexander Gerschenkron.[41]

In his mature years Gerschenkron has sought to synthesize
his outstanding knowledge of comparative economic history
by explaining some of the differences in growth experience
as systematic deviations from a common pattern, induced by

the varying incidence of one initial condition, degree of backwardness. Gerschenkron's hypothesis – one of his reviewers prefers to call it 'conception'[42] – is that the degree of *relative* backwardness of a country initiating industrialization (in comparison with advanced countries at the same point of time) has been a determinant of the type of industrialization it experienced. The greater the relative backwardness, the bigger the technological gap between its production techniques and those of (then) advanced countries, and the bigger therefore the discontinuity between its traditional techniques and form of industrial organization and those of the growing modern sector – *if* this adopts the most advanced techniques available elsewhere. Gerschenkron appears to think this likely both in order to meet foreign competition and – here paradoxically, and in sharp contrast with the assumptions of the Lewis 'surplus-labour' model – because in very backward countries the critical shortage of *skilled* and *factory-disciplined* labour dictates recourse to labour-saving, capital-intensive methods. Hence, while in such countries the relative backwardness makes it difficult to get started at all, once industrialization *does* begin it is liable to be rapid, to involve a sharper break in continuity than in countries starting from a less disadvantaged position, and to be marked by unusual emphasis on large-scale plants. Further, the low level of domestic incomes implies a relatively restricted demand for consumer goods and makes the sources of capital relied on in advanced countries – commercial banks, auto-financing and the stock market – inadequate, so that other forms of intermediation such as investment banks or, if backwardness is very pronounced, the State, have to play a relatively bigger role.

Gerschenkron documents his hypothesis only in a somewhat impressionistic way and claims that it is derived only from his study of, and perhaps only applicable to, nineteenth-century European industrial development. Nevertheless the importance of the period and continent, and Gerschenkron's unrivalled knowledge of comparative economic growth within them, clearly demand that his hypothesis be taken seriously. So far there has been only one attempt to apply a rigorous test.[43] The result is only moderately favourable, for of the three Gerschenkron 'effects' tested, only one (that alleging a positive correlation between measure of relative backwardness and subsequent rate of industrial growth) is unequivocally confirmed. A second relationship, that between relative backwardness and the share of producer goods industries, is highly significant and in the predicted direction if 'emphasis on producer goods industries' is interpreted as *share of manufacturing output attained* during the spurt, but not if it is interpreted as *rate of growth* of such industries during it. The third predicted relationship (between backwardness and increase in agricultural productivity) is not confirmed, though not contradicted either, by the test.

Professor Barsby's paper is certainly an interesting first attempt to test the Gerschenkron hypothesis in a rigorous fashion. Still, it has limits in that it tests only three components of the hypothesis, against the experience of only six countries. Further, as Barsby is the first to agree, the data admit of great deficiencies: one is frankly astonished, for example, by indices of agricultural labour productivity which show virtually as much improvement in Russia from 1884 to 1904 as in Denmark from 1870 to 1890. Apart from Professor Barsby's paper – which also suggests, very tentatively, that in so far as the relationships predicted by Gerschenkron hold, it may be for reasons other than his – there has been one extended and broadly-based attempt to test the heuristic power of Gerschenkron's model, namely Rosovsky's use of it as a basis for discussing the similarities and dissimilarities of the Japanese as compared with the European experience of industrialization.[44] The conclusion, broadly, is that starting from a position of marked relative backwardness, Japanese industrialization proceeded on Gerschenkron lines as regards its overall rate, its dependence on imported technology, and the relatively large role of the State. It diverged from the Gerschenkron path, however, by manifesting a relatively great stress on light industries and by its apparent ability to recruit a rapidly-growing and well-disciplined labour force.

The contrast with Russia in respect of both of these characteristics is certainly marked, and may perhaps be explained
partly in terms of the adoption in Japan of a style of industrialization which did minimum violence, either geographically or culturally, to the existing patterns of population
distribution and to social attitudes and values, and which
made the greatest possible use of traditional handicraft skills.
In both respects Russian industrialization in late Tsarist
times, almost as much as in the Soviet period, followed
precisely the opposite course. The reasons for this difference
may well lie primarily in the spheres of politics and of
ideology, though doubtless in the Russian case the relatively
greater importance of foreign capital and entrepreneurship
and the more critical importance of the geographical distribution of key resources were also factors.

It may therefore be, as some have suspected, that Gerschenkron's hypothesis has rather too exclusively the character of
a generalization from the Russian case, and that as it is tested
against other experiences its area of validity will in part at
least be narrowed down. But if we share Gerschenkron's
philosophy of history, this should occasion neither surprise
nor disappointment: 'Historical generalizations are not
universal propositions that are falsified as soon as a single
black swan has been observed. . . . Verifying historical
generalizations and establishing the area of their validity are
identical operations.'[45] It is for theory – though a theory
already, perhaps, informed by a provisional ordering of the
data – to suggest plausible explanatory hypotheses; for
empirical research to confirm or disconfirm them, or to
discover limits to their area of validity which, with the addition of further explanatory variables, it may then be possible
to push out once again.

The limitations of economic analysis

This concludes our brief survey of some modern attempts to
interpret the record of economic growth. Perhaps it will be
useful, in conclusion, to say something about what this
survey, and indeed the book generally, have *not* included.

Some readers will perhaps feel, for example, that attention has been far too narrowly confined to *economic* analyses and explanations of economic growth. There is a large body of opinion holding that the non-economic attributes of a society have an important bearing on its economic achievement. A case in point is the well-known hypothesis linking the growth of capitalism in the early modern centuries with the rise of Protestantism. This type of explanation is not favoured by historians and sociologists alone, however. It was the economist-authors of a well-known textbook on economic growth who asserted '. . . the really substantive barriers to development are mainly noneconomic . . .'.[46] Nor is it only in considering long-term growth and the transition from pre-industrial to industrial societies that the analysis of economic achievement may be furthered by considering non-economic factors; the role of such attributes as morale and sense of involvement has been shown by empirical studies at the micro-level to be of perhaps outstanding importance in determining labour productivity in modern industry.[47]

One cannot, however, readily accept the view, which seems to be implicit in some references to 'non-economic' and 'economic' determinants of economic achievement, that there is some quality of mutual exclusiveness about these two, such that those who propound an explanation in terms of 'non-economic' factors are in inevitable conflict with those who prefer an 'economic' explanation, and that if the former are right, the latter must necessarily be wrong, and vice versa. Rather, the truth seems to be that most frequently such protagonists are merely offering explanations *on different levels*. If we imagine a universe in which events are causally related, we can identify the causes of events $c_1, c_2, \ldots c_n$ as being, say, $b_1, b_2, \ldots b_n$. But $b_1, b_2, \ldots b_n$, in turn, have causes which we may call $a_1, a_2, \ldots a_n$. There is then both logical justification and (perhaps) sound reason for pointing to $a_1, a_2, \ldots a_n$ as 'causes' of $c_1, c_2, \ldots c_n$ respectively; but to do so does not imply any conflict with the view that $b_1, b_2, \ldots b_n$ are also 'causes'. If, for instance, an intelligent but sickly schoolboy fails his end-of-year examination, his teachers may rightly believe that this was brought about by repeated absences from school. These absences in turn, however, have their explanation in the boy's repeated and protracted illnesses, and his parents might well fasten on this medical condition as 'the cause' of his failure, doubtless because it is the point in the chain of causal regress at which they might have the opportunity to exert influence on the course of events. They might say to each other 'we must try to get him away for a good holiday this summer to build his strength up, if he is not to fail his examinations again next year'. Clearly these two explanations of the failure are in no sense incompatible: teachers and parents merely fix on differing *levels* of explanation reflecting their differing outlooks and points of involvement in the system.

The dichotomy between 'economic' and 'non-economic' explanations is usually of this type; they are sequential explanations on differing levels of the causal regress rather than competing and inconsistent explanations on the same level. This can be clearly seen if for instance we consider an explanation of the differing records of economic growth in two countries secured by breaking down achieved growth into two components, the investment ratio and the marginal capital/output ratio.

$$\frac{\Delta Y}{Y} = \frac{\Delta K}{Y} \cdot \frac{1}{ICOR}.$$

This expression is tautological, for the marginal capital/output ratio is *defined* as the increment of capital within a given period divided by the increment of output,

$$ICOR = \frac{\Delta K}{\Delta Y}.$$

Yet this tautology has often been pressed into service as a first step in 'explaining' differences in growth experience. Say, for example, that the two economies in question experienced growth at respective rates of $2\frac{1}{2}$ and 3 per cent per annum, and that their investment ratios were respectively 10 and 12 per cent per annum. Clearly the *ICOR* is the same

(4:1) in each case, the growth equations for the two being respectively

$$0.025 = 0.10 \times \tfrac{1}{4}$$

and

$$0.03 = 0.12 \times \tfrac{1}{4}.$$

This might seem a useful even though a very simple formulation, for it directs attention to the rate of capital formation rather than to the *ICOR* as the probable and proximate cause of the differing rates of growth.

Further investigation might, however, suggest that in the second country the cause of the higher investment ratio was superior savings brought about by a different age distribution in the population. (We are not concerned here with the plausibility of the causation proposed.) Since this difference in turn might have been generated by, e.g., medical factors, it could be regarded as a 'non-economic' or exogenous element in a scheme of economic explanation. But this would not imply any conflict or inconsistency between the two explanations of the difference in growth rates couched in terms, respectively, of investment rates and of differing age structures. These explanations would both, we may suppose, be right, but would simply fasten upon observed differences in characteristics located at different levels in the chain of causal regress. It seems natural to regard the former as an 'economic' explanation and the latter as 'non-economic', but this is a distinction imposed on the material by our conceptual scheme, our way of looking at things, which springs in turn only from the disciplinary boundaries which happen to have become conventional.

In this book we have concentrated chiefly on the 'economic' level of explanation only because this is what the author is most familiar with and what the reader (presumably) wants most to know about. But it is *not* intended to imply that 'economic' factors are more important than 'non-economic' ones, or that the latter would not be worth studying. Indeed, in analysing an economic problem in economic terms one very often feels that one has pursued the analysis so to say to saturation point, without achieving any great satisfaction of one's intellectual curiosity, to achieve which would require pursuing the quarry into the arena of the 'non-economic'. And this may often be practically important: the best hope of increasing output in some time of need, say in wartime, may for example lie in generating feelings of patriotism so as to improve labour productivity and increase savings, or in providing *crèches* and similar facilities so as to induce more married women to go out to work. It is at least arguable that there is usually more scope for raising output by changing social characteristics and attitudes of this sort in low-income than in highly-developed countries; this would presumably be the truth contained in such assertions as that by Buchanan and Ellis quoted a little earlier. In this sense the foregoing pages may indeed be unbalanced in that the sort of illumination they cast on economic growth is more relevant to developed than to less highly-developed societies. But that only points to what the author is very ready to assert, the need for more books like this one drawing on wider ranges of historical experience.

The other major omission from the preceding pages equally arises from the limitations of the author's competence and his assumption about what readers would be interested in, and also from deference to consideration of space. It is that economic growth and its determinants have been considered only on a high level of aggregation: in terms, that is, of the growth of aggregate output and of its major sectoral components, and of a few 'determinants' of growth, again very highly aggregated, such as labour, land and capital inputs and a 'residual'. In part this omission overlaps with the last one – if omissions can overlap – in that it involves a refusal to pursue the quarry far beyond the most proximate causes of the quality of economic performance. But whereas in the foregoing paragraphs the concern was to indicate an area of inquiry lying below this level of explanation, populated by 'non-economic' factors such as social attitudes and values, the present intention is to point to a huge body of historical evidence bearing on *economic* determinants of economic performance, but at a lower level of aggregation.

We have made little use, for example, of industry studies in the preceding pages.

This second omission, though equally enforced by the considerations mentioned above, is harder to justify than the first. For though one may not feel quite as warmly on the subject as Schumpeter, in his famous denunciation of 'the curse of aggregative thinking which never goes step by step, as it is necessary to do, into actual causation',[48] it is surely right to say that the power of aggregative analysis to yield intellectually satisfying answers to the questions we want to ask about economic growth is limited. This is only partly – though the point is fundamental – because the number of countries and the amount of macro-economic information we have about them are limited, whereas the differences in their circumstances are numerous and important. The first fact leads to a temptation to throw all the information we have on an aggregate level into one pool, disregarding relevant differences among the countries at our disposal. Often this leads to attempts to explain meaningless averages. We have seen, for example, that both the level and the trend of the capital/output ratio are far easier to explain if sectoral ratios for major areas of investment are considered separately, rather than merely national average ratios. We have pointed, too, to the improvement in power to predict patterns of industrial structure which Chenery achieved by a preliminary sorting of countries into sub-groups of more nearly similar characteristics.

Quite apart from this sort of consideration, however, there are difficulties of a more technical order – residing in the method of inquiry rather than in the material under scrutiny – which should discourage us from hoping too much from aggregative analysis. Briefly, it could be said that these difficulties arise because, after all, the economic magnitudes in question are statistical artefacts. Again it is Schumpeter who has sounded the warning note: 'However useful for many purposes, total output is a figment which . . . would not as such exist at all, were there no statisticians to create it.'[49] In the post-war decades we have become very alert to the problems of international comparisons of aggregate or *per capita* real income – problems which are much less forbidding, though indeed they are not completely absent, when we compare the prices in different countries of, say, a ton of steel. If we seek, as of course economic historians must, to introduce a temporal as well as an inter-country dimension into these comparisons, the difficulties become much greater; for the passage of time introduces new problems such as the invention of new commodities and quality changes which are absent or much less important in cross-country comparisons at a single point of time. It cannot be too strongly stated that quite apart from the *practical* difficulty of securing sufficient evidence, there is *in principle* no unique and fully satisfactory way, either actually or potentially, of resolving these problems. If aggregate output is itself an artefact, then a *comparative* and *historical* series of the course of such output for two or more countries is at least trebly artificial.

It is in fact a valuable contribution of quantitative research on economic growth – albeit at the same time a somewhat Pyrrhic victory – to have demonstrated the critical importance of the methods used to aggregate a collection of heterogeneous outputs into a single measure or to transform measures of value occurring in time series or in cross-section data into constant-price terms. How much may hang on the choice of weighting procedure adopted in calculating the course of real income over time has been demonstrated most dramatically by Western attempts to construct time series of the national income of the Soviet Union. It deserves repetition that while there is every reason to suppose that similar choices may also be crucial in making such estimates for other countries, little experiment with alternative weighting procedures for them has so far been undertaken. We have also seen how substantially the patterns may differ when we chart the historical course of the trade/income or capital/output ratios first in current and then in constant prices.

Nor, unfortunately, are the difficulties in the way of the quantitative analysis of historical growth from the side of prices confined to the familiar index number problem, and to the lack of any firm conceptual basis for choosing one procedure rather than another. Even when we have decided what we want to do, an appropriate price series may not be forthcoming. Price series for the nineteenth and earlier centuries, in particular, are scarce, and those that do exist are frequently largely based (because of the readier accessibility of raw data) on the prices of goods entering into foreign trade. For a variety of reasons these may be unrepresentative of the course of the internal price level, particularly if what one really wants is an index of prices relating to a particular type of domestic economic activity such as capital formation. It is worth reminding the reader that Phyllis Deane has recently proposed revised estimates of the rate of growth of G.N.P. in the United Kingdom, which for some periods of the later nineteenth century are little more than one-half of the previously accepted estimates. The chief reason for this difference lies in the use of a new price deflator, Professor Deane contending that the old deflator based on prices of exports and imports has been misleading since the internal price level fell much less than that of internationally-traded goods.[50]

In sum, both the conceptual and the practical problems of constructing long-term historical series of the major economic aggregates, and therefore of ratios between them, are daunting in the extreme. Without wishing to discourage further work or indeed to cut the ground from under one's feet – for, after all, progress *has* been made in unravelling these complexities, and the disabusing of simplistic notions is itself a contribution to scholarship – it must be said that one does sometimes wonder whether economists who borrow these long-term series from others, dividing this into that or regressing that on this, are always aware of the limitations of the data they are using.*

* They are certainly *sometimes* aware of this – indeed for a position of extreme scepticism, expressing almost complete agnosticism as to the feasibility of time series and cross-country comparisons of real income, see Richard Ruggles, 'Price Indexes and International Price Comparisons', in W. Fellner *et al.*, *Ten Economic Studies in the Tradition of Irving Fisher* (New York, Wiley, 1967).

By contrast, the study of some restricted sector, say an individual industry, over time can escape these problems to a considerable extent. The more nearly homogeneous the collection of output one is considering, for example, the less serious is the weighting problem in aggregation. Quality changes, too, are likely to be more readily discernible, perhaps measurable, and capable of being allowed for. There are, moreover, more positive attractions in sectoral studies. One is that the economic theory lying ready to hand is usually more sophisticated and useful than that relating to the macro-economics of long-term growth. Another is that the more specific the focus of quantitative study, the greater the possibility of making use of qualitative sources such as those bearing on the technology employed, the quality of management, and so on. We have seen that even economic historians well equipped for the econometric study of productivity change sometimes rebel against the wanton discarding of evidence which the inability of such techniques to handle non-measurable data compels; and it was similar (though not identical) considerations which led Professor Postan to assert that in the study of technological progress and innovation the 'proper unit of evidence' is the individual firm.[51]

Yet sectoral or industry studies on their own are surely not enough. The sort of framework provided by information about the major economic magnitudes is indispensable to any historical (or cross-country) investigation of comparative growth. There is little point in looking for explanations of growth in the performance of this or that industry unless we know what growth we are trying to explain. Nor does the most penetrating analysis of the performance of a particular sector or activity tell us much about its contribution to growth unless we have some notion of the opportunity cost of the factors employed in it. He would be a poor visiting expert who judged the progress of a developing country solely by the jet airport at which he arrived, the super-highway along which he was driven to the capital, or the opulent-seeming university campus on which he was housed. Both types of study, then, are necessary; and one can honourably disclaim any need to apologize for not having written a different sort of book while insisting to the reader that different sorts of books, nevertheless, are also necessary.

Notes

1. W. ASHWORTH, *A Short History of the International Economy 1850–1950* (London, Longmans, 1952), 7.

2. G. EISNER, *Jamaica, 1830–1930: A Study in Economic Growth* (Manchester, Manchester U.P., 1961), 25.

3. PAUL BAIROCH, *Révolution industrielle et sous-développement* (Paris, S.E.D.E.S., 1963), 54–7, 194–6, 205, 208.

4. cf. above, p. 265.

5. J. M. KEYNES, *The General Theory of Employment Interest and Money* (London, Macmillan, 1936), 383.

6. cf. above, pp. 60–1.

7. CHENERY (1960), 626.

8. CHENERY and TAYLOR (1968).

9. P. TEMIN, 'A Time-Series Test of Patterns of Industrial Growth', *Economic Development and Cultural Change*, 15 (January 1967), 174–82.

10. M. D. STEUER and C. VOIVODAS, 'Import Substitution and Chenery's Patterns of Industrial Growth – a Further Study', *Economia Internazionale*, 16 (February 1965), 47–77.

11. F. A. HAYEK, *The Constitution of Liberty* (London, Routledge & Kegan Paul, 1960), 208.

12. JOHN HICKS, *A Theory of Economic History* (London, Oxford U.P., 1969), especially 33–41, 68–80.

13. M. M. POSTAN, 'The Rise of a Money Economy', *Economic History Review*, XIV (1944), 123.

14. RICHARD A. EASTERLIN, 'Regional Income Trends, 1840–1950', in *American Economic History*, ed. SEYMOUR E. HARRIS (New York, McGraw-Hill, 1961), 529.

15. J. G. WILLIAMSON, 'Regional Inequality and the Process of National Development: a Description of the Patterns', *Economic Development and Cultural Change*, XIII (July 1965).

16. cf. above, pp. 168–9.

17. H. OBER, 'Occupational Wage Differentials, 1907–47', *Monthly Labor Review*, LXVII (August 1948), 127–34.

18. R. OZANNE, 'A Century of Occupational Differentials in Manufacturing', *Review of Economics and Statistics*, XLIV (August 1962), 292–9.

19. K. G. J. C. KNOWLES and D. J. ROBERTSON, 'Differences between the Wages of Skilled and Unskilled Workers, 1880–1950', *Bulletin of the Oxford Institute of Statistics*, 13 (April 1951), 109–27; GUY ROUTH, *Occupation and Pay in Great Britain 1906–60* (Cambridge, Cambridge U.P., 1965), 103. See also D. J. ROBERTSON, *The Economics of Wages* (London, Macmillan, 1961), 72–3.

20. GERHARD BRY, *Wages in Germany 1871–1945* (Princeton, N.J., N.B.E.R., 1960), 81–5 and Table A–14.

21. E. H. PHELPS BROWN and M. H. BROWNE, *A Century of Pay* (London, Macmillan, 1968), 47. BRY (*op. cit.*, 285), however, appears to take a different view of the facts.

22. LEWIS (1954).

23. CHARLES P. KINDLEBERGER, *Europe's Postwar Growth: The Role of Labour Supply* (Cambridge, Mass., Harvard U.P., 1967).

24. DENISON (1967).

25. JOHN C. H. FEI and GUSTAV RANIS, 'Innovation, Capital Accumulation, and Economic Development', *American Economic Review*, LIII (June 1963), 283–313.

26. G. RANIS, 'The Financing of Japanese Economic Development', *Economic History Review*, Sec. Ser. XI (April 1959), 440–54.

27. cf. above, p. 432.

28. W. G. HOFFMANN, *Stadien und Typen der Industrialisierung* (Kiel, Institut für Weltwirtschaft, 1931); trans. W. O. HENDERSON and W. H. CHALONER, *The Growth of Industrial Economies* (Manchester, Manchester U.P., 1958). Page references in the text are to the English edition.

29. W. G. HOFFMANN, 'Stadien und Typen der Industrialisierung', *Weltwirtschaftliches Archiv*, 103/2 (1969), 321–7.

30. ARMANDO M. LAGO, 'The Hoffmann Industrial Growth Development Path: An International Comparison', *ibid.*, 103/1 (1969), 41–57.

31. W. G. HOFFMANN, 'Antikritisches zu "Stadien und Typen der Industrialisierung"', *Weltwirtschaftliches Archiv*, 104/1 (1970), 127–37.

32. For a good survey, see BERT F. HOSELITZ, 'Theories of Stages of Economic Growth' in BERT F. HOSELITZ (ed.), *Theories of Economic Growth* (New York, Free Press of Glencoe, 1960).

33. LEWIS (1955), 15.

34. W. W. ROSTOW, *The Stages of Economic Growth* (Cambridge, Cambridge U.P., 1960). Page references in the text are to this edition.

35. CARLO M. CIPOLLA, *The Economic History of World Population* (Harmondsworth, Penguin, 1962), 29–30.

36. *The Causes of the Industrial Revolution in England*, ed. R. M. HARTWELL (London, Methuen, 1967), 1.

37. DAVID S. LANDES, *The Unbound Prometheus* (Cambridge, Cambridge U.P., 1969), 41.

38. W. W. ROSTOW, 'The Take-off into Self-Sustained Growth', *Economic Journal*, LXVI (March 1956), 25–48.

39. A. K. CAIRNCROSS, 'The Stages of Economic Growth', *Essays in Bibliography and Criticism*, XLV, *Economic History Review*, Sec. Ser. XIII (April 1961), 458.

40. R. W. FOGEL, *Railroads and American Economic Growth: Essays in Econometric History* (Baltimore, Md., Johns Hopkins Press, 1964), Ch. IV.

41. ALEXANDER GERSCHENKRON, *Economic Backwardness in Historical Perspective* (Cambridge, Mass., Harvard U.P. (Belknap Press), 1962), Ch. I.

42. RONDO CAMERON, in *Journal of Economic History*, XXVIII (December 1968), 682.

43. S. L. BARSBY, 'Economic Backwardness and the Characteristics of Development', *Journal of Economic History*, XXIX (September 1969), 449–72.

44. H. ROSOVSKY, *Capital Formation in Japan 1868–1940* (New York, Free Press of Glencoe, 1961), Ch. IV.

45. ALEXANDER GERSCHENKRON, *Continuity in History and Other Essays* (Cambridge, Mass., Harvard U.P. (Belknap Press), 1968), 97.

46. N. S. BUCHANAN and H. S. ELLIS, *Approaches to Economic Development* (New York, The Twentieth Century Fund, 1955), 407.

47. See above, pp. 368–9.

48. J. A. SCHUMPETER, *Business Cycles*, 2 vols (New York, McGraw-Hill, 1939), Vol. I, 233, fn. (1).

49. *ibid.*, Vol. II, 484.

50. See above, p. 17.

51. See pp. 370–1 above; POSTAN (1967), 167.

Key to References

ADLER, J. H., ed. (1967) *Capital Movements and Economic Development* (London, Macmillan, 1967).

ASHTON, T. S. (1955) *An Economic History of England: The Eighteenth Century* (London, Methuen, 1955).

ASHWORTH, W. (1962) *A Short History of the International Economy since 1850* (Harlow, Longmans, 1962), 2nd ed.

BERNSTEIN, M. D., ed. (1966) *Foreign Investment in Latin America: Cases and Attitudes* (New York, Knopf, 1966).

BUTLIN, N. G. (1962) *Australian Domestic Product, Investment and Foreign Borrowing 1861–1938/39* (Cambridge, Cambridge U.P., 1962).

BUTLIN, N. G. (1964) *Investment in Australian Economic Development 1861–1900* (Cambridge, Cambridge U.P., 1964).

CAIRNCROSS, A. K. (1962) *Factors in Economic Development* (London, Allen & Unwin, 1962).

CHENERY, HOLLIS B. (1960) Patterns of Industrial Growth, *American Economic Review*, L (September 1960), 624–54.

CHENERY, HOLLIS B. and TAYLOR, LANCE (1968) Development Patterns: Among Countries and Over Time, *Review of Economics and Statistics*, L (November 1968), 391–416.

DEANE, PHYLLIS (1968) New Estimates of the Gross National Product for the United Kingdom 1830–1914, *Review of Income and Wealth*, XIV (June 1968), 95–112.

DEANE, PHYLLIS, and COLE, W. A. (1967) *British Economic Growth 1688–1959* (Cambridge, Cambridge U.P., 1967), 2nd ed.

DENISON, EDWARD F. (1967) *Why Growth Rates Differ* (Washington D.C., Brookings Institution, 1967).

DUNNING, JOHN H. (1970) *Studies in International Investment* (London, Allen & Unwin, 1970).

EICHER, C., and WITT, L., eds (1964) *Agriculture in Economic Development* (New York, McGraw-Hill, 1964).

GILFILLAN, S. C. (1963) *The Sociology of Invention* (Cambridge, Mass., M.I.T. Press, 1963).

GOUROU, PIERRE (1961) *The Tropical World*, trans. E. D. LABORDE (Harlow, Longmans, 1961).

GRILICHES, ZVI (1957) Hybrid Corn: an Exploration in the Economics of Technological Change, *Econometrica*, 25 (October 1957), 501–22.

HABAKKUK, H. J., and POSTAN, M. M., eds (1965) *The Cambridge Economic History of Europe*, Vol. VI: *The Industrial Revolutions and After* (Cambridge, Cambridge U.P., 1965).

HALL, A. R., ed. (1968) *The Export of Capital from Britain 1870–1914* (London, Methuen, 1968).

HOFFMANN, W. G. (1965) *Das Wachstum der deutschen Wirtschaft seit der Mitte des 19. Jahrhunderts* (Berlin, Springer-Verlag, 1965).

I.C.E.H. (1962) Second International Conference of Economic History, Aix-en-Provence, 1962: École Pratique des Hautes Études, Sixième Section: *Congrès et colloques*, VIII, Vol. II (Mouton, 1965).

I.C.E.H. (1965) Third International Conference of Economic History, Munich, 1965: École Pratique des Hautes Études, Sixième Section: *Congrès et colloques*, X (Mouton, 1968).

ISLAM, NURUL (1960) *Foreign Capital and Economic Development: Japan, India, and Canada* (Charles E. Tuttle, Rutland, Vt., and Tokyo, 1960).

JONES, E. L., and WOOLF, S. J., eds. (1969) *Agrarian Change and Economic Development* (London, Methuen, 1969).

KENDRICK, JOHN W. (1961) *Productivity Trends in the United States* (N.B.E.R., Princeton, N.J., Princeton U.P., 1961).

KINDLEBERGER, CHARLES P. (1962) *Foreign Trade and the National Economy* (New Haven, Conn., Yale U.P., 1962).

KNAPP, J. (1957) Capital Exports and Growth, *Economic Journal*, 67 (September 1957), 432–44.

KUZNETS, S. (1960) Quantitative Aspects of the Economic Growth of Nations: V. Capital Formation Proportions: International Comparisons for Recent Years, *Economic Development and Cultural Change*, VIII (July 1960).

KUZNETS, S. (1961) Quantitative Aspects of the Economic Growth of Nations: VI. Long-Term Trends in Capital Formation Proportions, *Economic Development and Cultural Change*, IX (July 1961).

KUZNETS, S. (1966) *Modern Economic Growth: Rate, Structure and Spread* (New Haven, Conn., Yale U.P., 1966).

LEAGUE OF NATIONS (1945) League of Nations, Economic, Financial and Transit Department, *Industrialization and Foreign Trade* (1945).

LEVIN, JONATHAN V. (1960) *The Export Economies* (Cambridge, Mass., Harvard U.P., 1960).

LEWIS, W. ARTHUR (1954) Economic Development with Unlimited Supplies of Labour, *Manchester School of Economic and Social Studies*, XXII (May 1954), 139–91.

LEWIS W. ARTHUR (1955) *The Theory of Economic Growth* (London, Allen & Unwin, 1955).

LILLEY, S. (1948) *Men, Machines and History* (London, Cobbett Press, 1948). New edition (London, Lawrence & Wishart, 1965).

LUTZ, F. A. and HAGUE, D. C. (1961) *The Theory of Capital* (Proceedings of a Conference held by the International Economic Association, New York, St Martin's Press, 1961).

MADDISON, ANGUS (1964) *Economic Growth in the West* (Twentieth Century Fund, London, Allen & Unwin, 1964).

MADDISON, ANGUS (1969) *Economic Growth in Japan and the USSR* (London, Allen & Unwin, 1969).

MAIZELS, A. (1963) *Industrial Growth and World Trade* (Cambridge, Cambridge U.P., 1963).

MOORSTEEN, RICHARD, and POWELL, RAYMOND P. (1966) *The Soviet Capital Stock, 1928–1962* (Homewood, Ill., Richard D. Irwin, 1966).

MYRDAL, GUNNAR (1968) *Asian Drama: An Inquiry Into the Poverty of Nations* (New York, Pantheon, 1968).

NAKAMURA, JAMES I. (1966) *Agricultural Production and the Economic Development of Japan 1873–1922* (Princeton, N.J., Princeton U.P., 1966).

N.B.E.R. (1962) *The Rate and Direction of Inventive Activity: Economic and Social Factors* (N.B.E.R., Special Conference Series, No. 13, Princeton, N.J., Princeton U.P., 1962).

N.B.E.R. (1966) *Output, Employment and Productivity in the U.S. After 1800* (New York, N.B.E.R., Studies in Income and Wealth, Vol. 30, 1966).

NELSON, RICHARD R. (1959) The Economics of Invention: a Survey of the Literature, *Journal of Business*, XXXII (April 1959), 101–27.

NURKSE, RAGNAR (1953) *Problems of Capital Formation in Under-developed Countries* (Oxford, Blackwell, 1953).

NURKSE, RAGNAR (1961) *Patterns of Trade and Development* (Oxford, Blackwell, 1961).

PEARSON, LESTER B., chairman (1969) *Partners in Development: Report of the Commission on International Development* (London, Pall Mall Press, 1969).

PHELPS BROWN, E. H. and HOPKINS, SHEILA V. (1956) Seven Centuries of the Prices of Consumables, Compared with Builders' Wage-Rates, *Economica*, N.S. XXIII (November 1956), 296–314.

POSTAN, M. M. (1967) *An Economic History of Western Europe 1945–1964* (London, Methuen, 1967).

ROSTOW, W. W. (1960) *The Stages of Economic Growth, a non-Communist Manifesto* (Cambridge, Cambridge U.P., 1960).

SALTER, W. E. G. (1960) *Productivity and Technical Change* (Cambridge, Cambridge U.P., 1960).

SAUL, S. B., ed. (1970) *Technological Change: The United States and Britain in the Nineteenth Century* (London, Methuen, 1970).

SCHMOOKLER, JACOB (1966) *Invention and Economic Growth* (Cambridge, Mass., Harvard U.P., 1966).

UNITED NATIONS (1949) United Nations, Department of Economic Affairs, *International Capital Movements during the Inter-War Period* (Lake Success, N.Y., 1949).

Index of Persons

Index of Subjects and Places